The Original
U.S. CONGRESS
HANDBOOK

117th Congress Second Session 2022
Published Annually Since 1974

COLUMBIA BOOKS, Inc.
ARLINGTON, VA

THE ORIGINAL U.S. CONGRESS HANDBOOK ™
PUBLISHED BY COLUMBIA BOOKS, Inc.
ARLINGTON, VA

Acknowledgements the U.S. Congress, the U.S. Supreme Court, the White House staff, the Offices of the Governors, the U.S. Census Bureau and the Library of Congress.

Maps Map Resources

Pronunciations provided and copyrighted by inogolo.com

For information on obtaining photographs or data contact

Columbia Books, Inc.
1530 Wilson Blvd, Suite 400
Arlington, VA 22209
202.464.1662
www.columbiabooks.com and
www.uscongresshandbook.com
ISBN-10: 1-952374-14-6
ISBN-13: 978-1-952374-14-2

Managing Editor: Max Kratcoski
Editorial Director: Shawn Rahmani

Printed in United States.

Supreme Court photographs courtesy of the Supreme Court Historical Society

Publisher's cataloging in publication data
The Original U.S. Congress Handbook. - 117th Congress, Second Session (2022).

March 2022: State Version

TABLE OF CONTENTS

GUIDE TO STATE/LEGISLATOR PROFILES

Governor Title First name Surname (pronunciation)　　　　　　　　Phone

Photo	Address1	Capital
	Address2	Population (Rank)
	Website	Area (Rank)
	Fax	
	Term Ends	State Map
	Lt. Governor	

U.S. Senators

U.S. Representatives

Title First name Surname (pronunciation)　　　　　Party-State-District　　　　Phone

🐎 - Democrat and 🐘 - Republican

Names are displayed in red for Republican, blue for Democrat and green for Independent.

Photo	**Rm.**	**Web.**	**Fax**
	Bio. Birth Date • Birth City/State/Country • Professional Information • Military Service • Educational Institutions, Degrees and Years • Religion • Marital Status and Number of Children		
	Cmte. Committees		
	CoS.		**LD.**
	Sched.		**PS.**
	Dist Off. listing of state offices and phone numbers		

R: T: Percentage of the vote. Elected Year Next election year (Senators only)

Legend: **Rm** - Room; **Web** - Website; **CoS** - Chief of Staff; **LD** - Legis. Dir.; **Sched** - Scheduler; **PS** - Press Sec.; **R** - Rank; **T** - Term; **M** - Married; **Se** - Separated; **D** - Divorced; **W** - Widowed; **DP** - Domestic Partner; **S** - Single; **E** - Engaged; **ch** - child/ren; **gr-ch** - grandchild/ren; **(CD)** - district office staff member

Above positions are a description of the staffer's role and function. Actual job titles may vary.

NOTES

Ethics Guidelines for Lobbyists and Non-Lobbyists

The US House and US Senate prohibit a registered lobbyist from giving 'anything of value' to Members, officers or employees of the House or Senate. . This prohibition applies as well to reimbursing a non-lobbyist employee of a registered lobbying entity for 'anything of value' given to a covered legislative branch person. Further, the gift rules restrict to $100 per calendar year (and $49.99 maximum per occurrence) the value of any gift received by a Member, officer or employee of the Congress from a non-lobbyist, citizen advocate.

There are exceptions to the gift restrictions (citizen advocates) and gift ban (lobbyists).

Notwithstanding the rules and the exceptions, both the House and Senate Ethics Committees instruct Members and staff:

- NOT to accept any gifts that are linked to an official action (referred to as a "quid pro quo")
- Not to solicit a gift from anyone with business before Congress
- Not to allow third parties to pay for gifts, travel or entertainment for a Member or staffer, unless it is clearly permitted as an exception to the ban on gifts from lobbyists and lobbying entities
- Some Members have established stricter rules for their office staff in order to ensure that impermissible gifts are not accepted by those employed in that office.

As indicated above, there are exceptions to the gift rules. Some of the more common exceptions are listed below. Note that this list is not exhaustive.[2]

Gifts of nominal value, including food and drink of nominal value, not as part of a meal. Generally, items valued at less than $10 are allowed, as are certain specific items: "greeting cards, baseball caps, or T-shirts" (which may cost more than $10). Food and drink, not as part of a meal, are allowed for attendance at receptions.

Home state/district items. Products that are made or produced in the state or district represented by a member of Congress, , and are displayed or available to members, staff and visitors, at no cost, at the Member's office are allowed.

Attendance and meals at widely attended events are exempt from the gift rules as long as the following conditions exist: the event must include at least 25 people who are not "from the Hill" (i.e. congressional members and staff) who may be from a specific industry or have a specific interest, the invitation to the event must be from the event sponsor, and the event must be related to a member or staffer's official duties. A sporting or recreational event does qualify under the exception for a "widely attended event" and free tickets / food at such an event would not be permissible.

Personal friendship allows a member or staffer to accept a gift from a lobbyist , provided there is a history of friendship, including the exchange of gifts between the congressional member/staffer and the person giving the gift, and provided that the gift is paid with personal funds and not reimbursed or deducted as a business expense by the one giving the gift. And, of course, the gift cannot be in exchange for or related to any official action.

Items given by federal, state or local government refer to gifts that are paid for directly by any of the three levels of government. These cannot be paid for by an outside source and then given by a federal, state or local government. In addition, the House and Senate rules are different insofar as defining certain entities as 'agencies of the federal government' under the gift rules.

[1] This information should not be relied on as complete legal advice. Please contact legal counsel if you need further guidance.

[2] A full listing of the exceptions under the gift rule is available in the Lobbying Compliance Handbook: A Practitioner's Guide to HLOGA, published by Columbia Books, Inc.

Meals and transportation in the course of a site visit: the exception (specific to the House) allows a House member or staffer to accept a meal and local transportation to / from a site being visited by the House member/staffer, even if the source is a lobbying registrant.

Lobbyists and lobbying entities must certify compliance with the gift rules: Adhering to the gift rules is of prime importance. Registered organizations and individual lobbyists are required to file the LD-203 report semiannually, on which lobbyists and registrant organizations must certify under penalty of perjury that they did not knowingly violate the House and Senate gift rules by providing gifts and/ or travel to a Member, officer or employee of the House or Senate.

Congressional Demographics

Breakdown by Gender

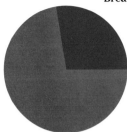

- Male (72.41%)
- Female (27.59%)

Breakdown by Ethnic Group

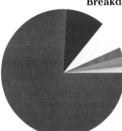

- White/Caucasian (75.97%)
- Black/African American (10.17%)
- Hispanic/Latino (7.39%)
- Asian/Pacific American (2.4%)
- Two or More Ethnicities (1.48%)
- Other (1.11%)
- Indian/Native American (0.74%)
- Not Specified (0.37%)
- Hawaiian/Pacific Islander (0.37%)

Breakdown by Marital Status

- Married (83.18%)
- Single (6.84%)
- Divorced (5.73%)
- Widower (1.11%)
- Widow (0.92%)
- Not Stated (0.92%)
- Separated (0.55%)
- Engaged (0.37%)
- Not Specified (0.37%)

Breakdown by Religion

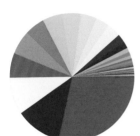

- Catholic (28.47%)
- Baptist (11.83%)
  Protestant - Unspecified Christian (9.43%)
- Methodist (6.28%)
- Jewish (6.1%)
- Christian - Non-Denominational (5.18%)
- Presbyterian (5.18%)
- Episcopalian (4.81%)
- Lutheran (4.25%)
- Not Known (3.51%)
  Unspecified/Other (3.51%)
- Evangelical (2.22%)
- Mormon (1.66%)
- Church of Christ (1.11%)
- Greek Orthodox (0.92%)
- African Methodist Episcopal (0.74%)
- Hinduism (0.55%)
- Islam (Muslim) (0.55%)
- Assembly of God (0.37%)
- Buddhism (0.37%)
- Congregationalist (0.37%)
- Seventh-Day Adventist (0.37%)
- Unitarian (0.37%)
- Anglican (0.18%)
- Christian Reformed Church (0.18%)
- Church of the United Brethren in Christ (0.18%)
- Disciples of Christ (0.18%)
- Eastern Orthodox (0.18%)
- None (0.18%)
- Pentecostal (0.18%)
- Quaker (0.18%)
- United Church of Christ (0.18%)
- Wesleyan (0.18%)

2022 Legislative Calendar

JANUARY 2022

S	M	T	W	T	F	S
						1
2	3	4	5	6	7	8
9	10	11	12	13	14	15
16	17	18	19	20	21	22
23	24	25	26	27	28	29
30	31					

FEBRUARY 2022

S	M	T	W	T	F	S
		1	2	3	4	5
6	7	8	9	10	11	12
13	14	15	16	17	18	19
20	21	22	23	24	25	26
27	28					

MARCH 2022

S	M	T	W	T	F	S
		1	2	3	4	5
6	7	8	9	10	11	12
13	14	15	16	17	18	19
20	21	22	23	24	25	26
27	28	29	30	31		

APRIL 2022

S	M	T	W	T	F	S
					1	2
3	4	5	6	7	8	9
10	11	12	13	14	15	16
17	18	19	20	21	22	23
24	25	26	27	28	29	30

MAY 2022

S	M	T	W	T	F	S
1	2	3	4	5	6	7
8	9	10	11	12	13	14
15	16	17	18	19	20	21
22	23	24	25	26	27	28
29	30	31				

JUNE 2022

S	M	T	W	T	F	S
			1	2	3	4
5	6	7	8	9	10	11
12	13	14	15	16	17	18
19	20	21	22	23	24	25
26	27	28	29	30		

JULY 2022

S	M	T	W	T	F	S
					1	2
3	4	5	6	7	8	9
10	11	12	13	14	15	16
17	18	19	20	21	22	23
24	25	26	27	28	29	30
31						

AUGUST 2022

S	M	T	W	T	F	S
	1	2	3	4	5	6
7	8	9	10	11	12	13
14	15	16	17	18	19	20
21	22	23	24	25	26	27
28	29	30	31			

SEPTEMBER 2022

S	M	T	W	T	F	S
				1	2	3
4	5	6	7	8	9	10
11	12	13	14	15	16	17
18	19	20	21	22	23	24
25	26	27	28	29	30	

OCTOBER 2022

S	M	T	W	T	F	S
						1
2	3	4	5	6	7	8
9	10	11	12	13	14	15
16	17	18	19	20	21	22
23	24	25	26	27	28	29
30	31					

NOVEMBER 2022

S	M	T	W	T	F	S
		1	2	3	4	5
6	7	8	9	10	11	12
13	14	15	16	17	18	19
20	21	22	23	24	25	26
27	28	29	30			

DECEMBER 2022

S	M	T	W	T	F	S
				1	2	3
4	5	6	7	8	9	10
11	12	13	14	15	16	17
18	19	20	21	22	23	24
25	26	27	28	29	30	31

☐ Federal Holiday ☐ House not in session
☐ Senate not in session

NOTES

U.S. SENATE LEADERSHIP

Republican Party   50   Democratic Party   48   Independent   2

A senator must be at least 30 years old, a U.S. citizen for nine years, and a resident of the state in which he or she is elected. Each state sends two senators to serve six-year terms. They are elected on a rotating schedule, with one-third of the Senate being elected every two years.

THE LEADERSHIP

Senate Majority Leader
Chuck E. Schumer (D-NY)   HSOB 322   **202.224.6542**

Senate Majority Whip; Assistant Majority Leader
Dick Durbin (D-IL)   HSOB 711   **202.224.2152**

Senate Republican Conference Chairman
John A. Barrasso (R-WY)   DSOB 307   **202.224.6441**

Senate Democratic Conference Chairman
Chuck E. Schumer (D-NY)   The Capitol S-221   **202.224.6542**

Senate Minority Leader
Mitch McConnell (R-KY)   RSOB 317   **202.224.2541**

Senate Minority Whip
John Thune (R-SD)   DSOB 511   **202.224.2321**

Senate Democratic Conference Secretary
Tammy Baldwin (D-WI)   HSOB 709   **202.224.5653**

THE OFFICERS

President of the Senate
Kamala D. Harris   Eisenhower   **202.456.0373**
                                 Executive Office
                                 Bldg.

President Pro Tempore
Patrick Leahy   The Capitol 126   **202.224.3744**

Secretary of the Senate
Ann Berry   The Capitol S-312   **202.224.3622**

Sergeant at Arms and Doorkeeper of the Senate
Karen H. Gibson   The Capitol S-151   **202.224.2341**

Senate Majority Secretary
Gary Myrick   The Capitol S-337   **202.224.3835**

Senate Minority Secretary
Robert Duncan   The Capitol S-309   **202.224.3735**

Senate Parliamentarian
Elizabeth C. MacDonough   The Capitol S-133   **202.224.6128**

Chaplain of the Senate
Barry C. Black   The Capitol S-332   **202.224.2510**

THE SENATE OFFICE BUILDINGS

When addressing correspondence to Members of the Senate, use the following abbreviations for office buildings. No street address is required. The Senate ZIP code is 20510.

S	Senate-north side of Capitol Building
DSOB	Dirksen Senate Office Building
	Constitution Avenue and First Street NE
HSOB	Hart Senate Office Building
	Constitution Avenue and Second Street NE
RSOB	Russell Senate Office Building
	Constitution and Delaware Avenues NE

SENATE ELECTION INFORMATION

As set forth in Article I, Section 3 of the Constitution, Senators are divided into three classes so that one-third may be elected every second year:

Class I - Senators whose next election occurs in 2025:

Democrats (21)	Republicans (10)	Independents (2)
Baldwin, Tammy (D-WI)	Barrasso, John A. (R-WY)	King, Angus S. (I-ME)
Brown, Sherrod C. (D-OH)	Blackburn, Marsha (R-TN)	Sanders, Bernie (I-VT)
Cantwell, Maria (D-WA)	Braun, Mike (R-IN)	
Cardin, Ben L. (D-MD)	Cramer, Kevin J. (R-ND)	
Carper, Tom R. (D-DE)	Cruz, Ted (R-TX)	
Casey, Bob (D-PA)	Fischer, Deb (R-NE)	
Feinstein, Dianne (D-CA)	Hawley, Josh (R-MO)	
Gillibrand, Kirsten E. (D-NY)	Romney, Mitt (R-UT)	
Heinrich, Martin T. (D-NM)	Scott, Rick (R-FL)	
Hirono, Mazie K. (D-HI)	Wicker, Roger F. (R-MS)	
Kaine, Tim M. (D-VA)		
Klobuchar, Amy (D-MN)		
Manchin, Joe (D-WV)		
Menendez, Bob (D-NJ)		
Murphy, Chris S. (D-CT)		
Rosen, Jacky S. (D-NV)		
Sinema, Kyrsten (D-AZ)		
Stabenow, Debbie (D-MI)		
Tester, Jon (D-MT)		
Warren, Elizabeth (D-MA)		
Whitehouse, Sheldon (D-RI)		

Class II - Senators whose next election occurs in 2027:

Democrats (13)	Republicans (20)	Independents (0)
Booker, Cory (D-NJ)	Capito, Shelley Moore (R-WV)	
Coons, Chris A. (D-DE)	Cassidy, Bill (R-LA)	
Durbin, Dick (D-IL)	Collins, Susan M. (R-ME)	
Hickenlooper, John W. (D-CO)	Cornyn, John (R-TX)	
Luján, Ben Ray Ray (D-NM)	Cotton, Tom B. (R-AR)	
Markey, Ed (D-MA)	Daines, Steve (R-MT)	
Merkley, Jeff A. (D-OR)	Ernst, Joni (R-IA)	
Ossoff, Jon (D-GA)	Graham, Lindsey (R-SC)	
Peters, Gary (D-MI)	Hagerty, Bill (R-TN)	
Reed, Jack F. (D-RI)	Hyde-Smith, Cindy (R-MS)	
Shaheen, Jeanne (D-NH)	Inhofe, James M. (R-OK)	
Smith, Tina (D-MN)	Lummis, Cynthia M. (R-WY)	
Warner, Mark R. (D-VA)	Marshall, Roger W. (R-KS)	
	McConnell, Mitch (R-KY)	
	Risch, James E. (R-ID)	
	Rounds, Mike (R-SD)	
	Sasse, Ben (R-NE)	
	Sullivan, Dan S. (R-AK)	
	Tillis, Thom R. (R-NC)	
	Tuberville, Tommy H. (R-AL)	

Class III - Senators whose next election occurs in 2023:

Democrats (14)	Republicans (20)	Independents (0)
Bennet, Michael F. (D-CO)	Blunt, Roy (R-MO)	
Blumenthal, Richard (D-CT)	Boozman, John N. (R-AR)	
Cortez Masto, Catherine (D-NV)	Burr, Richard M. (R-NC)	
Duckworth, Tammy (D-IL)	Crapo, Mike D. (R-ID)	
Hassan, Maggie (D-NH)	Grassley, Chuck (R-IA)	
Kelly, Mark (D-AZ)	Hoeven, John H. (R-ND)	
Leahy, Patrick (D-VT)	Johnson, Ron H. (R-WI)	
Murray, Patty (D-WA)	Kennedy, John N. (R-LA)	
Padilla, Alex (D-CA)	Lankford, James P. (R-OK)	
Schatz, Brian E. (D-HI)	Lee, Mike (R-UT)	
Schumer, Chuck E. (D-NY)	Moran, Jerry (R-KS)	
Van Hollen, Chris J. (D-MD)	Murkowski, Lisa A. (R-AK)	
Warnock, Raphael (D-GA)	Paul, Rand (R-KY)	
Wyden, Ron (D-OR)	Portman, Rob J. (R-OH)	
	Rubio, Marco (R-FL)	
	Scott, Tim E. (R-SC)	
	Shelby, Richard (R-AL)	
	Thune, John (R-SD)	
	Toomey, Pat J. (R-PA)	
	Young, Todd C. (R-IN)	

U.S. HOUSE OF REPRESENTATIVES LEADERSHIP

Democratic Party   226   Republican Party   214

A representative must be at least 25 years old, a U.S. citizen for seven years, and a resident of the state in which he or she is elected. The U.S. Census determines each state's allocation of the 435 representative seats, and each state legislature determines congressional district boundaries in that state. Every state has at least one representative, and all representatives are elected every even-numbered year.

Delegates and commissioners represent the U.S. territories, commonwealths and the federal district. Although they may not vote on the House floor, they can vote on legislation in their committees.

THE LEADERSHIP

Speaker of the House
Nancy Pelosi (D-CA)   The Capitol H-232   **202.225.4965**

House Majority Leader
Steny Hoyer (D-MD)   H-107   **202.225.3130**

House Majority Whip
James E. Clyburn (D-SC)   The Capitol H-329   **202.226.3210**

House Republican Conference Chairman
Elise Stefanik (R-NY)   RHOB 2211   **202.225.4611**

House Republican Policy Committee Chairman
Gary Palmer (R-AL)   CHOB 207   **202.225.4921**

House Minority Leader
Kevin McCarthy (R-CA)   H-204   **202.225.4000**

House Minority Whip
Steve Scalise (R-LA)   The Capitol H-148   **202.225.0197**

House Democratic Caucus Chairman
Hakeem Jeffries (D-NY)   LHOB B245   **202.225.1400**

THE OFFICERS

House Sergeant at Arms
Willie Walker   The Capitol H-124   **202.225.2456**

House Chief Administrative Officer
Catherine Szpindor   The Capitol HB-26   **202.225.5555**

Chaplain of the House
Margaret G. Kibben   The Capitol HB-25   **202.225.2509**

THE HOUSE OFFICE BUILDINGS

When addressing correspondence to Members of the House of Representatives, use the following abbreviations for office buildings. No street address is required. The ZIP code for the House is 20515.

CHOB   Cannon House Office Building
       First Street and Independence Avenue SE
FHOB   Ford House Office Building, 300 D St. SW
H   House-south side of Capitol Building
HB   House Basement-northwest side of Capitol Building
LHOB   Longworth House Office Building
       New Jersey and Independence Avenues SE
RHOB   Rayburn House Office Building
       South Capitol Street and Independence Avenue SW

SENATORS - 117th Congress

REPRESENTATIVES - 117th Congress

INDEX OF LEGISLATORS BY RANK

SENATE

HOUSE

NOTES

STATE/LEGISLATOR PROFILES - 117th Congress

ALABAMA

⚑ Governor Kay Ivey ("EYE"-vee)   p 334.242.7100

600 Dexter Avenue
Montgomery, AL 36130
Website alabama.gov
Fax 334.353.0004
Term Ends 2023
Lt. Governor
Will Ainsworth, R

C: Montgomery
P: 4,887,871 (24)
A: 50,645.39 mi^2 (28th)

U.S. Senators
Richard Shelby, R
Tommy H. Tuberville, R
U.S. Representatives
01 / Jerry L. Carl, R
02 / Barry Moore, R
03 / Mike D. Rogers, R
04 / Robert B. Aderholt, R
05 / Mo Brooks, R
06 / Gary Palmer, R
07 / Terri A. Sewell, **D**

⚑ Sen. Richard Shelby (SHELL-bee)   R-AL-Sr.   p 202.224.5744

Rm. RSOB 304 **Web.** shelby.senate.gov   **f** 202.224.3416
Bio. 05/06/1934 • Birmingham • U.S. Representative;
Attorney • Univ. of Alabama, B.A., 1957; Univ. of Alabama
School of Law, LL.B., 1963 • Presbyterian • M. Annette
Nevin Shelby, 2 ch; 2 gr-ch **Cmte.** Appropriations •
Banking, Housing & Urban Affairs • Environment & Public
Works • Joint Library • Rules & Administration
CoS. Watson Donald   **LD.** Clay Armentrout
                                        PS. Blair Taylor
Dist. Off. Birmingham 205.731.1384 • Huntsville
256.772.0460 • Mobile 251.694.4164 • Montgomery
334.223.7303 • Tuscaloosa 205.759.5047

R: 4 **T:** 6th 64%
Elected Year: 1986
Next Election: 2022

⚑ Sen. Tommy H. Tuberville (TOO-bur-vil)   R-AL-Jr.   p 202.224.4124

Rm. RSOB 142 **Web.** tuberville.senate.gov   **f** 202.224.3149
Bio. 09/18/1954 • Camden • Southern Arkansas Univ., B.S.,
1976 • Church of Christ • M. Suzanne Fette, 2 ch **Cmte.**
Agriculture, Nutrition & Forestry • Armed Services • Health,
Education, Labor & Pensions • Veterans' Affairs
CoS. Stephen E. Boyd   **LD.** Bradley F. Hayes
Sched. Taylor Stephens   **PS.** Ryann DuRant
Dist. Off. Birmingham 205.760.7307 • Dothan 334.547.7441
• Huntsville 256.692.7500 • Mobile 251.308.7233 •
Montgomery 334.523.7424

R: 97 **T:** 1st 60%
Elected Year: 2020
Next Election: 2026

⚑ Rep. Robert B. Aderholt (A-dur-holt)   R-AL-04   p 202.225.4876

Rm. CHOB 266 **Web.** aderholt.house.gov   **f** 202.225.5587
Bio. 07/22/1965 • Haleyville • Municipal Court Judge •
Birmingham-Southern College (AL), B.A., 1987; Samford
Univ. Cumberland Law School (AL), J.D., 1990 • Methodist •
M. Caroline McDonald Aderholt, 2 ch **Cmte.** Appropriations
• Joint Security & Cooperation in Europe
CoS. Kerry Knott   **LD.** Megan Medley
Sched. Chris Lawson   **PS.** Carson Clark (CD)
Dist. Off. Cullman 256.734.6043 • Gadsden 256.546.0201
• Jasper 205.221.2310 • Tuscumbia 256.381.3450

R: 33 **T:** 13th 82%
Elected Year: 1996

ALABAMA

⚑ Rep. Mo Brooks (brooks) R-AL-05 p 202.225.4801

Rm. RHOB 2185 **Web.** brooks.house.gov
Bio. 04/29/1954 • Charleston • State Legislator; County Commissioner • Duke Univ. (NC), B.A., 1975 • Christian Church • M. Martha Brooks, 4 ch; 10 gr-ch **Cmte.** Armed Services • Science, Space & Technology
CoS. Marshall Yates   **LD.** Sean E. Griffin
Sched. Madison Engelking   **PS.** Clay Mills
Dist. Off. Decatur 256.355.9400 • Florence 256.718.5155 • Huntsville 256.551.0190

R: 127 **T:** 6th 96%
Elected Year: 2010

⚑ Rep. Jerry L. Carl Jr. (karl) R-AL-01 p 202.225.4931

Rm. LHOB 1330 **Web.** carl.house.gov **f** 202.225.0562
Bio. 06/17/1958 • Mobile • Southern Baptist • M. Tina Carl, 3 ch **Cmte.** Armed Services • Natural Resources
CoS. Chad Carlough   **LD.** Laura Stagno
Sched. Talor Allen   **PS.** Zachary Weidlich
Dist. Off. Mobile 251.283.6280 • Summerdale 251.677.6630

R: 379 **T:** 1st 64%
Elected Year: 2020

⚑ Rep. Barry Moore (mor) R-AL-02 p 202.225.2901

Rm. LHOB 1504 **Web.** barrymoore.house.gov
Bio. 09/26/1966 • Enterprise • Enterprise State Junior College Foundation, A.D.; Auburn Univ., Bach. Deg., 1992; Auburn Univ., Bach. Deg., 1992 • Baptist • M. Heather Hopper, 4 ch **Cmte.** Agriculture • Veterans' Affairs
CoS. Shana Teehan   **LD.** Joshua Bradley
Sched. Maggie Thrailkill   **PS.** Bradley Jaye
Dist. Off. Andalusia 334.428.1129 • Dothan 334.547.6630 • Wetumpka 334.478.6330

R: 411 **T:** 1st 65%
Elected Year: 2020

⚑ Rep. Gary Palmer (PALL-mur) R-AL-06 p 202.225.4921

Rm. CHOB 170 **Web.** palmer.house.gov **f** 202.225.2082
Bio. 05/14/1954 • Hackleburg • Univ. of Alabama, B.S., 1977 • Presbyterian • M. Ann Cushing, 3 ch **Cmte.** Energy & Commerce • Select Committee on the Climate Crisis
CoS. William Smith   **LD.** Hunter Hobart
Sched. Ashley Sills   **PS.** Elizabeth Hance
Dist. Off. Birmingham 205.968.1290 • Clanton 205.280.6846 • Oneonta 205.625.4160

R: 229 **T:** 4th 97%
Elected Year: 2014

⚑ Rep. Mike D. Rogers (RAH-jurz) R-AL-03 p 202.225.3261

Rm. RHOB 2469 **Web.** mikerogers.house.gov **f** 202.226.8485
Bio. 07/16/1958 • Hammond • Jacksonville State Univ. (AL), B.A., 1981; Jacksonville State Univ. (AL), M.P.A., 1984; Birmingham School of Law (AL), J.D., 1991 • Baptist • M. Beth Rogers, 3 ch **Cmte.** Armed Services
CoS. Christopher Brinson   **LD.** Haley Wilson
Sched. Bronti Viskovich   **PS.** Shea Miller
Dist. Off. Opelika 334.745.6221 • Oxford 256.236.5655

R: 64 **T:** 10th 68%
Elected Year: 2002

⚑ Rep. Terri A. Sewell (SOO-wull) D-AL-07 p 202.225.2665

Rm. RHOB 2201 **Web.** sewell.house.gov **f** 202.226.9567
Bio. 01/01/1965 • Huntsville • Princeton Univ. (NJ), A.B., 1986; Oxford Univ. (England), M.A., 1988; Harvard Univ. Law School (MA), J.D., 1992 • Protestant - Unspecified Christian • D. Theodore Dixie **Cmte.** Ways & Means
CoS. Hillary Beard   **LD.** Robert Nuttall
Sched. Katie Brown   **PS.** Christopher Kosteva
Dist. Off. Birmingham 205.254.1960 • Montgomery 334.262.1919 • Selma 334.877.4414 • Tuscaloosa 205.752.5380

R: 150 **T:** 6th 97%
Elected Year: 2010

ALASKA

Governor Mike Dunleavy (DUHN-lee-vee)　　　　p 907.465.3500

Office of the Governor, P.O. Box 110001
Juneau, AK 99811
Website alaska.gov
Fax 907.465.3532
Term Ends 2022
Lt. Governor
Kevin Meyer, R

C: Juneau
P: 737,438 (49)
A: 570,640.61 mi² (1st)

U.S. Senators
Lisa A. Murkowski, R
Dan S. Sullivan, R
U.S. Representatives
01 / Don Young, R

Sen. Lisa A. Murkowski (mur-KOU-skee)　　R-AK-Sr.　　p 202.224.6665

Rm. HSOB 522 **Web.** murkowski.senate.gov **f** 202.224.5301
Bio. 05/22/1957 • Ketchikan • Attorney; State
Representative • Georgetown Univ. (DC), B.A., 1980;
Willamette Univ. College of Law (OR), J.D., 1985 • Roman
Catholic • M. Verne Martell, 2 ch **Cmte.** Appropriations •
Energy & Natural Resources • Health, Education, Labor &
Pensions • Indian Affairs
CoS. Kaleb D. Froehlich　　　**LD.** Annie Hoefler
Sched. Kristen Daimler-　　　**PS.** Karina Borger
　　Nothdurft

R: 18　**T:** 4th 44%　**Dist. Off.** Anchorage 907.271.3735 • Fairbanks
Elected Year: 2002　907.456.0233 • Juneau 907.586.7277 • Ketchikan
Next Election: 2022　907.225.6880 • Soldotna 907.262.4220 • Wasilla
　907.376.7665

Sen. Dan S. Sullivan (SULL-lih-vuhn)　　R-AK-Jr.　　p 202.224.3004

Rm. HSOB 302 **Web.** sullivan.senate.gov　**f** 202.224.6501
Bio. 11/13/1964 • Fairview Park • Harvard Univ., Bach.
Deg., 1987; Georgetown Univ. Law Center (DC), J.D., 1993;
Georgetown Univ. Law Center (DC), M.S., 1993 • Roman
Catholic • M. Julie Fate, 3 ch **Cmte.** Armed Services •
Commerce, Science & Transportation • Environment &
Public Works • Veterans' Affairs
CoS. Larry Burton　　　**LD.** Erik Elam
Sched. Avery Fogels　　　**PS.** Mike Reynard

R: 74　**T:** 2nd 54%　**Dist. Off.** Anchorage 907.271.5915 • Fairbanks
Elected Year: 2014　907.456.0261 • Juneau 907.586.7277 • Ketchikan
Next Election: 2026　907.225.6880 • Soldotna 907.283.4000 • Wasilla
　907.357.9956

Rep. Don Young (yung)　　　　R-AK-01　　p 202.225.5765

Rm. RHOB 2314 **Web.** donyoung.house.gov **f** 202.225.0425
Bio. 06/09/1933 • Meridian • State Legislator; School
Teacher • Army 1955-57 • Yuba Junior College (CA), A.A.,
1952; California State Univ., Chico, B.A., 1958 • Episcopalian
• M. Anne Garland Walton, 2 ch; 14 gr-ch; 1 great-gr-ch
Cmte. Natural Resources • Transportation & Infrastructure
CoS. Alex Ortiz　　　**LD.** Jesse von Stein
Sched. Paula Conru　　　**PS.** Zack Brown
Dist. Off. Anchorage 907.271.5978 • Fairbanks
907.456.0210

R: 1　**T:** 25th 54%
Elected Year: 1972

ARIZONA

Governor Douglas A. Ducey (DOO-see)　　　　p 602.542.4331

1700 W. Washington St.
Phoenix, AZ 85007
Website az.gov
Fax 602.542.7601
Term Ends 2023

C: Phoenix
P: 7,171,646 (14)
A: 113,593.91 mi² (6th)

ARIZONA

U.S. Senators
Kyrsten Sinema, **D**
Mark Kelly, **D**
U.S. Representatives
01 / Tom O'Halleran, **D**
02 / Ann L. Kirkpatrick, **D**
03 / Raul M. Grijalva, **D**
04 / Paul A. Gosar, R
05 / Andy Biggs, R
06 / David Schweikert, R
07 / Ruben Gallego, **D**
08 / Debbie Lesko, R
09 / Greg Stanton, **D**

⚲ Sen. Mark Kelly (KEH-lee)   D-AZ-Jr.   p 202.224.2235

Rm. HSOB 516 **Web.** kelly.senate.gov   **f** 202.228.2862
Bio. 02/21/1964 • Orange • United States Merchant Marine
Academy, B.S., 1986; United States Naval Postgraduate
School, M.S., 1994 • Catholic • M. Hon. Gabrielle Giffords,
2 ch (2 from previous marriage); 1 gr-ch **Cmte.** Aging
• Armed Services • Energy & Natural Resources •
Environment & Public Works • Joint Economic
CoS. Jennifer Cox   **LD.** Katie Campbell
Sched. Tony McComiskey   **PS.** Jacob Peters
Dist. Off. Phoenix 602.671.7901 • Prescott 928.420.7732 •
Tucson 520.475.5177

R: 91 **T:** 1st 51%
Elected Year: 2020
Next Election: 2022

⚲ Sen. Kyrsten Sinema (SIH-nih-muh)   D-AZ-Sr.   p 202.224.4521

Rm. HSOB 317 **Web.** sinema.senate.gov   **f** 202.228.0515
Bio. 07/12/1976 • Tucson • Brigham Young Univ. (UT),
Bach. Deg., 1995; Arizona State Univ., M.S., 1999; Arizona
State Univ. Law School, J.D., 2004; Arizona State Univ., Ph.D.,
2012 • None • S. **Cmte.** Banking, Housing & Urban Affairs •
Commerce, Science & Transportation • Homeland Security
& Government Affairs • Veterans' Affairs
CoS. Meg Joseph   **LD.** Michael Brownlie
Sched. Laura Piccioli   **PS.** John LaBombard
Dist. Off. Phoenix 602.598.7327 • Tucson 520.639.7080

R: 84 **T:** 1st 50%
Elected Year: 2018
Next Election: 2024

▨ Rep. Andy Biggs (bigz)   R-AZ-05   p 202.225.2635

Rm. CHOB 171 **Web.** biggs.house.gov
Bio. 11/07/1958 • Tucson • Brigham Young Univ. (UT),
B.A., 1982; Univ. of Arizona College of Pharmacy, J.D., 1984;
Arizona State Univ., M.A., 1999 • Mormon • M. Cindy Biggs, 6
ch **Cmte.** Judiciary • Oversight & Reform
CoS. Kate LaBorde   **LD.** Aaron L. Calkins
Sched. Sara Catherine   **PS.** Hilton Beckham
   Joseph
Dist. Off. Mesa 480.699.8239

R: 249 **T:** 3rd 59%
Elected Year: 2016

⚲ Rep. Ruben Gallego (gah-YEH-go)   D-AZ-07   p 202.225.4065

Rm. LHOB 1131 **Web.**
   rubengallego.house.gov
Bio. 11/20/1979 • Chicago • Harvard Univ., A.B., 2004 •
Catholic • M. Kate Gallego **Cmte.** Armed Services • Joint
Security & Cooperation in Europe • Natural Resources •
Veterans' Affairs
CoS. Grisella Martinez   **LD.** Mariel Jorgensen
Sched. Jose Contreras   **PS.** Jacques Petit
Dist. Off. Phoenix 602.256.0551

R: 216 **T:** 4th 77%
Elected Year: 2014

⚑ Rep. Paul A. Gosar (go-SAR)   R-AZ-04   p 202.225.2315

Rm. RHOB 2057 **Web.** gosar.house.gov   **f** 202.226.9739
Bio. 11/27/1958 • Rock Springs • Creighton Univ., B.S.,
1981; Creighton Boyne School of Dentistry (NE), D.D.S., 1985
• Roman Catholic • M. Maude Gosar, 3 ch
CoS. Thomas Van Flein   **LD.** Rory Burke
Sched. Leslie Foti   **PS.** Anthony Foti
Dist. Off. Gold Canyon 480.882.2697 • Prescott
928.445.1683

R: 135   **T:** 6th 70%
Elected Year: 2012

⚑ Rep. Raul M. Grijalva (gree-HAHL-vah)   D-AZ-03   p 202.225.2435

Rm. LHOB 1511 **Web.** grijalva.house.gov   **f** 202.225.1541
Bio. 02/19/1948 • Tucson • Pima County Supervisor;
Member, Tucson Unified School Board • Univ. of Arizona,
B.A., 1986 • Roman Catholic • M. Ramona Grijalva, 3 ch
Cmte. Education & Labor • Natural Resources
CoS. Amy Emerick Clerkin   **LD.** Norma Salazar-Ibarra
Sched. Carlos Martinez   **PS.** Jason T. Johnson
Dist. Off. Avondale 623.536.3388 • Somerton 928.343.7933
• Tucson 520.622.6788

R: 63   **T:** 10th 65%
Elected Year: 2012

⚑ Rep. Ann L. Kirkpatrick (kirk-PA-trik)   D-AZ-02   p 202.225.2542

Rm. CHOB 309
Bio. 03/24/1950 • McNary • State Legislator • Univ. of
Arizona, B.A., 1972; Univ. of Arizona James E. Rogers College
of Law (AZ), J.D., 1979 • Roman Catholic • M. Roger Curley,
2 ch **Cmte.** Appropriations
CoS. Abigail O'Brien   **LD.** Christian K. Walker
Sched. Sierra Yamanaka
  (CD)
Dist. Off. Sierra Vista 520.459.3115 • Tucson 520.881.3588

R: 203   **T:** 2nd 55%
Elected Year: 2018

⚑ Rep. Debbie Lesko (LEH-skoh)   R-AZ-08   p 202.225.4576

Rm. LHOB 1214 **Web.** lesko.house.gov   **f** 202.225.6328
Bio. 11/14/1959 • Sheboygan • Univ. of Wisconsin -
Madison, B.B.A. • Christian Church • M. Joe Lesko, 3 ch
Cmte. Energy & Commerce
CoS. Ross Branson   **LD.** Johnny Zwaanstra
Sched. Brendon Gallo   **PS.** Jacqueline Thomas
Dist. Off. Surprise 623.776.7911

R: 289   **T:** 3rd 60%
Elected Year: 2017

⚑ Rep. Tom O'Halleran (o-HA-lur-uhn)   D-AZ-01   p 202.225.3361

Rm. CHOB 318 **Web.** ohalleran.house.gov   **f** 202.225.3462
Bio. Chicago • Catholic • M. Pat O'Halleran, 3 ch; 3 gr-ch
Cmte. Agriculture • Energy & Commerce
CoS. Sally Adams   **LD.** Adam Finkel
Sched. Jarrett Kunz   **PS.** Kaitlin Hooker
Dist. Off. Flagstaff 928.286.5338 • Oro Valley 520.316.0839

R: 277   **T:** 3rd 52%
Elected Year: 2016

⚑ Rep. David Schweikert (SHWY-kurt)   R-AZ-06   p 202.225.2190

Rm. CHOB 304 **Web.** schweikert.house.gov   **f** 202.225.0096
Bio. 03/03/1962 • Los Angeles • Scottsdale Community
College (AZ), A.A., 1985; Arizona State Univ., B.S., 1988;
Arizona State Univ., M.B.A., 2005 • Roman Catholic • M.
Joyce Schweikert, 1 ch **Cmte.** Joint Economic • Ways &
Means
CoS. Kevin Knight (CD)   **LD.** Chad Michaels
Sched. Carolyn Prill
Dist. Off. Scottsdale 480.946.2411

R: 148   **T:** 6th 52%
Elected Year: 2012

ARIZONA

🏛 Rep. Greg Stanton (STAN-tuhn)   D-AZ-09   p 202.225.9888

Rm. CHOB 207   **Web.** stanton.house.gov
Bio. 03/08/1970 • Long Island • Marquette Univ. (WI), B.A.,
1992; Univ. of Michigan Law School, J.D., 1995 • Catholic •
M. Nicole Stanton, 2 ch   **Cmte.** Judiciary • Transportation &
Infrastructure
CoS. Seth Scott   **LD.** Tracee Gross Sutton
Sched. Sandy Moshi   **PS.** Allison Childress
Dist. Off.   Phoenix 602.956.2463

R: 350   **T:** 2nd   62%
Elected Year: 2018

ARKANSAS

🏛 Governor Asa Hutchinson (HUH-chin-suhn)   p 501.682.2345

State Capitol Room 250, 500   **C:** Little Rock
Woodlane Ave.   **P:** 3,013,825 (34)
Little Rock, AR 72201   **A:** 52,035.35 mi^2 (27th)
Website arkansas.gov
Fax 501.682.1382
Term Ends 2023
Lt. Governor
Tim Griffin, R

U.S. Senators
John N. Boozman, R
Tom B. Cotton, R
U.S. Representatives
01 / Rick Crawford, R
02 / French Hill, R
03 / Steve Womack, R
04 / Bruce Westerman, R

🏛 Sen. John N. Boozman (BOAZ-muhn)   R-AR-Sr.   p 202.224.4843

Rm. HSOB 141   **Web.** boozman.senate.gov   **f** 202.228.1371
Bio. 12/10/1950 • Shreveport • Optometrist • Univ. of
Arkansas, O.D., 1972; Southern College of Optometry
(TN), O.D., 1977 • Baptist • M. Cathy Marley Boozman,
3 ch; 2 gr-ch   **Cmte.** Agriculture, Nutrition & Forestry •
Appropriations • Environment & Public Works • Joint
Security & Cooperation in Europe • Veterans' Affairs
CoS. Toni-Marie Higgins   **LD.** Mackensie McKernan
Sched. Lauren Holly   **PS.** Sara Lasure
Dist. Off. El Dorado 870.863.4641 • Fort Smith
479.573.0189 • Jonesboro 870.268.6925 • Little Rock
501.372.7153 • Lowell 479.725.0400 • Mountain Home
870.424.0129 • Stuttgart 870.672.6941

R: 43   **T:** 2nd   60%
Elected Year: 2010
Next Election: 2022

🏛 Sen. Tom B. Cotton (KAH-tuhn)   R-AR-Jr.   p 202.224.2353

Rm. RSOB 326   **Web.** cotton.senate.gov   **f** 202.228.0908
Bio. 05/13/1977 • Dardanelle • Harvard Univ., A.B., 1998;
Harvard Law School (MA), J.D., 2002 • Methodist • M. Anna
Cotton, 2 ch   **Cmte.** Armed Services • Intelligence • Joint
Congressional-Executive Commission on China • Joint
Economic • Judiciary
CoS. Doug Coutts   **LD.** Edward Linczer
Sched. Joni Deoudes   **PS.** Caroline M. Tabler
Dist. Off. El Dorado 870.864.8582 • Jonesboro
870.933.6223 • Little Rock 501.223.9081 • Springdale
479.751.0879

R: 68   **T:** 2nd   67%
Elected Year: 2014
Next Election: 2026

ARKANSAS

⌂ Rep. Rick Crawford (KRAW-furd) R-AR-01 p 202.225.4076

Rm. RHOB 2422 **Web.** crawford.house.gov **f** 202.225.5602
Bio. 01/22/1966 • Homestead • Army 1985-89 • Arkansas
State Univ., Jonesboro, B.S., 1996 • Baptist • M. Stacy
Crawford, 2 ch **Cmte.** Agriculture • Permanent Select on
Intelligence • Transportation & Infrastructure
CoS. Jonah Shumate **LD.** Ashley Shelton
Sched. Courtney Handey **PS.** Sara Robertson
Dist. Off. Cabot 501.843.3043 • Dumas 870.377.5571 •
Jonesboro 870.203.0540 • Mountain Home 870.424.2075

R: 130 **T:** 6th 100%
Elected Year: 2010

⌂ Rep. French Hill (hill) R-AR-02 p 202.225.2506

Rm. LHOB 1533 **Web.** hill.house.gov **f** 202.225.5903
Bio. 12/05/1956 • Little Rock • Vanderbilt Univ. (TN),
B.S., 1979 • Roman Catholic • M. Martha Hill, 2 ch
Cmte. Financial Services • Joint Congressional Oversight
Commission
CoS. A. Brooke Bennett **LD.** Dylan Frost
Sched. Hannah Barr **PS.** Daniel Schneider
Dist. Off. Conway 501.358.3481 • Little Rock 501.324.5941

R: 220 **T:** 4th 55%
Elected Year: 2014

⌂ Rep. Bruce Westerman (WES-tur-muhn) R-AR-04 p 202.225.3772

Rm. CHOB 202 **Web.** westerman.house.gov **f** 202.225.1314
Bio. 11/18/1967 • Hot Springs • Univ. of Arkansas, B.S.,
1990; Yale Univ. (CT), M.S., 2001 • Southern Baptist •
M. Sharon French, 4 ch **Cmte.** Natural Resources •
Transportation & Infrastructure
CoS. Sarah Slocum Collins **LD.** Janet Rossi
  PS. Claire Y. Nance
Dist. Off. El Dorado 870.864.8946 • Hot Springs
501.609.9796 • Ozark 479.667.0075 • Pine Bluff
870.536.8178

R: 235 **T:** 4th 70%
Elected Year: 2014

⌂ Rep. Steve Womack (WOE-mak) R-AR-03 p 202.225.4301

Rm. RHOB 2412 **Web.** womack.house.gov **f** 202.225.5713
Bio. 02/18/1957 • Russellville • Mayor of Rogers, AR •
Arkansas Army National Guard, 1979-2009 • Arkansas Tech
Univ., B.A., 1979 • Southern Baptist • M. Terri Williams
Womack, 3 ch; 3 gr-ch **Cmte.** Appropriations
CoS. Madison Nash **LD.** Jessica Powell
Sched. Mariah Greenlee **PS.** Alexia Sikora
Dist. Off. Fort Smith 479.424.1146 • Harrison 870.741.6900
• Rogers 479.464.0446

R: 153 **T:** 6th 64%
Elected Year: 2010

CALIFORNIA

⚑ Governor Gavin Newsom (NEW-sum) p 916.445.2841

State Capitol Building, Suite 1173 **C:** Sacramento
Sacramento, CA 95814 **P:** 39,557,045 (1)
Website ca.gov **A:** 155,779.03 mi^2 (3rd)
Fax 916.558.3160
Term Ends 2023
Lt. Governor
Eleni Kounalakis, **D**

CALIFORNIA

CALIFORNIA

U.S. Senators
Dianne Feinstein, **D**
Alex Padilla, **D**

U.S. Representatives
01 / Doug LaMalfa, **R**
02 / Jared W. Huffman, **D**
03 / John Garamendi, **D**
04 / Tom McClintock, **R**
05 / Mike C. Thompson, **D**
06 / Doris Matsui, **D**
07 / Ami Bera, **D**
08 / Jay Obernolte, **R**
09 / Jerry McNerney, **D**
10 / Josh Harder, **D**
11 / Mark J. DeSaulnier, **D**
12 / Nancy Pelosi, **D**
13 / Barbara Lee, **D**
14 / Jackie Speier, **D**
15 / Eric Swalwell, **D**
16 / Jim Costa, **D**
17 / Ro Khanna, **D**
18 / Anna G. Eshoo, **D**
19 / Zoe Lofgren, **D**
20 / Jimmy Panetta, **D**
21 / David G. Valadao, **R**
22 / Vacant
23 / Kevin McCarthy, **R**

24 / Salud Carbajal, **D**
25 / Mike Garcia, **R**
26 / Julia Brownley, **D**
27 / Judy Chu, **D**
28 / Adam B. Schiff, **D**
29 / Tony Cardenas, **D**
30 / Brad J. Sherman, **D**
31 / Pete Aguilar, **D**
32 / Grace F. Napolitano, **D**
33 / Ted Lieu, **D**
34 / Jimmy Gomez, **D**
35 / Norma J. Torres, **D**
36 / Raul Ruiz, **D**
37 / Karen R. Bass, **D**
38 / Linda T. Sanchez, **D**

39 / Young O. Kim, **R**
40 / Lucille Roybal-Allard, **D**
41 / Mark A. Takano, **D**
42 / Ken S. Calvert, **R**
43 / Maxine Waters, **D**
44 / Nanette Diaz Barragan, **D**
45 / Katie Porter, **D**
46 / Lou Correa, **D**
47 / Alan S. Lowenthal, **D**
48 / Michelle Park Steel, **R**
49 / Mike Levin, **D**
50 / Darrell E. Issa, **R**
51 / Juan C. Vargas, **D**
52 / Scott H. Peters, **D**
53 / Sara Jacobs, **D**

🐾 Sen. Dianne Feinstein (FINE-stine) D-CA-Sr. p 202.224.3841

Rm. HSOB 331 **Web.** feinstein.senate.gov **f** 202.228.3954
Bio. 06/22/1933 • San Francisco • Mayor (San Francisco, CA) • Stanford Univ. (CA), Bach. Deg., 1955 • Jewish • M. Richard C. Blum, 1 ch; 3 stepch **Cmte.** Appropriations • Intelligence • Joint Congressional-Executive Commission on China • Judiciary • Rules & Administration
CoS. David A. Grannis **LD.** Rachel Bombach
Sched. Chesna Foord **PS.** Tom Mentzer
Dist. Off. Fresno 559.485.7430 • Los Angeles 310.914.7300 • San Diego 619.231.9712 • San Francisco 415.393.0707

R: 5 **T:** 6th 54%
Elected Year: 1992
Next Election: 2024

🐾 Sen. Alex Padilla (pa-DEE-yah) D-CA-Jr. p 202.224.3553

Rm. HSOB 112 **Web.** padilla.senate.gov **f** 202.224.2200
Bio. 03/22/1973 • Panorama City • Massachusetts Institute of Technology, B.S., 1994 • M. Angela Padilla, 3 ch **Cmte.** Budget • Environment & Public Works • Homeland Security & Government Affairs • Joint Printing • Judiciary • Rules & Administration
CoS. David Montes **LD.** Joshua Esquivel
Sched. Leah Schwartz **PS.** Vanessa Valdivia
Dist. Off. Fresno 559.497.5109 • Los Angeles 310.231.4494 • Sacramento 916.448.2787 • San Diego 619.239.3884 • San Francisco 415.981.9369

R: 98 **T:** 1st
Elected Year: 2021
Next Election: 2022

⚲ Rep. Pete Aguilar (ah-GEE-lar)   D-CA-31   p 202.225.3201

Rm. CHOB 109 **Web.** aguilar.house.gov   **f** 202.226.6962
Bio. 06/19/1979 • Fontana • Univ. of Redlands, B.R.E., 2001 • Roman Catholic • M. Alisha Aguilar, 2 ch   **Cmte.** Administration • Appropriations • Select Investigate Jan 6 Attack on the U.S. Capitol
CoS. Boris Medzhibovsky   **LD.** Victoria Rivas (CD)
                              PS. Owen Kilmer
Dist. Off. San Bernardino 909.890.4445

R: 205   **T:** 4th   61%
Elected Year: 2014

⚲ Rep. Nanette Diaz Barragan (BAIR-uh-guhn)   D-CA-44   p 202.225.8220

Rm. RHOB 2246 **Web.** barragan.house.gov   **f** 202.226.7290
Bio. 09/15/1976 • San Pedro • Univ. of California, Los Angeles, B.A., 2000; Univ. of Southern California, J.D., 2005 • Catholic • S.   **Cmte.** Energy & Commerce • Homeland Security
CoS. Liam Forsythe
Sched. Michelle Meza
Dist. Off. Carson 310.831.1799 • Compton 310.831.1799 • San Pedro 310.831.1799 • South Gate 310.831.1799

R: 247   **T:** 3rd   68%
Elected Year: 2016

⚲ Rep. Karen R. Bass (bass)   D-CA-37   p 202.225.7084

Rm. RHOB 2021 **Web.** bass.house.gov   **f** 202.225.2422
Bio. 10/03/1953 • Los Angeles • California State Univ. - Dominguez Hills, B.S., 1990 • Baptist • D., 2 ch (1 deceased); 4 stepch   **Cmte.** Foreign Affairs • Judiciary
CoS. Darryn Harris   **LD.** Chris Schloesser
Sched. Jonathan Aquino   **PS.** Zachary Seidl
Dist. Off. Los Angeles 323.965.1422

R: 126   **T:** 6th   86%
Elected Year: 2012

⚲ Rep. Ami Bera (BAIR-uh)   D-CA-07   p 202.225.5716

Rm. CHOB 172 **Web.** bera.house.gov   **f** 202.226.1298
Bio. 03/02/1965 • Los Angeles • Univ. of California, Irvine, B.S., 1987; Univ. of California, Irvine, B.S., 1987; Univ. of California, Irvine, M.D., 1991 • Unitarian • M. Janine Bera, 1 ch   **Cmte.** Foreign Affairs • Science, Space & Technology
CoS. Chad Obermiller   **LD.** Kelvin Lum
Sched. Madeleine Buchholz   **PS.** Travis Horne
Dist. Off. Sacramento 916.635.0505

R: 162   **T:** 5th   57%
Elected Year: 2012

⚲ Rep. Julia Brownley (BROWN-lee)   D-CA-26   p 202.225.5811

Rm. RHOB 2262 **Web.** juliabrownley.house.gov   **f** 202.225.1100
Bio. 08/28/1952 • Aiken • Mount Vernon College, B.A., 1975; American Univ. (DC), M.B.A., 1979 • Episcopalian • D., 2 ch   **Cmte.** Natural Resources • Select Committee on the Climate Crisis • Transportation & Infrastructure • Veterans' Affairs
CoS. Lenny Young   **LD.** Sharon Wagener
Sched. Ryan Dillon   **PS.** Carina Armenta
Dist. Off. Oxnard 805.379.1779 • Thousand Oaks 805.379.1779

R: 163   **T:** 5th   61%
Elected Year: 2012

⚑ Rep. Ken S. Calvert (CAL-vurt)   R-CA-42   p 202.225.1986

Rm. RHOB 2205 **Web.** calvert.house.gov   **f** 202.225.2004
Bio. 06/08/1953 • Corona • Real Estate Agent; Restaurateur • Chaffey Community College (CA), A.A., 1973; San Diego State Univ., B.A., 1975 • Protestant - Unspecified Christian • D.   **Cmte.** Appropriations
CoS. Rebecca Keightley   **LD.** Richie O'Connell
Sched. Johannah Murphy   **PS.** Jason Gagnon (CD)
Dist. Off. Corona 951.277.0042

R: 17   **T:** 15th   57%
Elected Year: 2012

CALIFORNIA

🖋 Rep. Salud Carbajal (KAR-bah-HAHL)   D-CA-24   p 202.225.3601

Rm. RHOB 2331 **Web.** carbajal.house.gov   **f** 202.225.5632
Bio. 11/18/1964 • Moroleon • Univ. of California, Santa
Barbara, B.A., 1990; Fielding Univ. (CA), Mast. Deg., 1994
• Catholic • M. Gina Carbajal, 2 ch **Cmte.** Agriculture •
Armed Services • Transportation & Infrastructure
CoS. Jeremy Tittle   **LD.** Johanna Montiel
Sched. Diana Villanueva   **PS.** Mannal Haddad
   (CD)
Dist. Off. San Luis Obispo 805.546.8348 • Santa Barbara
805.730.1710 • Santa Maria 805.730.1710

R: 253 **T:** 3rd 59%
Elected Year: 2016

🖋 Rep. Tony Cardenas (KAR-deh-nahss)   D-CA-29   p 202.225.6131

Rm. RHOB 2438 **Web.** cardenas.house.gov   **f** 202.225.0819
Bio. 03/31/1963 • Pacoima • Univ. of California, Santa
Barbara, B.S., 1986 • Christian Church • M. Norma
Cárdenas, 4 ch **Cmte.** Energy & Commerce
CoS. Ahmed Elsayed

PS. Clarissa Rojas
Dist. Off. Panorama City 818.221.3718

R: 165 **T:** 5th 57%
Elected Year: 2012

🖋 Rep. Judy Chu (choo)   D-CA-27   p 202.225.5464

Rm. RHOB 2423 **Web.** chu.house.gov   **f** 202.225.5467
Bio. 07/07/1953 • Los Angeles • Univ. of California,
Los Angeles, B.A., 1974; California School Professional
Psychology, Los Angeles, M.A., 1977; California School
Professional Psychology, Los Angeles, Ph.D., 1979 •
Unspecified/Other • M. Michael Eng **Cmte.** Budget • Small
Business • Ways & Means
CoS. Sonali Desai   **LD.** Ellen Hamilton
Sched. Jenna Christiansen **PS.** Benjamin Suarato
Dist. Off. Claremont 909.625.5394 • Pasadena
626.304.0110

R: 119 **T:** 7th 70%
Elected Year: 2012

🖋 Rep. Lou Correa (ko-RAY-ah)   D-CA-46   p 202.225.2965

Rm. RHOB 2301 **Web.** correa.house.gov
Bio. 01/24/1958 • Los Angeles • California State Univ.
Fullerton, B.S., 1980; Univ. of California, Los Angeles,
J.D., 1985; Univ. of California, Los Angeles, M.B.A., 1985
• Catholic • M. Esther Reynoso Correa, 4 ch **Cmte.**
Agriculture • Homeland Security • Judiciary
CoS. Laurie Beth Saroff   **LD.** Ngoc Nguyen
Sched. Jose Fontanez   **PS.** Marysol Ibarra
Dist. Off. Santa Ana 714.559.6190

R: 255 **T:** 3rd 69%
Elected Year: 2016

🖋 Rep. Jim Costa (KAHS-tuh)   D-CA-16   p 202.225.3341

Rm. RHOB 2081 **Web.** costa.house.gov   **f** 202.225.9308
Bio. 04/13/1952 • Fresno • State Legislator • California
State Univ., Fresno, B.S., 1974 • Roman Catholic • S. **Cmte.**
Agriculture • Foreign Affairs • Natural Resources
CoS. Juan E. Lopez   **LD.** John Lynch
Sched. Alex Rosenberg   **PS.** Adrian Thomas (CD)
Dist. Off. Fresno 559.495.1620 • Merced 209.384.1620

R: 73 **T:** 9th 59%
Elected Year: 2012

🖋 Rep. Mark J. DeSaulnier (deh-SOAN-yay)   D-CA-11   p 202.225.2095

Rm. CHOB 503 **Web.** desaulnier.house.gov   **f** 202.225.5609
Bio. 03/31/1952 • Lowell • College of The Holy Cross (MA),
B.A., 1974 • Roman Catholic • D., 2 ch **Cmte.** Education
& Labor • Oversight & Reform • Rules • Transportation &
Infrastructure
CoS. Betsy Arnold Marr   **LD.** Sarah Jackson
Sched. Brooklyn Alcott   **PS.** Mairead Glowacki
Dist. Off. Richmond 510.620.1000 • Walnut Creek
925.933.2660

R: 213 **T:** 4th 73%
Elected Year: 2014

Rep. Anna G. Eshoo (EH-shoo) D-CA-18 p 202.225.8104

Rm. CHOB 272 **Web.** eshoo.house.gov **f** 202.225.8890
Bio. 12/13/1942 • New Britain • San Mateo County Board of
Supervisors; Chief of Staff, CA Assembly Speaker • Canada
College (CA), A.A., 1975 • Roman Catholic • D., 2 ch **Cmte.**
Energy & Commerce
CoS. Matthew McMurray **LD.** Asad Ramzanali
Sched. Noor Shah **PS.** Katy Nystrom
Dist. Off. Palo Alto 650.323.2984

R: 19 **T:** 15th 63%
Elected Year: 2012

Rep. John Garamendi (gair-uh-MEN-dee) D-CA-03 p 202.225.1880

Rm. RHOB 2368 **Web.** garamendi.house.gov **f** 202.225.5914
Bio. 01/24/1945 • Camp Blanding • State Legislator; Lt
Governor (CA) • Univ. of California, Berkeley, B.A., 1966;
Harvard Univ. Law School (MA), M.B.A., 1970 • Christian
Church • M. Patricia Wilkinson Garamendi, 6 ch; 10 gr-ch
Cmte. Armed Services • Transportation & Infrastructure
CoS. Bradley Bottoms **LD.** Iain Hart
Sched. Henry Burke **PS.** Eric Olsen
Dist. Off. Davis 530.753.5301 • Fairfield 707.438.1822

R: 120 **T:** 7th 55%
Elected Year: 2012

Rep. Mike Garcia (gar-SEE-uh) R-CA-25 p 202.225.1956

Rm. LHOB 1535 **Web.** mikegarcia.house.gov **f** 202.226.0683
Bio. 04/24/1976 • Santa Clarita • U.S. Naval Academy (MD),
B.S., 1998; Georgetown Univ. (DC), M.A., 1998 • M. Rebecca
Garcia, 2 ch **Cmte.** Appropriations • Science, Space &
Technology
CoS. Alan N. Tennille **LD.** Will Turner
Sched. Hilda Harder **PS.** Molly Jenkins
Dist. Off. Palmdale 661.839.0532 • Santa Clarita
661.568.4855 • Simi Valley 805.760.9090

R: 367 **T:** 2nd 50%
Elected Year: 2019

Rep. Jimmy Gomez (GO-mehz) D-CA-34 p 202.225.6235

Rm. LHOB 1530 **Web.** gomez.house.gov **f** 202.225.2202
Bio. 11/25/1974 • Southern California • Univ. of California,
Los Angeles, B.A.; John F. Kennedy School of Government,
Harvard Univ., M.P.P. • M. Mary Hodge **Cmte.** Oversight &
Reform • Ways & Means
CoS. Bertha Alisia Guerrero **LD.** Omair Taher
  PS. Cameron Edinburgh
Dist. Off. Los Angeles 213.481.1425

R: 285 **T:** 3rd 53%
Elected Year: 2016

Rep. Josh Harder (HAR-dur) D-CA-10 p 202.225.4540

Rm. CHOB 209 **Web.** harder.house.gov
Bio. 08/01/1986 • Turlock • Stanford Univ. (CA), Bach.
Deg., 2008 • Christian Church • M. Pamela Harder **Cmte.**
Agriculture • Appropriations
CoS. Rachael L. Goldenberg **LD.** Adela Amador
Sched. Ryan Feldman **PS.** Andrew Mamo
Dist. Off. Modesto 209.579.5458

R: 321 **T:** 2nd 55%
Elected Year: 2018

Rep. Jared W. Huffman (HUF-muhn) D-CA-02 p 202.225.5161

Rm. LHOB 1527 **Web.** huffman.house.gov **f** 202.225.5163
Bio. 02/18/1964 • Independence • Univ. of California, Santa
Barbara, B.A., 1986; Boston College Law School (MA), J.S.D.,
1990 • Unspecified/Other • M. Susan Huffman, 2 ch **Cmte.**
Natural Resources • Select Committee on the Climate Crisis
• Transportation & Infrastructure
CoS. Jennifer Goedke **LD.** Shane Trimmer
Sched. Julia Diamond **PS.** Mary Hurrell
Dist. Off. Eureka 707.407.3585 • Fort Bragg 707.962.0933 •
Petaluma 707.981.8967 • San Rafael 415.258.9657 • Ukiah
707.671.7449

R: 171 **T:** 5th 76%
Elected Year: 2012

♔ Rep. Darrell E. Issa (EYE-suh) R-CA-50 p 202.225.5672

Rm. LHOB 2300 **Web.** issa.house.gov
Bio. 11/01/1953 • Cleveland • CEO, Auto Security Company
• Army 1970-72, 1976-80 • Kent State Univ. (OH), A.A.,
1976; Siena Heights Univ. (MI), B.A., 1976 • Christian - Non-
Denominational • Se. Kathy Issa, 1 ch **Cmte.** Foreign Affairs
• Judiciary
CoS. Veronica Wong   **LD.** Jennifer Haynes
Sched. Sally Lindsay   **PS.** Jonathan Wilcox
Dist. Off.   San Marcos 760.304.7575 • Temecula
760.304.7575

R: 71   **T:** 1st 54%
Elected Year: 2020

⚑ Rep. Sara Jacobs (JAY-kubz) D-CA-53 p 202.225.2040

Rm. LHOB 1232 **Web.** sarajacobs.house.gov **f** 202.225.2948
Bio. 02/01/1989 • Del Mar • Columbia Univ. (NY), B.A.;
Columbia Univ. (NY), Mast. Deg. • Jewish • S. **Cmte.**
Armed Services • Foreign Affairs • Select Economic
Disparity & Fairness in Growth
CoS. Amy Kuhn   **LD.** Brandon Mendoza
Sched. Katie Heller   **PS.** Will McDonald
Dist. Off.   San Diego 619.280.5353

R: 397   **T:** 1st 60%
Elected Year: 2020

⚑ Rep. Ro Khanna (KAH-nuh) D-CA-17 p 202.225.2631

Rm. CHOB 306
Bio. 09/13/1976 • Philadelphia • Univ. of Chicago (IL), A.B.,
1998; Yale Univ. Law School (CT), J.D., 2001 • Hinduism •
M. Ritu Ahuja, 2 ch **Cmte.** Agriculture • Armed Services •
Oversight & Reform
CoS. Geo Saba   **LD.** Kate Gould
Sched. Nicole Mata   **PS.** Marie Baldassarre
Dist. Off.   Santa Clara 408.436.2720

R: 270   **T:** 3rd 71%
Elected Year: 2016

♔ Rep. Young O. Kim (kim) R-CA-39 p 202.225.4111

Rm. LHOB 1306 **Web.** youngkim.house.gov **f** 202.225.1776
Bio. 10/18/1962 • Incheon • Univ. of Southern California,
B.S., 1985 • Christian - Non-Denominational • M. Charles
Kim, 4 ch **Cmte.** Foreign Affairs • Science, Space &
Technology • Small Business
CoS. Patrick Mocete   **LD.** Alex Cisneros
Sched. Alex Keledjian   **PS.** Callie Strock
Dist. Off.   Placentia 714.984.2440

R: 400   **T:** 1st 51%
Elected Year: 2020

♔ Rep. Doug LaMalfa (luh-MAL-fuh) R-CA-01 p 202.225.3076

Rm. CHOB 408 **Web.** lamalfa.house.gov
Bio. 07/02/1960 • Oroville • Butte College (CA), A.A., 1980;
California Polytechnic State Univ., San Luis Obispo, B.S.,
1982; California Polytechnic State Univ., San Luis Obispo,
B.S., 1982 • Evangelical • M. Jill LaMalfa, 4 ch **Cmte.**
Agriculture • Transportation & Infrastructure
CoS. Mark Spannagel   **LD.** John Veale
Sched. Courtney Jones   **PS.** Alexandra Lavy
Dist. Off.   Auburn 530.878.5035 • Chico 530.343.1000 •
Redding 530.223.5898

R: 177   **T:** 5th 57%
Elected Year: 2012

⚑ Rep. Barbara Lee (lee) D-CA-13 p 202.225.2661

Rm. RHOB 2470 **Web.** lee.house.gov   **f** 202.225.9817
Bio. 07/14/1946 • El Paso • Congressional Aide; Social
Worker • Mills College (CA), B.A., 1973; Univ. of California,
Berkeley, M.S.W., 1975 • Baptist • M. Clyde W. Oden, 2 ch; 5
gr-ch **Cmte.** Appropriations • Budget
CoS. Julie Nickson   **LD.** Gregory Adams
Sched. Chris Keosian   **PS.** Sean Ryan
Dist. Off.   Oakland 510.763.0370

R: 44   **T:** 13th 90%
Elected Year: 2012

🐾 Rep. Mike Levin (LEH-vin)   D-CA-49   p 202.225.3906

Rm. LHOB 1030 **Web.** mikelevin.house.gov
Bio. 10/20/1978 • Inglewood • Stanford Univ. (CA), B.A.,
2001; Duke Law School (NC), J.D., 2005 • Catholic • M.
Chrissy Levin, 2 ch **Cmte.** Natural Resources • Select
Committee on the Climate Crisis • Veterans' Affairs
CoS. Jonathan Gilbert   **LD.** Faith Williams
Sched. Jack Baisley   **PS.** Eric Mee
Dist. Off. Dana Point 949.281.2449 • Oceanside
760.599.5000

R: 329   **T:** 2nd   53%
Elected Year: 2018

🐾 Rep. Ted Lieu (loo)   D-CA-33   p 202.225.3976

Rm. CHOB 403 **Web.** lieu.house.gov   f 202.225.4099
Bio. 03/29/1969 • Taipei • Stanford Univ. (CA), B.S., 1991;
Stanford Univ. (CA), B.A., 1991; Georgetown Univ. Law
Center (DC), J.D., 1994 • Roman Catholic • M. Betty Lieu, 2
ch **Cmte.** Foreign Affairs • Judiciary
CoS. Marc A. Cevasco   **LD.** Corey Jacobson
Sched. Sameer Chintamani   **PS.** Jenna Bushnell
Dist. Off. Los Angeles 323.651.1040 • Manhattan Beach
310.321.7664

R: 223   **T:** 4th   68%
Elected Year: 2014

🐾 Rep. Zoe Lofgren (LAHF-gruhn)   D-CA-19   p 202.225.3072

Rm. LHOB 1401 **Web.** zoelofgren.house.gov   f 202.225.3336
Bio. 12/21/1947 • San Mateo • Attorney; Immigration Law
Professor • Stanford Univ. (CA), B.A., 1970; Santa Clara
Univ. Law School (CA), J.D., 1975 • Lutheran • M. John
Marshall Collins, 2 ch **Cmte.** Administration • Joint Library
• Joint Printing • Judiciary • Science, Space & Technology
• Select Committee on the Modernization of Congress •
Select Investigate Jan 6 Attack on the U.S. Capitol
CoS. Stacey E. Leavandosky
Sched. Andrew DeLuca   **PS.** Ally Kehoe
Dist. Off. San Jose 408.271.8700

R: 31   **T:** 14th   72%
Elected Year: 2012

🐾 Rep. Alan S. Lowenthal (LO-wuhn-thall)   D-CA-47   p 202.225.7924

Rm. CHOB 108 **Web.** lowenthal.house.gov   f 202.225.7926
Bio. 03/08/1941 • New York • Hobart College (NY), B.A.,
1962; Ohio State Univ., M.A., 1965; Ohio State Univ., Ph.D.,
1967 • Jewish • M. Deborah Malumed, 2 ch; 1 gr-ch **Cmte.**
Natural Resources • Transportation & Infrastructure
CoS. Chris Gorud
Sched. Alyssa Dinh   **PS.** Keith Higginbotham
Dist. Off. Garden Grove 714.243.4088 • Long Beach
562.436.3828

R: 178   **T:** 5th   63%
Elected Year: 2012

🐾 Rep. Doris Matsui (mat-SOO-ee)   D-CA-06   p 202.225.7163

Rm. RHOB 2311 **Web.** matsui.house.gov   f 202.225.0566
Bio. 09/25/1944 • Poston • Deputy Assistant, President
Clinton; Deputy Director, Public Liaison; Television
Executive; Civic Leader • Univ. of California, Berkeley,
B.A., 1966 • Methodist • E. Roger Sant, 1 ch; 2 gr-ch **Cmte.**
Energy & Commerce
CoS. Jeremy Marcus   **LD.** Christina McCauley
                      PS. Maureen Elinzano
Dist. Off. Sacramento 916.498.5600

R: 85   **T:** 9th   73%
Elected Year: 2012

🐾 Rep. Kevin McCarthy 1SG (muh-KAR-thee)   R-CA-23   p 202.225.2915

Rm. RHOB 2468 **Web.**   f 202.225.2908
kevinmccarthy.house.gov
Bio. 01/26/1965 • Bakersfield • Small Business Owner
• California State Univ., Bakersfield, B.A., 1989; Univ. of
California, Bakersfield, M.B.A., 1994 • Baptist • M. Judy
McCarthy, 2 ch
CoS. James Min   **LD.** Trevor Smith
Sched. Alex Gourdikian   **PS.** Matt Sparks
Dist. Off. Bakersfield 661.327.3611

R: 96   **T:** 8th   62%
Elected Year: 2012

CALIFORNIA

🏛 Rep. Tom McClintock (muh-KLIN-tahk)   R-CA-04   p 202.225.2511

Rm. RHOB 2312 **Web.** mcclintock.house.gov **f** 202.225.5444
Bio. 07/10/1956 • Bronxville • State Legislator • Univ.
of California, Los Angeles, B.S., 1978 • Baptist • W. Lori
McClintock, 2 ch **Cmte.** Budget • Judiciary • Natural
Resources
CoS. Chris Tudor   **LD.** Mary Doocy
Sched. Ally Hibben   **PS.** Jennifer Cressy
Dist. Off. Roseville 916.786.5560

R: 112   **T:** 7th   56%
Elected Year: 2008

🏛 Rep. Jerry McNerney (mik-NUR-nee)   D-CA-09   p 202.225.1947

Rm. RHOB 2265 **Web.** mcnerney.house.gov **f** 202.225.4060
Bio. 06/18/1951 • Albuquerque • Engineer • Univ. of New
Mexico, B.S., 1973; Univ. of New Mexico, M.S., 1975; Univ.
of New Mexico, Ph.D., 1981 • Roman Catholic • M. Mary
McNerney, 3 ch **Cmte.** Energy & Commerce • Science,
Space & Technology
CoS. Nicole Damasco
Sched. Alisa Alva-Campos   **PS.** Nikki Cannon
Dist. Off. Antioch 925.754.0716 • Stockton 209.476.8552

R: 97   **T:** 8th   58%
Elected Year: 2012

🏛 Rep. Grace F. Napolitano (nah-poe-lee-TAH-no)   D-CA-32   p 202.225.5256

Rm. LHOB 1610 **Web.** napolitano.house.gov **f** 202.225.0027
Bio. 12/04/1936 • Brownsville • Member, State Assembly;
Mayor (Norwalk, TX) • Roman Catholic • M. Frank
Napolitano, 5 ch (5 from previous marriage); 14 gr-ch; 2
great-gr-ch **Cmte.** Natural Resources • Transportation &
Infrastructure
CoS. Joe Sheehy   **LD.** Joseph Ciccone
Sched. Leandra Berdin   **PS.** Jerry O'Donnell
(CD)
Dist. Off. El Monte 626.350.0150

R: 47   **T:** 12th   67%
Elected Year: 2012

🏛 Rep. Jay Obernolte (oh-bur-NOAL-tee)   R-CA-08   p 202.225.5861

Rm. LHOB 1029 **Web.** obernolte.house.gov
Bio. 08/18/1970 • Chicago • California Institute of
Technology, B.S.; Univ. of California, Los Angeles, M.S. •
Christian - Non-Denominational • M. Heather Obernolte, 2
ch **Cmte.** Budget • Natural Resources • Science, Space &
Technology
CoS. Lorissa Bounds   **LD.** Rob Hicks
Sched. Caroline Donlon   **PS.** Emily Carlin
Dist. Off. Hesperia 760.247.1815

R: 416   **T:** 1st   56%
Elected Year: 2020

🏛 Rep. Jimmy Panetta (puh-NEH-tuh)   D-CA-20   p 202.225.2861

Rm. CHOB 406 **Web.** panetta.house.gov   **f** 202.225.6791
Bio. 10/01/1969 • Washington • Monterey Peninsula
College (CA), A.A., 1989; Univ. of California, Davis, B.A.,
1991; Santa Clara Univ. (CA), J.D., 1996 • Catholic • M.
Carrie Panetta, 2 ch **Cmte.** Agriculture • Armed Services •
Ways & Means
CoS. Pete Spiro   **LD.** Mark Dennin
Sched. Alexa Roth   **PS.** Hugh Daly
Dist. Off. Salinas 831.424.2229 • Santa Cruz 831.429.1976

R: 278   **T:** 3rd   77%
Elected Year: 2016

🏛 Rep. Nancy Pelosi (puh-LO-see)   D-CA-12   p 202.225.4965

Rm. LHOB 1236 **Web.** pelosi.house.gov   **f** 202.225.8259
Bio. 03/26/1940 • Baltimore • Chairman, California State
Democratic Party; Public Relations Consultant • Trinity
College (DC), A.B., 1962 • Roman Catholic • M. Paul F.
Pelosi, 5 ch; 9 gr-ch
CoS. Robert Edmonson
Sched. Adriana Hidalgo
(CD)
Dist. Off. San Francisco 415.556.4862

R: 8   **T:** 18th   78%
Elected Year: 2012

CALIFORNIA

⚑ Rep. Scott H. Peters (PEE-turz) D-CA-52 p 202.225.0508

Rm. LHOB 1201 **Web.** scottpeters.house.gov
Bio. 06/17/1958 • Springfield • Duke Univ. (NC), B.A., 1980; New York Univ. Law School, J.D., 1984 • Lutheran • M. Lynn Gorguze, 2 ch **Cmte.** Budget • Energy & Commerce • Joint Economic
CoS. Daniel Zawitoski **LD.** Baillee Brown
Sched. Lauren Barker **PS.** Alexandra Polaski
Dist. Off. San Diego 858.455.5550

R: 183 **T:** 5th 62%
Elected Year: 2012

⚑ Rep. Katie Porter (POR-tur) D-CA-45 p 202.225.5611

Rm. LHOB 1117 **Web.** porter.house.gov
Bio. 01/03/1974 • Des Moines • Yale Univ. (CT), B.A., 1996; Harvard Univ., J.D., 2001 • Episcopalian • D., 3 ch **Cmte.** Natural Resources • Oversight & Reform
CoS. Nora Walsh-DeVries
Sched. Emily Silk **PS.** Jordan Wong
Dist. Off. Irvine 949.668.6600

R: 341 **T:** 2nd 54%
Elected Year: 2018

⚑ Rep. Lucille Roybal-Allard (ROY-buhl-A-lurd) D-CA-40 p 202.225.1766

Rm. RHOB 2083 **Web.** roybal- **f** 202.226.0350
allard.house.gov
Bio. 06/12/1941 • Boyle Heights • Member, State Assembly; Public Relations and Fundraising Executive • California State Univ., Los Angeles, B.A., 1965 • Catholic • M. Edward T. Allard III, 2 ch; 2 stepch; 9 gr-ch **Cmte.** Appropriations
CoS. Victor Castillo **LD.** Carlos Condarco
Sched. Christine Ochoa
Dist. Off. Commerce 323.721.8790

R: 22 **T:** 15th 73%
Elected Year: 2012

⚑ Rep. Raul Ruiz (roo-EES) D-CA-36 p 202.225.5330

Rm. RHOB 2342 **Web.** ruiz.house.gov **f** 202.225.1238
Bio. 08/25/1972 • Zacatecas • Univ. of California, Los Angeles, B.S., 1994; Harvard Univ., M.P.P., 2001; Harvard Univ., M.D., 2001; Harvard Univ., M.PH, 2007 • Seventh-Day Adventist • M. Monica Ruiz, 2 ch (twins) **Cmte.** Energy & Commerce • Veterans' Affairs
CoS. Tim Del Monico **LD.** Erin Doty
Sched. Lauren Gedney **PS.** Kelly O'Keeffe
Dist. Off. Hemet 951.765.2304 • Palm Desert 760.424.8888

R: 186 **T:** 5th 60%
Elected Year: 2012

⚑ Rep. Linda T. Sanchez (SAN-chez) D-CA-38 p 202.225.6676

Rm. RHOB 2329 **Web.** **f** 202.226.1012
lindasanchez.house.gov
Bio. 01/28/1969 • Orange • Union Official; Attorney • Univ. of California, Berkeley, B.A., 1991; Univ. of California School of Law, Los Angeles (JD), J.D., 1995 • Roman Catholic • M. James M. Sullivan, 1 ch; 3 stepch **Cmte.** Ways & Means
CoS. Ricky Xuan Le **LD.** Cody Willming
Sched. Gabriela Morris- **PS.** Michael Cummings
Flores
Dist. Off. Norwalk 562.860.5050

R: 67 **T:** 10th 74%
Elected Year: 2012

⚑ Rep. Adam B. Schiff (shihf) D-CA-28 p 202.225.4176

Rm. RHOB 2309 **Web.** schiff.house.gov **f** 202.225.5828
Bio. 06/22/1960 • Framingham • State Senator; U.S. Attorney, Los Angeles • Stanford Univ. (CA), B.A., 1982; Harvard Univ. Law School (MA), J.D., 1985 • Jewish • M. Eve Sanderson Schiff, 2 ch **Cmte.** Permanent Select on Intelligence • Select Investigate Jan 6 Attack on the U.S. Capitol
CoS. Patrick Boland **LD.** Danielle Fulfs
Sched. Kyle Abrams **PS.** Lauren French
Dist. Off. Burbank 818.450.2900 • Los Angeles 323.315.5555

R: 56 **T:** 11th 73%
Elected Year: 2012

CALIFORNIA

⚲ Rep. Brad J. Sherman (SHUR-muhn) D-CA-30 p 202.225.5911

Rm. RHOB 2181 **Web.** sherman.house.gov **f** 202.225.5879
Bio. 10/24/1954 • Los Angeles • Harvard Law Instructor;
CPA • Univ. of California, Los Angeles, B.A., 1974; Harvard
Univ. Law School (MA), J.D., 1979 • Jewish • M. Lisa
Kaplan Sherman, 3 ch **Cmte.** Communications Standards
Commission • Financial Services • Foreign Affairs •
Science, Space & Technology
CoS. Don MacDonald **LD.** Johan Propst
Sched. Kathryn McCool **PS.** Arya Ansari
Dist. Off. Sherman Oaks 818.501.9200

R: 41 **T:** 13th 70%
Elected Year: 2012

⚲ Rep. Jackie Speier (speer) D-CA-14 p 202.225.3531

Rm. RHOB 2465 **Web.** speier.house.gov **f** 202.226.4183
Bio. 05/14/1950 • San Francisco County • State Legislator;
Attorney • Univ. of California, Davis, B.A., 1972; Univ. of
California Hastings College of Law, J.D., 1976 • Roman
Catholic • M. Barry Dennis, 2 ch **Cmte.** Armed Services •
Oversight & Reform • Permanent Select on Intelligence
CoS. Josh Connolly **LD.** Yana Mayayeva
Sched. Kate Adams **PS.** Tracy Manzer
Dist. Off. San Mateo 650.342.0300

R: 106 **T:** 8th 79%
Elected Year: 2012

⚑ Rep. Michelle Park Steel (steel) R-CA-48 p 202.225.2415

Rm. LHOB 1113 **Web.** steel.house.gov **f** 202.225.2595
Bio. 06/21/1955 • Seoul • Pepperdine Univ., B.S.;
Univ. of Southern California, M.B.A. • Christian - Non-
Denominational • M. Shawn Steel, 2 ch **Cmte.** Education
& Labor • Joint Congressional-Executive Commission on
China • Transportation & Infrastructure
CoS. Arie Dana **LD.** Kenneth Clifford
Sched. Shelby Kaplan **PS.** Danielle Stewart
Dist. Off. Huntington Beach 714.960.6483

R: 423 **T:** 1st 51%
Elected Year: 2020

⚲ Rep. Eric Swalwell (SWALL-well) D-CA-15 p 202.225.5065

Rm. CHOB 174 **Web.** swalwell.house.gov **f** 202.226.3805
Bio. 11/16/1980 • Sac City • Univ. of Maryland - College
Park, B.A., 2003; Univ. of Maryland School of Law, J.D., 2006
• Christian - Non-Denominational • M. Brittany Ann Watts,
2 ch **Cmte.** Homeland Security • Judiciary • Permanent
Select on Intelligence
CoS. Yardena Wolf **LD.** Sarah Shapiro
Sched. Karina Gallardo **PS.** Jessica Gail
Dist. Off. Castro Valley 510.370.3322

R: 188 **T:** 5th 71%
Elected Year: 2012

⚲ Rep. Mark A. Takano (tah-KAH-no) D-CA-41 p 202.225.2305

Rm. CHOB 420 **Web.** takano.house.gov **f** 202.225.7018
Bio. 12/10/1960 • Riverside • Harvard College (MA), A.B.,
1983; School of Education, Univ. of California, Riverside,
M.F.A., 2010 • Methodist • S. **Cmte.** Education & Labor •
Veterans' Affairs
CoS. Richard McPike **LD.** Justin Maturo
Sched. Desiree Wroten **PS.** Lana Abbasi (CD)
Dist. Off. Riverside 951.222.0203

R: 189 **T:** 5th 64%
Elected Year: 2012

⚲ Rep. Mike C. Thompson (TOMP-suhn) D-CA-05 p 202.225.3311

Rm. CHOB 268 **Web.** **f** 202.225.4335
mikethompson.house.gov
Bio. 01/24/1951 • St. Helena • State Senator; CA State
Assembly Fellow • Army 1969-73 • California State Univ.,
Chico, B.A., 1982; California State Univ., Chico, M.A., 1996 •
Roman Catholic • M. Janet Thompson, 2 ch; 3 gr-ch **Cmte.**
Joint Taxation • Ways & Means
CoS. Melanie Rhinehart Van **LD.** Adam Durand
Tassell
Sched. Emma Tomaszewski **PS.** Jack Stelzner
Dist. Off. Napa 707.226.9898 • Santa Rosa 707.542.7182 •
Vallejo 707.645.1888

R: 50 **T:** 12th 76%
Elected Year: 2012

CALIFORNIA

Rep. Norma J. Torres (toe-ress)　　　D-CA-35　　p 202.225.6161

Rm. RHOB 2227 **Web.** torres.house.gov　　**f** 202.225.8671
Bio. 04/04/1965 • Escuintla • National Labor College (MD),
B.A., 2012 • Roman Catholic • M. Louis Torres, 3 ch **Cmte.**
Appropriations • Rules
CoS. Matthew Alpert　　　　**LD.** Serena Gobbi
Sched. Leah Carey　　　　　**PS.** Michaela Johnson
Dist. Off. Ontario 909.481.6474

R: 233　**T:** 4th　69%
Elected Year: 2014

Rep. David G. Valadao (va-luh-DAY-o)　　　R-CA-21　　p 202.225.4695

Rm. LHOB 1728 **Web.** valadao.house.gov
Bio. 04/14/1977 • Hanford • Catholic • M. Terra Valadao, 3
ch **Cmte.** Appropriations
CoS. Andrew Renteria　　　　**LD.** Amanda Hall
Sched. Hailee Howard
Dist. Off. Bakersfield 661.864.7736 • Hanford 559.460.6070

R: 243　**T:** 1st　50%
Elected Year: 2020

Rep. Juan C. Vargas (VAR-guhs)　　　D-CA-51　　p 202.225.8045

Rm. RHOB 2244 **Web.** vargas.house.gov　　**f** 202.225.2772
Bio. 03/07/1961 • National City • Univ. of San Diego, B.A.,
1983; Harvard Univ. Law School (MA), J.D., 1991 • Roman
Catholic • M. Adrienne D'Ascoli, 2 ch **Cmte.** Financial
Services • Foreign Affairs
CoS. Larry Cohen　　　　**LD.** Scott Hinkle
Sched. Brittany Murray　　**PS.** Gabriella Salazar
Dist. Off. Chula Vista 619.422.5963 • El Centro
760.312.9900

R: 190　**T:** 5th　68%
Elected Year: 2012

Rep. Maxine Waters (WAH-durs)　　　D-CA-43　　p 202.225.2201

Rm. RHOB 2221 **Web.** waters.house.gov　　**f** 202.225.7854
Bio. 08/15/1938 • St. Louis • Head Start Teacher; Delegate
to Democratic National Convention • California State Univ.,
Los Angeles, B.A., 1970 • Christian Church • M. Amb. Sidney
Williams, 2 ch; 2 gr-ch **Cmte.** Financial Services
　　　　　　　　　　　　　　LD. Patrick Fergusson
Sched. Darlene Murray
Dist. Off. Hawthrone 323.757.8900

R: 13　**T:** 16th　72%
Elected Year: 2012

COLORADO

Governor Jared S. Polis (POLL-lis)　　　　　p 303.866.2471

136 State Capitol　　　　　**C:** Denver
Denver, CO 80203-1792　　**P:** 5,695,564 (21)
Website colorado.gov　　**A:** 103,641.75 mi^2 (8th)
Fax 303.866.2003
Term Ends 2023
Lt. Governor
Dianne Primavera, D

U.S. Senators
Michael F. Bennet, D
John W. Hickenlooper, D
U.S. Representatives
01 / Diana L. DeGette, D
02 / Joe Neguse, D
03 / Lauren Boebert, R
04 / Ken R. Buck, R
05 / Doug Lamborn, R
06 / Jason Crow, D
07 / Ed G. Perlmutter, D

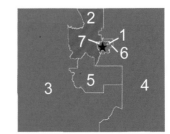

COLORADO

COLORADO

Sen. Michael F. Bennet (BEH-nuht)   D-CO-Sr.   p 202.224.5852

Rm. RSOB 261 **Web.** bennet.senate.gov   **f** 202.228.5097
Bio. 11/28/1964 • New Delhi • Schools Superintendent; Political Aide • Wesleyan Univ. (CT), B.A., 1987; Yale Univ. Law School (CT), J.D., 1993 • Episcopalian • M. Susan Daggett Bennet, 3 ch **Cmte.** Agriculture, Nutrition & Forestry • Finance • Intelligence
CoS. Kristin Mollet   **LD.** Brian Appel
Sched. Dani Kimball (CD)   **PS.** Olivia Bercow
Dist. Off. Alamosa 719.587.0096 • Colorado Springs 719.328.1100 • Denver 303.455.7600 • Durango 970.259.1710 • Fort Collins 970.224.2200 • Grand Junction 970.241.6631 • Pueblo 719.542.7550

R: 36   **T:** 3rd   50%
Elected Year: 2009
Next Election: 2022

Sen. John W. Hickenlooper (HIH-kuhn-loo-pur)   D-CO-Jr.   p 202.224.5941

                                        f 202.224.3115
Bio. 02/07/1952 • Narberth • Wesleyan Univ. (CT), 1974; Wesleyan Univ. (CT), M.S., 1980 • Quaker • M. Robin Pringle, 1 ch (1 from previous marriage) **Cmte.** Commerce, Science & Transportation • Energy & Natural Resources • Health, Education, Labor & Pensions • Small Business & Entrepreneurship
CoS. Kirtan Mehta (CD)   **LD.** Kate Cassling (CD)
Sched. Rayhaan Merani (CD)   **PS.** Alyssa Roberts (CD)
Dist. Off. Colorado Springs 719.632.6706 • Denver 303.244.1628 • Durango 970.880.7236 • Fort Collins 970.484.3502 • Grand Junction 970.822.4530 • Greeley 970.352.5546

R: 93   **T:** 1st   54%
Elected Year: 2020
Next Election: 2026

Rep. Lauren Boebert (BOE-burt)   R-CO-03   p 202.225.4761

Rm. LHOB 1609 **Web.** boebert.house.gov
Bio. 12/15/1986 • Orlando • Christian - Non-Denominational • M. Jayson Boebert, 4 ch **Cmte.** Budget • Natural Resources
CoS. Jeff Small   **LD.** Paige Agostin
Sched. Kristine Nichols   **PS.** Ben Stout
Dist. Off. Durango 970.317.6130 • Grand Junction 970.208.0460 • Pueblo 719.696.6970

R: 374   **T:** 1st   51%
Elected Year: 2020

Rep. Ken R. Buck (buck)   R-CO-04   p 202.225.4676

Rm. RHOB 2455 **Web.** buck.house.gov
Bio. 02/16/1959 • Ossining • Princeton Univ. (NJ), A.B., 1981; Univ. of Wyoming (WY), J.D., 1985 • Wesleyan • M. Perry Lynn, 2 ch (2 from previous marriage) **Cmte.** Foreign Affairs • Judiciary
CoS. James Braid
Sched. Lucy Harrington   **PS.** Collin B. Cummings
Dist. Off. Castle Rock 720.639.9165 • Greeley 970.702.2136

R: 211   **T:** 4th   60%
Elected Year: 2014

Rep. Jason Crow (kroe)   D-CO-06   p 202.225.7882

Rm. LHOB 1229 **Web.** crow.house.gov
Bio. 03/15/1979 • Beaver Dam • Univ. of Wisconsin - Madison, B.A., 2002; Univ. of Denver (CO), J.D., 2009 • Christian - Non-Denominational • M. Deserai Crow, 2 ch **Cmte.** Armed Services • Permanent Select on Intelligence • Small Business
CoS. Macey Matthews   **LD.** Emily Kolano
Sched. Liz Natonski   **PS.** Kaylin Dines
Dist. Off. Aurora 720.748.7514

R: 306   **T:** 2nd   57%
Elected Year: 2018

COLORADO

꙳ Rep. Diana L. DeGette (deh-GET) D-CO-01 p 202.225.4431

Rm. RHOB 2111 **Web.** degette.house.gov **f** 202.225.5657
Bio. 07/29/1957 • Tachikawa • Attorney; State
Representative • Colorado College, B.A., 1979; New York
Univ. Law School, J.D., 1982 • Presbyterian • M. Lino
Lipinsky, 2 ch **Cmte.** Energy & Commerce • Natural
Resources
CoS. Joeana Middleton **LD.** Thomas J. Woodburn
(CD)
Sched. Hannah Katz (CD) **PS.** Ryan Brown
Dist. Off. Denver 303.844.4988

R: 36 **T:** 13th 74%
Elected Year: 1996

꙳ Rep. Doug Lamborn (LAM-born) R-CO-05 p 202.225.4422

Rm. RHOB 2371 **Web.** lamborn.house.gov **f** 202.226.2638
Bio. 05/24/1954 • Leavenworth • Attorney • Univ. of
Kansas School of Journalism, B.S., 1978; Univ. of Kansas
School of Law, J.D., 1985 • Christian Church • M. Jeanie
Lamborn, 5 ch **Cmte.** Armed Services • Natural Resources
CoS. Dale Anderson **LD.** James Thomas
Sched. Meghan Selip **PS.** Cassandra Sebastian
(CD)
Dist. Off. Colorado Springs 719.520.0055

R: 95 **T:** 8th 58%
Elected Year: 2006

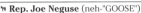

꙳ Rep. Joe Neguse (neh-"GOOSE") D-CO-02 p 202.225.2161

Rm. LHOB 1419 **Web.** neguse.house.gov
Bio. 05/13/1984 • Bakersfield • Univ. of Colorado, Boulder,
Bach. Deg., 2005; Univ. of Colorado, Boulder, J.D., 2009
• Christian Church • M. Andrea Neguse, 1 ch **Cmte.**
Judiciary • Natural Resources • Rules • Select Committee
on the Climate Crisis
CoS. Jennifer Van der Heide **LD.** Carissa Bunge
Sched. Priya Robb (CD) **PS.** Sally Tucker
Dist. Off. Boulder 303.335.1045 • Fort Collins 970.372.3971

R: 335 **T:** 2nd 62%
Elected Year: 2018

꙳ Rep. Ed G. Perlmutter (PERL-muh-ter) D-CO-07 p 202.225.2645

Rm. LHOB 1226 **Web.** perlmutter.house.gov **f** 202.225.5278
Bio. 05/01/1953 • Denver • Law Firm Director • Univ. of
Colorado, Boulder, B.A., 1975; Univ. of Colorado School of
Law, J.D., 1978 • Protestant - Unspecified Christian • M.
Nancy Perlmutter, 3 ch **Cmte.** Financial Services • Rules
• Science, Space & Technology • Select Committee on the
Modernization of Congress
CoS. Danielle Radovich **LD.** Jeffrey O'Neil
Piper (CD)
Sched. Alison Wright **PS.** Ashley Verville (CD)
Dist. Off. Lakewood 303.274.7944

R: 98 **T:** 8th 59%
Elected Year: 2006

CONNECTICUT

꙳ Governor Ned Lamont (LAH-mawnt) p 860.566.4840

State Capitol, 210 Capitol Ave. **C:** Hartford
Hartford, CT 06106 **P:** 3,572,665 (29)
Website ct.gov **A:** 4,842.49 mi^2 (48th)
Fax 860.524.7395
Term Ends 2023
Lt. Governor
Susan Bysiewicz, **D**

U.S. Senators
Richard Blumenthal, **D**
Chris S. Murphy, **D**
U.S. Representatives
01 / John B. Larson, **D**
02 / Joe Courtney, **D**
03 / Rosa DeLauro, **D**
04 / Jim A. Himes, **D**
05 / Jahana Hayes, **D**

CONNECTICUT

CONNECTICUT

⚑ Sen. Richard Blumenthal (BLOOM-un-thawl) D-CT-Sr. p 202.224.2823

Rm. HSOB 706 **Web.** blumenthal.senate.gov **f** 202.224.9673
Bio. 02/13/1946 • Brooklyn • State Attorney General; State
Legislator • Marine Corps Reserve, 1970-75 • Harvard
College (MA), A.B., 1967; Yale Univ. Law School (CT),
J.D., 1973 • Jewish • M. Cynthia Allison Malkin, 4 ch
Cmte. Aging • Armed Services • Commerce, Science &
Transportation • Joint Security & Cooperation in Europe •
Judiciary • Veterans' Affairs
CoS. Joel Kelsey **LD.** Brian Steele
Sched. Michael Lawson **PS.** Maria McElwain
Dist. Off. Bridgeport 203.330.0598 • Hartford 860.258.6940

R: 49 **T:** 2nd 63%
Elected Year: 2010
Next Election: 2022

⚑ Sen. Chris S. Murphy (MUR-fee) D-CT-Jr. p 202.224.4041

Rm. HSOB 136 **Web.** murphy.senate.gov **f** 202.224.9750
Bio. 08/03/1973 • White Plains • State Legislator; Attorney
• Williams College, B.A., 1996; Univ. of Connecticut School
of Law, J.D., 2002 • Protestant - Unspecified Christian • M.
Catherine Holahan Murphy, 2 ch **Cmte.** Appropriations •
Foreign Relations • Health, Education, Labor & Pensions
CoS. Allison Herwitt **LD.** Chris Mewett
Sched. Maya Ashwal **PS.** Jamie Geller
Dist. Off. Hartford 860.549.8463

R: 54 **T:** 2nd 60%
Elected Year: 2012
Next Election: 2024

⚑ Rep. Joe Courtney (KORT-nee) D-CT-02 p 202.225.2076

Rm. RHOB 2449 **Web.** courtney.house.gov **f** 202.225.4977
Bio. 04/06/1953 • West Hartford • Attorney • Tufts Univ.
(MA), B.A., 1975; Univ. of Connecticut School of Law, J.D.,
1978 • Roman Catholic • M. Audrey Courtney, 2 ch **Cmte.**
Armed Services • Education & Labor
CoS. Neil McKiernan **LD.** Maria Costigan
Sched. Rachel Newstadt **PS.** Patrick Cassidy
Dist. Off. Enfield 860.741.6011 • Norwich 860.886.0139

R: 92 **T:** 8th 59%
Elected Year: 2006

⚑ Rep. Rosa DeLauro (deh-LOOR-o) D-CT-03 p 202.225.3661

Rm. RHOB 2413 **Web.** delauro.house.gov **f** 202.225.4890
Bio. 03/02/1943 • New Haven • Executive Director, Emily's
List; Congressional Aide • Marymount College (NY), B.A.,
1964; Columbia Univ. (NY), M.A., 1966 • Roman Catholic •
M. Stanley Greenberg, 3 ch; 4 gr-ch **Cmte.** Appropriations
CoS. Liz Albertine **LD.** Christian Lovell
Sched. Hadar Arazi **PS.** Katelynn Thorpe
Dist. Off. New Haven 203.562.3718

R: 12 **T:** 16th 59%
Elected Year: 1990

⚑ Rep. Jahana Hayes (hayz) D-CT-05 p 202.225.4476

Rm. LHOB 1415 **Web.** hayes.house.gov
Bio. 03/08/1973 • Waterbury • Naugatuck Valley
Community College (CT), A.A., 2002; Southern Connecticut
State Univ., B.S., 2005; Univ. of Saint Joseph (CT), M.A., 2012
• Methodist • M. Milford Hayes, 4 ch **Cmte.** Agriculture •
Education & Labor
CoS. Alex Ginis **LD.** Madeline Daly
  PS. Annmarie Goyzueta
Dist. Off. Waterbury 860.223.8412

R: 322 **T:** 2nd 55%
Elected Year: 2018

Rep. Jim A. Himes (hymz)   D-CT-04   p 202.225.5541

Rm. RHOB 2137   **Web.** himes.house.gov   **f** 202.225.9629
Bio. 07/05/1966 • Lima • Financial Executive • Harvard Univ., B.A., 1988; Oxford Univ. (England), M.Phil, 1990 • Presbyterian • M. Mary Himes, 2 ch   **Cmte.** Financial Services • Permanent Select on Intelligence • Select Economic Disparity & Fairness in Growth
CoS. Mark Snyder   **LD.** Hannah Aiken
Sched. Elizabeth Stanley   **PS.** Patrick Malone
Dist. Off. Bridgeport 203.333.6600 • Stamford 203.353.9400

R: 110   **T:** 7th 62%
Elected Year: 2008

Rep. John B. Larson (LAR-suhn)   D-CT-01   p 202.225.2265

Rm. LHOB 1501   **Web.** larson.house.gov   **f** 202.225.1031
Bio. 07/22/1948 • Hartford • State Senator; Businessman • Central Connecticut State Univ. (CT), B.S., 1971 • Catholic • M. Leslie Best Larson, 3 ch   **Cmte.** Ways & Means
CoS. Scott Stephanou   **LD.** Nancy Perry
Sched. Sarah Gianni   **PS.** Mary Yatrousis
Dist. Off. Hartford 860.278.8888

R: 46   **T:** 12th 64%
Elected Year: 1998

DELAWARE

Governor John C. Carney Jr. (KAR-nee)   p 302.744.4101

150 Martin Luther King Jr. Blvd.,   **C:** Dover
2nd Floor   **P:** 967,171 (46)
Dover, DE 19901   **A:** 1,948.66 mi^2 (50th)
Website delaware.gov
Fax 302.739.2775
Term Ends 2025
Lt. Governor
Bethany Hall-Long, **D**

U.S. Senators
Tom R. Carper, **D**
Chris A. Coons, **D**
U.S. Representatives
01 / Lisa Blunt Rochester, **D**

Sen. Tom R. Carper (KAR-pur)   D-DE-Sr.   p 202.224.2441

Rm. HSOB 513   **Web.** carper.senate.gov   **f** 202.228.2190
Bio. 01/23/1947 • Beckley • Governor; U.S. Representative • Navy 1968-73; Navy Reserve 1973-91 • Ohio State Univ., B.A., 1968; Univ. of Delaware, Newark, M.B.A., 1975 • Presbyterian • M. Martha Ann Stacy Carper, 2 ch   **Cmte.** Environment & Public Works • Finance • Homeland Security & Government Affairs
CoS. Jan Beukelman   **LD.** Lucy Xiao
Sched. Lydia Wehrley   **PS.** Rachel Levitan
Dist. Off. Dover 302.674.3308 • Georgetown 302.856.7690 • Wilmington 302.573.6291

R: 14   **T:** 4th 60%
Elected Year: 2000
Next Election: 2024

Sen. Chris A. Coons (koonz)   D-DE-Jr.   p 202.224.5042

Rm. RSOB 218   **Web.** coons.senate.gov   **f** 202.228.3075
Bio. 09/09/1963 • Greenwich • Amherst College (MA), B.A., 1985; Yale Univ. Law School (CT), J.D., 1992; Yale Univ. Divinity School (CT), Mast. Deg., 1992 • Presbyterian • M. Annie Lingenfelter, 3 ch   **Cmte.** Appropriations • Ethics • Foreign Relations • Judiciary • Small Business & Entrepreneurship
CoS. Jonathan Stahler   **LD.** Brian Winseck
Sched. Chelsea Moser   **PS.** Will A. Baskin-Gerwitz
Dist. Off. Dover 302.736.5601 • Wilmington 302.573.6345

R: 39   **T:** 3rd 60%
Elected Year: 2010
Next Election: 2026

DELAWARE

🐦 **Rep. Lisa Blunt Rochester** (RAH-chess-tur)   D-DE-01   p 202.225.4165
Rm. LHOB 1724 **Web.** bluntrochester.house.gov
Bio. 02/10/1962 • Philadelphia • Fairleigh Dickinson Univ., Bach. Deg., 1985; Univ. of Delaware, M.A., 2003 • Christian Church • W., 2 ch **Cmte.** Energy & Commerce
CoS. Jacqueline Sanchez   **LD.** Kevin Diamond
Sched. Quristin Walker   **PS.** Andrew Donnelly
Dist. Off. Georgetown 302.858.4773 • Wilmington 302.830.2330

R: 250 **T:** 3rd 58%
Elected Year: 2016

FLORIDA

FLORIDA

🏛 **Governor Ron D. DeSantis** (dee-SAN-tis)   p 850.488.7146
The Capitol
400 S. Monroe St.
Tallahassee, FL 32399-0001
Website flgov.com
Fax 850.487.0801
Term Ends 2023
Lt. Governor
Jeanette Nunez, R

C: Tallahassee
P: 21,299,325 (3)
A: 53,624.55 mi^2 (26th)

U.S. Senators
Marco Rubio, R
Rick Scott, R
U.S. Representatives
01 / Matt Gaetz, R
02 / Neal P. Dunn, R
03 / Kat Cammack, R
04 / John Rutherford, R
05 / Al J. Lawson, D
06 / Mike G. Waltz, R
07 / Stephanie Murphy, D
08 / Bill Posey, R
09 / Darren M. Soto, D
10 / Val B. Demings, D
11 / Daniel A. Webster, R
12 / Gus M. Bilirakis, R
13 / Charlie J. Crist, D
14 / Kathy A. Castor, D
15 / Scott Franklin, R
16 / Vern G. Buchanan, R
17 / Greg Steube, R
18 / Brian Mast, R
19 / Byron Donalds, R
20 / Sheila Cherfilus-McCormick, D
21 / Lois J. Frankel, D
22 / Ted E. Deutch, D
23 / Debbie Wasserman Schultz, D
24 / Frederica S. Wilson, D
25 / Mario Diaz-Balart, R
26 / Carlos Gimenez, R
27 / Maria E. Salazar, R

🏛 **Sen. Marco Rubio** (ROO-bee-o)   R-FL-Sr.   p 202.224.3041
Rm. RSOB 284 **Web.** rubio.senate.gov   **f** 202.228.0285
Bio. 05/28/1971 • Miami • State Legislator; Spkr., Florida House of Representatives • Univ. of Florida, B.S., 1993; Univ. of Miami, J.D., 1996 • Roman Catholic • M. Jeanette Dousdebes, 4 ch **Cmte.** Aging • Appropriations • Foreign Relations • Intelligence • Joint Congressional-Executive Commission on China • Joint Security & Cooperation in Europe • Small Business & Entrepreneurship
CoS. Mike Needham   **LD.** Lauren Reamy
Sched. Bridget Spurlock   **PS.** Ansley Bradwell
Dist. Off. Fort Myers 239.318.6464 • Jacksonville 904.354.4300 • Miami 305.596.4224 • Orlando 407.254.2573 • Palm Beach Gardens 561.775.3360 • Pensacola 850.433.2603 • Tallahassee 850.599.9100 • Tampa 813.853.1099

R: 46 **T:** 2nd 52%
Elected Year: 2010
Next Election: 2022

FLORIDA

Sen. Rick Scott (skaht) — R-FL-Jr. — p 202.224.5274

Rm. HSOB 502 **Web.** rickscott.senate.gov **f** 202.224.0104
Bio. Bloomington • Univ. of Missouri - Kansas City, B.S., 1975; Southern Methodist Univ. Law School (TX), J.D., 1978 • Christian Church • M. Ann Scott, 2 ch; 6 gr-ch **Cmte.** Aging • Armed Services • Budget • Commerce, Science & Transportation • Homeland Security & Government Affairs • Small Business & Entrepreneurship
CoS. Craig Carbone **LD.** Jon Foltz
Sched. Megan Bailey **PS.** McKinley Lewis
Dist. Off. Coral Gables 786.501.7141 • Jacksonville 904.479.7227 • Kissimmee 407.586.7879 • Naples 239.231.7890 • Orlando 407.872.7161 • Pensacola 850.760.5151 • Tallahassee 850.942.8415 • Tampa 813.225.7040 • West Palm Beach 561.514.0189

R: 90 **T:** 1st 50%
Elected Year: 2018
Next Election: 2024

Rep. Gus M. Bilirakis (bih-lih-RAK-uhss) — R-FL-12 — p 202.225.5755

Rm. RHOB 2354 **Web.** bilirakis.house.gov **f** 202.225.4085
Bio. 02/08/1963 • Gainesville • Attorney; State Legislator • Univ. of Florida, B.S., 1986; Stetson Univ. College of Law (FL), J.D., 1989 • Greek Orthodox • M. Eva Lialios Bilirakis, 4 ch **Cmte.** Energy & Commerce
CoS. Liz Hittos **LD.** Jonathan Vecchi
Sched. Savannah Bolender **PS.** Summer Robertson
Dist. Off. New Port Richey 727.232.2921 • Tarpon Springs 727.940.5860

R: 87 **T:** 8th 63%
Elected Year: 2012

Rep. Vern G. Buchanan (byoo-KA-nuhn) — R-FL-16 — p 202.225.5015

Rm. RHOB 2110 **Web.** buchanan.house.gov **f** 202.226.0828
Bio. 05/08/1951 • Detroit • Automobile Dealer; Owner, Reinsurance Co. • Michigan Air National Guard 1969-1975 • Cleary Univ. (MI), B.B.A., 1975; Univ. of Detroit (MI), M.B.A., 1986 • Baptist • M. Sandy Harris Buchanan, 2 ch **Cmte.** Joint Taxation • Ways & Means
CoS. Sean Brady **LD.** Aaron Bill
Sched. Chase Babair **PS.** Savannah Glasgow
Dist. Off. Bradenton 941.747.9081 • Sarasota 941.951.6643

R: 88 **T:** 8th 56%
Elected Year: 2012

Rep. Kat Cammack (KAM-mek) — R-FL-03 — p 202.225.5744

Rm. LHOB 1626 **Web.** cammack.house.gov **f** 202.225.3973
Bio. 02/16/1988 • Denver • Naval War College (RI), Mast. Deg.; Metropolitan State Univ. of Denver (CO), Bach. Deg., 2011 • Christian - Non-Denominational • M. Matt Harrison **Cmte.** Agriculture • Communications Standards Commission • Homeland Security • Select Economic Disparity & Fairness in Growth
CoS. Larry Calhoun **LD.** Joshua Woodward
Sched. Alexander Strizak **PS.** Adeline Sandridge
Dist. Off. Gainesville 352.505.0838 • Orange Park 904.276.9626

R: 378 **T:** 1st 57%
Elected Year: 2020

Rep. Kathy A. Castor (KAS-tur) — D-FL-14 — p 202.225.3376

Rm. RHOB 2052 **Web.** castor.house.gov **f** 202.225.5652
Bio. 08/20/1966 • Miami • County Commissioner • Emory Univ. - Atlanta (GA), B.A., 1988; Florida State Univ. School of Law, J.D., 1991 • Presbyterian • M. Bill Lewis, 2 ch **Cmte.** Energy & Commerce • Select Committee on the Climate Crisis
CoS. Lara Hopkins
Sched. Maria Robayo **PS.** Rikki Miller
Dist. Off. Tampa 813.871.2817

R: 89 **T:** 8th 60%
Elected Year: 2012

Rep. Sheila Cherfilus-McCormick () — D-FL-20 — p 202.225.1313

Rm. RHOB 2365 **Web.** cherfilus-mccormick.house.gov **f** 202.225.1171
Bio. • Howard Univ., B.S., 2001; Saint Thomas Univ. College of Law (FL), J.D., 2010 • **Cmte.** Education & Labor • Veterans' Affairs
Dist. Off. Tamarac 954.733.2800 • West Palm Beach 561.461.6767

R: 434 **T:** 1st 79%
Elected Year: 2021

Rep. Charlie J. Crist (Krist) D-FL-13 p 202.225.5961

Rm. CHOB 215 **Web.** crist.house.gov **f** 202.225.9764
Bio. 07/24/1956 • Altoona • 44th Governor of Florida;
Attorney General, State of Florida; Deputy Secretary, FL
Dept. of Business and Professional Regulation; Candidate,
FL State Senate; Candidate, FL State Senate; Member, FL
Senate; FL Commissioner of Education • Florida State
Univ., B.S., 1978; Cumberland School of Law, Stamford Univ.
(AL), J.D., 1981 • Methodist • M. Carole Rome Crist, 2 stepch
Cmte. Appropriations • Science, Space & Technology
CoS. Austin Durrer **LD.** Christopher Fisher
Dist. Off. Seminole 727.318.6770 • St. Petersburg
727.318.6770

R: 256 **T:** 3rd 53%
Elected Year: 2016

Rep. Val B. Demings (DEH-mingz) D-FL-10 p 202.225.2176

Rm. CHOB 217 **Web.** demings.house.gov **f** 202.226.6559
Bio. Jacksonville • Webster Univ. (MO), M.P.A.; Florida
State Univ., B.S., 1979 • African Methodist Episcopal • M.
Jerry L. Demings, 3 ch; 5 gr-ch **Cmte.** Homeland Security •
Judiciary • Permanent Select on Intelligence
CoS. Wendy D. Anderson **LD.** Aimee Collins-
Mandeville
Sched. Wendy Featherson **PS.** Daniel Gleick
Dist. Off. Orlando 321.388.9808

R: 257 **T:** 3rd 64%
Elected Year: 2016

Rep. Ted E. Deutch (doych) D-FL-22 p 202.225.3001

Rm. RHOB 2323 **Web.** teddeutch.house.gov **f** 202.225.5974
Bio. 05/07/1966 • Bethlehem • Univ. of Michigan, B.A.,
1988; Univ. of Michigan Law School, J.D., 1990 • Jewish •
M. Jill Deutch, 3 ch (twins) **Cmte.** Ethics • Foreign Affairs •
Judiciary
CoS. Joshua Rogin **LD.** Joshua Lipman
Sched. Alex Rocha (CD) **PS.** Aviva Abusch
Dist. Off. Boca Raton 561.470.5440 • Coral Springs
954.255.8336 • Fort Lauderdale 954.255.8336 • Margate
954.972.6454

R: 121 **T:** 7th 59%
Elected Year: 2016

Rep. Mario Diaz-Balart (DEE-az-buh-LART) R-FL-25 p 202.225.4211

Rm. CHOB 374 **Web.** **f** 202.225.8576
mariodiazbalart.house.gov
Bio. 09/25/1961 • Fort Lauderdale • State Legislator;
President, Marketing and PR Firm • Roman Catholic • M. Tia
Diaz-Balart, 1 ch **Cmte.** Appropriations
CoS. Cesar A. Gonzalez **LD.** Chris Sweet
 PS. Laura Hernandez
Dist. Off. Doral 305.470.8555 • Naples 239.348.1620

R: 62 **T:** 10th 100%
Elected Year: 2002

Rep. Byron Donalds (DAH-nuld) R-FL-19 p 202.225.2536

Rm. CHOB 523 **Web.** donalds.house.gov
Bio. 10/28/1978 • Brooklyn • Florida State Univ., B.S.,
2002 • Christian Church • M. Erika Donalds, 3 ch **Cmte.**
Budget • Oversight & Reform • Select Economic Disparity &
Fairness in Growth • Small Business
CoS. Tyler Haymore **LD.** Alexandria Smith
Sched. Abby Delahoyde **PS.** Harrison Fields
Dist. Off. Cape Coral 239.599.6033 • Naples 239.252.6225

R: 382 **T:** 1st 61%
Elected Year: 2020

Rep. Neal P. Dunn (dun) R-FL-02 p 202.225.5235

Rm. CHOB 316 **Web.** dunn.house.gov **f** 202.225.5615
Bio. New Haven • Washington and Lee Univ. (VA), Bach.
Deg.; George Washington Univ. Medical School (DC), M.D.
• Catholic • M. Leah Dunn, 3 ch; 3 gr-ch **Cmte.** Energy &
Commerce
CoS. Michael Lowry **LD.** Matt Blackwell
Sched. Meghan Myhill (CD) **PS.** Leah Courtney
Dist. Off. Panama City 850.785.0812 • Tallahassee
850.891.8610

R: 258 **T:** 3rd 98%
Elected Year: 2016

📍 Rep. Lois J. Frankel (FRANK-uhl) D-FL-21 p 202.225.9890

Rm. RHOB 2305 **Web.** frankel.house.gov **f** 202.225.1224
Bio. 05/16/1948 • New York • Boston Univ. (MA), B.A.,
1970; Georgetown Univ. Law Center (DC), J.D., 1973 •
Jewish • D., 1 ch **Cmte.** Appropriations • Veterans' Affairs
CoS. Joshua D. Cohen **LD.** Bradley Solyan
Sched. Kate Regan **PS.** Morgan Routman
Dist. Off. Boca Raton 561.998.9045

R: 169 **T:** 5th 59%
Elected Year: 2016

📍 Rep. Scott Franklin (FRANK-luhn) R-FL-15 p 202.225.1252

Rm. LHOB 1517 **Web.** franklin.house.gov **f** 202.226.0585
Bio. 08/23/1964 • Thomaston • U.S. Naval Academy (MD),
B.S., 1986; Embry-Riddle Aeronautical Univ., M.B.A., 1994;
Univ. of Pennsylvania Wharton School of Business (PA), B.S.,
2003 • Presbyterian • M. Amy Wood, 3 ch **Cmte.** Armed
Services • Oversight & Reform
CoS. Melissa Kelly **LD.** Charles Truxal
Sched. Katharine A. Tate **PS.** Russel Read
Dist. Off. Lakeland 863.644.8215

R: 387 **T:** 1st 55%
Elected Year: 2020

📍 Rep. Matt Gaetz ("gates") R-FL-01 p 202.225.4136

Rm. LHOB 1721 **Web.** gaetz.house.gov **f** 202.225.3414
Bio. 05/07/1982 • Hollywood • Florida State Univ., B.S.,
2003 • Baptist • M. Ginger Luckey, 1 adopted ch **Cmte.**
Armed Services • Judiciary
CoS. Jillian Lane Wyant **LD.** Isabela Belchior
  PS. Joel Valdez
Dist. Off. Fort Walton Beach 850.479.1183 • Pensacola
850.479.1183

R: 262 **T:** 3rd 65%
Elected Year: 2016

📍 Rep. Carlos Gimenez (hym-MEHN-ez) R-FL-26 p 202.225,2778

Rm. CHOB 419 **Web.** gimenez.house.gov
Bio. Havana • Barry Univ., Bach. Deg. • Catholic •
M. Lourdes Portela, 3 ch; 6 gr-ch **Cmte.** Homeland
Security • Science, Space & Technology • Transportation &
Infrastructure
CoS. Alex Ferro **LD.** Chase Clanahan
  PS. Danny Jativa
Dist. Off. Florida City 305.222.0160 • Key West
305.292.4485 • Miami 305.222.0160

R: 389 **T:** 1st 52%
Elected Year: 2020

📍 Rep. Al J. Lawson Jr. (LAW-suhn) D-FL-05 p 202.225.0123

Rm. RHOB 2437 **Web.** lawson.house.gov **f** 202.225.2256
Bio. Midway • Florida Agricultural and Mechanical Univ.,
B.S., 1970; Florida State Univ., M.S., 1973 • Episcopalian • M.
Delores J. Brooks Lawson, 2 ch; 2 gr-ch **Cmte.** Agriculture
• Financial Services
CoS. Deborah Fairhurst **LD.** Amber Milenkevich
  PS. Ayanna Young
Dist. Off. Jacksonville 904.354.1652 • Tallahassee
850.558.9450

R: 273 **T:** 3rd 65%
Elected Year: 2016

📍 Rep. Brian Mast ("mast") R-FL-18 p 202.225.3026

Rm. RHOB 2182 **Web.** mast.house.gov **f** 202.225.8398
Bio. 07/10/1980 • Grand Rapids • Harvard Univ., Bach.
Deg., 2016 • Christian Church • M. Brianna Mast, 3 ch
Cmte. Foreign Affairs • Joint Congressional-Executive
Commission on China • Transportation & Infrastructure
CoS. James Langenderfer **LD.** Steve Koncar
Sched. Hannah Thomas **PS.** AnnMarie Graham
Dist. Off. North Palm Beach 561.530.7778 • Port St Lucie
772.336.2877 • Stuart 772.403.0900

R: 274 **T:** 3rd 56%
Elected Year: 2016

FLORIDA

🎗 Rep. Stephanie Murphy (MUR-fee)

D-FL-07   p 202.225.4035

Rm. LHOB 1710 **Web.** stephaniemurphy.house.gov   **f** 202.226.0821
Bio. 09/16/1978 • Ho Chi Minh City, Vietnam • College of William and Mary (VA), B.A., 2000; Georgetown Univ. (DC), M.S., 2004 • Christian Church • M. Sean Murphy, 2 ch
Cmte. Armed Services • Select Investigate Jan 6 Attack on the U.S. Capitol • Ways & Means
CoS. Bradley Neal Howard   **LD.** John Laufer
Sched. Lauren Calmet   **PS.** MacKensie Kvalvik
Dist. Off. Orlando 888.205.5421 • Sanford 888.205.5421

R: 276   **T:** 3rd 55%
Elected Year: 2016

🎗 Rep. Bill Posey (POE-zee)

R-FL-08   p 202.225.3671

Rm. RHOB 2150 **Web.** posey.house.gov   **f** 202.225.3516
Bio. 12/18/1947 • Washington • State Legislator; Realtor • Brevard Community College (FL), A.A., 1969 • Methodist • M. Katie Ingram Posey, 2 ch; 3 gr-ch **Cmte.** Financial Services • Science, Space & Technology
CoS. Stuart Burns   **LD.** Valentina J. Valenta
Sched. Allison Turk   **PS.** George Cecala
Dist. Off. Melbourne 321.632.1776

R: 114   **T:** 7th 61%
Elected Year: 2013

🎗 Rep. John Rutherford (RUH-thur-furd)

R-FL-04   p 202.225.2501

Rm. LHOB 1711 **Web.** rutherford.house.gov **f** 202.225.2504
Bio. Omaha • Florida Junior College, A.A., 1972; Florida State Univ., B.S., 1974 • Catholic • M. Patricia Rutherford, 2 ch; 6 gr-ch **Cmte.** Appropriations • Ethics
CoS. Jenifer Bradley   **LD.** Hannah Strub
Sched. Carole Anne Spohn   **PS.** Alex Lanfranconi
Dist. Off. Jacksonville 904.831.5205

R: 280   **T:** 3rd 61%
Elected Year: 2016

🎗 Rep. Maria E. Salazar (SA-luh-zar)

R-FL-27   p 202.225.3931

Rm. LHOB 1616 **Web.** salazar.house.gov
Bio. 11/01/1961 • Miami • Univ. of Miami (FL)-Teacher's Certificate, B.A., 1983; Harvard Univ. John F. Kennedy School of Government (MA), M.P.A., 1995 • Christian - Non-Denominational • M. Jaime Court, 2 ch **Cmte.** Foreign Affairs • Small Business
CoS. Tom Moran   **LD.** John Mark Kolb
    PS. Valerie Chicola
Dist. Off. Miami 305.668.2285

R: 421   **T:** 1st 51%
Elected Year: 2020

🎗 Rep. Darren M. Soto (so-toe)

D-FL-09   p 202.225.9889

Rm. RHOB 2353 **Web.** soto.house.gov   **f** 202.225.9742
Bio. 02/25/1978 • Ringwood • Rutgers Univ. (NJ), B.A., 2000; George Washington Univ. School of Law (DC), J.D., 2004 • Catholic • M. Amanda Soto **Cmte.** Energy & Commerce • Natural Resources
CoS. Christine A. Biron   **LD.** Nicole McLaren
Sched. Dilenny Reyes   **PS.** Belen Sassone
Dist. Off. Haines City 407.452.1171 • Kissimmee 407.452.1171 • Lake Wales 407.452.1171 • Orlando 202.322.4476 • Winter Haven 407.452.1171

R: 282   **T:** 3rd 56%
Elected Year: 2016

🎗 Rep. Greg Steube (STOO-bee)

R-FL-17   p 202.225.5792

Rm. RHOB 2457 **Web.** steube.house.gov   **f** 202.225.3132
Bio. 05/19/1978 • Bradenton • Univ. of Florida, B.S., 2001; Univ. of Florida Levin College of Law, J.D., 2003 • Methodist • M. Jennifer Mary Retzer, 1 ch **Cmte.** Foreign Affairs • Judiciary
CoS. Alex Blair   **LD.** Twinkle Patel
    PS. Sadie Thorman
Dist. Off. Lake Placid 941.499.3214 • Punta Gorda 941.499.3214 • Venice 941.499.3214

R: 353   **T:** 2nd 65%
Elected Year: 2018

▶ Rep. Mike G. Waltz (walts)   R-FL-06   p 202.225.2706

Rm. CHOB 213 **Web.** waltz.house.gov
Bio. 01/31/1974 • Boynton Beach • Virginia Military
Institute, B.A., 1996 • Christian Church • D., 1 ch   **Cmte.**
Armed Services • Science, Space & Technology
CoS. Micah T. Ketchel   **LD.** Walker B. Barrett
Sched. Deborah Hansen   **PS.** James Hewitt
Dist. Off. Deland 386.279.0707 • Palm Coast 386.302.0442
• Port Orange 386.238.9711

R: 362   **T:** 2nd   61%
Elected Year: 2018

⇥ Rep. Debbie Wasserman Schultz (WAH-sur-   D-FL-23   p 202.225.7931
muhn shullts)

                   f 202.226.2052
Rm. LHOB 1114 **Web.**
wassermanschultz.house.gov
Bio. 09/27/1966 • Forest Hills • State Legislator; College
Administrator • Univ. of Florida, B.A., 1988; Univ. of Florida,
M.A., 1990 • Jewish • M. Steve Schultz, 3 ch   **Cmte.**
Appropriations • Oversight & Reform
CoS. Tracie Pough   **LD.** Lauren Wolman
Sched. Lauren Mylott   **PS.** David Damron
Dist. Off. Aventura 305.936.5724 • Sunrise 954.845.1179

R: 84   **T:** 9th   58%
Elected Year: 2012

▶ Rep. Daniel A. Webster (WEB-stur)   R-FL-11   p 202.225.1002

Rm. RHOB 2184 **Web.** webster.house.gov
Bio. 04/27/1949 • Charleston • State Legislator; Spkr.,
House of Representatives • Georgia Institute of Technology,
B.E.E., 1971 • Baptist • M. Sandy Jordan, 6 ch; 14 gr-ch
Cmte. Natural Resources • Science, Space & Technology •
Transportation & Infrastructure
CoS. Jaryn Emhof   **LD.** Scott Mackenzie
Sched. Natali Werner
Dist. Off. Brooksville 352.241.9230 • Inverness
352.241.9204 • Leesburg 352.241.9220 • The Villages
352.383.3552

R: 151   **T:** 6th   67%
Elected Year: 2016

⇥ Rep. Frederica S. Wilson (WILL-suhn)   D-FL-24   p 202.225.4506

Rm. RHOB 2445 **Web.** wilson.house.gov   **f** 202.226.0777
Bio. 11/05/1942 • Miami • State Legislator • Fisk
Univ. (TN), B.S., 1963; Univ. of Miami, M.Ed., 1972 •
Episcopalian • W., 3 ch; 5 gr-ch   **Cmte.** Education & Labor
• Transportation & Infrastructure
CoS. Jean Roseme   **LD.** Derron Bennett
                    PS. Joyce Jones
Dist. Off. Hollywood 954.921.3682 • Miami Gardens
305.690.5905 • West Park 954.989.2688

R: 152   **T:** 6th   76%
Elected Year: 2012

GEORGIA

▶ Governor Brian Kemp (kemp)   p 404.656.1776

206 Washington Street, 111 State   **C:** Atlanta
Capitol   **P:** 10,519,475 (8)
Atlanta, GA 30334   **A:** 57,513.37 mi^2 (21st)
Website georgia.gov
Fax 404.657.7332
Term Ends 2023
Lt. Governor
Geoff Duncan, R

GEORGIA

U.S. Senators
Jon Ossoff, **D**
Raphael Warnock, **D**
U.S. Representatives
01 / Buddy Carter, **R**
02 / Sanford D. Bishop, **D**
03 / Drew Ferguson, **R**
04 / Hank C. Johnson, **D**
05 / Nikema Williams, **D**
06 / Lucy McBath, **D**
07 / Carolyn Bourdeaux, **D**
08 / Austin Scott, **R**
09 / Andrew Clyde, **R**
10 / Jody B. Hice, **R**
11 / Barry D. Loudermilk, **R**
12 / Rick W. Allen, **R**
13 / David A. Scott, **D**
14 / Marjorie Taylor Greene, **R**

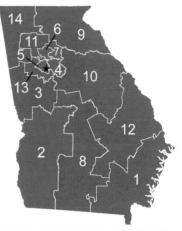

⚓ Sen. Jon Ossoff (OSS-off)　　　　D-GA-Sr.　p 202.224.3521

Rm. RSOB 455 **Web.** ossoff.senate.gov　**f** 202.224.2575
Bio. 02/16/1987 • Atlanta • Georgetown Univ. School
of Medicine (DC), Bach. Deg., 2009; London School of
Economics (England), M.S., 2013 • Jewish • M. Alisha
Kramer **Cmte.** Banking, Housing & Urban Affairs
• Homeland Security & Government Affairs • Joint
Congressional-Executive Commission on China • Judiciary
• Rules & Administration
CoS. Reynaldo Benitez　　　**LD.** Caitlin Frazer
Sched. Caroline Ehlich　　　**PS.** Jake Best
Dist. Off. Atlanta 470.786.7800

R: 99　**T:** 1st 50%
Elected Year: 2021
Next Election: 2026

⚓ Sen. Raphael Warnock (WAR-naak)　　D-GA-Jr.　p 202.224.3643

Rm. RSOB 388 **Web.** warnock.senate.gov　**f** 202.228.0724
Bio. 07/23/1969 • Savannah • Morehouse College (GA),
B.A.; Union Theological Seminary, a school affiliated with
Columbia Univ. (NY), M.Phil; Union Theological Seminary,
a school affiliated with Columbia Univ. (NY), Ph.D. • Baptist
• Se. Oulèye Ndoye, 2 ch **Cmte.** Aging • Agriculture,
Nutrition & Forestry • Banking, Housing & Urban Affairs •
Commerce, Science & Transportation • Joint Economic
CoS. Mark Libell　　　　**LD.** Joshua Delaney
Sched. Stuart Guillory　　**PS.** Michael Brewer
Dist. Off. Atlanta 770.694.7828

R: 100　**T:** 1st 51%
Elected Year: 2021
Next Election: 2022

🏛 Rep. Rick W. Allen (A-luhn)　　　　R-GA-12　p 202.225.2823

Rm. CHOB 570 **Web.** allen.house.gov　**f** 202.225.3377
Bio. Augusta • Auburn Univ. School of Architecture and
Fine Arts (GA), B.S., 1973 • Methodist • M. Robin Reeve, 4
ch; 12 gr-ch **Cmte.** Agriculture • Education & Labor
CoS. Lauren E. Hodge　　　**LD.** Mary Christina Riley
　　　　　　　　　　　　　　PS. Andrea Porwoll
Dist. Off. Augusta 706.228.1980 • Dublin 478.272.4030 •
Statesboro 912.243.9452 • Vidalia 912.403.3311

R: 206　**T:** 4th 58%
Elected Year: 2014

⚓ Rep. Sanford D. Bishop Jr. (BIH-shuhp)　　D-GA-02　p 202.225.3631

Rm. RHOB 2407 **Web.** bishop.house.gov　**f** 202.225.2203
Bio. 02/04/1947 • Mobile • Attorney; State Legislator •
Army ROTC 1969-71 • Morehouse College (GA), B.A., 1968;
Emory Univ. Law School (GA), J.D., 1971 • Baptist • M.
Vivian Creighton Bishop, 1 ch; 1 gr-ch **Cmte.** Agriculture •
Appropriations
CoS. Kenneth Cutts (CD)　　　**LD.** Jonathan Halpern
Sched. Jack Bryan　　　　　**PS.** Haig Hovsepian
Dist. Off. Albany 229.439.8067 • Columbus 706.320.9477 •
Macon 478.803.2631

R: 16　**T:** 15th 59%
Elected Year: 1992

⌐ Rep. Carolyn Bourdeaux (bor-DOW)　　　D-GA-07　　p 202.225.4272

Rm. LHOB 1319 **Web.** bourdeaux.house.gov **f** 202.225.4696
Bio. 06/03/1979 • Roanoke • Yale Univ. (CT), B.A., 1992;
Univ. of Southern California, M.P.A., 1999; Syracuse Univ.
(NY), Ph.D., 2003 • Christian Church • M. Jeff Skodnick, 1 ch
Cmte. Small Business • Transportation & Infrastructure
CoS. Estefania L. Rodriguez　　**LD.** Matthew Jackson
Sched. Harlow Poteete　　　　**PS.** Andrew Scibetta
Dist. Off. Lawrenceville 770.232.3005

R: 375 **T:** 1st 51%
Elected Year: 2020

⌐ Rep. Buddy Carter (KAR-tur)　　　　R-GA-01　　p 202.225.5831

Rm. RHOB 2432 **Web.**　　　　　　　　**f** 202.226.2269
buddycarter.house.gov
Bio. Port Wentworth • Young Harris College, A.S., 1977;
Univ. of Georgia School of Pharmacy (GA), B.S., 1980 •
Methodist • M. Amy Coppage, 3 ch; 3 gr-ch **Cmte.** Budget
• Energy & Commerce • Select Committee on the Climate
Crisis
CoS. Chris Crawford　　　　**LD.** Robert L. Wehagen
Sched. Brooke Miller　　　　**PS.** Harley Adsit
Dist. Off. Brunswick 912.265.9010 • Savannah
912.352.0101

R: 212 **T:** 4th 58%
Elected Year: 2014

⌐ Rep. Andrew Clyde (klyd)　　　　　R-GA-09　　p 202.225.9893

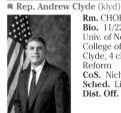

Rm. CHOB 521 **Web.** clyde.house.gov　　**f** 202.226.1224
Bio. 11/22/1963 • Ontario • Bethel College (IN), B.S.;
Univ. of Notre Dame (IN), B.A., 1985; Univ. of Georgia Terry
College of Business, M.B.A., 1999 • Baptist • M. Jennifer
Clyde, 4 ch **Cmte.** Homeland Security • Oversight &
Reform
CoS. Nicholas Brown
Sched. Lindsay Roberts　　　**PS.** Madeline Corso
Dist. Off. Gainesville 470.768.6520

R: 381 **T:** 1st 79%
Elected Year: 2020

⌐ Rep. Drew Ferguson IV (FUR-guh-suhn)　　R-GA-03　　p 202.225.5901

Rm. LHOB 1032 **Web.** ferguson.house.gov **f** 202.225.2515
Bio. 11/15/1967 • West Point • Univ. of Georgia, Bach. Deg.,
1988; Medical College of Georgia, D.M.D., 1992 • Catholic •
M. Elizabeth Ferguson, 4 ch **Cmte.** Ways & Means
CoS. David Sours　　　　**LD.** Allie White
Sched. Alissa Knight　　　　**PS.** Nadgey Louis-Charles
Dist. Off. Newnan 770.683.2033

R: 260 **T:** 3rd 65%
Elected Year: 2016

⌐ Rep. Marjorie Taylor Greene (green)　　R-GA-14　　p 202.225.5211

Rm. LHOB 1023 **Web.** greene.house.gov
Bio. 05/27/1974 • Milledgeville • Univ. of Georgia, B.B.A. •
Christian - Non-Denominational • M. Perry Greene, 3 ch
CoS. Ed Buckham　　　　**LD.** Taylor LaJoie
Sched. Gavin Thompson　　　**PS.** Nick Dyer
Dist. Off. Dalton 706.226.5320 • Rome 706.290.1776

R: 392 **T:** 1st 75%
Elected Year: 2020

⌐ Rep. Jody B. Hice (hice)　　　　　R-GA-10　　p 202.225.4101

Web. jodyhice.com　　　　　　　　　**f** 202.226.0776
Bio. Atlanta • Asbury College (KY), B.A., 1982;
Southwestern Baptist Theological Seminary (TX), M.Div.,
1986 • Southern Baptist • M. Dee Hice, 2 ch; 4 gr-ch **Cmte.**
Natural Resources • Oversight & Reform
CoS. Tim Reitz (CD)
Sched. Taylor Ford (CD)　　　**PS.** Sarah Selip (CD)
Dist. Off. Greensboro 762.445.1776 • Monroe 770.207.1776
• Thomson 770.207.1776

R: 219 **T:** 4th 62%
Elected Year: 2014

GEORGIA

Rep. Hank C. Johnson Jr. (JAHN-suhn)   D-GA-04   p 202.225.1605

Rm. RHOB 2240 **Web.**   **f** 202.226.0691
hankjohnson.house.gov
Bio. 10/02/1954 • Washington • Judge; Attorney • Clark College (GA), B.A., 1976; Texas Southern Univ., Thurgood Marshall School of Law, J.D., 1979 • Buddhism • M. Mereda Davis Johnson, 2 ch **Cmte.** Judiciary • Oversight & Reform • Transportation & Infrastructure
CoS. Scott R. Goldstein   **LD.** Khaula Kaiser
Sched. LaVeeta Branche   **PS.** Andy Phelan (CD)
(CD)
Dist. Off. Decatur 770.987.2291

R: 93 **T:** 8th 80%
Elected Year: 2006

Rep. Barry D. Loudermilk (LOU-dur-milk)   R-GA-11   p 202.225.2931

Rm. RHOB 2133 **Web.** loudermilk.house.gov **f** 202.225.2944
Bio. Riverdale • Community College of the Air Force (AL), A.A.S., 1987; Wayland Baptist Univ. (TX), B.S., 1992 • Baptist • M. Desiree Loudermilk, 3 ch; 2 gr-ch **Cmte.** Administration • Financial Services • Joint Library • Joint Printing
CoS. Robert Adkerson   **LD.** Colin Carr
Sched. Ashley Adkerson   **PS.** Brandon Cockerham
Dist. Off. Atlanta 770.429.1776 • Cartersville 770.429.1776 • Woodstock 770.429.1776

R: 224 **T:** 4th 60%
Elected Year: 2014

Rep. Lucy McBath (mik-BATH)   D-GA-06   p 202.225.4501

Rm. LHOB 1513 **Web.** mcbath.house.gov
Bio. 06/01/1960 • Joliet • Virginia State Univ., B.A., 1982 • Christian Church • M. Curtis McBath, 2 ch (2 deceased)
Cmte. Education & Labor • Judiciary
CoS. Rebecca Walldorff   **LD.** Michael Williams
                      PS. Tanner Palin
Dist. Off. Atlanta 470.773.6330

R: 332 **T:** 2nd 55%
Elected Year: 2018

Rep. Austin Scott (skaht)   R-GA-08   p 202.225.6531

Rm. RHOB 2417 **Web.** austinscott.house.gov **f** 202.225.3013
Bio. 12/10/1969 • Augusta • State Legislator • Univ. of Georgia Terry College of Business, B.B.A., 1993 • M. Vivien Scott, 2 ch **Cmte.** Agriculture • Armed Services
CoS. Jason Lawrence
                      PS. Alex Enlow
Dist. Off. Tifton 229.396.5175 • Warner Robins 478.971.1776

R: 149 **T:** 6th 65%
Elected Year: 2010

Rep. David A. Scott (skaht)   D-GA-13   p 202.225.2939

Rm. CHOB 468 **Web.** davidscott.house.gov   **f** 202.225.4628
Bio. 06/27/1946 • Aynor • State Legislator • Florida Agricultural and Mechanical Univ., B.A., 1967; Univ. of Pennsylvania Wharton School of Business Aresty Institute, M.B.A., 1969 • Baptist • M. Alfredia Aaron Scott, 2 ch; 2 gr-ch
Cmte. Agriculture • Financial Services
CoS. Catherine Kuerbitz   **LD.** Christofer Horta
Sched. Kathleen Burke   **PS.** Ralph Jones
Dist. Off. Jonesboro 770.210.5073 • Smyrna 770.432.5405

R: 68 **T:** 10th 77%
Elected Year: 2002

Rep. Nikema Williams (WILL-yuhmz)   D-GA-05   p 202.225.3801

Rm. LHOB 1406 **Web.**
nikemawilliams.house.gov
Bio. 07/30/1978 • Smiths Station • Talladega College, B.A. • Methodist • M. Leslie Williams, 1 ch **Cmte.** Financial Services • Select Committee on the Modernization of Congress • Transportation & Infrastructure
CoS. Melanee Farrah   **LD.** Max Ernst
Sched. Kristina Kimball   **PS.** Ed Hula
(CD)
Dist. Off. Atlanta 404.659.0116

R: 427 **T:** 1st 85%
Elected Year: 2020

HAWAII

🏵 **Governor David Y. Ige** (EE-gay) p 808.586.0034

Executive Chambers, State Capitol **C:** Honolulu
Honolulu, HI 96813 **P:** 1,420,491 (41)
Website hawaii.gov **A:** 6,422.81 mi² (47th)
Fax 808.586.0006
Term Ends 2022
Lt. Governor
Josh Green, D

U.S. Senators
Brian E. Schatz, **D**
Mazie K. Hirono, **D**
U.S. Representatives
01 / Ed E. Case, **D**
02 / Kaiali'i Kahele, **D**

🏵 **Sen. Mazie K. Hirono** (hee-RO-no) D-HI-Jr. p 202.224.6361

Rm. HSOB 109 **Web.** hirono.senate.gov **f** 202.224.2126
Bio. 11/03/1947 • Fukushima • Lawyer • Univ. of Hawaii,
Manoa, B.A., 1970; Georgetown Univ. Law Center (DC),
J.D., 1978 • Buddhism • M. Leighton Kim Oshima, 1 stepch
Cmte. Armed Services • Energy & Natural Resources •
Judiciary • Small Business & Entrepreneurship • Veterans'
Affairs
CoS. Alan Yamamoto **LD.** Jed Daniel D'Ercole
Sched. Blaine Nolan **PS.** Madeleine Russak
Dist. Off. Honolulu 808.522.8970

R: 55 **T:** 2nd 69%
Elected Year: 2012
Next Election: 2024

🏵 **Sen. Brian E. Schatz** (shahts) D-HI-Sr. p 202.224.3934

Rm. HSOB 722 **Web.** schatz.senate.gov **f** 202.228.1153
Bio. 10/20/1972 • Ann Arbor • Pomona College, B.A.,
1994 • Jewish • M. Linda Kwok Kai Yun, 2 ch **Cmte.**
Appropriations • Commerce, Science & Transportation •
Ethics • Foreign Relations • Indian Affairs
CoS. Eric Einhorn **LD.** Arun Revana
Sched. Diane Miyasato- **PS.** Michael Inacay
Vizmanos
Dist. Off. Honolulu 808.523.2061

R: 51 **T:** 3rd 70%
Elected Year: 2012
Next Election: 2022

🏵 **Rep. Ed E. Case** (kayss) D-HI-01 p 202.225.2726

Rm. RHOB 2210 **Web.** case.house.gov
Bio. 09/27/1952 • Hilo • Williams College, B.A., 1975; Univ.
of California Hastings College of Law, J.D., 1981 • Protestant
- Unspecified Christian • M. Audrey Nakamura, 4 ch **Cmte.**
Appropriations • Natural Resources
CoS. Timothy M. Nelson
Sched. Wisdom Matsuzaki **PS.** Nestor R. Garcia (CD)
Dist. Off. Honolulu 808.650.6688

R: 204 **T:** 2nd 72%
Elected Year: 2018

HAWAII

⋊ Rep. Kaiali'i Kahele (ka-hehl-eh) D-HI-02 p 202.225.4906

Rm. LHOB 1205 **Web.** kahele.house.gov **f** 202.225.4987
Bio. 03/28/1974 • Miloli'i • Univ. of Hawaii, Manoa, B.A.,
1998 • Unspecified/Other • M. Maria Fe Day, 3 ch **Cmte.**
Armed Services • Transportation & Infrastructure
CoS. Christine Wagner **LD.** Kana Smith
  PS. Michael Ahn

Dist. Off. Hilo 808.746.6220

R: 399 **T:** 1st 63%
Elected Year: 2020

IDAHO

IDAHO

⚑ Governor Brad Little (LIH-tull) p 208.334.2100

State Capitol, PO Box 83720 **C:** Boise
Boise, ID 83720 **P:** 1,754,208 (40)
Website idaho.gov **A:** 82,643.20 mi^2 (11th)
Fax 208.334.3454
Term Ends 2023
Lt. Governor
Janice McGeachin, R

U.S. Senators
Mike D. Crapo, R
James E. Risch, R
U.S. Representatives
01 / Russ M. Fulcher, R
02 / Mike K. Simpson, R

⚑ Sen. Mike D. Crapo (KRAY-poe) R-ID-Sr. p 202.224.6142

Rm. DSOB 239 **Web.** crapo.senate.gov **f** 202.228.1375
Bio. 05/20/1951 • Idaho Falls • U.S. Representative;
Attorney • Brigham Young Univ. (UT), B.A., 1973; Harvard
Univ. Law School (MA), J.D., 1977 • Mormon • M. Susan
Diane Hasleton Crapo, 5 ch; 8 gr-ch **Cmte.** Banking,
Housing & Urban Affairs • Budget • Finance • Joint Taxation
CoS. Susan H. Wheeler **LD.** Molly Carpenter
Sched. Kathleen Amacio **PS.** Melanie Baucom
  Lawhorn
Dist. Off. Boise 208.334.1776 • Coeur D'Alene

R: 13 **T:** 4th 66% 208.664.5490 • Idaho Falls 208.522.9779 • Lewiston
Elected Year: 1998 208.743.1492 • Pocatello 208.236.6775 • Twin Falls
Next Election: 2022 208.734.2515

⚑ Sen. James E. Risch (rish) R-ID-Jr. p 202.224.2752

Rm. RSOB 483 **Web.** risch.senate.gov **f** 202.224.2573
Bio. 05/03/1943 • Milwaukee • Governor of Idaho; Lt.
Governor of Idaho; State Legislator • Univ. of Idaho, B.S.,
1965; Univ. of Idaho, Law School, J.D., 1968 • Roman
Catholic • M. Vicki L. Choborda, 3 ch; 7 gr-ch **Cmte.**
Energy & Natural Resources • Ethics • Foreign Relations •
Intelligence • Small Business & Entrepreneurship
CoS. Ryan White **LD.** Charles Adams
Sched. Alexa Green **PS.** Marty Cozza
Dist. Off. Boise 208.342.7985 • Coeur d'Alene 208.667.6130

R: 34 **T:** 3rd 63% • Idaho Falls 208.523.5541 • Lewiston 208.743.0792 •
Elected Year: 2008 Pocatello 208.236.6817 • Twin Falls 208.734.6780
Next Election: 2026

IDAHO

🏛 Rep. Russ M. Fulcher (FUHL-chur) R-ID-01 p 202.225.6611

Rm. LHOB 1520 **Web.** fulcher.house.gov
Bio. 03/09/1962 • Meridian • Boise State Univ., B.B.A., 1984; Boise State Univ., M.B.A., 1988; Boise State Univ., M.B.A., 1988; Micron Univ., E.E., 1993 • Protestant - Unspecified Christian • M. Kara Fulcher, 3 ch **Cmte.** Education & Labor • Natural Resources
CoS. Cliff Bayer **LD.** Steve Ackerman
Sched. Daniel Tellez **PS.** Alexah Rogge
Dist. Off. Coeur d'Alene 208.667.0127 • Lewiston 208.743.1388 • Meridian 208.888.3188

R: 312 **T:** 2nd 68%
Elected Year: 2018

🏛 Rep. Mike K. Simpson (SIMP-suhn) R-ID-02 p 202.225.5531

Rm. RHOB 2084 **Web.** simpson.house.gov **f** 202.225.8216
Bio. 09/08/1950 • Burley • Dentist; State Representative; Speaker of State House • Washington Univ. School of Dental Medicine (MO), D.D.S., 1977; Utah State Univ., B.S., 2002 • Mormon • M. Kathy Johnson Simpson **Cmte.** Appropriations
CoS. Lindsay J. Slater **LD.** Sarah Cannon
Sched. Jocelyn Bryant **PS.** Nicole Wallace (CD)
Dist. Off. Boise 208.334.1953 • Idaho Falls 208.523.6701 • Twin Falls 208.734.7219

R: 49 **T:** 12th 64%
Elected Year: 1998

ILLINOIS

🏛 Governor J.B. Pritzker (PRIT-skur) p 217.782.0244

207 State House
Springfield, IL 62706
Website illinois.gov
Fax 217.524.4049
Term Ends 2023
Lt. Governor
Juliana Stratton, **D**

C: Springfield
P: 12,741,080 (6)
A: 55,518.76 mi^2 (24th)

U.S. Senators
Dick Durbin, **D**
Tammy Duckworth, **D**
U.S. Representatives
01 / Bobby L. Rush, **D**
02 / Robin L. Kelly, **D**
03 / Marie Newman, **D**
04 / Jesús G. Garcia, **D**
05 / Mike Quigley, **D**
06 / Sean Casten, **D**
07 / Danny K. Davis, **D**
08 / Raja Krishnamoorthi, **D**
09 / Jan D. Schakowsky, **D**
10 / Brad S. Schneider, **D**
11 / Bill Foster, **D**
12 / Mike Bost, **R**
13 / Rodney L. Davis, **R**
14 / Lauren A. Underwood, **D**
15 / Mary Miller, **R**
16 / Adam D. Kinzinger, **R**
17 / Cheri Bustos, **D**
18 / Darin M. LaHood, **R**

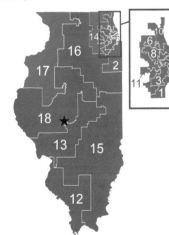

🏛 Sen. Tammy Duckworth (DUK-wurth) D-IL-Jr. p 202.224.2854

Rm. HSOB 524 **f** 202.228.0618
Bio. 03/12/1968 • Bangkok • Veterans Affairs • National Guard • Capella Univ., Ph.D.; Univ. of Hawaii, B.A., 1989; George Washington Univ. Elliot School of International Affairs (DC), M.A., 1992 • Unspecified/Other • M. Major Bryan Bowlsbey, 2 ch **Cmte.** Armed Services • Commerce, Science & Transportation • Environment & Public Works • Small Business & Entrepreneurship
CoS. Kalina Bakalov-Thompson **LD.** Benjamin Rhodeside
Sched. Kelsey Becker **PS.** Ben Garmisa
Dist. Off. Belleville 618.722.7070 • Carbondale 618.677.7000 • Chicago 312.886.3506 • Rock Island 309.606.7060 • Springfield 217.528.6124

R: 77 **T:** 1st 55%
Elected Year: 2016
Next Election: 2022

ILLINOIS

🏛 Sen. Dick Durbin (DUR-bin) D-IL-Sr. p 202.224.2152

Rm. HSOB 711 **Web.** durbin.senate.gov **f** 202.228.0400
Bio. 11/21/1944 • East St. Louis • U.S. Representative;
Attorney • Georgetown Univ. (DC), B.S., 1966; Georgetown
Univ. Law Center (DC), J.D., 1969 • Roman Catholic • M.
Loretta Schaefer Durbin, 3 ch (1 deceased); 3 gr-ch **Cmte.**
Agriculture, Nutrition & Forestry • Appropriations • Judiciary
CoS. Patrick J. Souders **LD.** Jasmine Hunt
Sched. Claire A. Reuschel **PS.** Emily Hampsten
Dist. Off. Carbondale 618.351.1122 • Chicago
312.353.4952 • Rock Island 309.786.5173 • Springfield
217.492.4062

R: 9 **T:** 5th 55%
Elected Year: 1996
Next Election: 2026

🏛 Rep. Mike Bost (bahst) R-IL-12 p 202.225.5661

Rm. LHOB 1211 **Web.** bost.house.gov **f** 202.225.0285
Bio. Murphysboro • Southern Baptist • M. Tracy Stanton
Bost, 3 ch; 11 gr-ch **Cmte.** Transportation & Infrastructure
• Veterans' Affairs
CoS. Matt McCullough **LD.** Noah Barger
Sched. Tyler Cianciotti **PS.** Alexandra Naughton
Dist. Off. Alton 618.622.0766 • Carbondale 618.457.5787
• Granite City 618.622.0766 • Mount Vernon 618.513.5294 •
O'Fallon 618.622.0766

R: 209 **T:** 4th 60%
Elected Year: 2014

🏛 Rep. Cheri Bustos (BOO-stoass) D-IL-17 p 202.225.5905

Rm. LHOB 1233 **Web.** bustos.house.gov **f** 202.225.5396
Bio. 10/17/1961 • Springfield • Univ. of Maryland - College
Park, B.A., 1983; Univ. of Illinois - Springfield, M.A., 1985 •
Roman Catholic • M. Gerry Bustos, 3 ch; 2 gr-ch **Cmte.**
Agriculture • Appropriations
CoS. Trevor Reuschel **LD.** Leighton Huch
Sched. Mitchell Dunn **PS.** Heather Sager
Dist. Off. Peoria 309.966.1813 • Rock Island 309.786.3406
• Rockford 309.786.3406

R: 164 **T:** 5th 52%
Elected Year: 2012

🏛 Rep. Sean Casten (KASS-tuhn) D-IL-06 p 202.225.4561

Rm. RHOB 2440 **Web.** casten.house.gov
Bio. 11/23/1971 • Dublin • Middlebury College (VT), B.A.,
1993; Dartmouth College, M.S., 1998 • Unspecified/Other •
M. Kara Casten, 2 ch **Cmte.** Financial Services • Science,
Space & Technology • Select Committee on the Climate
Crisis
CoS. Chloe Hunt

PS. Emilia Rowland
Dist. Off. Barrington • Glen Ellyn 630.520.9450

R: 302 **T:** 2nd 53%
Elected Year: 2018

🏛 Rep. Danny K. Davis (DAY-vuhs) D-IL-07 p 202.225.5006

Rm. RHOB 2159 **Web.** davis.house.gov **f** 202.225.5641
Bio. 09/06/1941 • Parkdale • Cook County Commissioner;
Alderman, Chicago City Council • Arkansas Agricultural
and Mechanical College, B.A., 1961; Chicago State Univ. (IL),
M.A., 1968; Union Institute and Univ., Ph.D., 1977 • Baptist •
M. Vera G. Davis, 2 ch (1 deceased); 4 gr-ch (1 deceased)
Cmte. Oversight & Reform • Ways & Means
CoS. Turnia Romero **LD.** Jill Hunter-Williams
Sched. Joseph Peters **PS.** Ira Cohen (CD)
Dist. Off. Chicago 773.533.7520

R: 35 **T:** 13th 80%
Elected Year: 1996

🏛 Rep. Rodney L. Davis (DAY-vuhs) R-IL-13 p 202.225.2371

Rm. RHOB 2079 **Web.** **f** 202.226.0791
rodneydavis.house.gov
Bio. 01/05/1970 • Des Moines • Millikin Univ. (IL), B.A.,
1992 • Roman Catholic • M. Shannon Davis, 3 ch **Cmte.**
Administration • Agriculture • Joint Library • Joint Printing
• Select Committee on the Modernization of Congress •
Transportation & Infrastructure
CoS. Bret Manley **LD.** Jimmy Ballard
Sched. Brianna Nagle **PS.** Aaron DeGroot (CD)
Dist. Off. Champaign 217.403.4690 • Decatur 217.791.6224
• Edwardsville 618.205.8660 • Normal 309.252.8834 •
Springfield 217.791.6224 • Taylorville 217.824.5117

R: 168 **T:** 5th 55%
Elected Year: 2012

ILLINOIS

Rep. Bill Foster (FAHSS-tur)   D-IL-11   p 202.225.3515

Rm. RHOB 2366 **Web.** foster.house.gov   **f** 202.225.9420
Bio. 10/07/1955 • Madison • Physicist • Univ. of Wisconsin,
B.A., 1976; Harvard Univ., Ph.D., 1983 • Unspecified/Other •
M. Aesook Byon, 2 ch **Cmte.** Financial Services • Science,
Space & Technology
CoS. Samantha Warren   **LD.** Kim Soffen
Sched. Jenae Jackson   **PS.** Greg Cybulski
Dist. Off. Aurora 630.585.7672 • Joliet 815.280.5876

R: 124 **T:** 5th 63%
Elected Year: 2012

Rep. Jesús G. Garcia (gar-SEE-uh)   D-IL-04   p 202.225.8203

Rm. LHOB 1519 **Web.** chuygarcia.house.gov
Bio. 04/12/1956 • Durango • Univ. of Illinois, Chicago, B.A.,
1999; Univ. of Illinois, Chicago, M.A., 2002 • Catholic • M.
Evelyn Garcia, 3 ch **Cmte.** Financial Services • Natural
Resources • Transportation & Infrastructure
CoS. Don Andres   **LD.** Alex Campbell
Sched. Julissa Santoy   **PS.** Fabiola Rodriguez-
                                       Ciampoli
Dist. Off. Chicago 773.342.0774 • Chicago 773.475.0833

R: 313 **T:** 2nd 84%
Elected Year: 2018

Rep. Robin L. Kelly (KEH-lee)   D-IL-02   p 202.225.0773

Rm. RHOB 2416 **Web.** robinkelly.house.gov   **f** 202.225.4583
Bio. 04/30/1956 • New York • Bradley Univ., B.A., 1977;
Bradley Univ., M.A., 1982; Northern Illinois Univ., Ph.D., 2004
• Christian - Non-Denominational • M. Nathaniel Horn, 2 ch
Cmte. Energy & Commerce • Oversight & Reform
CoS. Mia Keeys   **LD.** Matt McMurray
Sched. Alan Banks (CD)   **PS.** Rachel Kingery
Dist. Off. Chicago 773.321.2001 • Matteson 708.679.0078

R: 198 **T:** 5th 79%
Elected Year: 2012

Rep. Adam D. Kinzinger (KIN-zing-ur)   R-IL-16   p 202.225.3635

Rm. RHOB 2245 **Web.** kinzinger.house.gov   **f** 202.225.3521
Bio. 02/27/1978 • Kankakee • Air Force; Air National Guard
• Illinois State Univ., B.A., 2000 • Christian Church • M.
Sofia Boza-Holman, 1 ch **Cmte.** Energy & Commerce •
Foreign Affairs • Select Investigate Jan 6 Attack on the U.S.
Capitol
CoS. Austin Weatherford   **LD.** Sebastian De Luca
Sched. Patrick Doggett (CD) **PS.** Maura Gillespie
Dist. Off. Ottawa 815.431.9271 • Rockford 815.708.8032 •
Watseka 815.432.0580

R: 144 **T:** 6th 65%
Elected Year: 2012

Rep. Raja Krishnamoorthi (krish-nuh-MOR-thee) D-IL-08   p 202.225.3711

Rm. CHOB 115   **f** 202.225.7830
Bio. 07/19/1973 • New Delhi • Princeton Univ. (NJ),
B.A., 1995; Harvard Univ., J.D., 2000 • Hinduism • M.
Priya Krishnamoorthi, 2 ch **Cmte.** Oversight & Reform •
Permanent Select on Intelligence
CoS. Brian Kaissi   **LD.** Rebecca Lauer
Sched. Nicole Malec   **PS.** Wilson Baldwin
Dist. Off. Schaumburg 847.413.1959

R: 271 **T:** 3rd 73%
Elected Year: 2016

Rep. Darin M. LaHood (luh-"HOOD")   R-IL-18   p 202.225.6201

Rm. LHOB 1424 **Web.** lahood.house.gov   **f** 202.225.9249
Bio. 07/05/1968 • Peoria • Loras College, B.A., 1990; John
Marshall Law School, J.D., 1997 • Catholic • M. Kristen
LaHood, 3 ch **Cmte.** Permanent Select on Intelligence •
Ways & Means
CoS. Steve Pfrang   **LD.** Mary Ellen Richardson
Sched. Alexis Alavi   **PS.** John Rauber
Dist. Off. Bloomington 309.205.9556 • Jacksonville
217.245.1431 • Peoria 309.671.7027 • Springfield
217.670.1653

R: 238 **T:** 4th 70%
Elected Year: 2014

ILLINOIS

⚑ Rep. Mary Miller (MIH-lur) R-IL-15 p 202.225.5271

Rm. LHOB 1529 **Web.** marymiller.house.gov **f** 202.225.5880
Bio. 08/27/1959 • Naperville • Northeastern Illinois Univ.,
B.S., 1981 • Christian - Non-Denominational • M. Chris
Miller, 7 ch; 16 gr-ch **Cmte.** Agriculture • Education &
Labor
CoS. Benjamin E. DeMarzo **LD.** Christina Rabuse
Sched. William Wadsworth **PS.** Erin O'Malley
Dist. Off. Danville 217.703.6100 • Effingham 217.240.3155
• Harrisburg

R: 409 **T:** 1st 73%
Elected Year: 2020

⚑ Rep. Marie Newman (NOO-muhn) D-IL-03 p 202.225.5701

Rm. LHOB 1022 **Web.** newman.house.gov
Bio. 04/13/1964 • Chicago • Univ. of Wisconsin - Madison,
B.A. • Catholic • M. Jim Newman, 2 ch **Cmte.** Small
Business • Transportation & Infrastructure
CoS. Nancy Juarez **LD.** Marcus Garza
Sched. Rylee Stirn **PS.** Patrick Mullane
Dist. Off. Chicago 773.948.6223

R: 415 **T:** 1st 56%
Elected Year: 2020

⚑ Rep. Mike Quigley (KWIG-lee) D-IL-05 p 202.225.4061

Rm. RHOB 2078 **Web.** quigley.house.gov **f** 202.225.5603
Bio. 10/17/1958 • Indianapolis • Member, Cook County
Board of Commissioners • Roosevelt Univ. (IL), B.A., 1981;
Univ. of Chicago (IL), M.P.P., 1985; Loyola Univ. Law School
(IL), J.D., 1989 • Christian - Non-Denominational • M.
Barbara Quigley, 2 ch **Cmte.** Appropriations • Permanent
Select on Intelligence
CoS. Allison M. Jarus
Sched. Isabella Lee (CD) **PS.** Victoria Oms
Dist. Off. Chicago 773.267.5926

R: 118 **T:** 7th 71%
Elected Year: 2008

⚑ Rep. Bobby L. Rush (rush) D-IL-01 p 202.225.4372

Rm. RHOB 2188 **Web.** rush.house.gov **f** 202.226.0333
Bio. 11/23/1946 • Albany • Minister; Chicago City
Councilman • Army 1963-68 • Roosevelt Univ. (IL), B.A.,
1973; Univ. of Illinois, Chicago, M.A., 1994; McCormick
Theological Seminary (IL), M.Th., 1998 • Baptist • M.
Carolyn Thomas Rush, 7 ch (1 deceased) **Cmte.** Agriculture
• Energy & Commerce
CoS. Nishith Pandya **LD.** Lauren Citron
Sched. N. Lenette Myers **PS.** Naomi Savin
Dist. Off. Chicago 773.779.2400

R: 23 **T:** 15th 74%
Elected Year: 1992

⚑ Rep. Jan D. Schakowsky (shuh-KOU-skee) D-IL-09 p 202.225.2111

Rm. RHOB 2367 **Web.** **f** 202.226.6890
schakowsky.house.gov
Bio. 05/26/1944 • Chicago • Nonprofit Coordinator; State
Legislator • Univ. of Illinois, B.A., 1965 • Jewish • M.
Robert Creamer, 3 ch; 6 gr-ch **Cmte.** Budget • Energy &
Commerce
CoS. Syd Terry **LD.** Kate Durkin
Sched. Kim Muzeroll **PS.** Miguel Ayala
Dist. Off. Chicago 773.506.7100 • Glenview 847.328.3409

R: 48 **T:** 12th 71%
Elected Year: 1998

⚑ Rep. Brad S. Schneider (SHNY-dur) D-IL-10 p 202.225.4835

Rm. CHOB 300 **Web.** schneider.house.gov **f** 202.225.0837
Bio. 08/20/1961 • Denver • Northwestern Univ., B.S., 1983;
Kellogg Graduate School of Management, Northwestern
Univ. (IL), M.B.A., 1988 • Jewish • M. Julie Dann, 2 ch
Cmte. Foreign Affairs • Ways & Means
CoS. Casey O'Shea **LD.** Jessica Bernton
Sched. Daniela Altamirano **PS.** Matt Fried
Crosby
Dist. Off. Lincolnshire 847.383.4870

R: 242 **T:** 3rd 64%
Elected Year: 2016

⚑ Rep. Lauren A. Underwood (UN-dur-"wood")   D-IL-14   p 202.225.2976

Rm. LHOB 1130 **Web.** underwood.house.gov
Bio. 10/04/1986 • Mayfield Heights • Univ. of Michigan, B.S., 2008; Johns Hopkins Univ., M.S.N., 2009; Johns Hopkins Univ., M.PH, 2009 • Christian Church • S. **Cmte.** Appropriations • Veterans' Affairs
CoS. Andrea Harris   **LD.** Caroline Paris-Behr
Sched. Kleya Dhenin   **PS.** Chanda Daniels
Dist. Off. Crystal Lake 630.549.2190 • West Chicago 630.549.2190

R: 360 **T:** 2nd 51%
Elected Year: 2018

INDIANA

⚑ Governor Eric Holcomb (HOL-kum)   p 317.232.4567

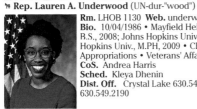

State House, Room 206
Indianapolis, IN 46204
Website in.gov
Fax 317.232.3443
Term Ends 2025
Lt. Governor
Suzanne Crouch, R

C: Indianapolis
P: 6,691,878 (17)
A: 35,826.02 mi^2 (38th)

U.S. Senators
Todd C. Young, R
Mike Braun, R
U.S. Representatives
01 / Frank J. Mrvan, D
02 / Jackie Swihart Walorski, R
03 / Jim F. Banks, R
04 / Jim Baird, R
05 / Victoria Spartz, R
06 / Greg Pence, R
07 / Andre D. Carson, D
08 / Larry D. Bucshon, R
09 / Trey Hollingsworth, R

⚑ Sen. Mike Braun ("brown")   R-IN-Jr.   p 202.224.4814

Rm. RSOB 374 **Web.** braun.senate.gov   **f** 202.224.5011
Bio. 03/24/1954 • Jasper • Wabash College (IN), B.A., 1976; Harvard Univ., M.B.A., 1978 • Catholic • M. Braun Braun, 4 ch **Cmte.** Aging • Agriculture, Nutrition & Forestry • Appropriations • Budget • Health, Education, Labor & Pensions
CoS. Joshua Kelley   **LD.** Katie Bailey
Sched. Jessica Wedgewood   **PS.** Zach Riddle
Dist. Off. Fort Wayne 260.427.2164 • Hammond 219.937.9650 • Indianapolis 317.822.8240

R: 88 **T:** 1st 51%
Elected Year: 2018
Next Election: 2024

⚑ Sen. Todd C. Young (yung)   R-IN-Sr.   p 202.224.5623

Rm. DSOB 185 **Web.** young.senate.gov   **f** 202.224.1845
Bio. 08/24/1972 • Lancaster • Attorney • Marine Corps, 1990-2000 • U.S. Naval Academy (MD), B.S., 1995; Univ. of Chicago's Graduate School of Business, M.B.A., 2000; Univ. of London's Institute of U.S. Studies, M.A., 2001; Indiana Univ. Law School, J.D., 2006 • Christian Church • M. Jennifer B. Young, 4 ch **Cmte.** Commerce, Science & Transportation • Finance • Foreign Relations • Small Business & Entrepreneurship
CoS. John Connell   **LD.** Lauren O'Brien
Sched. Lindsay McDonough   **PS.** Heidi Reutebuch
Dist. Off. Evansville 812.288.3999 • Fort Wayne 260.422.7397 • Indianapolis 317.226.6700 • New Albany 812.542.4820

R: 76 **T:** 1st 52%
Elected Year: 2016
Next Election: 2022

INDIANA

♟ Rep. Jim Baird (baird)   R-IN-04   p 202.225.5037

Rm. LHOB 1314 **Web.** baird.house.gov   **f** 202.226.0544
Bio. 06/04/1945 • Covington • Purdue Univ. (IN), B.S., 1967;
Purdue Univ. (IN), M.S., 1969; Univ. of Kentucky, Ph.D., 1975
• Methodist • M. Denise Baird, 3 ch **Cmte.** Agriculture •
Science, Space & Technology
CoS. Quincy Cunningham   **LD.** Cory Harris
Sched. Alyssa Jennings   **PS.** Katie Milner
Dist. Off. Danville 317.563.5567

R: 300   **T:** 2nd   67%
Elected Year: 2018

♟ Rep. Jim E. Banks (banks)   R-IN-03   p 202.225.4436

Rm. LHOB 1713 **Web.** banks.house.gov   **f** 202.226.9870
Bio. 07/16/1979 • Columbia City • Indiana Univ.,
Bloomington, Bach. Deg., 2004; Grace College, M.B.A., 2013
• Evangelical • M. Amanda Banks, 3 ch **Cmte.** Armed
Services • Education & Labor • Veterans' Affairs
CoS. David Keller   **LD.** Lindsay Ratliff
    PS. Mitchell Hailstone
Dist. Off. Fort Wayne 260.702.4750

R: 246   **T:** 3rd   68%
Elected Year: 2016

♟ Rep. Larry D. Bucshon (boo-SHAHN)   R-IN-08   p 202.225.4636

Rm. RHOB 2313 **Web.** bucshon.house.gov   **f** 202.225.3284
Bio. 05/31/1962 • Taylorsville • Heart Surgeon • Navy
Reserve, 1989-98 • Univ. of Illinois - Urbana, B.S., 1984; Univ.
of Illinois Medical School - Chicago, M.D., 1988 • Lutheran •
M. Kathryn Bucshon, 4 ch **Cmte.** Energy & Commerce
CoS. Kyle Jackson   **LD.** Dylan M. Moore
Sched. Liz T. Davis   **PS.** Charlotte Taylor
Dist. Off. Evansville 812.465.6484 • Jasper 812.482.4255 •
Terre Haute 812.232.0523 • Vincennes 855.519.1629

R: 128   **T:** 6th   67%
Elected Year: 2010

♞ Rep. Andre D. Carson (KAR-suhn)   D-IN-07   p 202.225.4011

Rm. RHOB 2135 **Web.** carson.house.gov   **f** 202.225.5633
Bio. 10/16/1974 • Indianapolis • Marketing Executive
• Concordia Univ. of Wisconsin, B.S., 2003; Indiana
Wesleyan Univ., M.A., 2005 • Islam (Muslim) • M. Mariama
Carson, 1 ch **Cmte.** Permanent Select on Intelligence •
Transportation & Infrastructure
CoS. Kim Rudolph   **LD.** Andrea Martin
Sched. Holly Woytcke   **PS.** Copeland Tucker
Dist. Off. Indianapolis 317.283.6516

R: 105   **T:** 8th   62%
Elected Year: 2007

♟ Rep. Trey Hollingsworth III (HAH-lingz-wurth)   R-IN-09   p 202.225.5315

Rm. LHOB 1641 **Web.**   **f** 202.226.6866
hollingsworth.house.gov
Bio. 09/12/1983 • Clinton • Univ. of Pennsylvania, B.S.E.,
2004; Georgetown Univ. (DC), M.P.P., 2014 • Christian
Church • M. Kelly Hollingsworth, 1 ch **Cmte.** Financial
Services
CoS. Rebecca Shaw
Sched. Blaine Kistler   **PS.** Carter Moelk
Dist. Off. Franklin 317.851.8710 • Jeffersonville
812.288.3999

R: 267   **T:** 3rd   61%
Elected Year: 2016

♞ Rep. Frank J. Mrvan (MER-van)   D-IN-01   p 202.225.2461

Rm. LHOB 1607 **Web.** mrvan.house.gov   **f** 202.225.2493
Bio. 04/16/1969 • Hammond • Ball State Univ., Bach.
Deg. • M. Jane Mrvan, 2 ch **Cmte.** Education & Labor •
Veterans' Affairs
CoS. Mark Lopez   **LD.** Travis Wheeler
Sched. Alejandro Rodriguez   **PS.** Kevin Spicer
Dist. Off. Merrillville 219.795.1844

R: 413   **T:** 1st   57%
Elected Year: 2020

INDIANA

🏛 **Rep. Greg Pence** (pence)　　　　R-IN-06　　p 202.225.3021

Rm. CHOB 211　**Web.** pence.house.gov
Bio. Columbus • Loyola Univ. Chicago (IL), Bach. Deg.,
1981; Loyola Univ. Chicago (IL), M.B.A., 1986 • Catholic • M.
Denice Pence, 4 ch; 5 gr-ch　**Cmte.** Energy & Commerce
CoS. Kyle Robertson　　　　**LD.** Hillary Lassiter
Sched. Mallory Cogar　　　　**PS.** Hannah Osantowske
Dist. Off. Columbus 812.799.5230 • Greenfield
812.799.5233 • Muncie 765.702.2434 • Richmond
765.660.1083

R: 339　**T:** 2nd　69%
Elected Year: 2018

🏛 **Rep. Victoria Spartz** (spartss)　　　　R-IN-05　　p 202.225.2276

Rm. LHOB 1523　**Web.** spartz.house.gov
Bio. 10/06/1978 • Nosivka • National Univ. of Economics
(Ukraine), B.S.; National Univ. of Economics (Ukraine),
M.B.A.; Kelley School of Business (IN), Mast. Deg. • Eastern
Orthodox • M. Jason Spartz, 2 ch　**Cmte.** Education & Labor
• Judiciary
CoS. Renee Hudson　　　　**LD.** Phillip Pinegar
Sched. Mariel Bailey
Dist. Off. Anderson 765.639.0671 • Carmel 317.848.0201

R: 422　**T:** 1st　50%
Elected Year: 2020

🏛 **Rep. Jackie Swihart Walorski** (wah-LOR-skee)　R-IN-02　p 202.225.3915

Rm. CHOB 466　**Web.** walorski.house.gov　**f** 202.225.6798
Bio. 08/17/1963 • South Bend • Taylor Univ. (IN), B.A., 1985
• Assembly of God • M. Dean Swihart　**Cmte.** Ethics • Ways
& Means
CoS. Timothy P. Cummings　　**LD.** Martin Schultz
Sched. Julie Macmann
Dist. Off. Mishawaka 574.204.2645 • Rochester
574.223.4373

R: 194　**T:** 5th　62%
Elected Year: 2012

IOWA

🏛 **Governor Kim Reynolds** (REH-nuhldz)　　　　p 515.281.5211

State Capitol
1007 E. Grand Ave.
Des Moines, IA 50319
Website iowa.gov
Fax 515.725.3527
Term Ends 2023
Lt. Governor
Adam Gregg, R

C: Des Moines
P: 3,156,145 (32)
A: 55,856.99 mi^2 (23rd)

U.S. Senators
Chuck Grassley, R
Joni Ernst, R
U.S. Representatives
01 / Ashley Hinson, R
02 / Mariannette Miller-Meeks, R
03 / Cindy Axne, D
04 / Randy Feenstra, R

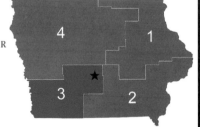

INDIANA

IOWA

IOWA

♣ Sen. Joni Ernst (urnst)　　　　　　R-IA-Jr.　　p 202.224.3254

Rm. HSOB 730　**Web.** ernst.senate.gov　**f** 202.224.9369
Bio. Red Oak • Iowa State Univ. (IA), B.S., 1992; Columbus
College (IA), M.P.A., 1995 • Lutheran • D. Gail Ernst, 1 ch;
2 stepch　**Cmte.** Agriculture, Nutrition & Forestry • Armed
Services • Environment & Public Works • Small Business &
Entrepreneurship
CoS. Lisa Goeas　　　　　**LD.** Corey Becker
Sched. Courtney Klein　　　**PS.** Brendan Conley
Dist. Off.　Cedar Rapids 319.365.4504 • Council Bluffs
712.352.1167 • Davenport 563.322.0677 • Des Moines
515.284.4574 • Sioux City 712.252.1550

R: 72　**T:** 2nd 52%
Elected Year: 2014
Next Election: 2026

♣ Sen. Chuck Grassley (GRASS-lee)　　　R-IA-Sr.　　p 202.224.3744

Rm. HSOB 135　**Web.** grassley.senate.gov　**f** 202.224.6020
Bio. 09/17/1933 • New Hartford • U.S. Representative;
Farmer • Univ. of Northern Iowa, B.A., 1955; Univ. of
Northern Iowa, M.A., 1956 • Baptist • M. Barbara Ann
Speicher Grassley, 5 ch　**Cmte.** Agriculture, Nutrition &
Forestry • Budget • Finance • Joint Taxation • Judiciary
CoS. Aaron Cummings　　　**LD.** James Rice
Sched. Jennifer Heins　　　**PS.** Taylor J. Foy
Dist. Off.　Cedar Rapids 319.363.6832 • Council Bluffs
712.322.7103 • Davenport 563.322.4331 • Des Moines
515.288.1145 • Sioux City 712.233.1860 • Waterloo
319.232.6657

R: 2　**T:** 7th 60%
Elected Year: 1980
Next Election: 2022

♣ Rep. Cindy Axne (AKSS-nee)　　　　D-IA-03　　p 202.225.5476

Rm. LHOB 1034　**Web.** axne.house.gov　**f** 202.225.3301
Bio. 04/20/1965 • Des Moines • Univ. of Iowa, B.A., 1987;
Northwestern Univ., M.B.A., 2002 • Catholic • M. John Axne,
2 ch　**Cmte.** Agriculture • Financial Services
CoS. Joe Diver　　　　　　**LD.** Denise Fleming
　　　　　　　　　　　　　　PS. Ian Mariani
Dist. Off.　Council Bluffs 712.890.3117 • Creston
641.278.1828 • Des Moines 515.400.8180

R: 299　**T:** 2nd 49%
Elected Year: 2018

♣ Rep. Randy Feenstra (FEEN-strah)　　　R-IA-04　　p 202.225.4426

Rm. LHOB 1440　**Web.** feenstra.house.gov　**f** 202.225.3193
Bio. 01/14/1969 • Hull • Iowa State Univ. (IA), M.P.A.; Dordt
College, B.A., 1991 • Protestant - Unspecified Christian •
M. Lynette Feenstra, 4 ch　**Cmte.** Agriculture • Budget •
Science, Space & Technology
CoS. Matthew Z. Leopold　　**LD.** Tim Medeiros
Sched. Josie Wagler　　　　**PS.** Billy Fuerst
Dist. Off.　Fort Dodge 515.302.7060 • Sioux City
712.224.4692

R: 384　**T:** 1st 62%
Elected Year: 2020

♣ Rep. Ashley Hinson (HIN-suhn)　　　R-IA-01　　p 202.225.2911

Rm. LHOB 1429　**Web.** hinson.house.gov
Bio. 06/27/1983 • Iowa • Univ. of Southern California, B.A.
• Christian Church • M. Matthew Arenholz, 2 ch　**Cmte.**
Appropriations • Budget
CoS. Jimmy Peacock　　　　**LD.** Brittany Madni
Sched. Jude Al-Hmoud　　　**PS.** Sophie Seid
Dist. Off.　Cedar Rapids 319.364.2288 • Dubuque
563.557.7789 • Waterloo 319.266.6925

R: 395　**T:** 1st 51%
Elected Year: 2020

⚑ Rep. Mariannette Miller-Meeks (MIH-lur meeks)   R-IA-02   p 202.225.6576

Rm. LHOB 1716 **Web.**   **f** 202.226.0757
millermeeks.house.gov
Bio. 09/06/1955 • Herlong • Texas Christian Univ., B.S.N., 1976; Univ. of Southern California, M.S., 1980; Univ. of Texas Health Science Center, San Antonia, M.S., 1980 • Roman Catholic • M. Curt Meeks, 2 ch **Cmte.** Education & Labor • Homeland Security • Veterans' Affairs
CoS. Tracie S. Gibler   **LD.** Kyle Jacobs
Sched. Austin Harris   **PS.** Will Kiley
Dist. Off. Davenport 563.232.0930 • Ottumwa 641.244.7020

R: 410   **T:** 1st   50%
Elected Year: 2020

KANSAS

⚑ Governor Laura Kelly (KEH-lee)   p 785.296.3232

Kansas State Capitol   **C:** Topeka
300 S.W. Tenth Ave., Suite 241-S   **P:** 2,911,505 (36)
Topeka, KS 66612   **A:** 81,758.64 mi^2 (13th)
Website kansas.gov
Fax 785.296.7973
Term Ends 2023
Lt. Governor
David Toland, **D**

U.S. Senators
Jerry Moran, R
Roger W. Marshall, R
U.S. Representatives
01 / Tracey R. Mann, R
02 / Jake A. LaTurner, R
03 / Sharice Davids, D
04 / Ron Estes, R

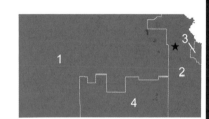

⚑ Sen. Roger W. Marshall (MAR-shull)   R-KS-Jr.   p 202.224.4774

Rm. RSOB 479A   **f** 202.224.3514
Bio. El Dorado • Butler Community College, A.S., 1980; Kansas State Univ., B.S., 1982; Univ. of Kansas, M.D., 1987 • Christian Church • M. Laina Marshall, 4 ch; 2 gr-ch
Cmte. Agriculture, Nutrition & Forestry • Energy & Natural Resources • Health, Education, Labor & Pensions • Small Business & Entrepreneurship
CoS. Brent Robertson   **LD.** Pace McMullan
Sched. Walton Stivender   **PS.** Michawn Marie Rich
Dist. Off. Garden City 620.765.7800 • Overland Park 913.879.7070 • Salina 785.829.9000 • Topeka 785.414.7501 • Wichita 316.803.6120

R: 96   **T:** 1st   53%
Elected Year: 2020
Next Election: 2026

⚑ Sen. Jerry Moran (moor-AHN)   R-KS-Sr.   p 202.224.6521

Rm. DSOB 521 **Web.** moran.senate.gov   **f** 202.228.6966
Bio. 05/29/1954 • Great Bend • State Senator; Attorney • Univ. of Kansas, B.S., 1976; Univ. of Kansas, J.D., 1981 • Methodist • M. Robba Addison Moran, 2 ch **Cmte.** Appropriations • Banking, Housing & Urban Affairs • Commerce, Science & Transportation • Health, Education, Labor & Pensions • Indian Affairs • Veterans' Affairs
CoS. James Kelly (CD)   **LD.** Judd Gardner
Sched. Emily Whitfield   **PS.** Tom Brandt
Dist. Off. Garden City 620.260.3025 • Hays 785.628.6401 • Manhattan 785.539.8973 • Olathe 913.393.0711 • Pittsburg 620.232.2286 • Wichita 316.269.9257

R: 41   **T:** 2nd   62%
Elected Year: 2010
Next Election: 2022

KANSAS

⌂ Rep. Sharice Davids (DAY-vidz) D-KS-03 p 202.225.2865

Rm. LHOB 1541 **Web.** davids.house.gov **f** 202.225.2807
Bio. 05/22/1980 • Frankfurt • Johnson County Community
College (KS), A.A., 2003; Univ. of Missouri - Kansas City,
B.A., 2007; Cornell Univ. Law School (NY), J.D., 2010 •
Unspecified/Other • S. **Cmte.** Joint Economic • Small
Business • Transportation & Infrastructure
CoS. Allison Teixeira Sulier **LD.** Brandon Naylor
Sched. Zac Donley **PS.** Ellie Turner
Dist. Off. Kansas City 913.766.3993 • Overland Park
913.621.0832

R: 307 **T:** 2nd 54%
Elected Year: 2018

⌂ Rep. Ron Estes (ESS-tess) R-KS-04 p 202.225.6216

Rm. RHOB 2411 **Web.** estes.house.gov **f** 202.225.3489
Bio. 07/19/1956 • Topeka • Tennessee Technological Univ.,
B.S.; Tennessee Technological Univ., M.B.A. • Lutheran • M.
Susan Oliver, 3 ch **Cmte.** Joint Economic • Ways & Means
CoS. Josh Bell **LD.** Nicholas O'Boyle
Sched. Haley Olchyk **PS.** Roman Rodriguez (CD)
Dist. Off. Wichita 316.262.8992

R: 284 **T:** 3rd 64%
Elected Year: 2016

⌂ Rep. Jake A. LaTurner (lah-TUR-nur) R-KS-02 p 202.225.6601

Rm. LHOB 1630 **Web.** laturner.house.gov
Bio. 02/17/1988 • Galena • Pittsburg State Univ., B.A.,
2011 • Catholic • M. Suzanne LaTurner, 4 ch **Cmte.**
Homeland Security • Oversight & Reform • Science, Space
& Technology
CoS. Braden Dreiling **LD.** Jake Middlebrooks
Sched. Marisa Burleson **PS.** Michael Howard
Dist. Off. Pittsburg 620.308.7450 • Topeka 785.205.5253

R: 401 **T:** 1st 55%
Elected Year: 2020

⌂ Rep. Tracey R. Mann (man) R-KS-01 p 202.225.2715

Rm. CHOB 522 **Web.** mann.house.gov **f** 202.225.5124
Bio. 12/17/1976 • Quinter • Kansas State Univ., Bach. Deg.
• Evangelical • M. Audrey Haynes, 4 ch **Cmte.** Agriculture
• Veterans' Affairs
CoS. Brandon Harder **LD.** Riley Pagett
Sched. Emily Woods **PS.** Michaela Todd
Dist. Off. Dodge City 620.682.7340 • Manhattan
785.370.7277

R: 405 **T:** 1st 71%
Elected Year: 2020

KENTUCKY

⌂ Governor Andy Beshear (Beh-SHEER) p 502.564.2611

State Capitol **C:** Frankfort
700 Capitol Ave., Suite 100 **P:** 4,468,402 (26)
Frankfort, KY 40601 **A:** 39,486.27 mi² (37th)
Website kentucky.gov
Fax 502.564.0437
Term Ends 2023
Lt. Governor
Jacqueline Coleman, **D**

U.S. Senators
Mitch McConnell, **R**
Rand Paul, **R**
U.S. Representatives
01 / James R. Comer, **R**
02 / Brett Guthrie, **R**
03 / John A. Yarmuth, **D**
04 / Thomas H. Massie, **R**
05 / Hal D. Rogers, **R**
06 / Andy Barr, **R**

Sen. Mitch McConnell (mih-KAH-null)   R-KY-Sr.   p 202.224.2541

Rm. RSOB 317 **Web.** mcconnell.senate.gov **f** 202.224.2499
Bio. 02/20/1942 • Tuscumbia • Deputy Assistant Attorney
General (President Ford) • Univ. of Louisville (KY),
B.A., 1964; Univ. of Kentucky Law School, J.D., 1967 •
Baptist • M. Elaine Chao, 3 ch from previous marriage
Cmte. Agriculture, Nutrition & Forestry • Appropriations •
Intelligence • Rules & Administration
CoS. Terry Carmack   **LD.** Tiffany Ge
Sched. Emily Louden   **PS.** Robert Steurer
Dist. Off. Bowling Green 270.781.1673 • Fort Wright
859.578.0188 • Lexington 859.224.8286 • London
606.864.2026 • Louisville 502.582.6304 • Paducah
270.442.4554

R: 3 **T:** 7th 58%
Elected Year: 1984
Next Election: 2026

Sen. Rand Paul (pall)   R-KY-Jr.   p 202.224.4343

Rm. RSOB 167 **Web.** paul.senate.gov **f** 202.228.6917
Bio. 01/07/1963 • Pittsburgh • Duke Univ. (NC), M.D.,
1988 • Presbyterian • M. Kelley Paul, 3 ch **Cmte.** Foreign
Relations • Health, Education, Labor & Pensions •
Homeland Security & Government Affairs • Small Business
& Entrepreneurship
CoS. William Henderson   **LD.** John Maniscalco
Sched. Claire London   **PS.** Madeline Meeker
Dist. Off. Bowling Green 270.782.8303

R: 48 **T:** 2nd 57%
Elected Year: 2010
Next Election: 2022

Rep. Andy Barr IV (bar)   R-KY-06   p 202.225.4706

Rm. RHOB 2430 **Web.** barr.house.gov **f** 202.225.2122
Bio. 07/24/1973 • Lexington • Univ. of Virginia, B.A., 1996;
Univ. of Kentucky College of Law, J.D., 2001 • Episcopalian
• W. Eleanor Carol Leavell, 2 ch **Cmte.** Financial Services
• Foreign Affairs
CoS. Mary Rosado   **LD.** Hunt VanderToll
Sched. Carissa Taylor   **PS.** Alexander Bellizzi
Dist. Off. Lexington 859.219.1366

R: 160 **T:** 5th 57%
Elected Year: 2012

Rep. James R. Comer Jr. (KOAM-ur)   R-KY-01   p 202.225.3115

Rm. RHOB 2410 **f** 202.225.3547
Bio. 08/19/1972 • Carthage • Western Kentucky Univ., B.S.,
1993 • Baptist • M. Tamera Jo, 3 ch **Cmte.** Education &
Labor • Oversight & Reform
CoS. Caroline Cash   **LD.** Sarah Coffman
Sched. Jason Tyler   **PS.** Matt Smith
Dist. Off. Madisonville 270.487.9509 • Paducah
270.408.1865 • Tompkinsville 270.487.9509

R: 240 **T:** 4th 75%
Elected Year: 2015

Rep. Brett Guthrie (GUH-three)   R-KY-02   p 202.225.3501

Rm. RHOB 2434 **Web.** guthrie.house.gov **f** 202.226.2019
Bio. 02/18/1964 • Florence • State Legislator • Army • U.S.
Military Academy (NY), B.S., 1987; Yale Univ. (CT), M.P.A.,
1997 • Church of Christ • M. Elizabeth Clemons, 3 ch **Cmte.**
Energy & Commerce
CoS. Sophie Trainor   **LD.** Brian Fahey
Khanahmadi
Sched. Jennifer Beil   **PS.** S.K. Bowen
Dist. Off. Bowling Green 270.842.9896 • Owensboro
270.842.9896 • Radcliff 270.842.9896

R: 109 **T:** 7th 71%
Elected Year: 2008

♖ Rep. Thomas H. Massie (MASS-ee) R-KY-04 p 202.225.3465

Rm. RHOB 2453 **Web.** massie.house.gov **f** 202.225.0003
Bio. 01/13/1971 • Huntington • Massachusetts Institute of Technology, B.S., 1993; Massachusetts Institute of Technology, M.M.E., 1996 • Methodist • M. Rhonda Massie, 4 ch **Cmte.** Transportation & Infrastructure
CoS. Matt Gurtler **LD.** Seana Cranston
Sched. Madeline Malone **PS.** John Kennedy
Dist. Off. Ashland 606.324.9898 • Crescent Springs 859.426.0080 • LaGrange 502.265.9119

R: 157 **T:** 6th 67%
Elected Year: 2011

♖ Rep. Hal D. Rogers (RAH-jurz) R-KY-05 p 202.225.4601

Rm. RHOB 2406 **Web.** halrogers.house.gov **f** 202.225.0940
Bio. 12/31/1937 • Barrier • Commonwealth's Attorney • Kentucky and North Carolina National Guards 1956-63 • Univ. of Kentucky, Bach. Deg., 1962; Univ. of Kentucky Law School, J.D., 1964 • Baptist • M. Cynthia Doyle Rogers, 3 ch (from a previous marriage) **Cmte.** Appropriations
CoS. Jakob Johnsen **LD.** Austin Gage
Sched. Kelley Kurtz **PS.** Danielle Smoot (CD)
Dist. Off. Hazard 606.439.0794 • Prestonsburg 606.886.0844 • Somerset 606.679.8346

R: 2 **T:** 21st 84%
Elected Year: 1980

↘ Rep. John A. Yarmuth (YAR-muhth) D-KY-03 p 202.225.5401

Rm. CHOB 402 **Web.** yarmuth.house.gov **f** 202.225.5776
Bio. 11/04/1947 • Louisville • Newspaper Publisher • Yale Univ. (CT), B.A., 1969 • Jewish • M. Catherine Yarmuth, 1 ch **Cmte.** Budget
CoS. Julie Carr **LD.** Katy Rowley
Sched. Claire Elliott **PS.** Christopher Schuler
Dist. Off. Louisville 502.582.5129 • Louisville 502.933.5863

R: 102 **T:** 8th 63%
Elected Year: 2006

LOUISIANA

↘ Governor John Bel Edwards (EHD-wurdz) p 225.342.7015

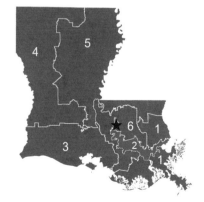

PO Box 94004
Baton Rouge, LA 70804-9004
Website louisiana.gov
Fax 225.342.7099
Term Ends 2024
Lt. Governor
Billy Nungesser, R

C: Baton Rouge
P: 4,659,978 (25)
A: 43,204.04 mi^2 (33rd)

U.S. Senators
Bill Cassidy, R
John N. Kennedy, R
U.S. Representatives
01 / Steve Scalise, R
02 / Troy Carter, **D**
03 / Clay Higgins, R
04 / Mike Johnson, R
05 / Julia Letlow, R
06 / Garret N. Graves, R

Sen. Bill Cassidy (KA-sih-dee) R-LA-Sr. p 202.224.5824

Rm. HSOB 520 **Web.** cassidy.senate.gov **f** 202.224.9735
Bio. 09/28/1957 • Highland Park • State Legislator
• Louisiana State Univ., B.S., 1979; Louisiana State
Univ. Medical School, M.D., 1983 • Christian - Non-
Denominational • M. Laura Layden Cassidy, 3 ch **Cmte.**
Energy & Natural Resources • Finance • Health, Education,
Labor & Pensions • Joint Economic • Veterans' Affairs
CoS. James Quinn **LD.** Katie Hadji
Sched. Emilie Jones **PS.** Ty Bofferding
Dist. Off. Alexandria 318.448.7176 • Baton Rouge
225.929.7711 • Lafayette 337.261.1400 • Lake Charles
337.493.5398 • Metairie 504.838.0130 • Monroe
318.324.2111 • Shreveport 318.798.3215

R: 66 **T:** 2nd 59%
Elected Year: 2014
Next Election: 2026

Sen. John N. Kennedy (KEH-nuh-dee) R-LA-Jr. p 202.224.4623

Rm. RSOB 416 **Web.** kennedy.senate.gov **f** 202.228.0447
Bio. 11/21/1951 • Centreville • Vanderbilt Univ. (TN), B.A.,
1973; Univ. of Virginia School of Law, J.D., 1977; Oxford
Univ. (England), B.CL, 1979 • Methodist • M. Rebecca Stulb
Kennedy, 1 ch **Cmte.** Appropriations • Banking, Housing
& Urban Affairs • Budget • Judiciary • Small Business &
Entrepreneurship
CoS. David Stokes **LD.** Nathan Flagg
Sched. Mary Kirchner **PS.** Jess S. Andrews
Dist. Off. Alexandria 318.445.2892 • Baton Rouge
225.926.8033 • Houma 985.851.0956 • Lafayette
337.269.5980 • Lake Charles 337.436.6255 • Mandeville
985.809.8153 • Monroe 318.361.1489 • New Orleans
504.581.6190 • Shreveport 318.670.5192

R: 79 **T:** 1st 61%
Elected Year: 2016
Next Election: 2022

Rep. Troy Carter (KAR-tur) D-LA-02 p 202.225.6636

Rm. CHOB 506 **Web.** troycarter.house.gov **f** 202.225.1988
Bio. New Orleans • Xavier Univ. of Louisiana, B.A. •
Baptist • M. Melanie Sanders, 2 ch **Cmte.** Small Business •
Transportation & Infrastructure
CoS. James Bernhard
Sched. Freedom **PS.** Zoe Bluffstone
Richardson
Dist. Off. Baton Rouge 504.381.3970 • Gretna 504.381.3999
• New Orleans 504.288.3777 • New Orleans 504.381.3970 •
Reserve 504.381.3970

R: 429 **T:** 1st 55%
Elected Year: 2020

Rep. Garret N. Graves (grayvz) R-LA-06 p 202.225.3901

Rm. RHOB 2402 **Web.** **f** 202.225.7313
garretgraves.house.gov
Bio. 01/31/1972 • Baton Rouge • Roman Catholic • M.
Carissa Graves, 3 ch **Cmte.** Natural Resources • Select
Committee on the Climate Crisis • Transportation &
Infrastructure
CoS. Paul Sawyer **LD.** Maggie Ayrea
Sched. Alexandra Erwin **PS.** Zach Barnett
Dist. Off. Baton Rouge 225.442.1731 • Gonzales
225.450.1672 • Livingston 225.686.4413 • Thibodaux
985.448.4103

R: 217 **T:** 4th 71%
Elected Year: 2014

Rep. Clay Higgins (HIH-guhnz) R-LA-03 p 202.225.2031

Rm. CHOB 572 **Web.** clayhiggins.house.gov **f** 202.225.5724
Bio. 08/24/1961 • New Orleans • Christian - Non-
Denominational • M. Becca Higgins, 4 ch (1 deceased)
Cmte. Homeland Security • Oversight & Reform
CoS. Kathee Facchiano **LD.** Ward Cormier
Sched. Laura Ahrens **PS.** Andrew David
Dist. Off. Lafayette 337.703.6105 • Lake Charles
337.656.2833

R: 266 **T:** 3rd 68%
Elected Year: 2016

LOUISIANA

♟ Rep. Mike Johnson (JAHN-suhn)   R-LA-04   p 202.225.2777
f 202.225.8039

Rm. CHOB 568 **Web.** mikejohnson.house.gov
Bio. 01/30/1972 • Shreveport • Louisiana State Univ., B.S., 1995; Louisiana State Univ. Law School, J.D., 1998 • Southern Baptist • M. Kelly Lary Johnson, 4 ch **Cmte.** Armed Services • Judiciary
CoS. Hayden Haynes   **LD.** Garrett Fultz
Sched. Claire Bienvenu   **PS.** Taylor S. Haulsee
Dist. Off. Bossier City 318.840.0309 • Leesville 337.423.4232 • Natchitoches 318.951.4316

R: 269 **T:** 3rd 60%
Elected Year: 2016

♟ Rep. Julia Letlow ()   R-LA-05   p 202.225.8490

Rm. LHOB 1408 **Web.** letlow.house.gov
Bio. Monroe • Univ. of Louisiana Monroe, B.A., 2002; Univ. of Louisiana Monroe, M.A., 2005; Univ. of South Florida, Ph.D., 2011 • Presbyterian • W., 2 ch **Cmte.** Agriculture • Education & Labor
CoS. Ted Verrill   **LD.** Lindsay Linhares
Sched. Caroline Courville   **PS.** Mitch Rabalais
Dist. Off. Alexandria 318.319.6465 • Amite 985.284.5200 • Monroe 318.570.6440

R: 428 **T:** 1st 65%
Elected Year: 2020

♟ Rep. Steve Scalise (skuh-LEESS)   R-LA-01   p 202.225.3015

Rm. RHOB 2049 **Web.** scalise.house.gov   f 202.226.0386
Bio. 10/06/1965 • New Orleans • State Legislator • Louisiana State Univ., B.S., 1989; Louisiana State Univ., B.S., 1989 • Catholic • M. Jennifer Letulle Scalise, 2 ch **Cmte.** Energy & Commerce
CoS. Megan Bel Miller   **LD.** Claire Trokey
Sched. Jacqueline Battaglia   **PS.** Hunter Lovell
Dist. Off. Hammond 985.340.2185 • Houma 985.879.2300 • Mandeville 985.893.9064 • Metairie 504.837.1259

R: 107 **T:** 8th 72%
Elected Year: 2007

MAINE

☙ Governor Janet Mills (millz)   p 207.287.3531

One State House Station
Augusta, ME 04333-0001
Website maine.gov
Fax 207.287.1034
Term Ends 2023

C: Augusta
P: 1,338,404 (43)
A: 30,842.99 mi^2 (39th)

U.S. Senators
Susan M. Collins, R
Angus S. King, I
U.S. Representatives
01 / Chellie M. Pingree, D
02 / Jared F. Golden, D

MAINE

♜ Sen. Susan M. Collins (KAH-luhnz) R-ME-Sr. p 202.224.2523

Rm. DSOB 413 **Web.** collins.senate.gov **f** 202.224.2693
Bio. 12/07/1952 • Caribou • Association Director; Small
Business Administration Director • St. Lawrence Univ.
(NY), B.A., 1975 • Roman Catholic • M. Thomas Daffron
Cmte. Aging • Appropriations • Health, Education, Labor &
Pensions • Intelligence
CoS. Steve Abbott **LD.** Katie Brown
Sched. Darci Greenacre **PS.** Annie Clark
Dist. Off. Augusta 207.622.8414 • Bangor 207.945.0417 •
Biddeford 207.283.1101 • Caribou 207.493.7873 • Lewiston
207.784.6969 • Portland 207.780.3575

R: 11 **T:** 5th 51%
Elected Year: 1996
Next Election: 2026

♞ Sen. Angus S. King Jr. (king) I-ME-Jr. p 202.224.5344

Caucuses with Democratic Party **f** 202.224.1946
Rm. HSOB 133 **Web.** king.senate.gov
Bio. 03/31/1944 • Alexandria • Governor • Dartmouth
College, A.B., 1966; Univ. of Virginia Law School, J.D., 1969
• Episcopalian • M. Mary J. Herman, 5 ch; 5 gr-ch **Cmte.**
Armed Services • Energy & Natural Resources • Intelligence
• Joint Congressional-Executive Commission on China •
Joint Printing • Rules & Administration
CoS. Kathleen Connery **LD.** Morgan Cashwell
Dawe
Sched. Claire Bridgeo **PS.** Matthew Felling
Dist. Off. Augusta 207.622.8292 • Bangor 207.945.8000 •
Biddeford 207.352.5216 • Portland 207.245.1565 • Presque
Isle 207.764.5124

R: 57 **T:** 2nd 54%
Elected Year: 2012
Next Election: 2024

♞ Rep. Jared F. Golden (GOAL-duhn) D-ME-02 p 202.225.6306

Rm. LHOB 1222 **Web.** golden.house.gov **f** 202.225.2943
Bio. 07/25/1982 • Leeds • Bates College (ME), B.A., 2011
• Unspecified/Other • M. Isobel Golden **Cmte.** Armed
Services • Small Business
CoS. Aisha Woodward **LD.** Eric Kanter
Sched. Ainsley Jamieson **PS.** Nick Zeller
Dist. Off. Bangor 207.249.7400 • Caribou 207.492.6009 •
Lewiston 207.241.6767

R: 315 **T:** 2nd 53%
Elected Year: 2018

♞ Rep. Chellie M. Pingree (PING-gree) D-ME-01 p 202.225.6116

Rm. RHOB 2162 **Web.** pingree.house.gov **f** 202.225.5590
Bio. 04/02/1955 • Minneapolis • State Legislator • College
of the Atlantic (ME), B.A., 1979 • Lutheran • Se. Donald
Sussman, 3 ch (3 from previous marriage); 3 gr-ch **Cmte.**
Agriculture • Appropriations
CoS. Jesse Connolly (CD) **LD.** Evan Johnston
Sched. Karen Sudbay (CD) **PS.** Victoria Bonney
Dist. Off. Portland 207.774.5019 • Waterville 207.873.5713

R: 113 **T:** 7th 62%
Elected Year: 2008

MARYLAND

♜ Governor Larry Hogan (HO-guhn) p 410.974.3901

100 State Circle **C:** Annapolis
Annapolis, MD 21401 **P:** 6,042,718 (19)
Website maryland.gov **A:** 9,707.38 mi^2 (42nd)
Fax 401.974.3275
Term Ends 2023
Lt. Governor
Boyd Rutherford, R

U.S. Senators
Ben L. Cardin, D
Chris J. Van Hollen, D
U.S. Representatives
01 / Andy P. Harris, R
02 / Dutch Ruppersberger, D
03 / John P. Sarbanes, D
04 / Anthony G. Brown, D
05 / Steny Hoyer, D
06 / David Trone, D
07 / Kweisi Mfume, D

MARYLAND

08 / Jamie Raskin, **D**

⚓ Sen. Ben L. Cardin (KAR-din)　　　　D-MD-Sr.　　p 202.224.4524

Rm. HSOB 509 **Web.** cardin.senate.gov　　**f** 202.224.1651
Bio. 10/05/1943 • Baltimore • U.S. Representative;
Attorney • Univ. of Pittsburgh (PA), B.A., 1964; Univ. of
Maryland School of Law, J.D., 1967; Villa Julie College (MD),
LL.D., 2007 • Jewish • M. Myrna Edelman Cardin, 2 ch (1
deceased); 2 gr-ch **Cmte.** Environment & Public Works •
Finance • Foreign Relations • Joint Security & Cooperation
in Europe • Small Business & Entrepreneurship
CoS. Christopher W. Lynch　　**LD.** Gray Maxwell
Sched. Debbie Yamada　　**PS.** Sue Walitsky
Dist. Off. Baltimore 410.962.4436 • Bowie 301.860.0414
• Cumberland 301.777.2957 • Rockville 301.762.2974 •
Salisbury 410.546.4250

R: 23　**T:** 3rd　65%
Elected Year: 2006
Next Election: 2024

⚓ Sen. Chris J. Van Hollen Jr. (van-HAH-luhn)　D-MD-Jr.　p 202.224.4654

Rm. HSOB 110 **Web.** vanhollen.senate.gov　　**f** 202.228.0629
Bio. 01/10/1959 • Karachi • State Senator; Representative
• Swarthmore College (PA), B.A., 1982; John F. Kennedy
School of Government, Harvard Univ., M.P.P., 1985;
Georgetown Univ. (DC), J.D., 1990 • Episcopalian • M.
Katherine Wilkens Van Hollen, 3 ch **Cmte.** Appropriations
• Banking, Housing & Urban Affairs • Budget • Foreign
Relations
CoS. Tricia Russell　　**LD.** Sarah Schenning
Sched. Liana Pardini　　**PS.** Francesca Amodeo
Dist. Off. Annapolis 410.263.1325 • Baltimore 667.212.4610
• Cambridge 410.221.2074 • Hagerstown 301.797.2826 •
Largo 301.322.6560 • Rockville 301.545.1500

R: 75　**T:** 1st　61%
Elected Year: 2016
Next Election: 2022

⚓ Rep. Anthony G. Brown (brown)　　　　D-MD-04　　p 202.225.8699

Rm. LHOB 1323 **Web.**
anthonybrown.house.gov
Bio. 11/21/1961 • Huntington • Mbr., Board of Governors;
Council of State Gov't Toll Fellow; Mbr., MD House of
Delegates; MD House Majority Whip • U.S. Army CPT;
U.S. Army Reserves LTC • Harvard College (MA), B.A.,
1984; Harvard Univ. Law School (MA), J.D., 1992 • Roman
Catholic • M. Karmen Bailey Walker Brown, 2 ch; 1 stepch
Cmte. Armed Services • Transportation & Infrastructure
CoS. Matthew Verghese　　**LD.** James DeAtley
　　　　　　　　　　　　PS. Christian Unkenholz
Dist. Off. Annapolis 410.266.3249 • Largo 301.458.2600

R: 251　**T:** 3rd　80%
Elected Year: 2016

⚓ Rep. Andy P. Harris (HAIR-iss)　　　　R-MD-01　　p 202.225.5311

Rm. RHOB 2334 **Web.** harris.house.gov
Bio. 01/25/1957 • Brooklyn • Johns Hopkins Univ., B.S.,
1977; Johns Hopkins Univ., M.D., 1980; Johns Hopkins Univ.
Bloomburg School of Hygiene and Public Health (MD),
M.H.S., 1995 • Roman Catholic • M. Nicole Harris, 5 ch; 6 gr-
ch **Cmte.** Appropriations
CoS. Bryan Shuy　　**LD.** Tim Daniels
Sched. Victoria Cesaro　　**PS.** Walter Smoloski
Dist. Off. Bel Air 410.588.5670 • Chester 410.643.5425 •
Salisbury 443.944.8624

R: 137　**T:** 6th　63%
Elected Year: 2010

⚓ Rep. Steny Hoyer (HOY-yur)　　　　D-MD-05　　p 202.225.4131

Rm. LHOB 1705 **Web.** hoyer.house.gov　　**f** 202.225.4300
Bio. 06/14/1939 • New York • Attorney; Member, State
Board of Education • Univ. of Maryland - College Park,
B.S., 1963; Georgetown Univ. Law Center (DC), J.D., 1966 •
Baptist • W., 3 ch; 3 gr-ch; 2 great-gr-ch
CoS. Alexis Covey-Brandt　　**LD.** James P. Leuschen
Sched. Bridget Brennan　　**PS.** Maya Valentine
Dist. Off. Greenbelt 301.474.0119 • White Plains
301.843.1577

R: 4　**T:** 21st　69%
Elected Year: 1980

⌕ Rep. Kweisi Mfume (oom-FOO-mae)　　D-MD-07　p 202.225.4741

Rm. RHOB 2263 **Web.** mfume.house.gov　**f** 202.225.3178
Bio. 10/24/1948 • Baltimore • Morgan State Univ., B.S., 1976; Johns Hopkins Univ., M.A., 1984 • M. Tiffany McMillan, 5 ch　**Cmte.** Education & Labor • Oversight & Reform • Small Business
CoS. Eric Bryant
Sched. Kia Brown　　　　**PS.** Ramon Korionoff
Dist. Off. Baltimore 410.685.9199 • Catonsville 410.818.2120 • Ellicott City 443.364.5413

R: 125　**T:** 2nd　72%
Elected Year: 2019

⌕ Rep. Jamie Raskin (RAS-kin)　　　D-MD-08　p 202.225.5341

Rm. RHOB 2242 **Web.** raskin.house.gov
Bio. 12/13/1962 • Washington • Harvard College (MA), B.A., 1983; Harvard Univ. Law School (MA), J.D., 1987 • Unspecified/Other • M. Sarah Raskin, 3 ch (1 deceased)
Cmte. Administration • Joint Printing • Judiciary • Oversight & Reform • Rules • Select Investigate Jan 6 Attack on the U.S. Capitol
CoS. Julie Tagen　　　　**LD.** Lauren Doney
Sched. James Montfort　　**PS.** Jacob Wilson
Dist. Off. Rockville 301.354.1000

R: 279　**T:** 3rd　68%
Elected Year: 2016

⌕ Rep. Dutch Ruppersberger III (ROO-purs-bur-　D-MD-02　p 202.225.3061
gur)

Rm. RHOB 2206 **Web.**　　　　**f** 202.225.3094
ruppersberger.house.gov
Bio. 01/31/1946 • Baltimore • Member, City Council; Assistant State Attorney • Univ. of Maryland - College Park, B.A., 1967; Univ. of Baltimore School of Law (MD), J.D., 1970 • Methodist • M. Kay Murphy Ruppersberger, 2 ch; 5 gr-ch
Cmte. Appropriations
CoS. Tara Oursler　　　　**LD.** Walter Gonzales
Sched. Victoria Graham　　**PS.** Jaime Lennon (CD)
Dist. Off. Timonium 410.628.2701

R: 65　**T:** 10th　68%
Elected Year: 2002

⌕ Rep. John P. Sarbanes (SAR-baynz)　　D-MD-03　p 202.225.4016

Rm. RHOB 2370 **Web.** sarbanes.house.gov　**f** 202.225.9219
Bio. 05/22/1962 • Baltimore • School Superintendent • Princeton Univ. Woodrow Wilson School of Public and International Affairs (NJ), B.A., 1984; Harvard Univ., J.D., 1988 • Greek Orthodox • M. Dina Sarbanes, 3 ch　**Cmte.** Energy & Commerce • Oversight & Reform
CoS. Dvora Lovinger　　　**LD.** Kathleen Teleky
Sched. Kelly Moura　　　　**PS.** Natalie Young
Dist. Off. Annapolis 410.295.1679 • Burtonsville 301.421.4078 • Towson 410.832.8890

R: 99　**T:** 8th　70%
Elected Year: 2006

⌕ Rep. David Trone (troan)　　　　D-MD-06　p 202.225.2721

Rm. LHOB 1110 **Web.** trone.house.gov
Bio. 09/21/1955 • Cheverly • Furman Univ. (SC), B.A., 1977; Univ. of Pennsylvania, Wharton School of Finance and Commerce, M.B.A., 1985 • Lutheran • M. June Trone, 4 ch
Cmte. Appropriations • Joint Economic • Veterans' Affairs
CoS. Lane Lofton　　　　**LD.** Krista O'Neill
Sched. Matt Pastore　　　**PS.** Sasha Galbreath
Dist. Off. Cumberland 240.382.6464 • Frederick 240.803.6119 • Gaithersburg 301.926.0300 • Hagerstown 240.382.6464

R: 359　**T:** 2nd　59%
Elected Year: 2018

MASSACHUSETTS

MASSACHUSETTS

🏛 **Governor Charlie Baker** (BAY-kur)   p 617.725.4005

Massachusetts State House, Room 280
Boston, MA 02133
Website mass.gov
Fax 617.727.9725
Term Ends 2023
Lt. Governor
Karyn Polito, R

C: Boston
P: 6,902,149 (15)
A: 7,800.03 mi^2 (45th)

U.S. Senators
Ed Markey, **D**
Elizabeth Warren, **D**
U.S. Representatives
01 / Richard E. Neal, **D**
02 / Jim P. McGovern, **D**
03 / Lori Trahan, **D**
04 / Jake D. Auchincloss, **D**
05 / Katherine Clark, **D**
06 / Seth W. Moulton, **D**
07 / Ayanna Pressley, **D**
08 / Stephen F. Lynch, **D**
09 / Bill R. Keating, **D**

🏛 **Sen. Ed Markey** (MAR-kee)   D-MA-Jr.   p 202.224.2742

Rm. DSOB 255 **Web.** markey.senate.gov   f 202.224.8525
Bio. 07/11/1946 • Malden • Representative • Army
Reserves 1968-73 • Boston College (MA), B.A., 1968; Boston
College Law School (MA), J.D., 1972 • Roman Catholic
• M. Susan Blumenthal **Cmte.** Commerce, Science &
Transportation • Environment & Public Works • Foreign
Relations • Small Business & Entrepreneurship
CoS. John E. Walsh   **LD.** Jeremy D'Aloisio
Sched. Sarah Butler   **PS.** Taylor St. Germain
Dist. Off. Boston 617.565.8519 • Springfield 413.785.4610

R: 62 **T:** 3rd 66%
Elected Year: 2013
Next Election: 2026

🏛 **Sen. Elizabeth Warren** (WAR-ruhn)   D-MA-Sr.   p 202.224.4543

Rm. HSOB 309 **Web.** warren.senate.gov   f 202.228.2072
Bio. 06/22/1949 • Oklahoma City • Univ. of Houston (TX),
B.A., 1970; Rutgers Univ. (NJ), J.D., 1976 • Methodist • M.
Bruce H. Mann, 2 ch; 3 gr-ch **Cmte.** Aging • Armed Services
• Banking, Housing & Urban Affairs • Finance
CoS. Jonathan Donenberg   **LD.** Beth Pearson
Sched. Laura Gerrard   **PS.** Alex Sarabia
Dist. Off. Boston 617.565.3170 • Springfield 413.788.2690

R: 60 **T:** 2nd 60%
Elected Year: 2012
Next Election: 2024

🏛 **Rep. Jake D. Auchincloss** (AW-kin-klaws)   D-MA-04   p 202.225.5931

Rm. LHOB 1524 **Web.** auchincloss.house.gov f 202.225.0182
Bio. 01/29/1988 • Newton • Harvard Univ., B.A., 2010;
Massachusetts Institute of Technology, M.B.A., 2016 • Jewish
• M. Michelle Auchincloss **Cmte.** Financial Services •
Transportation & Infrastructure
CoS. Tim Hysom   **LD.** Jessica Hatcher
Sched. Joe Valente   **PS.** Matt Corridoni
Dist. Off. Attleboro 508.431.1110 • Newton 617.332.3333

R: 371 **T:** 1st 61%
Elected Year: 2020

⚑ Rep. Katherine Clark (klark)   D-MA-05   p 202.225.2836
Rm. RHOB 2448 **Web.**   **f** 202.226.0092
katherineclark.house.gov
Bio. 07/17/1963 • New Haven • Saint Lawrence Univ., B.A.,
1985; Cornell Univ. Law School (NY), J.D., 1989; Harvard
Univ. John F. Kennedy School of Government (MA), M.P.A.,
1997 • Protestant - Unspecified Christian • M. Rodney
Dowell, 3 ch **Cmte.** Appropriations
CoS. Brooke Scannell   **LD.** Steve Thornton
Sched. Judah Piepho   **PS.** Kathryn Alexander
Dist. Off. Framingham 508.319.9757 • Malden
617.354.0292

R: 200   **T:** 5th 74%
Elected Year: 2012

⚑ Rep. Bill R. Keating (KEE-ting)   D-MA-09   p 202.225.3111
Rm. RHOB 2351 **Web.** keating.house.gov   **f** 202.225.5658
Bio. 09/06/1952 • Norwood • Boston College (MA), B.A.,
1974; Boston College (MA), M.B.A., 1982; Suffolk Univ.
School of Law (MA), J.D., 1985 • Roman Catholic • M. Tevis
Keating, 2 ch **Cmte.** Armed Services • Foreign Affairs
CoS. Garrett Donovan   **LD.** Natasha Silva
Sched. David Oleksak   **PS.** Lauren McDermott
Dist. Off. Hyannis 508.771.6868 • New Bedford
508.999.6462 • Plymouth 508.746.9000

R: 142   **T:** 6th 61%
Elected Year: 2012

⚑ Rep. Stephen F. Lynch (linch)   D-MA-08   p 202.225.8273
Rm. RHOB 2109 **Web.** lynch.house.gov   **f** 202.225.3984
Bio. 03/31/1955 • Boston • State Legislator • Wentworth
Institute of Technology (MA), B.S., 1988; Boston College
Law School (MA), J.D., 1991; Harvard Univ. John F. Kennedy
School of Government (MA), M.P.A., 1999 • Roman
Catholic • M. Margaret Shaughnessy Lynch, 1 ch **Cmte.**
Financial Services • Oversight & Reform • Transportation &
Infrastructure
CoS. Kevin Ryan   **LD.** Bruce Fernandez
Sched. Megan Hollingshead   **PS.** Molly Rose Tarpey (CD)
Dist. Off. Boston 617.428.2000 • Brockton 508.586.5555 •
Quincy 617.657.6305

R: 57   **T:** 11th 81%
Elected Year: 2012

⚑ Rep. Jim P. McGovern (mih-GUH-vurn)   D-MA-02   p 202.225.6101
Rm. CHOB 370 **Web.** mcgovern.house.gov   **f** 202.225.5759
Bio. 11/20/1959 • Worcester • Congressional Aide •
American Univ. (DC), B.A., 1981; American Univ. (DC),
M.P.A., 1984 • Roman Catholic • M. Lisa Murray McGovern,
2 ch **Cmte.** Agriculture • Joint Congressional-Executive
Commission on China • Rules
CoS. Jennifer Chandler   **LD.** Cindy Buhl
Sched. Daniel Holt   **PS.** Matt Bonaccorsi
Dist. Off. Leominster 978.466.3552 • Northampton
413.341.8700 • Worcester 508.831.7356

R: 39   **T:** 13th 65%
Elected Year: 2012

⚑ Rep. Seth W. Moulton (MOAL-tuhn)   D-MA-06   p 202.225.8020
Rm. LHOB 1127 **Web.** moulton.house.gov   **f** 202.225.5915
Bio. 10/24/1978 • Salem • Phillips Academy, (MA), M.P.A.,
1997; Harvard Univ., B.S., 2001; Harvard Univ. School of
Business (MA), M.B.A., 2011; Harvard Univ. John F. Kennedy
School of Government (MA), M.P.A., 2011 • Christian - Non-
Denominational • M. Liz Boardman, 1 ch **Cmte.** Armed
Services • Budget • Transportation & Infrastructure
CoS. Alexis L'Heureux   **LD.** Joseph Rodriguez
Sched. Cari Berlin   **PS.** Ron Eckstein
Dist. Off. Salem 978.531.1669

R: 227   **T:** 4th 65%
Elected Year: 2014

⚑ Rep. Richard E. Neal (neel)   D-MA-01   p 202.225.5601
Rm. CHOB 372 **Web.** neal.house.gov   **f** 202.225.8112
Bio. 02/14/1949 • Worcester • Mayor (Springfield, MA);
President, Springfield City Council • American International
College (MA), B.A., 1972; Univ. of Hartford Barney School of
Business (CT), M.P.A., 1976 • Roman Catholic • M. Maureen
Conway Neal, 4 ch **Cmte.** Joint Taxation • Ways & Means
CoS. Elizabeth O'Hara   **LD.** Kara Getz
Sched. Timothy Ranstrom   **PS.** Margaret Boyle (CD)
Dist. Off. Pittsfield 413.442.0946 • Springfield 413.785.0325

R: 10   **T:** 17th 97%
Elected Year: 2012

MASSACHUSETTS

ꙮ Rep. Ayanna Pressley (PRESS-lee) D-MA-07 p 202.225.5111

Rm. LHOB 1108 **Web.** pressley.house.gov **f** 202.225.9322
Bio. 02/03/1974 • Cincinnati • Baptist • M. Conan Harris pressley, 1 stepch **Cmte.** Financial Services • Oversight & Reform
CoS. Sarah Groh **LD.** Aissa Canchola
Sched. Lona Watts **PS.** Ricardo Sanchez
Dist. Off. Hyde Park 617.850.0040

R: 342 **T:** 2nd 87%
Elected Year: 2018

ꙮ Rep. Lori Trahan (truh-HAN) D-MA-03 p 202.225.3411

Rm. RHOB 2439 **Web.** trahan.house.gov
Bio. Lowell • Georgetown Univ. (DC), B.S., 1995 • Catholic • M. David Trahan, 2 ch; 3 stepch **Cmte.** Energy & Commerce • Natural Resources
CoS. Mark McDevitt **LD.** Elya Taichman
Sched. Lisa Degou **PS.** Francis Grubar
Dist. Off. Acton 978.459.0101 • Fitchburg 978.459.0101 • Hudson 978.459.0101 • Lawrence 978.258.1138 • Lowell 978.459.0101

R: 358 **T:** 2nd 98%
Elected Year: 2018

MICHIGAN

ꙮ Governor Gretchen Whitmer (WHIT-mur) p 517.373.3400

PO Box 30013
Lansing, MI 48909
Website michigan.gov
Fax 517.335.6863
Term Ends 2023
Lt. Governor
Garlin Gilchrist, **D**

C: Lansing
P: 9,995,915 (10)
A: 56,538.85 mi^2 (22nd)

U.S. Senators
Debbie Stabenow, **D**
Gary Peters, **D**
U.S. Representatives
01 / Jack W. Bergman, R
02 / Bill P. Huizenga, R
03 / Peter Meijer, R
04 / John Moolenaar, R
05 / Dan T. Kildee, D
06 / Fred S. Upton, R
07 / Tim L. Walberg, R
08 / Elissa B. Slotkin, D
09 / Andy Levin, D
10 / Lisa McClain, R
11 / Haley Stevens, D
12 / Debbie Dingell, D
13 / Rashida Tlaib, D
14 / Brenda L. Lawrence, D

ꙮ Sen. Gary Peters Sr. (PEE-turz) D-MI-Jr. p 202.224.6221

Rm. HSOB 724 **Web.** peters.senate.gov **f** 202.224.7387
Bio. 12/01/1958 • Pontiac • State Legislator; Professor • Navy Reserves • Alma College (MI), B.A., 1980; Univ. of Detroit (MI), M.B.A., 1984; Wayne State Univ. Law School (MI), J.D., 1989; Michigan State Univ., M.A., 2007 • Episcopalian • M. Colleen Ochoa, 3 ch **Cmte.** Armed Services • Commerce, Science & Transportation • Homeland Security & Government Affairs
CoS. Caitlyn Stephenson **LD.** Catherine Barrett
Sched. Angeli Chawla **PS.** Sarah Schakow
Dist. Off. Detroit 313.226.6020 • Grand Rapids 616.233.9150 • Lansing 517.377.1508 • Marquette 906.226.4554 • Rochester 248.608.8040 • Saginaw 989.754.0112 • Traverse City 231.947.7773

R: 65 **T:** 2nd 50%
Elected Year: 2014
Next Election: 2026

Sen. Debbie Stabenow (STAB-uh-nou)   D-MI-Sr.   p 202.224.4822

Rm. HSOB 731 **Web.** stabenow.senate.gov   **f** 202.228.0325
Bio. 04/29/1950 • Gladwin • U.S. Representative; State
Legislator; Social Worker • Michigan State Univ., B.A., 1972;
Michigan State Univ., M.S.W., 1975 • Methodist • D., 2 ch; 4
gr-ch **Cmte.** Agriculture, Nutrition & Forestry • Budget •
Environment & Public Works • Finance • Joint Taxation
CoS. Matt VanKuiken   **LD.** Emily Carwell
Sched. Ellen Rodman (CD)   **PS.** Patricia Curran
Dist. Off. Detroit 313.961.4330 • East Lansing 517.203.1760
• Flint 810.720.4172 • Grand Rapids 616.975.0052 •
Marquette 906.228.8756 • Traverse City 231.929.1031

R: 15 **T:** 4th 52%
Elected Year: 2000
Next Election: 2024

Rep. Jack W. Bergman (BAIRG-mahn)   R-MI-01   p 202.225.4735

Rm. CHOB 566 **Web.** bergman.house.gov   **f** 202.225.4710
Bio. 02/02/1947 • Shakopee • Gustavus Adolphus College,
B.A., 1969; Univ. of West Florida, M.B.A., 1975 • Lutheran •
M. Cindy Bergman, 5 ch; 8 gr-ch **Cmte.** Armed Services •
Veterans' Affairs
CoS. Tony Lis   **LD.** Michelle Jelnicky
Sched. Amelia Burns   **PS.** James Hogge
Dist. Off. Gwinn 906.273.2227 • Manistique 906.286.4191
• Traverse City 231.944.7633

R: 248 **T:** 3rd 62%
Elected Year: 2016

Rep. Debbie Dingell (DING-gull)   D-MI-12   p 202.225.4071

Rm. CHOB 116 **Web.**   **f** 202.226.0371
  debbiedingell.house.gov
Bio. 11/23/1953 • Detroit • Georgetown Univ. (DC),
B.S., 1975; Georgetown Univ. (DC), M.S., 1996 • Roman
Catholic • M. Hon. John D. Dingell Jr., 4 ch **Cmte.** Energy &
Commerce • Natural Resources
CoS. Dan Black   **LD.** Kevin Rambosk
Sched. Elizabeth Hood   **PS.** Mackenzie Smith
Dist. Off. Dearborn 313.278.2936 • Ypsilanti 734.481.1100

R: 214 **T:** 4th 66%
Elected Year: 2014

Rep. Bill P. Huizenga (HY-zeng-uh)   R-MI-02   p 202.225.4401

Rm. RHOB 2232 **Web.** huizenga.house.gov   **f** 202.226.0779
Bio. 01/31/1969 • Zeeland • Calvin College (MI), B.A., 1991
• Christian Reformed Church • M. Natalie Huizenga, 5 ch
Cmte. Financial Services
CoS. Jon DeWitte   **LD.** Palmer Rafferty
Sched. Sarah Lisman   **PS.** Brian Patrick
Dist. Off. Grand Haven 616.414.5516 • Grandville
616.570.0917

R: 140 **T:** 6th 59%
Elected Year: 2010

Rep. Dan T. Kildee (KILL-dee)   D-MI-05   p 202.225.3611

Rm. CHOB 200 **Web.** dankildee.house.gov   **f** 202.225.6393
Bio. 08/11/1958 • Flint • Central Michigan Univ., B.S. •
Roman Catholic • M. Jennifer Kildee, 3 ch; 2 gr-ch **Cmte.**
Budget • Science, Space & Technology • Ways & Means
CoS. Mitchell Rivard   **LD.** Jordan Dickinson
Sched. Elizabeth Virga   **PS.** Kelly Montgomery
Dist. Off. Flint 810.238.8627

R: 174 **T:** 5th 55%
Elected Year: 2012

Rep. Brenda L. Lawrence (LAW-renss)   D-MI-14   p 202.225.5802

Rm. RHOB 2463 **Web.** lawrence.house.gov   **f** 202.226.2356
Bio. Detroit • Central Michigan Univ., Bach. Deg., 2005 •
Christian - Non-Denominational • M. McArthur Lawrence, 2
ch; 1 gr-ch **Cmte.** Appropriations • Oversight & Reform
CoS. Curtis Doster   **LD.** Zach Weber
Sched. Merone Kahassai   **PS.** Cody Sibulo
Dist. Off. Detroit 313.880.2400 • Southfield 248.356.2052

R: 222 **T:** 4th 79%
Elected Year: 2014

Rep. Andy Levin (LEH-vin) — D-MI-09 — p 202.225.4961

Rm. CHOB 312 **Web.** andylevin.house.gov **f** 202.226.1033
Bio. 08/10/1960 • Berkley • Williams College, B.A., 1983;
Univ. of Michigan, M.A., 1990; Harvard Law School (MA),
J.D., 1994 • Jewish • M. Mary Freeman, 4 ch **Cmte.**
Education & Labor • Foreign Affairs
CoS. Ven Neralla **LD.** Erica Fein
Sched. Taryn Brown **PS.** Janae Washington
Dist. Off. Warren 586.498.7122

R: 328 **T:** 2nd 58%
Elected Year: 2018

Rep. Lisa McClain (mih-klain) — R-MI-10 — p 202.225.2106

Rm. CHOB 218 **Web.** mcclain.house.gov **f** 202.226.1169
Bio. 04/07/1966 • Stockbridge • Lansing Community
College, Assc. Deg.; Northwood Univ. (MI), B.B.A. • Roman
Catholic • M. Mike McClain, 3 ch **Cmte.** Armed Services •
Education & Labor
CoS. Nick Hawatmeh **LD.** Erik Kinney
Sched. Caleb Baca **PS.** Stacey Daniels
Dist. Off. Washington 586.697.9300

R: 407 **T:** 1st 66%
Elected Year: 2020

Rep. Peter Meijer (MAI-ur) — R-MI-03 — p 202.225.3831

Rm. LHOB 1508 **Web.** meijer.house.gov **f** 202.225.5144
Bio. 01/10/1988 • Grand Rapids • Univ. of the District
of Columbia, B.A., 2012; New York Univ., M.B.A., 2017 •
Christian Church • M. Gabriella Meijer **Cmte.** Foreign
Affairs • Homeland Security • Science, Space & Technology
CoS. Ken Monahan **LD.** Maggie Woodin
Sched. Errical Bryant **PS.** Emily Taylor
Dist. Off. Grand Rapids 616.451.8383

R: 408 **T:** 1st 53%
Elected Year: 2020

Rep. John Moolenaar (MULL-leh-nar) — R-MI-04 — p 202.225.3561

Rm. CHOB 117 **Web.** moolenaar.house.gov **f** 202.225.9679
Bio. 05/08/1961 • Midland • Hope College (MI), B.S., 1983;
Harvard Univ., M.P.A., 1989 • Christian - Non-Denominational
• M. Amy Moolenaar, 6 ch **Cmte.** Appropriations
CoS. Lindsay Ryan **LD.** Edward Kim
Sched. Michelle Chavez **PS.** David Russell
Dist. Off. Cadillac 231.942.5070 • Midland 989.631.2552

R: 225 **T:** 4th 65%
Elected Year: 2014

Rep. Elissa B. Slotkin (SLAHT-kin) — D-MI-08 — p 202.225.4872

Rm. LHOB 1210 **Web.** slotkin.house.gov **f** 202.225.5820
Bio. 07/10/1976 • Holly • Columbia Univ. School of
International and Public Affairs, Mast. Deg.; Cornell Univ.
(NY), B.A., 1998 • Jewish • M. Dave Slotkin, 2 stepch **Cmte.**
Armed Services • Homeland Security • Veterans' Affairs
CoS. Matt Hennessey **LD.** Danielle Most
Sched. Megan Birleson **PS.** Austin Cook
Dist. Off. Lansing 517.993.0510

R: 348 **T:** 2nd 51%
Elected Year: 2018

Rep. Haley Stevens (STEE-vuhnz) — D-MI-11 — p 202.225.8171

Rm. LHOB 1510 **Web.** stevens.house.gov
Bio. 06/24/1983 • Oakland County • American Univ.
(DC), Bach. Deg., 2005; American Univ. (DC), M.A., 2007 •
Christian Church • M. Rob Gulley **Cmte.** Education & Labor
• Science, Space & Technology
CoS. Justin German **LD.** Liam Steadman
Sched. John Martin **PS.** Larkin Parker
Dist. Off. Livonia 734.853.3040

R: 354 **T:** 2nd 50%
Elected Year: 2018

⚑ Rep. Rashida Tlaib (tuh-LEEB)　　　　D-MI-13　　p 202.225.5126

Rm. LHOB 1628 **Web.** tlaib.house.gov
Bio. 07/24/1976 • Detroit • Wayne State Univ. (MI), B.A., 1998; Western Michigan Univ., J.D., 2004 • Islam (Muslim) • M. Fayez Tlaib, 2 ch **Cmte.** Financial Services • Joint Congressional-Executive Commission on China • Natural Resources • Oversight & Reform
CoS. Britteny Jenkins　　　**LD.** Tom Clancy
Sched. Amanda Kaye　　　**PS.** Adrienne Salazar
Dist. Off. Detroit 313.463.6220 • Inkster 313.463.6220 • River Rouge 313.463.6220

R: 357 **T:** 2nd 78%
Elected Year: 2018

⚑ Rep. Fred S. Upton (UP-tuhn)　　　　R-MI-06　　p 202.225.3761

Rm. RHOB 2183 **Web.** upton.house.gov　　**f** 202.225.4986
Bio. 04/23/1953 • St. Joseph • Congressional Staffer • Univ. of Michigan, B.A., 1975 • Congregationalist • M. Amey Rulon-Miller Upton, 2 ch **Cmte.** Energy & Commerce
CoS. Joan Hillebrands　　　**LD.** Mark Ratner
Sched. Suzanne Scruggs
Dist. Off. Kalamazoo 269.385.0039 • St. Joseph 269.982.1986

R: 7 **T:** 18th 56%
Elected Year: 1992

⚑ Rep. Tim L. Walberg (WALL-burg)　　　R-MI-07　　p 202.225.6276

Rm. RHOB 2266 **Web.** walberg.house.gov　　**f** 202.225.6281
Bio. 04/12/1951 • Chicago • Minister; College Administrator • Taylor Univ. (IN), B.S., 1975; Fort Wayne Bible College, B.R.E., 1975; Wheaton College (IL), M.A., 1978 • Protestant - Unspecified Christian • M. Susan Walberg, 3 ch; 2 gr-ch
Cmte. Education & Labor • Energy & Commerce
CoS. R.J. Laukitis　　　**LD.** Joanna Brown
Sched. Mary Elizabeth　　　**PS.** Dan Kotman
Stringer
Dist. Off. Jackson 517.780.9075

R: 123 **T:** 6th 59%
Elected Year: 2010

MINNESOTA

⚑ Governor Tim J. Walz (wallz)　　　　　　　p 651.201.3400

130 State Capitol, 75 Rev. Dr.　**C:** St. Paul
Martin Luther King Jr. Blvd.　**P:** 5,611,179 (22)
St. Paul, MN 55155　　　**A:** 79,626.59 mi^2 (14th)
Website state.mn.us
Fax 651.797.1850
Term Ends 2023
Lt. Governor
Peggy Flanagan, **D**

U.S. Senators
Amy Klobuchar, **D**
Tina Smith, **D**
U.S. Representatives
01 / Jim Hagedorn, R
02 / Angie D. Craig, **D**
03 / Dean Phillips, **D**
04 / Betty McCollum, **D**
05 / Ilhan Omar, **D**
06 / Tom Emmer, R
07 / Michelle L. Fischbach, R
08 / Pete A. Stauber, R

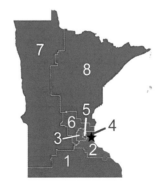

MINNESOTA

🔸 Sen. Amy Klobuchar (KLOE-buh-shar)　　D-MN-Sr.　p 202.224.3244

Rm. DSOB 425　**Web.** klobuchar.senate.gov　**f** 202.228.2186
Bio. 05/25/1960 • Plymouth • Attorney; Hennepin County
Attorney • Yale Univ. (CT), B.A., 1982; Univ. of Chicago (IL),
J.D., 1985 • Congregationalist • M. John Bessler, 1 ch　**Cmte.**
Agriculture, Nutrition & Forestry • Commerce, Science &
Transportation • Joint Economic • Joint Library • Joint
Printing • Judiciary • Rules & Administration
CoS. Doug Calidas　　**LD.** Jonathan Sclarsic
Sched. Savanna Peterson　**PS.** Jane Meyer
Dist. Off. Minneapolis 612.727.5220 • Moorhead
218.287.2219 • Rochester 507.288.5321 • Virginia
218.741.9690

R: 27　**T:** 3rd　60%
Elected Year: 2006
Next Election: 2024

🔸 Sen. Tina Smith (smith)　　D-MN-Jr.　p 202.224.5641

Rm. HSOB 720　**Web.** smith.senate.gov　**f** 202.224.0044
Bio. 03/04/1958 • Albuquerque • Stanford Univ. (CA),
B.A.; Dartmouth College Tuck School of Business (NH),
M.B.A. • M. Archie Smith, 2 ch　**Cmte.** Agriculture, Nutrition
& Forestry • Banking, Housing & Urban Affairs • Health,
Education, Labor & Pensions • Indian Affairs • Joint Security
& Cooperation in Europe
CoS. Jeff Lomonaco　　**LD.** Gohar Sedighi
Sched. Michael Weiss　　**PS.** Shea Necheles
Dist. Off. Duluth 218.722.2390 • Moorhead 218.284.8721 •
Rochester 507.288.2003 • Saint Paul 651.221.1016

R: 81　**T:** 3rd　49%
Elected Year: 2018
Next Election: 2026

🔸 Rep. Angie D. Craig (krayg)　　D-MN-02　p 202.225.2271

Rm. RHOB 2442　**Web.** craig.house.gov
Bio. 02/14/1972 • West Helena • Univ. of Memphis,
B.A., 1994 • Lutheran • M. Cheryl Greene, 4 ch　**Cmte.**
Agriculture • Energy & Commerce • Select Economic
Disparity & Fairness in Growth • Small Business
CoS. Nick Coe　　**LD.** Will Mitchell
Sched. Maria Ferrara　　**PS.** David G. McGonigal
Dist. Off. Burnsville 651.846.2120

R: 304　**T:** 2nd　48%
Elected Year: 2018

🔺 Rep. Tom Emmer Jr. (EH-mur)　　R-MN-06　p 202.225.2331

Rm. CHOB 315　**Web.** emmer.house.gov　**f** 202.225.6475
Bio. 03/03/1961 • South Bend • Univ. of Alaska, Fairbanks,
B.A., 1984; William Mitchell College of Law (MN), J.D., 1988
• Roman Catholic • M. Jacqueline Samuel Emmer, 7 ch
Cmte. Financial Services
CoS. Christopher Maneval　　**LD.** Jeff Kuckuck
Sched. Christine Callaghan　**PS.** Theresa Meyer
Dist. Off. Otsego 763.241.6848

R: 215　**T:** 4th　66%
Elected Year: 2014

🔺 Rep. Michelle L. Fischbach (FISH-baak)　　R-MN-07　p 202.225.2165

Rm. LHOB 1237　**Web.** fischbach.house.gov　**f** 202.225.1593
Bio. 11/03/1965 • Minnesota • St. Cloud State College
(MN), B.A., 1989; William Mitchell College of Law (MN),
J.D., 2010 • Catholic • M. Scott Fischbach, 2 ch　**Cmte.**
Agriculture • Judiciary • Rules
CoS. David FitzSimmons　**LD.** Nick Lunneberg
Sched. Eleanor Traynham　**PS.** Lauren Weber
Dist. Off. Moorhead 218.422.2090 • Willmar 320.403.6100

R: 385　**T:** 1st　53%
Elected Year: 2020

MINNESOTA

📌 Rep. Jim Hagedorn (HAG-uh-dorn) R-MN-01 p 202.225.2472

Rm. LHOB 1433 **Web.** hagedorn.house.gov
Bio. 08/04/1962 • Blue Earth • George Mason Univ., B.A.,
1992 • Lutheran • S. **Cmte.** Agriculture • Small Business
CoS. Kris Skrzycki **LD.** Noah Yantis
Sched. Karin Mantor **PS.** Lia Palazzo
Dist. Off. Mankato 507.323.6090 • Rochester 507.323.6090

R: 320 **T:** 2nd 49%
Elected Year: 2018

📌 Rep. Betty McCollum (mih-KAW-lum) D-MN-04 p 202.225.6631

Rm. RHOB 2256 **Web.** mccollum.house.gov **f** 202.225.1968
Bio. 07/12/1954 • Minneapolis • Teacher; Representative •
Saint Catherine Univ., B.S., 1986 • Roman Catholic • D., 2 ch
Cmte. Appropriations • Natural Resources
CoS. Bill Harper (CD) **LD.** Ben Peterson
Sched. Erin Melody **PS.** Amanda Yanchury
Dist. Off. St. Paul 651.224.9191

R: 55 **T:** 11th 63%
Elected Year: 2000

📌 Rep. Ilhan Omar (O-mar) D-MN-05 p 202.225.4755

Rm. LHOB 1730 **Web.** omar.house.gov
Bio. 10/04/1982 • Mogadishu • North Dakota State Univ.,
B.A., 2011 • Islam (Muslim) • M. Ahmed Hirsi, 3 ch **Cmte.**
Education & Labor • Foreign Affairs
CoS. Connor McNutt **LD.** Kelly Misselwitz
Sched. Philip Bennett **PS.** Jeremy Slevin
Dist. Off. Minneapolis 612.333.1272

R: 337 **T:** 2nd 64%
Elected Year: 2018

📌 Rep. Dean Phillips (FIH-lips) D-MN-03 p 202.225.2871

Rm. RHOB 2452 **Web.** phillips.house.gov **f** 202.225.6351
Bio. 01/20/1969 • St. Paul • Brown Univ. (RI), B.A., 1991;
Univ. of Minnesota, M.B.A., 2000 • Jewish • D., 2 ch
Cmte. Ethics • Foreign Affairs • Select Committee on the
Modernization of Congress • Small Business
CoS. Tim Bertocci **LD.** Beverly Hart
Sched. Jessica Larsen **PS.** Bryan Doyle
Dist. Off. Minnetonka 952.656.5176

R: 340 **T:** 2nd 56%
Elected Year: 2018

📌 Rep. Pete A. Stauber (STAW-bur) R-MN-08 p 202.225.6211

Rm. CHOB 461 **Web.** stauber.house.gov
Bio. 05/10/1966 • Duluth • Lake Superior State Univ.,
B.S., 1988 • Catholic • M. Jodi Stauber, 4 ch **Cmte.**
Natural Resources • Small Business • Transportation &
Infrastructure
CoS. Desiree Koetzle **LD.** Jeff Bishop
 PS. Kelsey Mix
Dist. Off. Brainerd 218.355.0862 • Cambridge 763.310.6208
• Chisholm 218.355.0726 • Hermantown 218.481.6396

R: 351 **T:** 2nd 57%
Elected Year: 2018

MISSISSIPPI

📌 Governor Tate Reeves (reevz) p 601.359.3150

PO Box 139
Jackson, MS 39205
Website mississippi.gov
Fax 601.359.3741
Term Ends 2024
Lt. Governor
Delbert Hosemann, R

C: Jackson
P: 2,986,530 (35)
A: 46,923.36 mi^2 (31st)

MISSISSIPPI

MISSISSIPPI

U.S. Senators
Roger F. Wicker, **R**
Cindy Hyde-Smith, **R**
U.S. Representatives
01 / Trent Kelly, **R**
02 / Bennie G. Thompson, **D**
03 / Michael P. Guest, **R**
04 / Steven M. Palazzo, **R**

⚑ Sen. Cindy Hyde-Smith ("hide" smith)　　R-MS-Jr.　　p 202.224.5054

Rm. HSOB 702　**Web.** hydesmith.senate.gov　**f** 202.224.5321
Bio. Brookhaven • Copiah-Lincoln Community College (MS), A.A., 1979; Univ. of Southern Mississippi, B.C.J, 1981 • Baptist • M. Michael Roberts, 1 ch　**Cmte.** Agriculture, Nutrition & Forestry • Appropriations • Energy & Natural Resources • Rules & Administration
CoS. Doug E. Davis　　　**LD.** Tim Wolverton
Sched. Alex Calhoon　　**PS.** Chris Gallegos
Dist. Off. Gulfport 228.867.9710 • Jackson 601.965.4459 • Oxford 662.236.1018

R: 82　**T:** 4th　54%
Elected Year: 2018
Next Election: 2026

⚑ Sen. Roger F. Wicker (WIH-kur)　　R-MS-Sr.　　p 202.224.6253

Rm. DSOB 555　**Web.** wicker.senate.gov　**f** 202.228.0378
Bio. 07/05/1951 • Pontotoc • State Senator; Attorney • Air Force 1976-80 • Univ. of Mississippi, B.A., 1973; Univ. of Mississippi, J.D., 1975 • Baptist • M. Gayle Long Wicker, 3 ch; 5 gr-ch　**Cmte.** Armed Services • Commerce, Science & Transportation • Environment & Public Works • Joint Printing • Joint Security & Cooperation in Europe • Rules & Administration
CoS. Michelle Barlow　　**LD.** Robert Murray
　　Richardson
Sched. Jen Jett　　　　**PS.** Palmer Brigham
Dist. Off. Gulfport 228.871.7017 • Hernando 662.429.1002 • Jackson 601.965.4644 • Tupelo 662.844.5010

R: 31　**T:** 4th　59%
Elected Year: 2007
Next Election: 2024

⚑ Rep. Michael P. Guest ("guest")　　R-MS-03　　p 202.225.5031

Rm. CHOB 418　**Web.** guest.house.gov　**f** 202.225.5797
Bio. 02/04/1970 • Woodbury • Mississippi State Univ., B.A., 1992; Univ. of Mississippi, J.D., 1995 • Baptist • M. Haley Guest, 2 ch　**Cmte.** Ethics • Homeland Security • Transportation & Infrastructure
CoS. Jordan Downs　　　**LD.** Elizabeth Joseph
Sched. Debra Boutwell　　**PS.** Rob Pillow
　　(CD)
Dist. Off. Brandon 769.241.6120 • Brookhaven 601.823.3400 • Meridian 601.693.6681 • Starkville 662.324.0007

R: 319　**T:** 2nd　65%
Elected Year: 2018

⚑ Rep. Trent Kelly (KEH-lee)　　R-MS-01　　p 202.225.4306

Rm. RHOB 2243　**Web.** trentkelly.house.gov　**f** 202.225.3549
Bio. 03/01/1966 • Union • East Central Community College (MS), A.A., 1986; Univ. of Mississippi Business School, B.A., 1989; Univ. of Mississippi Law School, J.D., 1994; Army War College, M.A., 2010 • Methodist • M. Sheila Kelly Hampton, 3 ch　**Cmte.** Agriculture • Armed Services • Budget • Permanent Select on Intelligence
CoS. Paul Howell　　　**LD.** Rodney Hall
Sched. Reed Craddock　　**PS.** Susan Parker (CD)
Dist. Off. Columbus 662.327.0748 • Corinth 662.687.1525 • Eupora 662.687.1545 • Hernando 662.449.3090 • Oxford 662.687.1540 • Tupelo 662.841.8808

R: 237　**T:** 4th　69%
Elected Year: 2014

⚑ Rep. Steven M. Palazzo (puh-LAZ-o)   R-MS-04   p 202.225.5772

Rm. RHOB 2349 **Web.** palazzo.house.gov **f** 202.225.7074
Bio. 02/21/1970 • Gulfport • Univ. of Southern Mississippi,
B.B.A., 1994; Univ. of Southern Mississippi, M.S., 1996
• Roman Catholic • M. Lisa Palazzo, 3 ch **Cmte.**
Appropriations

CoS. Patrick Large	**LD.** Courtney Stevens
Sched. Leslie Churchwell	**PS.** Britney Dickerson
(CD)	

Dist. Off. Gulfport 228.864.7670 • Hattiesburg 601.582.3246
• Pascagoula 228.202.8104

R: 147 T: 6th 100%
Elected Year: 2010

⚑ Rep. Bennie G. Thompson (TOMP-suhn)   D-MS-02   p 202.225.5876

Rm. RHOB 2466 **Web.** **f** 202.225.5898
benniethompson.house.gov
Bio. 01/28/1948 • Bolton • County Supervisor, Hinds Co.,
MS; Mayor (Bolton, MS) • Tougaloo College (MS), B.A.,
1968; Jackson State Univ. (MS), M.S., 1972 • Methodist
• M. London Johnson Thompson, 1 ch; 2 gr-ch **Cmte.**
Homeland Security • Select Investigate Jan 6 Attack on the
U.S. Capitol

CoS. Timla Washington	**LD.** Claytrice Henderson
Sched. Earvin Miers	**PS.** Cedric Watkins

R: 26 T: 15th 66%
Elected Year: 1992

Dist. Off. Bolton 601.866.9003 • Greenville 662.335.9003 •
Greenwood 662.455.9003 • Jackson 601.946.9003 • Marks
662.326.9003 • Mound Bayou 662.741.9003

MISSOURI

⚑ Governor Michael L. Parson (PAR-suhn)   p 573.751.3222

State Capitol
PO Box 720
Jefferson City, MO 65102-9500
Website mo.gov
Fax 573.526.3291
Term Ends 2025
Lt. Governor
Mike Kehoe, R

C: Jefferson City
P: 6,126,452 (18)
A: 68,741.60 mi^2 (18th)

U.S. Senators
Roy Blunt, R
Josh Hawley, R
U.S. Representatives
01 / Cori Bush, D
02 / Ann L. Wagner, R
03 / Blaine Luetkemeyer, R
04 / Vicky Jo Hartzler, R
05 / Emanuel Cleaver, D
06 / Sam B. Graves, R
07 / Billy Long, R
08 / Jason T. Smith, R

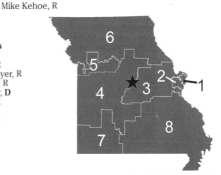

⚑ Sen. Roy Blunt (blunt)   R-MO-Sr.   p 202.224.5721

Rm. RSOB 260 **Web.** blunt.senate.gov **f** 202.224.8149
Bio. 01/10/1950 • Niangua • Missouri Secretary of State;
President of Southwest Baptist University • Southwest
Baptist Univ. (MO), B.A., 1970; Southwest Missouri State
Univ., M.A., 1972 • Baptist • M. Abigail Blunt, 4 ch; 6
gr-ch **Cmte.** Appropriations • Commerce, Science &
Transportation • Intelligence • Joint Library • Joint Printing
• Rules & Administration

CoS. Stacy McHatton	**LD.** Dan Burgess
McBride (CD)	
Sched. Richard B. Eddings	**PS.** Katie Boyd

R: 40 T: 2nd 49%
Elected Year: 2010
Next Election: 2022

Dist. Off. Cape Girardeau 573.334.7044 • Columbia
573.442.8151 • Kansas City 816.471.7141 • Springfield
417.877.7814 • St. Louis 314.725.4484

MISSOURI

⬛ Sen. Josh Hawley (Haw - l ee) R-MO-Jr. p 202.224.6154

Rm. RSOB 212 **Web.** hawley.senate.gov **f** 202.228.0526
Bio. 12/31/1979 • Springdale • Stanford Univ. (CA), A.B.,
2002; Yale Law School (CT), J.D., 2006 • Evangelical • M.
Erin Morrow, 3 ch **Cmte.** Armed Services • Homeland
Security & Government Affairs • Judiciary • Small Business
& Entrepreneurship
CoS. Eric Teetsel **LD.** Chris Weihs
Sched. Ellen James **PS.** Philip Letsou
Dist. Off. Cape Girardeau 573.334.5995 • Columbia
573.554.1919 • Kansas City 816.960.4694 • Springfield
417.869.4433 • St. Louis 314.354.7060

R: 89 **T:** 1st 51%
Elected Year: 2018
Next Election: 2024

⬛ Rep. Cori Bush (bush) D-MO-01 p 202.225.2406

Rm. CHOB 563 **Web.** bush.house.gov **f** 202.226.3717
Bio. 07/21/1976 • St. Louis • Christian - Non-
Denominational • D., 2 ch **Cmte.** Judiciary • Oversight &
Reform
CoS. Abbas Alawieh **LD.** Lynese Wallace
Sched. Stephanie Herndon **PS.** Julia Albertson
Dist. Off. St. Louis 314.955.9980

R: 377 **T:** 1st 79%
Elected Year: 2020

⬛ Rep. Emanuel Cleaver II (KLEE-vur) D-MO-05 p 202.225.4535

Rm. RHOB 2335 **Web.** cleaver.house.gov **f** 202.225.4403
Bio. 10/26/1944 • Waxahachie • Pastor; Mayor (Kansas City,
MO) • Prairie View Agricultural and Mechanical Univ. (TX),
B.S., 1972; St. Paul School of Theology, Kansas City (MO),
M.Div., 1974 • Methodist • M. Dianne Cleaver, 4 ch (twins); 3
gr-ch **Cmte.** Financial Services • Homeland Security • Joint
Security & Cooperation in Europe • Select Committee on
the Modernization of Congress
CoS. Christina Mahoney **LD.** Harden Spencer
Sched. Herline Mathieu **PS.** Matthew Helfant
Dist. Off. Higginsville 660.584.7373 • Independence
816.833.4545 • Kansas City 816.842.4545

R: 72 **T:** 9th 59%
Elected Year: 2004

⬛ Rep. Sam B. Graves Jr. (grayvz) R-MO-06 p 202.225.7041

Rm. LHOB 1135 **Web.** graves.house.gov **f** 202.225.8221
Bio. 11/07/1963 • Tarkio • State Representative • Univ. of
Missouri, B.S., 1986 • Baptist • M. Lesley Graves, 3 ch **Cmte.**
Armed Services • Transportation & Infrastructure
CoS. Nancy Peele **LD.** Julie Devine
Sched. Amanda Sollazzo **PS.** Bryan Nichols (CD)
Dist. Off. Hannibal 573.221.3400 • Kansas City
816.792.3976 • St. Joseph 816.749.0800

R: 52 **T:** 11th 67%
Elected Year: 2000

⬛ Rep. Vicky Jo Hartzler (HARTS-lur) R-MO-04 p 202.225.2876

Rm. RHOB 2235 **Web.** hartzler.house.gov **f** 202.225.0148
Bio. 10/13/1960 • Harrisonville • High School Teacher;
State Representative • Univ. of Missouri, B.S., 1983; Central
Missouri State Univ., M.S., 1992 • Evangelical • M. Lowell
Hartzler, 3 ch **Cmte.** Agriculture • Armed Services • Joint
Congressional-Executive Commission on China
CoS. Christopher Connelly **LD.** Chrissi Lee
Sched. Jillian Vogl **PS.** Kevin Knoth
Dist. Off. Columbia 573.442.9311 • Harrisonville
816.884.3411 • Lebanon 417.532.5582

R: 138 **T:** 6th 68%
Elected Year: 2010

MISSOURI

⚑ Rep. Billy Long (long) R-MO-07 p 202.225.6536

Rm. RHOB 2454 **Web.** long.house.gov **f** 202.225.5604
Bio. 08/11/1955 • Springfield • Business Owner; Talk Radio
Show Host • Presbyterian • M. Barbara Long, 2 ch **Cmte.**
Energy & Commerce
CoS. Joe Lillis **LD.** Tanner Warbinton
Sched. Sean Manzelli **PS.** Michael Appelbaum
Dist. Off. Joplin 417.781.1041 • Springfield 417.889.1800

R: 145 **T:** 6th 69%
Elected Year: 2010

⚑ Rep. Blaine Luetkemeyer (LOOT-keh-my-ur) R-MO-03 p 202.225.2956

Rm. RHOB 2230 **Web.** **f** 202.225.5712
luetkemeyer.house.gov
Bio. 05/07/1952 • Jefferson City • State Representative;
Banker • Lincoln Univ. (MO), B.A., 1974 • Catholic • M.
Jackie Luetkemeyer, 3 ch; 4 gr-ch **Cmte.** Financial Services
• Small Business
CoS. Chad Ramey **LD.** Meghan Schmidtlein
Sched. Ann Vogel **PS.** Georgeanna Sullivan
Dist. Off. Jefferson City 573.635.7232 • Washington
636.239.2276 • Wentzville 636.327.7055

R: 111 **T:** 7th 69%
Elected Year: 2012

⚑ Rep. Jason T. Smith (smith) R-MO-08 p 202.225.4404

Rm. RHOB 2418 **Web.** jasonsmith.house.gov **f** 202.226.0326
Bio. 06/16/1980 • St. Louis • Missouri State Univ., B.S.,
2001; Oklahoma City Univ. Law School (OK), J.D., 2004 •
Assembly of God • NS. **Cmte.** Budget • Ways & Means
CoS. Matthew Meyer **LD.** Hilary Pinegar
Sched. Marshall Stallings **PS.** Matt Schuck
Dist. Off. Cape Girardeau 573.335.0101 • Farmington
573.756.9755 • Poplar Bluff 573.609.2996 • Rolla
573.364.2455 • West Plains 417.255.1515

R: 199 **T:** 5th 77%
Elected Year: 2012

⚑ Rep. Ann L. Wagner (WAG-nur) R-MO-02 p 202.225.1621

Rm. RHOB 2350 **Web.** wagner.house.gov **f** 202.225.2563
Bio. 09/13/1962 • St. Louis • Univ. of Missouri, B.S., 1984 •
Roman Catholic • M. Raymond T. Wagner Jr., 3 ch **Cmte.**
Financial Services • Foreign Affairs
CoS. Charlie Keller **LD.** Jamie Robinette
Sched. Emily Ann Smith **PS.** Arthur Bryant
Dist. Off. Ballwin 636.779.5449

R: 193 **T:** 5th 52%
Elected Year: 2012

MONTANA

MONTANA

⚑ Governor Greg Gianforte (JEE-uhn-for-tay) p 406.444.3111

Montana State Capitol Building **C:** Helena
PO Box 200801 **P:** 1,062,305 (44)
Helena, MT 59620-0801 **A:** 145,545.78 mi^2 (4th)
Website mt.gov
Fax 406.444.5529
Term Ends 2025
Lt. Governor
Kristen Juras, R

U.S. Senators
Jon Tester, **D**
Steve Daines, **R**
U.S. Representatives
01 / Matt M. Rosendale, **R**

Sen. Steve Daines (daynz)   R-MT-Jr.   p 202.224.2651

Rm. HSOB 320   **Web.** daines.senate.gov   **f** 202.228.1236
Bio. 08/20/1962 • Van Nuys • Montana State Univ.,
Bozeman, B.S., 1984 • Presbyterian • M. Cindy Daines, 4 ch
Cmte. Banking, Housing & Urban Affairs • Energy & Natural
Resources • Finance • Indian Affairs • Joint Congressional-
Executive Commission on China
CoS. Jason Thielman   **LD.** Darin C. Thacker
Sched. Caitlin Affolter   **PS.** Katie Schoettler
Dist. Off. Billings 406.245.6822 • Bozeman 406.587.3446
• Great Falls 406.453.0148 • Helena 406.443.3189 •
Kalispell 406.257.3765 • Missoula 406.549.8198 • Sidney
406.482.9010

R: 69   **T:** 2nd   55%
Elected Year: 2014
Next Election: 2026

Sen. Jon Tester (TEHSS-tur)   D-MT-Sr.   p 202.224.2644

Rm. HSOB 311   **Web.** tester.senate.gov   **f** 202.224.8594
Bio. 08/21/1956 • Havre • Farmer • Univ. of Great Falls
(MT), B.S., 1978 • Christian Church • M. Sharla Tester, 2 ch;
2 gr-ch   **Cmte.** Appropriations • Banking, Housing & Urban
Affairs • Commerce, Science & Transportation • Indian
Affairs • Veterans' Affairs
CoS. Dylan Laslovich   **LD.** Justin Folsom
Sched. Corine Weiler   **PS.** Sarah Feldman
Dist. Off. Billings 406.252.0550 • Bozeman 406.586.4450
• Butte 406.723.3277 • Great Falls 406.452.9585 •
Helena 406.449.5401 • Kalispell 406.257.3360 • Missoula
406.728.3003

R: 29   **T:** 3rd   50%
Elected Year: 2006
Next Election: 2024

Rep. Matt M. Rosendale Sr. (RO-zuhn-dayl)   R-MT-01   p 202.225.3211

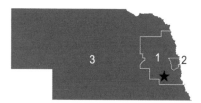

Rm. LHOB 1037   **Web.** rosendale.house.gov
Bio. 07/07/1960 • Baltimore • Catholic • M. Jean
Rosendale, 3 ch   **Cmte.** Natural Resources • Veterans'
Affairs
CoS. Trevor Whetstone   **LD.** Sean Brislin
Sched. Aashka Varma
Dist. Off. Billings 406.413.6720 • Great Falls 406.770.6260
• Helena 406.502.1435

R: 419   **T:** 1st   56%
Elected Year: 2020

NEBRASKA

Governor Pete Ricketts (RIH-kuhtss)   p 402.471.2244

State Capitol
PO Box 94848
Lincoln, NE 68509-4848
Website nebraska.gov
Fax 402.471.6031
Term Ends 2023
Lt. Governor
Mike Foley, R

C: Lincoln
P: 1,929,268 (38)
A: 76,824.26 mi^2 (15th)

U.S. Senators
Deb Fischer, R
Ben Sasse, R
U.S. Representatives
01 / Jeff L. Fortenberry, R
02 / Don J. Bacon, R
03 / Adrian M. Smith, R

NEBRASKA

⚑ Sen. Deb Fischer (FIH-shur)   R-NE-Sr.   p 202.224.6551

Rm. RSOB 454 **Web.** fischer.senate.gov   **f** 202.228.1325
Bio. 03/01/1951 • Lincoln • Univ. of Nebraska, Lincoln, B.S.,
1988 • Presbyterian • M. Bruce G. Fischer, 3 ch; 3 gr-ch
Cmte. Agriculture, Nutrition & Forestry • Armed Services
• Commerce, Science & Transportation • Ethics • Rules &
Administration
CoS. Emily Leviner   **LD.** Corey Inglee
Sched. Allison Haindfield   **PS.** Brianna Puccini
Dist. Off. Kearney 308.234.2361 • Lincoln 402.441.4600 •
Norfolk 402.200.8816 • Omaha 402.391.3411 • Scottsbluff
308.630.2329

R: 61 **T:** 2nd 58%
Elected Year: 2012
Next Election: 2024

⚑ Sen. Ben Sasse (sass)   R-NE-Jr.   p 202.224.4224

Rm. RSOB 107 **Web.** sasse.senate.gov
Bio. 02/22/1972 • Plainview • Yale Univ. (CT), M.A.; Yale
Univ. (CT), M.Phil; Harvard Univ. Law School (MA), A.B.,
1994; Saint John's College (MD), M.A., 1998; Yale Univ. (CT),
Ph.D., 2004 • Lutheran • M. Melissa Sasse, 3 ch **Cmte.**
Budget • Finance • Intelligence • Judiciary
CoS. Raymond Sass   **LD.** Patrick Lehman
Sched. Kelicia Rice   **PS.** James Wegmann
Dist. Off. Kearney 308.233.3677 • Lincoln 402.476.1400 •
Omaha 402.550.8040 • Scottsbluff 308.632.6032

R: 73 **T:** 2nd 67%
Elected Year: 2014
Next Election: 2026

⚑ Rep. Don J. Bacon (BAY-kun)   R-NE-02   p 202.225.4155

Rm. LHOB 1024 **Web.** bacon.house.gov
Bio. 08/16/1963 • Momence • Northern Illinois Univ., B.A.,
1984; Univ. of Phoenix, M.S., 1995; National War College
(DC), Mast. Deg., 2004; Univ. of Virginia Darden School of
Business, M.S., 2009 • Christian - Non-Denominational • M.
Angie Bacon, 4 ch **Cmte.** Agriculture • Armed Services
CoS. Mark Edward Dreiling   **LD.** Jeff Kratz
Sched. Amanda Kepplin   **PS.** Abbey Schieffer
Dist. Off. Omaha 402.938.0300

R: 245 **T:** 3rd 51%
Elected Year: 2016

⚑ Rep. Jeff L. Fortenberry (FOR-tuhn-bair-ee)   R-NE-01   p 202.225.4806

Rm. LHOB 1514 **Web.** fortenberry.house.gov **f** 202.225.5686
Bio. 12/27/1960 • Baton Rouge • Lincoln City Council;
Senate Aide • Franciscan Univ. (OH), M.Th.; Louisiana
State Univ., B.A., 1982; Georgetown Univ. (DC), M.P.P., 1986;
Franciscan Univ. (OH), M.A., 1996 • Roman Catholic • M.
Celeste Gregory Fortenberry, 5 ch
CoS. Andy Braner   **LD.** Alan Feyerherm
Sched. Caty Matthews   **PS.** James Crotty
Dist. Off. Fremont 402.727.0888 • Lincoln 402.438.1598 •
Norfolk 402.379.2064

R: 75 **T:** 9th 60%
Elected Year: 2004

⚑ Rep. Adrian M. Smith (smith)   R-NE-03   p 202.225.6435

Rm. CHOB 502 **Web.** adriansmith.house.gov **f** 202.225.0207
Bio. 12/19/1970 • Scottsbluff • State Legislator; Realtor •
Univ. of Nebraska, Lincoln, B.S., 1993 • Evangelical • M.
Andrea Smith, 1 ch **Cmte.** Ways & Means
CoS. Monica Didiuk   **LD.** Joshua Jackson
Sched. Becca Salter   **PS.** Tiffany Haverly
Dist. Off. Grand Island 308.384.3900 • Scottsbluff
308.633.6333

R: 100 **T:** 8th 79%
Elected Year: 2006

NEVADA

NEVADA

🔊 **Governor Steve Sisolak** (Siso-lak)   p 775.684.5670

State Capitol
101 N. Carson St.
Carson City, NV 89701
Website nv.gov
Fax 775.684.5683
Term Ends 2023
Lt. Governor
Kate Marshall, **D**

C: Carson City
P: 3,034,392 (33)
A: 109,781.15 mi² (7th)

U.S. Senators
Catherine Cortez Masto, **D**
Jacky S. Rosen, **D**
U.S. Representatives
01 / Dina Titus, **D**
02 / Mark E. Amodei, R
03 / Susie K. Lee, **D**
04 / Steven A. Horsford, **D**

🔊 **Sen. Catherine Cortez Masto** (kor-TEZ-MASS-toe) D-NV-Sr.   p 202.224.3542

Bio. 03/29/1964 • Las Vegas • Univ. of Nevada, Reno, B.S., 1986; Gonzaga Univ. School of Law, J.D., 1990 • Catholic • M. Paul Masto **Cmte.** Banking, Housing & Urban Affairs • Energy & Natural Resources • Finance • Indian Affairs
CoS. Scott Fairchild (CD)   **LD.** Joleen Rivera (CD)
Sched. Anaisy Tolentino   **PS.** Joshua Marcus-Blank
 (CD)   (CD)
Dist. Off. Las Vegas 702.388.5020 • Reno 775.686.5750

R: 80 **T:** 1st 47%
Elected Year: 2016
Next Election: 2022

🔊 **Sen. Jacky S. Rosen** (RO-zuhn)   D-NV-Jr.   p 202.224.6244

Rm. HSOB 713 **Web.** rosen.senate.gov   **f** 202.228.6753
Bio. 08/02/1957 • Chicago • Univ. of Minnesota, B.A., 1979 • Jewish • M. Larry Rosen, 1 ch **Cmte.** Aging • Armed Services • Commerce, Science & Transportation • Health, Education, Labor & Pensions • Homeland Security & Government Affairs • Small Business & Entrepreneurship
CoS. Dara Cohen   **LD.** Grant Dubler
Sched. Nicole Echeto   **PS.** Renzo Olivari
Dist. Off. Las Vegas 702.388.0205 • Reno 775.337.0110

R: 86 **T:** 1st 50%
Elected Year: 2018
Next Election: 2024

🔊 **Rep. Mark E. Amodei** (AM-uh-day)   R-NV-02   p 202.225.6155

Rm. CHOB 104 **Web.** amodei.house.gov   **f** 202.225.5679
Bio. 06/12/1958 • Carson City • Univ. of Nevada, Reno, B.A., 1980; Univ. of the Pacific McGeorge School of Law (CA), J.D., 1983 • Presbyterian • D., 2 ch **Cmte.** Appropriations
CoS. Molly Lowe   **LD.** Ken Brooke
Sched. Tyler Phillip Platt   **PS.** Lynn Hatcher
Dist. Off. Elko 775.777.7705 • Reno 775.686.5760

R: 154 **T:** 6th 57%
Elected Year: 2011

Rep. Steven A. Horsford (HORSS-furd) D-NV-04 p 202.225.9894

Rm. CHOB 562 **Web.** horsford.house.gov **f** 202.225.9783
Bio. 04/29/1973 • Las Vegas • NV State Senator • Univ. of
Nevada, Reno, B.A., 2014 • Baptist • M. Dr. Sonya Horsford,
3 ch **Cmte.** Armed Services • Budget • Ways & Means
CoS. Asha Jones (CD) **LD.** LaVontae Brooks
Sched. Alex Swann
Dist. Off. North Las Vegas 702.963.9360

R: 296 **T:** 2nd 51%
Elected Year: 2018

Rep. Susie K. Lee (lee) D-NV-03 p 202.225.3252

Rm. CHOB 365 **Web.** susielee.house.gov **f** 202.225.2185
Bio. 11/07/1966 • Canton • Carnegie Mellon Univ., B.S.,
1989; Carnegie Mellon Univ., M.P.A., 1990 • Catholic • M.
Dan Lee, 2 ch **Cmte.** Appropriations
CoS. Brandon Cox **LD.** Lauren Toy
Sched. Annie Campbell **PS.** Zoe Sheppard
Dist. Off. Las Vegas 702.963.9336

R: 327 **T:** 2nd 49%
Elected Year: 2018

Rep. Dina Titus (TY-tuhs) D-NV-01 p 202.225.5965

Rm. RHOB 2464 **Web.** titus.house.gov **f** 202.225.3119
Bio. 05/23/1950 • Thomasville • State Legislator; Professor
• College of William and Mary (VA), A.B., 1970; Univ.
of Georgia, M.A., 1973; Florida State Univ., Ph.D., 1976
• Greek Orthodox • M. Thomas Clayton Wright **Cmte.**
Foreign Affairs • Homeland Security • Transportation &
Infrastructure
CoS. Jay Gertsema **LD.** Joel A. Cohen
Sched. Reid Fauble **PS.** Blake Williams
Dist. Off. Las Vegas 702.220.9823

R: 159 **T:** 5th 62%
Elected Year: 2012

NEW HAMPSHIRE

Governor Chris Sununu (suh-NOO-noo) p 603.271.2121

State House **C:** Concord
107 N. Main St. **P:** 1,356,458 (42)
Concord, NH 03301 **A:** 8,952.55 mi^2 (44th)
Website nh.gov
Fax 603.271.7640
Term Ends 2023

U.S. Senators
Jeanne Shaheen, **D**
Maggie Hassan, **D**
U.S. Representatives
01 / Chris C. Pappas, **D**
02 / Ann McLane Kuster, **D**

NEW HAMPSHIRE

Sen. Maggie Hassan (HAS-suhn) D-NH-Jr. p 202.224.3324

Rm. HSOB 324 **Web.** hassan.senate.gov **f** 202.228.0581
Bio. 02/27/1958 • Boston • Brown Univ. (RI), A.B., 1980;
Northeastern Univ. Law School (MA), J.D., 1985 • United
Church of Christ • M. Thomas Hassan, 2 ch **Cmte.** Finance
• Health, Education, Labor & Pensions • Homeland Security
& Government Affairs • Joint Economic • Veterans' Affairs
CoS. Marc P. Goldberg **LD.** Dave Christie
Sched. Catherine E. Toner **PS.** Laura Epstein
Dist. Off. Berlin 603.752.6190 • Concord 603.622.2204
• Manchester 603.622.2204 • Nashua 603.880.3314 •
Portsmouth 603.433.4445

R: 78 **T:** 1st 48%
Elected Year: 2016
Next Election: 2022

Sen. Jeanne Shaheen (shuh-HEEN) D-NH-Sr. p 202.224.2841

Rm. HSOB 506 **Web.** shaheen.senate.gov **f** 202.228.3194
Bio. 01/28/1947 • St. Charles • Governor, NH; State
Legislator; Teacher • Shippensburg Univ. (PA), B.A., 1969;
Univ. of Mississippi, M.S., 1973 • Protestant - Unspecified
Christian • M. William Shaheen, 3 ch; 7 gr-ch **Cmte.**
Appropriations • Armed Services • Ethics • Foreign
Relations • Joint Security & Cooperation in Europe • Small
Business & Entrepreneurship
CoS. Chad Kreikemeier **LD.** Ariel Marshall
Sched. Meaghan D'Arcy **PS.** Sarah Weinstein
Dist. Off. Berlin 603.752.6300 • Claremont 603.542.4872
• Dover 603.750.3004 • Keene 603.358.6604 • Manchester
603.647.7500 • Nashua 603.883.0196

R: 32 **T:** 3rd 57%
Elected Year: 2008
Next Election: 2026

Rep. Ann McLane Kuster (mih-KLAIN KUH-stur) D-NH-02 p 202.225.5206

Rm. CHOB 320 **Web.** kuster.house.gov **f** 202.225.2946
Bio. 09/05/1956 • Concord • Dartmouth College, A.B.,
1978; Georgetown Univ. Law Center (DC), J.D., 1984 •
Christian Church • M. Brad Kuster, 2 ch **Cmte.** Agriculture
• Energy & Commerce
CoS. Patrick Devney **LD.** Travis Krogman
Sched. Miriam Young **PS.** Jen Fox
Dist. Off. Concord 603.226.1002 • Littleton 603.444.7700 •
Nashua 603.595.2006

R: 176 **T:** 5th 54%
Elected Year: 2012

Rep. Chris C. Pappas (PAP-puhss) D-NH-01 p 202.225.5456

Rm. CHOB 319 **Web.** pappas.house.gov
Bio. 06/04/1980 • Manchester • Harvard College (MA),
B.A., 2002 • Greek Orthodox • E. Vann Bentley **Cmte.**
Transportation & Infrastructure • Veterans' Affairs
CoS. Steven Carlson **LD.** Nandini Narayan
Sched. Alex Siegal **PS.** Kristen Morris
Dist. Off. Dover 603.285.4300 • Manchester 603.935.6710

R: 338 **T:** 2nd 51%
Elected Year: 2018

NEW JERSEY

Governor Phil Murphy (MUR-fee) p 609.292.6000

The State House
PO Box 001
Trenton, NJ 08625
Website nj.gov
Fax 609.292.3454
Term Ends 2022
Lt. Governor
Sheila Oliver, **D**

C: Trenton
P: 8,908,520 (11)
A: 7,354.08 mi^2 (46th)

NEW JERSEY

U.S. Senators
Bob Menendez, **D**
Cory Booker, **D**
U.S. Representatives
01 / Donald W. Norcross, **D**
02 / Jefferson Van Drew, **R**
03 / Andy Kim, **D**
04 / Chris H. Smith, **R**
05 / Josh S. Gottheimer, **D**
06 / Frank J. Pallone, **D**
07 / Tom Malinowski, **D**
08 / Albio Sires, **D**
09 / Bill J. Pascrell, **D**
10 / Donald M. Payne, **D**
11 / Mikie Sherrill, **D**
12 / Bonnie Watson Coleman, **D**

🔊 **Sen. Cory Booker** ("BOOK"-ur) D-NJ-Jr. p 202.224.3224

Rm. HSOB 717 **Web.** booker.senate.gov **f** 202.224.8378
Bio. 04/27/1969 • Washington • Stanford Univ. (CA), B.A., 1991; Stanford Univ. (CA), M.A., 1992; Yale Law School (CT), J.D., 1997 • Baptist • S. **Cmte.** Agriculture, Nutrition & Forestry • Foreign Relations • Judiciary • Small Business & Entrepreneurship
CoS. Veronica Duron **LD.** Leah Hill
Schcd. Andrew Serrano **PS.** Jeff Giertz
Dist. Off. Camden 856.338.8922 • Newark 973.639.8700

R: 63 **T:** 3rd 57%
Elected Year: 2013
Next Election: 2026

🔊 **Sen. Bob Menendez** (meh-NEN-dehz) D-NJ-Sr. p 202.224.4744

Rm. HSOB 528 **Web.** menendez.senate.gov **f** 202.228.2197
Bio. 01/01/1954 • New York • State Senator; Mayor of Union City • St. Peter's College (NJ), B.A., 1976; Rutgers Univ. Law School (NJ), J.D., 1979 • Roman Catholic • M. Nadine Arslanian, 2 ch (2 from previous marriage) **Cmte.** Banking, Housing & Urban Affairs • Finance • Foreign Relations
CoS. Jason Tuber **LD.** Rebecca Schatz
Schcd. Maria Almeida (CD) **PS.** Francisco Pelayo
Dist. Off. Barrington 856.757.5353 • Jersey City 973.645.3030

R: 22 **T:** 3rd 54%
Elected Year: 2006
Next Election: 2024

🔊 **Rep. Josh S. Gottheimer** (GAHT-hy-mur) D-NJ-05 p 202.225.4465

Rm. CHOB 203 **Web.** gottheimer.house.gov **f** 202.225.9048
Bio. 03/08/1975 • Livingston • Univ. of Pennsylvania, B.A., 1997; Harvard Law School (MA), J.D., 2004 • Jewish • M. Marla Brooke Tusk Gottheimer, 2 ch **Cmte.** Financial Services • Homeland Security
CoS. Clay Schroers **LD.** Jordan Colvin
Sched. Jacqueline Sobol **PS.** Alexandra Caffrey
Dist. Off. Glen Rock 201.389.1100 • Hackensack 973.814.4076 • Newton 973.940.1117 • Ringwood 973.814.4076 • Vernon Township 973.814.4076 • Washington 973.814.4076

R: 265 **T:** 3rd 53%
Elected Year: 2016

🔊 **Rep. Andy Kim** (kim) D-NJ-03 p 202.225.4765

Rm. RHOB 2444 **Web.** kim.house.gov **f** 202.225.0778
Bio. 07/12/1982 • Boston • Univ. of Chicago (IL), B.A., 2004; Oxford Univ. (UK), M.Phil, 2007; Univ. of Oxford (UK), Ph.D., 2010 • Presbyterian • M. Kammy Kim, 2 ch **Cmte.** Armed Services • Foreign Affairs • Small Business
CoS. Amy Pfeiffer **LD.** Hillary Caron
Sched. Hafiza Kazi **PS.** Forrest Rilling
Dist. Off. Marlton 856.703.2700 • Toms River 732.504.0490 • Willingboro 856.703.2700

R: 326 **T:** 2nd 53%
Elected Year: 2018

NEW JERSEY

🔖 **Rep. Tom Malinowski** (ma-lih-NOU-skee) D-NJ-07 p 202.225.5361

Rm. LHOB 1318 **Web.** malinowski.house.gov **f** 202.225.9460
Bio. 09/23/1965 • Slupsk • Univ. of California, Berkeley, B.A., 1987; Oxford Univ. (UK), M.Phil, 1991 • Unspecified/Other • D., 1 ch **Cmte.** Foreign Affairs • Homeland Security • Joint Congressional-Executive Commission on China • Transportation & Infrastructure
CoS. Colston Reid   **LD.** Eliza Ramirez
Sched. Catherine Magos   **PS.** Naree Ketudat
Dist. Off. Somerville 908.547.3307

R: 331 **T:** 2nd 51%
Elected Year: 2018

🔖 **Rep. Donald W. Norcross** (NOR-krawss) D-NJ-01 p 202.225.6501

Rm. RHOB 2427 **Web.** norcross.house.gov **f** 202.225.6583
Bio. 12/13/1958 • Camden • Camden County College (NJ), A.S., 1979 • Lutheran • M. Andrea Doran, 3 ch; 2 gr-ch **Cmte.** Armed Services • Education & Labor • Science, Space & Technology
CoS. Todd Sloves   **LD.** Katherine Lee
Sched. Maggie Madsen   **PS.** Britton Burdick
Dist. Off. Camden 856.427.7000 • Cherry Hill 856.427.7000

R: 202 **T:** 5th 63%
Elected Year: 2013

🔖 **Rep. Frank J. Pallone Jr.** (puh-LOAN) D-NJ-06 p 202.225.4671

Rm. RHOB 2107 **Web.** pallone.house.gov **f** 202.225.9665
Bio. 10/30/1951 • Long Branch • State Senator; Member, City Council • Middlebury College (VT), B.A., 1973; Tufts Univ. Fletcher School of Law and Diplomacy (MA), M.A., 1974; Rutgers Univ. Law School (NJ), J.D., 1978 • Roman Catholic • M. Sarah Hospodor Pallone, 3 ch **Cmte.** Energy & Commerce
CoS. Liam Fitzsimmons   **LD.** James Johnson
Sched. Alexander Gristina   **PS.** Mary Werden
Dist. Off. Long Branch 732.571.1140 • New Brunswick 732.249.8892

R: 9 **T:** 17th 61%
Elected Year: 1992

🔖 **Rep. Bill J. Pascrell Jr.** (PASS-krell) D-NJ-09 p 202.225.5751

Rm. RHOB 2409 **Web.** pascrell.house.gov **f** 202.225.5782
Bio. 01/25/1937 • Paterson • Attorney • Army 1961-62; Army Reserves 1962-67 • Fordham Univ. (NY), B.S., 1959; Fordham Univ. (NY), M.A., 1961 • Roman Catholic • M. Elsie Marie Botto Pascrell, 3 ch; 3 gr-ch **Cmte.** Ways & Means
CoS. Benjamin Rich   **LD.** Dylan Sodaro
Sched. Bob Evans   **PS.** Mark Greenbaum
Dist. Off. Englewood 201.935.2248 • Lyndhurst 201.935.2248 • Passaic 973.472.4510 • Paterson 973.523.5152

R: 40 **T:** 13th 66%
Elected Year: 2012

🔖 **Rep. Donald M. Payne Jr.** (pain) D-NJ-10 p 202.225.3436

Rm. CHOB 106 **Web.** payne.house.gov **f** 202.225.4160
Bio. 12/17/1958 • Newark • Baptist • M. Bea Payne, 3 ch (triplets) **Cmte.** Homeland Security • Transportation & Infrastructure
CoS. LaVerne Alexander   **LD.** Sam Morgante
Sched. Shannon Casey   **PS.** Patrick Wright
Dist. Off. Hillside 862.229.2994 • Jersey City 201.369.0392 • Newark 973.645.3213

R: 158 **T:** 6th 83%
Elected Year: 2012

🔖 **Rep. Mikie Sherrill** (SHAIR-uhl) D-NJ-11 p 202.225.5034

Rm. LHOB 1414 **Web.** sherrill.house.gov **f** 202.225.3186
Bio. 01/19/1972 • Alexandria • U.S. Naval Academy (MD), B.S., 1994; London School of Economics and Political Science, Mast. Deg., 2003; Georgetown Univ. (DC), J.D., 2007 • Catholic • M. Jason Hedberg, 4 ch **Cmte.** Armed Services • Education & Labor • Science, Space & Technology
CoS. Jean Roehrenbeck   **LD.** Isaac Loeb
Sched. Julie Jochem   **PS.** Bryan Doherty
Dist. Off. Parsippany 973.526.5668

R: 347 **T:** 2nd 53%
Elected Year: 2018

NEW JERSEY

⚑ Rep. Albio Sires (SEER-ehz)　　　　　D-NJ-08　　p 202.225.7919

Rm. RHOB 2268　**Web.** sires.house.gov　**f** 202.226.0792
Bio. 01/26/1951 • Bejucal • State Legislator; Insurance
Executive • Saint Peter's College (NJ), B.A., 1974;
Middlebury College (VT), M.A., 1985 • Roman Catholic • M.
Adrienne Sires, 1 stepch　**Cmte.** Budget • Foreign Affairs •
Transportation & Infrastructure
CoS. Gene Martorony　　**LD.** Clare Plassche
Sched. Judi Wolford　　**PS.** Erica Daughtrey (CD)
Dist. Off. Elizabeth 908.820.0692 • Jersey City 201.309.0301
• West New York 201.558.0800

R: 86　**T:** 9th 74%
Elected Year: 2012

⚑ Rep. Chris H. Smith (smith)　　　　　R-NJ-04　　p 202.225.3765

Rm. RHOB 2373　**Web.** chrissmith.house.gov　**f** 202.225.7768
Bio. 03/04/1953 • Rahway • State Legislator; Wholesaler
• Trenton State College (NJ), B.A., 1975 • Roman Catholic
• M. Marie Hahn Smith, 4 ch　**Cmte.** Foreign Affairs • Joint
Congressional-Executive Commission on China
CoS. Mary Noonan　　**LD.** Mary Vigil
Sched. Angela Ryan　　**PS.** Michael Finan
Dist. Off. Freehold 732.780.3035 • Hamilton 609.585.7878
• Plumsted 609.585.7878

R: 3　**T:** 21st 60%
Elected Year: 1980

⚑ Rep. Jefferson Van Drew (van-DROO)　　R-NJ-02　　p 202.225.6572

Rm. RHOB 2447　**Web.** vandrew.house.gov
Bio. 02/23/1953 • New York • Rutgers Univ. (NJ), B.S.,
1975; Fairleigh Dickinson Univ., D.D.S., 1979 • Catholic
• M. Ricarda Drew, 2 ch　**Cmte.** Homeland Security •
Transportation & Infrastructure
CoS. Allison Murphy　　**LD.** Scott Fischer
Sched. Alyson Kerr (CD)　　**PS.** Ashley Brown
Dist. Off. Mays Landing 609.625.5008

R: 361　**T:** 2nd 52%
Elected Year: 2018

⚑ Rep. Bonnie Watson Coleman (WAHT-suhn　　D-NJ-12　　p 202.225.5801
KOAL-muhn)

Rm. CHOB 168　**Web.**　　　　　　**f** 202.225.6025
watsoncoleman.house.gov
Bio. Camden • Thomas Edison State College (NJ), B.A.,
1985 • Baptist • M. William E. Coleman Jr., 1 ch; 2 stepch; 3
gr-ch　**Cmte.** Appropriations • Homeland Security
CoS. Kari Osmond (CD)　　**LD.** Alex Huang
Sched. Jaimee Gilmartin　　**PS.** Mike Shanahan
(CD)
Dist. Off. Ewing 609.883.0026

R: 234　**T:** 4th 66%
Elected Year: 2014

NEW MEXICO

⚑ Governor Michelle Lujan Grisham (LOO-hahn GRIH-　　p 505.476.2200
shuhm)

State Capitol　　　　　　　　　　　**C:** Santa Fe
490 Old Sante Fe Trail, Room 400　**P:** 2,095,428 (37)
Santa Fe, NM 87501　　　　　　　**A:** 121,298.19 mi^2 (5th)
Website newmexico.gov
Fax 505.476.2226
Term Ends 2023
Lt. Governor
Howie Morales, **D**

NEW MEXICO

U.S. Senators
Martin T. Heinrich, **D**
Ben Ray Ray Luján, **D**
U.S. Representatives
01 / Melanie A. Stansbury, **D**
02 / Yvette Herrell, R
03 / Teresa Isabel Leger
Fernandez, **D**

⚓ Sen. Martin T. Heinrich (HYN-rihk) D-NM-Sr. p 202.224.5521

Rm. HSOB 303 **Web.** heinrich.senate.gov **f** 202.228.2841
Bio. 10/17/1971 • Fallon • Businessman • Univ. of Missouri,
B.S., 1995 • Lutheran • M. Julie Heinrich, 2 ch **Cmte.**
Appropriations • Energy & Natural Resources • Intelligence
• Joint Economic
CoS. Rebecca Avitia **LD.** Dominic Saavedra
Sched. Caitlin Terry **PS.** Whitney Potter
Dist. Off. Albuquerque 505.346.6601 • Farmington
505.325.5030 • Las Cruces 575.523.6561 • Roswell
575.622.7113 • Santa Fe 505.988.6647

R: 56 **T:** 2nd 54%
Elected Year: 2012
Next Election: 2024

⚓ Sen. Ben Ray Ray Luján Jr. (LOO-hahn) D-NM-Jr. p 202.224.6621

Rm. RSOB 498 **f** 202.224.3370
Bio. 06/07/1972 • Santa Fe • Chairman, New Mexico
Public Regulation Commission • New Mexico Highlands
Univ., B.A., 2007 • Roman Catholic • S. **Cmte.** Agriculture,
Nutrition & Forestry • Budget • Commerce, Science &
Transportation • Health, Education, Labor & Pensions •
Indian Affairs
CoS. Carlos Sanchez **LD.** Graham Mason
Sched. Rebekah Kirkwood **PS.** Katherine Schneider
Dist. Off. Las Cruces 575.526.5475 • Las Vegas • Portales
575.252.6188 • Santa Fe

R: 94 **T:** 1st 52%
Elected Year: 2020
Next Election: 2026

⚑ Rep. Yvette Herrell (HERR-ehl) R-NM-02 p 202.225.2365

Rm. LHOB 1305 **Web.** herrell.house.gov **f** 202.225.9599
Bio. 03/16/1964 • Ruidoso • Christian - Non-
Denominational • S. **Cmte.** Natural Resources • Oversight
& Reform
CoS. Michael Horanburg **LD.** Brian Kennedy
Sched. Casey Conlee (CD) **PS.** Billy Gribbin
Dist. Off. Las Cruces 575.323.6390 • Roswell 575.578.6290

R: 394 **T:** 1st 54%
Elected Year: 2020

⚓ Rep. Teresa Isabel Leger Fernandez (LEDGE-er D-NM-03 p 202.225.6190
fehr-NAHN-dess)

Rm. LHOB 1432 **Web.** fernandez.house.gov **f** 202.225.1528
Bio. 07/01/1959 • Las Vegas • Yale Univ. (CT), B.A., 1982;
Stanford Univ. Law School (CA), J.D., 1987 • Catholic • D.,
3 ch **Cmte.** Administration • Education & Labor • Joint
Printing • Natural Resources
CoS. Nathan R. Schelble **LD.** Elizabeth Arevalo
Sched. Chris Garcia **PS.** Nairka Joe Trevino-
  Muller
Dist. Off. Las Vegas 505.570.7558 • Rio Rancho
505.415.7810 • Santa Fe 505.428.4680

R: 402 **T:** 1st 59%
Elected Year: 2020

Rep. Melanie A. Stansbury () D-NM-01 p 202.225.6316

Rm. LHOB 1421 **Web.** stansbury.house.gov
Bio. 01/31/1979 • Albuquerque • Saint Mary's College of California, B.S.; Cornell Univ. (NY), M.S.; Cornell Univ. (NY), Ph.D. • NS. **Cmte.** Natural Resources • Science, Space & Technology
CoS. Scott Forrester   **LD.** Ian Fluellen
Sched. Maya Pinon   **PS.** Julia Friedmann
Dist. Off. Albuquerque 505.346.6781

R: 430   **T:** 1st 60%
Elected Year: 2020

NEW YORK

Governor Kathy Hochul () p 518.474.8390

State Capitol
Executive Chambers
Albany, NY 12224
Website ny.gov
Fax 518.474.1513
Term Ends 2023
Lt. Governor
Brian A. Benjamin, **D**

C: Albany
P: 19,542,209 (4)
A: 47,126.45 mi^2 (30th)

U.S. Senators
Chuck E. Schumer, **D**
Kirsten E. Gillibrand, **D**
U.S. Representatives
01 / Lee M. Zeldin, **R**
02 / Andrew R. Garbarino, **R**
03 / Thomas R. Suozzi, **D**
04 / Kathleen M. Rice, **D**
05 / Gregory W. Meeks, **D**
06 / Grace Meng, **D**
07 / Nydia M. Velazquez, **D**
08 / Hakeem Jeffries, **D**
09 / Yvette D. Clarke, **D**
10 / Jerry L. Nadler, **D**
11 / Nicole Malliotakis, **R**
12 / Carolyn B. Maloney, **D**
13 / Adriano Espaillat, **D**
14 / Alexandria Ocasio-Cortez, **D**
15 / Ritchie John Torres, **D**
16 / Jamaal A. Bowman, **D**
17 / Mondaire Jones, **D**
18 / Sean Patrick Maloney, **D**
19 / Antonio Delgado, **D**
20 / Paul D. Tonko, **D**
21 / Elise Stefanik, **R**
22 / Claudia Tenney, **R**
23 / Tom W. Reed, **R**
24 / John M. Katko, **R**
25 / Joseph D. Morelle, **D**
26 / Brian M. Higgins, **D**
27 / Chris Jacobs, **R**

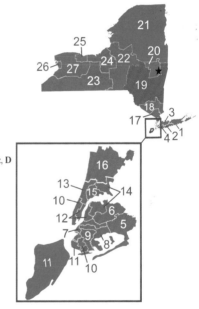

Sen. Kirsten E. Gillibrand (JIH-luh-brand) D-NY-Jr. p 202.224.4451

Rm. RSOB 478 **Web.** gillibrand.senate.gov   **f** 202.228.0282
Bio. 12/09/1966 • Albany • Attorney • Dartmouth College, Hanover (NH), B.A., 1988; Univ. of California, Los Angeles, J.D., 1991 • Roman Catholic • M. Jonathan Gillibrand, 2 ch
Cmte. Aging • Agriculture, Nutrition & Forestry • Armed Services • Intelligence
CoS. Jess C. Fassler   **LD.** Amanda Lauren Miller
Sched. Catherine Ming   **PS.** Evan T. Lukaske
Dist. Off. Albany 518.431.0120 • Buffalo 716.854.9725 • Lowville 315.376.6118 • Melville 631.249.2825 • New York 212.688.6262 • Rochester 585.263.6250 • Syracuse 315.448.0470 • Yonkers 845.875.4585

R: 37   **T:** 4th 67%
Elected Year: 2009
Next Election: 2024

NEW YORK

⚓ Sen. Chuck E. Schumer (SHOO-mur) D-NY-Sr. p 202.224.6542

Rm. HSOB 322 **Web.** schumer.senate.gov **f** 202.228.3027
Bio. 11/23/1950 • Brooklyn • U.S. Representative; Attorney
• Harvard Univ., B.A., 1971; Harvard Univ., J.D., 1974 •
Jewish • M. Iris Weinshall, 2 ch; 1 gr-ch **Cmte.** Intelligence
• Rules & Administration
CoS. Michael Lynch **LD.** Meghan Taira
Sched. Kellie Karney **PS.** Allison Biasotti
Dist. Off. Albany 518.431.4070 • Binghamton 607.772.6792
• Buffalo 716.846.4111 • Melville 631.753.0978 • New
York 212.486.4430 • Peekskill 914.734.1532 • Rochester
585.263.5866 • Syracuse 315.423.5471

R: 12 **T:** 4th 71%
Elected Year: 1998
Next Election: 2022

⚓ Rep. Jamaal A. Bowman (BO-muhn) D-NY-16 p 202.225.2464

Rm. LHOB 1605 **Web.** bowman.house.gov **f** 202.225.5513
Bio. 04/01/1976 • New York City • Manhattanville College,
Ed.D.; Univ. of New Haven, B.A., 1999; Mercy College of
New York, M.A., 2007 • Unspecified/Other • M. Melissa
Oppenheimer, 3 ch **Cmte.** Education & Labor • Science,
Space & Technology
CoS. Sarah Iddrissu **LD.** Fae Rabin
Sched. Lucia Rodriguez **PS.** Marcus Frias
Dist. Off. Bronx 718.530.7710 • Mount Vernon
914.371.9220

R: 376 **T:** 1st 84%
Elected Year: 2020

⚓ Rep. Yvette D. Clarke (klark) D-NY-09 p 202.225.6231

Rm. RHOB 2058 **Web.** clarke.house.gov **f** 202.226.0112
Bio. 11/21/1964 • Brooklyn • State Representative • African
Methodist Episcopal • S. **Cmte.** Energy & Commerce •
Homeland Security
CoS. Christopher Cox **LD.** Steven Blattner
Sched. Tenesha Hare **PS.** Jeanette Lenoir
Dist. Off. Brooklyn 718.287.1142

R: 90 **T:** 8th 83%
Elected Year: 2012

⚓ Rep. Antonio Delgado (del-GAH-"doe") D-NY-19 p 202.225.5614

Rm. LHOB 1007 **Web.** delgado.house.gov **f** 202.225.1168
Bio. 01/28/1977 • Schenectady • Colgate Univ., B.A., 1999;
Oxford Univ. (UK), M.A., 2001; Harvard Law School (MA),
J.D., 2005 • Unspecified/Other • M. Lacey Delgado, 2 ch
Cmte. Agriculture • Small Business • Transportation &
Infrastructure
CoS. Jessie Andrews **LD.** Robert Dougherty
Sched. Christine Bienes
Dist. Off. Delhi 607.376.0090 • Hudson 518.267.4123 •
Kingston 845.443.2930 • Liberty 845.295.6020 • Oneonta
607.376.0091

R: 309 **T:** 2nd 55%
Elected Year: 2018

⚓ Rep. Adriano Espaillat (eh-spy-YAHT) D-NY-13 p 202.225.4365

Rm. RHOB 2332 **Web.** espaillat.house.gov **f** 202.226.9731
Bio. 09/27/1954 • Santiago • Univ. of New York Queens
College (NY), B.S., 1978 • Roman Catholic • M. Marthera
Madera Espaillat, 2 ch **Cmte.** Appropriations • Education &
Labor
CoS. Aneiry Batista (CD) **LD.** Monica Garay
Sched. Carlos Vivaldi **PS.** Candace Person
Lanauze
Dist. Off. Bronx 646.740.3632 • New York 212.497.5959 •
New York 212.663.3900

R: 259 **T:** 3rd 91%
Elected Year: 2016

⚑ Rep. Andrew R. Garbarino (gar-ba-REE-noh) R-NY-02 p 202.225.7896

Rm. LHOB 1516 **Web.** garbarino.house.gov **f** 202.226.2279
Bio. 09/27/1984 • West Islip • George Washington Univ.
(DC), B.A.; Hofstra Univ. School of Law, J.D. • Roman
Catholic • S. **Cmte.** Homeland Security • Small Business
CoS. Deena Tauster **LD.** Scott A. Rausch
Sched. Emily Burdick **PS.** Kristen Cianci
Dist. Off. Massapequa Park 516.541.4225

R: 388 **T:** 1st 53%
Elected Year: 2020

🏛 Rep. Brian M. Higgins (HIH-guhnz)   D-NY-26   p 202.225.3306

Rm. RHOB 2459 **Web.** higgins.house.gov   **f** 202.226.0347
Bio. 10/06/1959 • Buffalo • Member, State Assembly;
Member, City Council • Buffalo State College (NY), B.S.,
1984; Buffalo State College (NY), M.A., 1985; Harvard Univ.
John F. Kennedy School of Government (MA), M.A., 1996
• Catholic • M. Mary Jane Hannon, 2 ch **Cmte.** Budget •
Ways & Means
CoS. Matthew Fery   **LD.** Lyndsey Barnes
Sched. Max Hernandez   **PS.** Theresa Kennedy (CD)
Dist. Off. Buffalo 716.852.3501 • Niagara Falls 716.282.1274

R: 79   **T:** 9th 70%
Elected Year: 2012

🏛 Rep. Chris Jacobs (JAY-kubz)   R-NY-27   p 202.225.5265

Rm. CHOB 214 **Web.** jacobs.house.gov   **f** 202.225.5910
Bio. 11/28/1966 • Buffalo • State Univ. of New York, Buffalo,
J.D.; Boston College (MA), B.A.; American Univ. (DC), M.B.A.
• NS. **Cmte.** Agriculture • Budget
CoS. Kyle Kizzier   **LD.** Derek Judd
Sched. Hannah Crossman   **PS.** Christian Chase
Dist. Off. Geneseo 585.519.4002 • Williamsville
716.634.2324

R: 369   **T:** 2nd 60%
Elected Year: 2019

🏛 Rep. Hakeem Jeffries (JEHF-reez)   D-NY-08   p 202.225.5936

Rm. RHOB 2433 **Web.** jeffries.house.gov   **f** 202.225.1018
Bio. 08/04/1970 • Brooklyn • State Univ. of New York,
Binghamton, B.A., 1992; Georgetown Univ. (DC), M.P.P.,
1994; New York Univ. Law School, J.D., 1997 • Baptist • M.
Kennisandra Jeffries, 2 ch **Cmte.** Budget • Judiciary
CoS. Tasia Jackson   **LD.** Zoe Oreck
Sched. Lauren Milnes   **PS.** Andy Eichar
Dist. Off. Brooklyn 718.237.2211 • Brooklyn 718.373.0033

R: 172   **T:** 5th 85%
Elected Year: 2012

🏛 Rep. Mondaire Jones (joanz)   D-NY-17   p 202.225.6506

Rm. LHOB 1017 **Web.** jones.house.gov   **f** 202.225.0546
Bio. 05/18/1987 • Nyack • Stanford Univ. (CA), B.A.,
2009; Harvard Univ., J.D., 2013 • Baptist • S. **Cmte.**
Communications Standards Commission • Education &
Labor • Ethics • Judiciary
CoS. Zach Fisch   **LD.** Michael Perez
Sched. Sabir Muhammad   **PS.** George Flynn
Dist. Off. New City 845.826.8090 • White Plains
914.323.5550

R: 398   **T:** 1st 59%
Elected Year: 2020

🏛 Rep. John M. Katko (KAT-ko)   R-NY-24   p 202.225.3701

Rm. RHOB 2457 **Web.** katko.house.gov   **f** 202.225.4042
Bio. 11/09/1962 • Syracuse • Niagara Univ., B.A., 1984;
Syracuse Univ. - College of Law (NY), J.D., 1988 • Roman
Catholic • M. Robin Katko, 3 ch **Cmte.** Homeland Security
• Transportation & Infrastructure
CoS. Erin Elliott (CD)   **LD.** Tristan Southard
Sched. Emily Bazydlo   **PS.** Dan Kranz
Dist. Off. Auburn 315.253.4068 • Lyons 315.253.4068 •
Oswego 315.423.5657 • Syracuse 315.423.5657

R: 221   **T:** 4th 53%
Elected Year: 1996

🏛 Rep. Nicole Malliotakis (MAL-ee-uh-TAHK-uhs) R-NY-11   p 202.225.3371

Rm. CHOB 417 **Web.** malliotakis.house.gov
Bio. 11/11/1980 • New York • Seton Hall Univ. (NJ), B.A.,
2001; Wagner College, M.B.A., 2010 • Greek Orthodox • S.
Cmte. Foreign Affairs • Transportation & Infrastructure
CoS. Alex B. Bolton   **LD.** Michael DeFilippis
Sched. Courtney Watson   **PS.** Natalie Baldassarre
Dist. Off. Brooklyn 718.306.1620 • Staten Island
718.568.2870

R: 404   **T:** 1st 53%
Elected Year: 2020

NEW YORK

Rep. Carolyn B. Maloney (muh-LOAN-ee)   D-NY-12   p 202.225.7944

Rm. RHOB 2308 **Web.** maloney.house.gov   **f** 202.225.4709
Bio. 02/19/1946 • Greensboro • NYC Board of Education;
NYC Council Member • Greensboro College (NC), Bach.
Deg., 1968 • Presbyterian • W., 2 ch **Cmte.** Financial
Services • Oversight & Reform
CoS. Emily Crerand   **LD.** Eric May
Sched. Rebecca Tulloch   **PS.** Sara Severens
Dist. Off. Astoria 718.932.1804 • New York 212.860.0606

R: 21   **T:** 15th   82%
Elected Year: 2012

Rep. Sean Patrick Maloney (muh-LO-nee)   D-NY-18   p 202.225.5441

Rm. CHOB 464 **Web.**
seanmaloney.house.gov
Bio. 07/30/1966 • Sherbrooke • Univ. of Virginia, B.A., 1988;
Univ. of Virginia School of Law, J.D., 1992 • Roman Catholic
• M. Randy Florke, 3 ch **Cmte.** Agriculture • Permanent
Select on Intelligence • Transportation & Infrastructure
CoS. Matthew McNally   **LD.** Austin Yager
Sched. Allie Kopel   **PS.** Mia Ehrenberg
Dist. Off. Newburgh 845.561.1259

R: 179   **T:** 5th   56%
Elected Year: 2012

Rep. Gregory W. Meeks (meeks)   D-NY-05   p 202.225.3461

Rm. RHOB 2310 **Web.** meeks.house.gov   **f** 202.226.4169
Bio. 09/25/1953 • Harlem • Assistant District Attorney; State
Legislator • Adelphi Univ. (NY), B.A., 1975; Howard Univ.
Law School (DC), J.D., 1978 • African Methodist Episcopal •
M. Simone-Marie Meeks, 3 ch **Cmte.** Financial Services •
Foreign Affairs
CoS. Ernie Jolly   **LD.** Amber Unwala
Sched. Reginald Belon   **PS.** Melissa Barosy
Dist. Off. Arverne 347.230.4032 • Jamaica 718.725.6000

R: 43   **T:** 12th   99%
Elected Year: 2012

Rep. Grace Meng (mehng)   D-NY-06   p 202.225.2601

Rm. RHOB 2209 **Web.** meng.house.gov   **f** 202.225.1589
Bio. 10/01/1975 • Queens • Univ. of Michigan, B.A., 1997;
Yeshiva Univ. Benjamin N. Cardozo School of Law (NY),
J.D., 2002 • Christian Church • M. Wayne Kye, 2 ch **Cmte.**
Appropriations
CoS. Maeve Healy   **LD.** Mark Olson
Sched. Aaron Feldman   **PS.** Jordan Goldes (CD)
Dist. Off. Flushing 718.358.6364 • Forest Hills 718.358.6364

R: 180   **T:** 5th   68%
Elected Year: 2012

Rep. Joseph D. Morelle (mor-REH-lee)   D-NY-25   p 202.225.3615

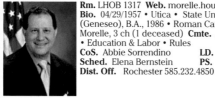

Rm. LHOB 1317 **Web.** morelle.house.gov   **f** 202.225.7822
Bio. 04/29/1957 • Utica • State Univ. of New York
(Geneseo), B.A., 1986 • Roman Catholic • M. Mary Beth
Morelle, 3 ch (1 deceased) **Cmte.** Armed Services • Budget
• Education & Labor • Rules
CoS. Abbie Sorrendino   **LD.** Joanne Stiles
Sched. Elena Bernstein   **PS.** Dana Vernetti (CD)
Dist. Off. Rochester 585.232.4850

R: 293   **T:** 3rd   59%
Elected Year: 2017

Rep. Jerry L. Nadler (NAD-lur)   D-NY-10   p 202.225.5635

Rm. RHOB 2132 **Web.** nadler.house.gov   **f** 202.225.6923
Bio. 06/13/1947 • Brooklyn • State Representative; NY State
Legislative Staffer • Columbia Univ. (NY), Bach. Deg., 1969;
Fordham Univ. School of Law (NY), J.D., 1978 • Jewish • M.
Joyce L. Miller, 1 ch **Cmte.** Judiciary
CoS. John Doty   **LD.** Andrew Heineman
Sched. Asha Armstrong   **PS.** Daniel Rubin
Dist. Off. Brooklyn 718.373.3198 • New York 212.367.7350

R: 14   **T:** 15th   75%
Elected Year: 2012

⚑ Rep. Alexandria Ocasio-Cortez (o-kah-SEE-o KOR-tehz) D-NY-14 p 202.225.3965

Rm. CHOB 229 **Web.** ocasio-cortez.house.gov
Bio. 10/13/1989 • Bronx • Boston Univ. (MA), B.A., 2011 • Catholic • S. **Cmte.** Financial Services • Oversight & Reform • Select Economic Disparity & Fairness in Growth
CoS. Gerardo Bonilla   **LD.** Mariam Jalloul Chavez
Sched. Tanushri Shankar   **PS.** Lauren Hitt
Dist. Off. Jackson Heights 718.662.5970 • The Bronx 718.662.5970

R: 336 **T:** 2nd 72%
Elected Year: 2018

⚑ Rep. Tom W. Reed II (reed) R-NY-23 p 202.225.3161

Web. reed.house.gov   **f** 202.226.6599
Bio. 11/18/1971 • Joliet • Attorney • Alfred Univ. (NY), Bach. Deg., 1993; Ohio Northern Univ. College of Law, J.D., 1996 • Roman Catholic • M. Jean Reed, 2 ch **Cmte.** Ways & Means
CoS. Joe Rizzo (CD)   **LD.** Luke Wallwork (CD)
Sched. Isabel Quinones   **PS.** Frank Acomb (CD) (CD)
Dist. Off. Corning 607.654.7566 • Geneva 315.759.5229 • Jamestown 716.708.6369 • Olean 716.379.8434

R: 122 **T:** 7th 58%
Elected Year: 2012

⚑ Rep. Kathleen M. Rice ("rice") D-NY-04 p 202.225.5516

Rm. RHOB 2435 **Web.**   **f** 202.225.5758
kathleenrice.house.gov
Bio. 02/15/1965 • New York City • Catholic Univ. of America (DC), B.A., 1987; Touro Law Center, J.D., 1991 • Roman Catholic • S. **Cmte.** Energy & Commerce • Homeland Security
CoS. Liz Amster   **LD.** Michael Demakos
Sched. Madeline Roberts   **PS.** Nora Kohli
Dist. Off. Garden City 516.739.3008

R: 230 **T:** 4th 56%
Elected Year: 2014

⚑ Rep. Elise Stefanik (steh-FAH-nik) R-NY-21 p 202.225.4611

Rm. RHOB 2211 **Web.** stefanik.house.gov   **f** 202.226.0621
Bio. 07/02/1984 • Albany • Harvard Univ., A.B., 2006 • Roman Catholic • M. Matthew Manda, 1 ch **Cmte.** Armed Services • Education & Labor • Permanent Select on Intelligence
CoS. Patrick Stewart Hester   **LD.** Marek Laco
Sched. Emma Cunningham   **PS.** Palmer Brigham
Dist. Off. Glens Falls 518.743.0964 • Plattsburgh 518.561.2324 • Watertown 315.782.3150

R: 232 **T:** 4th 59%
Elected Year: 2014

⚑ Rep. Thomas R. Suozzi (SWAH-zee) D-NY-03 p 202.225.3335

Rm. CHOB 407 **Web.** suozzi.house.gov   **f** 202.225.4669
Bio. 08/31/1962 • Glen Cove • Boston College (MA), B.S., 1984; Fordham Univ. School of Law (NY), J.D., 1989 • Roman Catholic • M. Helene Suozzi, 3 ch **Cmte.** Joint Congressional-Executive Commission on China • Ways & Means
CoS. Diane Shust   **LD.** Conor Walsh
Sched. Sydney Harvey   **PS.** Dylan Smith
Dist. Off. Huntington 631.923.4100 • Little Neck 718.631.0400

R: 283 **T:** 3rd 56%
Elected Year: 2016

⚑ Rep. Claudia Tenney (TEH-nee) R-NY-22 p 202.225.3665

Rm. LHOB 1410 **Web.** tenney.house.gov   **f** 202.225.1891
Bio. 02/04/1961 • New Hartford • Colgate Univ., B.A., 1983; Univ. of Cincinnati, J.D., 1987 • Presbyterian • D., 1 ch
Cmte. Foreign Affairs • Small Business
CoS. Nick Stewart   **LD.** Haim Engelman
Sched. Tiffany Boguslawski
Dist. Off. Binghamton 607.242.0200 • Utica 315.732.0713

R: 370 **T:** 1st 49%
Elected Year: 2020

NEW YORK

🔾 **Rep. Paul D. Tonko** (TAHN-ko)　　　　D-NY-20　　p 202.225.5076

Rm. RHOB 2369　**Web.** tonko.house.gov　**f** 202.225.5077
Bio. 06/18/1949 • Amsterdam • Engineer • Clarkson Univ.
(NY), B.S., 1971 • Roman Catholic • S.　**Cmte.** Energy
& Commerce • Natural Resources • Science, Space &
Technology
CoS. Jeff Morgan　　　　　**LD.** Emily Silverberg
Sched. David Mastrangelo　　**PS.** Rachel Dejean (CD)
Dist. Off. Albany 518.465.0700 • Amsterdam 518.843.3400
• Schenectady 518.374.4547

R: 117　**T:** 7th　61%
Elected Year: 2012

🔾 **Rep. Ritchie John Torres** (toe-ress)　　　D-NY-15　　p 202.225.4361

Rm. CHOB 317　**Web.** ritchietorres.house.gov　**f** 202.225.6001
Bio. 03/12/1988 • Bronx • Christian - Non-Denominational •
S.　**Cmte.** Financial Services • Homeland Security
CoS. Angel Vazquez　　　　**LD.** Sophie Pollock
　　　　　　　　　　　　　　　PS. Raymond Rodriguez
Dist. Off. Bronx 718.503.9610

R: 425　**T:** 1st　89%
Elected Year: 2020

🔾 **Rep. Nydia M. Velazquez** (veh-LAS-kez)　　D-NY-07　　p 202.225.2361

Rm. RHOB 2302　**Web.** velazquez.house.gov　**f** 202.226.0327
Bio. 03/28/1953 • Yabucoa • Director, Dept. of Puerto Rican
Community Affairs; Congressional Staffer • Univ. of Puerto
Rico (Rio Piedras), B.A., 1974; New York Univ., M.A., 1976 •
Roman Catholic • M. Paul Bader　**Cmte.** Financial Services
• Natural Resources • Small Business
CoS. Melissa Jung　　　　　**LD.** Jonathan Martinez
　　　　　　　　　　　　　　　PS. Evelyn Quartz
Dist. Off. Brooklyn 718.599.3658 • New York 212.619.2606

R: 25　**T:** 15th　85%
Elected Year: 2012

🔾 **Rep. Lee M. Zeldin** (ZEL-duhn)　　　　R-NY-01　　p 202.225.3826

Rm. RHOB 2441　**Web.** zeldin.house.gov
Bio. 01/30/1980 • East Meadow • Albany Law School,
J.D., 2003 • Jewish • M. Diana Zeldin, 2 ch (twins)　**Cmte.**
Financial Services • Foreign Affairs
CoS. Andrea Grace　　　　　**LD.** Sarah Talmage
Sched. Ashley Phillips　　　　**PS.** Jacob Murphy
Dist. Off. Patchogue 631.289.1097 • Riverhead
631.209.4235

R: 236　**T:** 4th　56%
Elected Year: 2014

NORTH CAROLINA

NORTH CAROLINA

🔾 **Governor Roy Cooper** (KOO-pur)　　　　　　　p 919.814.2000

Office of the Governor, 20301　Mail **C:** Raleigh
Service Center　　　　　　　**P:** 10,383,620 (9)
Raleigh, NC 27699-0301　　　**A:** 48,617.96 mi^2 (29th)
Website nc.gov
Fax 919.733.2120
Term Ends 2025
Lt. Governor
Mark Robinson, **R**

U.S. Senators
Richard M. Burr, **R**
Thom R. Tillis, **R**
U.S. Representatives
01 / G.K. Butterfield, **D**
02 / Deborah K. Ross, **D**
03 / Gregory F. Murphy, **R**
04 / David E. Price, **D**
05 / Virginia A. Foxx, **R**
06 / Kathy E. Manning, **D**
07 / David C. Rouzer, **R**　　10 / Patrick T. McHenry, **R**
08 / Richard Hudson, **R**　　 11 / Madison Cawthorn, **R**
09 / Dan Bishop, **R**　　　　 12 / Alma S. Adams, **D**

⚑ Sen. Richard M. Burr (bur) R-NC-Sr. p 202.224.3154

Rm. RSOB 217 **Web.** burr.senate.gov **f** 202.228.2981
Bio. 11/30/1955 • Charlottesville • U.S. Representative;
Businessman • Wake Forest Univ. (NC), B.A., 1978 •
Methodist • M. Brooke Fauth Burr, 2 ch **Cmte.** Aging
• Finance • Health, Education, Labor & Pensions •
Intelligence
CoS. Natasha Hickman
Sched. Michael Sorensen **PS.** Caitlin A. Carroll
Dist. Off. Asheville 828.350.2437 • Rocky Mount
252.977.9522 • Wilmington 910.251.1058 • Winston-Salem
336.631.5125

R: 20 **T:** 3rd 51%
Elected Year: 2004
Next Election: 2022

⚑ Sen. Thom R. Tillis (TIH-liss) R-NC-Jr. p 202.224.6342

Rm. DSOB 113 **Web.** tillis.senate.gov **f** 202.228.2563
Bio. 08/30/1960 • Jacksonville • Univ. of Maryland Univ.
College, B.S., 1996 • Catholic • M. Susan Tillis, 2 ch **Cmte.**
Armed Services • Banking, Housing & Urban Affairs • Joint
Security & Cooperation in Europe • Judiciary • Veterans'
Affairs
CoS. Ted Lehman **LD.** Shil Patel
Sched. Angela Schulze **PS.** Adam Webb
Dist. Off. Charlotte 704.509.9087 • Greenville 252.329.0371
• Hendersonville 828.693.8750 • High Point 336.885.0685 •
Raleigh 919.856.4630

R: 71 **T:** 2nd 49%
Elected Year: 2014
Next Election: 2026

⚑ Rep. Alma S. Adams (AD-uhmz) D-NC-12 p 202.225.1510

Rm. RHOB 2436 **Web.** adams.house.gov **f** 202.225.1512
Bio. 05/27/1946 • High Point • North Carolina Agricultural
and Technical State Univ., B.S., 1968; North Carolina
Agricultural and Technical State Univ., M.S., 1972; Ohio
State Univ., Ph.D., 1981 • Baptist • D., 2 ch; 4 gr-ch **Cmte.**
Agriculture • Education & Labor • Financial Services
CoS. John Christie **LD.** Christopher DeVore
Sched. Sandra Brown **PS.** Sam Spencer (CD)
Dist. Off. Charlotte 704.344.9950

R: 201 **T:** 5th 100%
Elected Year: 2013

⚑ Rep. Dan Bishop (BIH-shuhp) R-NC-09 p 202.225.1976

Rm. LHOB 1207 **Web.** danbishop.house.gov **f** 202.225.3389
Bio. 07/01/1964 • Charlotte • Univ. of North Carolina, B.S.,
1986; Univ. of North Carolina School of Law, J.D., 1990 • M.
Jo bishop, 1 ch **Cmte.** Homeland Security • Judiciary
CoS. James Hampson **LD.** Scott Knittle
Sched. Conley Lowrance **PS.** Clay Shoemaker
Dist. Off. Lumberton 910.671.3000 • Monroe 704.218.5300

R: 365 **T:** 2nd 56%
Elected Year: 2018

⚑ Rep. Ted P. Budd ("bud") R-NC-13 p 202.225.4531

Rm. CHOB 103 **Web.** budd.house.gov
Bio. 10/21/1971 • Winston-Salem • Appalachian State Univ.
(NC), B.S., 1994; Dallas Theological Seminary (TX), M.Th.,
1998; Wake Forest Univ. (NC), M.B.A., 2007 • Christian -
Non-Denominational • M. Amy Kate, 3 ch **Cmte.** Financial
Services
CoS. Chad Yelinski **LD.** Eric Heigis
Sched. Elizabeth Dews- **PS.** Curtis Kalin
Haymore
Dist. Off. Advance 336.998.1313 • Asheboro 336.610.3300
• Graham 336.639.7323

R: 252 **T:** 3rd 68%
Elected Year: 2016

NORTH CAROLINA

↯ Rep. G.K. Butterfield Jr. (BUT-ur-"field") D-NC-01 p 202.225.3101

Rm. RHOB 2080 **Web.** butterfield.house.gov **f** 202.225.3354
Bio. 04/27/1947 • Wilson • North Carolina Supreme Court
Judge; Attorney • Army 1968-70 • North Carolina Central
Univ., B.A., 1971; North Carolina Central Univ. School of Law,
J.D., 1974 • Baptist • D., 3 ch; 3 gr-ch **Cmte.** Administration
• Energy & Commerce • Joint Library
CoS. Kyle Parker **LD.** Caitlin Van Sant
Sched. Lindsey Bowen **PS.** De'Marcus Finnell
Dist. Off. Wilson 252.237.9816

R: 70 **T:** 10th 54%
Elected Year: 2003

⚑ Rep. Madison Cawthorn (KAW-thowrn) R-NC-11 p 202.225.6401

Rm. CHOB 102 **Web.** cawthorn.house.gov
Bio. 08/01/1995 • Asheville • Christian - Non-
Denominational • M. Cristina Bayardelle **Cmte.** Education
& Labor • Veterans' Affairs
CoS. Blake Harp **LD.** Catherine Treadwell
Sched. Stephen Smith **PS.** Luke Ball
Dist. Off. Burnsville 828.808.2148 • Franklin 828.452.6022
• Hendersonville 828.435.7310 • Waynesville 828.452.6022

R: 380 **T:** 1st 55%
Elected Year: 2020

⚑ Rep. Virginia A. Foxx (fahks) R-NC-05 p 202.225.2071

Rm. RHOB 2462 **Web.** foxx.house.gov **f** 202.225.2995
Bio. 06/29/1943 • Bronx • Business Owner; Board of
Education • Univ. of North Carolina Chapel Hill (UNC),
Bach. Deg., 1968; Univ. of North Carolina Chapel Hill (UNC),
M.A., 1972; Univ. of North Carolina, Greensboro, Ed.D., 1985
• Roman Catholic • M. Thomas A. Foxx, 1 ch; 2 gr-ch **Cmte.**
Education & Labor • Oversight & Reform
CoS. Carson Middleton **LD.** Bryan McVae
Sched. Hannah Cooke **PS.** Alex Ives
Dist. Off. Boone 828.265.0240 • Clemmons 336.778.0211

R: 76 **T:** 9th 67%
Elected Year: 2004

⚑ Rep. Richard Hudson Jr. (HUD-suhn) R-NC-08 p 202.225.3715

Rm. RHOB 2112 **Web.** hudson.house.gov **f** 202.225.4036
Bio. 11/04/1971 • Franklin • Univ. of North Carolina,
Charlotte, B.A., 1996 • Methodist • M. Renee Hudson, 1 ch
Cmte. Energy & Commerce • Joint Security & Cooperation
in Europe
CoS. Billy Constangy **LD.** Elliott Guffin
Sched. Jessica D. Harrison **PS.** Greg Steele
Dist. Off. Concord 704.786.1612 • Fayetteville 910.997.2070

R: 170 **T:** 5th 53%
Elected Year: 2012

↯ Rep. Kathy E. Manning (MAN-ing) D-NC-06 p 202.225.3065

Rm. CHOB 415 **Web.** manning.house.gov **f** 202.225.8611
Bio. 12/03/1956 • Detroit • Harvard Univ., B.A., 1978; Univ.
of Michigan Law School, J.D., 1978 • Jewish • M. Randall
Kaplan, 3 ch **Cmte.** Education & Labor • Foreign Affairs
CoS. Sarah Curtis **LD.** Jayme Holliday
Sched. Carolyn Calder **PS.** Hailey Barringer
Dist. Off. Greensboro 336.333.5005

R: 406 **T:** 1st 62%
Elected Year: 2020

⚑ Rep. Patrick T. McHenry (mik-HEN-ree) R-NC-10 p 202.225.2576

Rm. RHOB 2004 **Web.** mchenry.house.gov **f** 202.225.0316
Bio. 10/22/1975 • Charlotte • Realtor; Campaign Aide •
Belmont Abbey College (NC), B.A., 2000 • Roman Catholic
• M. Giulia Cangiano McHenry, 2 ch **Cmte.** Financial
Services
CoS. Jeff Butler **LD.** Doug Nation
Sched. Grace Tricomi **PS.** Taylor Theodossiou
Dist. Off. Hickory 828.327.6100 • Mooresville 800.477.2576
• Rural Hall 800.477.2576

R: 81 **T:** 9th 69%
Elected Year: 2004

NORTH CAROLINA

🏛 Rep. Gregory F. Murphy (MUR-fee) R-NC-03 p 202.225.3415
Rm. CHOB 313 **Web.** gregmurphy.house.gov **f** 202.225.3286
Bio. 03/05/1963 • Raleigh • Davidson College, B.S., 1985;
Univ. of North Carolina School of Medicine, Chapel Hill,
M.D., 1989 • M. Wendy Murphy, 3 ch **Cmte.** Education &
Labor • Ways & Means
CoS. Dave Natonski   **LD.** John Wilson
Sched. Jessica Santos   **PS.** Kate Currie
Dist. Off. Edenton 252.368.8866 • Greenville 252.931.1003
• Jacksonville 910.937.6929 • New Bern 252.636.6612

R: 366 **T:** 2nd 63%
Elected Year: 2018

🏛 Rep. David E. Price (price) D-NC-04 p 202.225.1784
Rm. RHOB 2108 **Web.** price.house.gov **f** 202.225.2014
Bio. 08/17/1940 • Erwin • Professor of Political Sciences &
Policy Sciences • Univ. of North Carolina, B.A., 1961; Yale
Univ. (CT), B.D., 1964; Yale Univ. (CT), Ph.D., 1969 • Baptist
• M. Lisa Kanwit Price, 2 ch; 2 gr-ch **Cmte.** Appropriations
• Budget
CoS. Justin Wein   **LD.** Nora Blalock
Sched. Sarah Aldridge   **PS.** Katelynn Vogt
Dist. Off. Durham 919.967.7924

R: 11 **T:** 13th 67%
Elected Year: 1996

🏛 Rep. Deborah K. Ross (rawss) D-NC-02 p 202.225.3032
Rm. LHOB 1208 **Web.** ross.house.gov **f** 202.225.0181
Bio. 06/20/1963 • Philadelphia • Brown Univ. (RI), B.A.,
1985; Univ. of North Carolina Law School (NC), J.D., 1990 •
Unitarian • M. Stephen (Steve) J. Wrinn **Cmte.** Judiciary •
Rules • Science, Space & Technology
CoS. Matt Lee   **LD.** Shirley Dai
Sched. Nate Matteson   **PS.** Josie Feron
Dist. Off. Raleigh 919.334.0840

R: 420 **T:** 1st 63%
Elected Year: 2020

🏛 Rep. David C. Rouzer (ROU-zur) R-NC-07 p 202.225.2731
Rm. RHOB 2333 **Web.** rouzer.house.gov **f** 202.225.5773
Bio. 02/16/1972 • Landstuhl, Germany • North Carolina
State Univ., B.A., 1994; North Carolina State Univ., B.S., 1994
• Southern Baptist • S. **Cmte.** Agriculture • Transportation
& Infrastructure
CoS. Anna McCormack   **LD.** Jason Cooke
Sched. Courtney Eubanks   **PS.** Erin McBride
Dist. Off. Bolivia 910.253.6111 • Four Oaks 919.938.3040 •
Wilmington 910.395.0202

R: 231 **T:** 4th 60%
Elected Year: 2014

NORTH DAKOTA

🏛 Governor Doug Burgum (BUR-guhm) p 701.328.2200
600 E. Boulevard Ave.   **C:** Bismarck
Bismarck, ND 58505-0001   **P:** 760,077 (48)
Website nd.gov   **A:** 69,000.67 mi² (17th)
Fax 701.328.2205
Term Ends 2024
Lt. Governor
Brent Sanford, R

U.S. Senators
John H. Hoeven, R
Kevin J. Cramer, R
U.S. Representatives
01 / Kelly M. Armstrong, R

NORTH DAKOTA

⚑ Sen. Kevin J. Cramer (KRAY-mur)   R-ND-Jr.   p 202.224.2043

Rm. RSOB 400   **Web.** cramer.senate.gov
Bio. 01/21/1961 • Rolette • Concordia College (MN), B.A., 1983; Univ. of Mary (ND), M.A., 2003 • Evangelical • M. Kris Neumann, 5 ch (1 deceased); 5 gr-ch   **Cmte.** Armed Services • Banking, Housing & Urban Affairs • Budget • Environment & Public Works • Veterans' Affairs
CoS. Mark Gruman   **LD.** Micah Chambers
Sched. Rachel Buening   **PS.** Molly Block
Dist. Off. Bismarck 701.699.7020 • Fargo 701.232.5094 • Grand Forks 701.699.7030 • Minot 701.837.6141 • Williston 701.441.7230

R: 85   **T:** 1st   55%
Elected Year: 2018
Next Election: 2024

⚑ Sen. John H. Hoeven III (HO-vuhn)   R-ND-Sr.   p 202.224.2551

Rm. RSOB 338   **Web.** hoeven.senate.gov   **f** 202.224.7999
Bio. 03/13/1957 • Bismarck • Former Chair, Gov.'s Ethanol Coalition; Chair, Midwestern Governors Assn.; Chair, District 47 North Dakota Republican Party; Chair, Interstate Oil and Gas Compact Commission • Dartmouth College, Hanover (NH), B.A., 1979; Northwestern Univ. Kellogg School of Management (IL), M.B.A., 1981 • Roman Catholic • M. Mikey Hoeven, 2 ch; 3 gr-ch   **Cmte.** Agriculture, Nutrition & Forestry • Appropriations • Energy & Natural Resources • Indian Affairs
CoS. Tony Eberhard   **LD.** Daniel Auger
Sched. Sydney Fitzpatrick   **PS.** Kami Capener
Dist. Off. Bismarck 701.250.4618 • Fargo 701.239.5389 • Grand Forks 701.746.8972 • Minot 701.838.1361 • Watford City 701.609.2727

R: 45   **T:** 2nd   79%
Elected Year: 2010
Next Election: 2022

⚑ Rep. Kelly M. Armstrong (ARM-strong)   R-ND-01   p 202.225.2611

Rm. LHOB 1740   **Web.** armstrong.house.gov   **f** 202.226.3410
Bio. 10/08/1976 • Dickinson • Univ. of North Dakota, B.A., 2000; Univ. of North Dakota School of Law, J.D., 2003 • Lutheran • M. Kjersti Armstrong, 2 ch   **Cmte.** Energy & Commerce • Ethics • Select Committee on the Climate Crisis
CoS. Rosalyn Leighton   **LD.** Nicholas Tortorici
                    PS. Conner Swanson
Dist. Off. Bismarck 701.354.6700 • Fargo 701.353.6665

R: 298   **T:** 2nd   69%
Elected Year: 2018

OHIO

⚑ Governor Mike DeWine (duh-WINE)   p 614.466.3555

Riffe Center
77 S. High St., 30th Floor
Columbus, OH 43215
Website ohio.gov
Fax 614.466.9354
Term Ends 2023
Lt. Governor
Jon A. Husted, R

C: Columbus
P: 11,689,442 (7)
A: 40,860.79 mi^2 (35th)

U.S. Senators
Sherrod C. Brown, **D**
Rob J. Portman, **R**
U.S. Representatives
01 / Steve Chabot, **R**
02 / Brad R. Wenstrup, **R**
03 / Joyce B. Beatty, **D**
04 / Jim D. Jordan, **R**
05 / Bob E. Latta, **R**
06 / Bill Johnson, **R**
07 / Bob B. Gibbs, **R**
08 / Warren Davidson, **R**
09 / Marcy C. Kaptur, **D**
10 / Mike R. Turner, **R**
11 / Shontel Brown, **D**
12 / Troy Balderson, **R**
13 / Tim J. Ryan, **D**
14 / Dave P. Joyce, **R**
15 / Mike Carey, **R**
16 / Anthony E. Gonzalez, **R**

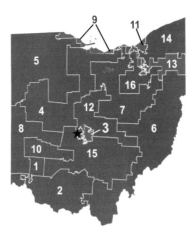

📧 Sen. Sherrod C. Brown ("brown")　　　　D-OH-Sr.　　p 202.224.2315

Rm. HSOB 503　**Web.** brown.senate.gov　**f** 202.228.6321
Bio. 11/09/1952 • Mansfield • Professor; Representative •
Yale Univ. (CT), B.A., 1974; Ohio State Univ., M.A., 1979; Ohio
State Univ., M.P.A., 1981 • Lutheran • M. Connie Schultz,
2 ch; 2 stepch; 6 gr-ch　**Cmte.** Agriculture, Nutrition &
Forestry • Banking, Housing & Urban Affairs • Finance •
Veterans' Affairs
CoS. Sarah Benzing　　　　**LD.** Jeremy Hekhuis
Sched. Diana Baron　　　　**PS.** Trudy Perkins
Dist. Off. Cincinnati 513.684.1021 • Cleveland
216.522.7272 • Columbus 614.469.2083 • Lorain
440.242.4100

R: 25　**T:** 3rd　53%
Elected Year: 2006
Next Election: 2024

📧 Sen. Rob J. Portman (PORT-muhn)　　　　R-OH-Jr.　　p 202.224.3353

Rm. RSOB 448　**Web.** portman.senate.gov　**f** 202.224.9075
Bio. 12/19/1955 • Cincinnati • Dartmouth College, B.A.,
1979; Univ. of Michigan Law School, J.D., 1984 • Methodist •
M. Jane Portman, 3 ch　**Cmte.** Finance • Foreign Relations •
Homeland Security & Government Affairs • Joint Economic
CoS. Kevin Smith　　　　**LD.** Sarah Peery
　　　　　　　　　　　　　　PS. Drew Nirenberg
Dist. Off. Cincinnati 513.684.3265 • Cleveland
216.522.7095 • Columbus 614.469.6774 • Toledo
419.259.3895

R: 42　**T:** 2nd　58%
Elected Year: 2010
Next Election: 2022

📧 Rep. Troy Balderson (ball-dur-sun)　　　　R-OH-12　　p 202.225.5355

Rm. RHOB 2429　**Web.** balderson.house.gov　**f** 202.226.4523
Bio. 01/16/1962 • Zanesville • Christian Church • D.
Angie Albright, 1 ch　**Cmte.** Agriculture • Transportation &
Infrastructure
CoS. Laura Engquist　　　　**LD.** Nate Zimpher
Sched. Katie Tomko　　　　**PS.** Clark Siddle (CD)
Dist. Off. Worthington 614.523.2555

R: 291　**T:** 3rd　55%
Elected Year: 2017

📧 Rep. Joyce B. Beatty (BAY-dee)　　　　D-OH-03　　p 202.225.4324

Rm. RHOB 2303　**Web.** beatty.house.gov　**f** 202.225.1984
Bio. 03/12/1950 • Dayton • Central State Univ. (OH), B.A.,
1972; Wright State Univ. (OH), M.S., 1974 • Baptist • M.
Justice Otto Beatty Jr., 2 stepch; 2 gr-ch　**Cmte.** Financial
Services • Joint Economic
CoS. Todd Valentine　　　　**LD.** Nicholas Semanko
Sched. Blaike Bibbs　　　　**PS.** Mary Ellen Garrett
Dist. Off. Columbus 614.220.0003

R: 161　**T:** 5th　71%
Elected Year: 2012

Rep. Shontel Brown ("brown") — D-OH-11 — p 202.225.7032

Rm. RHOB 2344 **Web.** shontelbrown.house.gov — **f** 202.225.1339
Bio. Cleveland • Cuyahoga Community College, Assc. Deg., 2012 • NS. **Cmte.** Agriculture • Oversight & Reform
CoS. Veleter Mazyck — **LD.** Julian Sham
Sched. Jasmine Lastery-Butler — **PS.** Conor Fryer
Dist. Off. Akron 330.835.4758 • Warrensville Heights 216.522.4900

R: 432 **T:** 1st 79%
Elected Year: 2020

Rep. Mike Carey (KAIR-ree) — R-OH-15 — p 202.225.2015

Rm. RHOB 2234 **Web.** carey.house.gov
Bio. Sabina • Marion Military Institute, A.S., 1991; Ohio State Univ., B.A., 1993 • Christian - Non-Denominational • M. Meghan Carey, 2 ch **Cmte.** Budget
CoS. David Distefano — **LD.** Kaitlyn Dwyer
Sched. Matthew Johnson — **PS.** Blaine Kelly (CD)
Dist. Off. Hilliard 614.771.4968

R: 433 **T:** 1st 58%
Elected Year: 2020

Rep. Steve Chabot (SHA-buht) — R-OH-01 — p 202.225.2216

Rm. RHOB 2408 **Web.** chabot.house.gov — **f** 202.225.3012
Bio. 01/22/1953 • Cincinnati • College of William and Mary (VA), B.A., 1975; Northern Kentucky Univ. Salmon P. Chase College of Law (KY), J.D., 1978 • Roman Catholic • M. Donna Chabot, 2 ch; 2 gr-ch **Cmte.** Foreign Affairs • Judiciary
CoS. Jonathan Lowe — **LD.** Erick Harris
Sched. Athena McAllister — **PS.** Mackenzie Martinez
Dist. Off. Cincinnati 513.684.2723 • Lebanon 513.421.8704

R: 45 **T:** 6th 52%
Elected Year: 2010

Rep. Warren Davidson (DAY-vid-suhn) — R-OH-08 — p 202.225.6205

Rm. RHOB 2113 **Web.** davidson.house.gov — **f** 202.225.0704
Bio. 03/01/1970 • Troy • Univ. of Notre Dame (IN), M.B.A.; U.S. Military Academy - West Point (NY), B.A., 1995 • Unspecified/Other • M. Lisa Davidson, 2 ch **Cmte.** Financial Services • Select Economic Disparity & Fairness in Growth
CoS. Douglas Branch — **LD.** Connor White
Sched. Martha Davis
Dist. Off. Springfield 937.322.1120 • Troy 937.339.1524 • West Chester 513.779.5400

R: 239 **T:** 4th 69%
Elected Year: 2015

Rep. Bob B. Gibbs (gibz) — R-OH-07 — p 202.225.6265

Rm. RHOB 2217 **Web.** gibbs.house.gov — **f** 202.225.3394
Bio. 06/14/1954 • Peru • Ohio State Univ. Agricultural Technical Institute, A.A.S., 1974 • Methodist • M. Jody Gibbs, 3 ch **Cmte.** Oversight & Reform • Transportation & Infrastructure
CoS. Hillary Gross — **LD.** Brian Bates
Sched. Hannah Hughes — **PS.** Dallas Gerber
Dist. Off. Ashland 419.207.0650 • Canton 330.737.1631

R: 134 **T:** 6th 68%
Elected Year: 2012

Rep. Anthony E. Gonzalez (gon-SAH-les) — R-OH-16 — p 202.225.3876

Rm. RHOB 2458 **Web.** anthonygonzalez.house.gov — **f** 202.225.3059
Bio. 09/18/1984 • Avon Lake • Ohio State Univ., B.A., 2007; Stanford Univ. (CA), M.B.A., 2014 • Catholic • M. Elizabeth Gonzalez, 1 ch **Cmte.** Financial Services • Science, Space & Technology • Select Committee on the Climate Crisis
CoS. Timothy Lolli — **LD.** Stephen Hostelley
Sched. Carol Kresse
Dist. Off. Canton 330.599.7037 • Strongsville 440.783.3696

R: 316 **T:** 2nd 63%
Elected Year: 2018

OHIO

⌨ Rep. Bill Johnson (JAHN-suhn)   R-OH-06   p 202.225.5705

Rm. RHOB 2336 **Web.** billjohnson.house.gov **f** 202.225.5907
Bio. 11/10/1954 • Roseboro • Troy Univ. (AL), B.S., 1979;
Georgia Institute of Technology, M.S., 1984 • Protestant -
Unspecified Christian • M. LeeAnn Johnson, 4 ch; 6 gr-ch
Cmte. Energy & Commerce
CoS. Mike Smullen   **LD.** Sam Hattrup
Sched. McKenna Simpson   **PS.** Benjamin Keeler (CD)
Dist. Off. Cambridge 740.432.2366 • Ironton 740.534.9431
• Marietta 740.376.0868 • Salem 330.337.6951

R: 141 **T:** 6th 74%
Elected Year: 2010

⌨ Rep. Jim D. Jordan (JOR-duhn)   R-OH-04   p 202.225.2676

Rm. RHOB 2056 **Web.** jordan.house.gov   **f** 202.226.0577
Bio. 02/17/1964 • Urbana • State Representative • Univ. of
Wisconsin, B.S., 1986; Ohio State Univ., M.A., 1991; Capital
Univ. (OH), J.D., 2001 • Evangelical • M. Polly Jordan, 4 ch; 2
gr-ch **Cmte.** Judiciary • Oversight & Reform
CoS. Kevin Christopher   **LD.** Jared Dilley
Eichinger
Sched. Emma Summers   **PS.** Russell Dye
Dist. Off. Bucyrus 419.663.1426 • Lima 419.999.6455 •
Norwalk 419.663.1426

R: 94 **T:** 8th 68%
Elected Year: 2006

⌨ Rep. Dave P. Joyce (joyss)   R-OH-14   p 202.225.5731

Rm. RHOB 2065 **Web.** joyce.house.gov   **f** 202.225.3307
Bio. 03/17/1957 • Cleveland • Univ. of Dayton (OH), B.S.,
1979; Univ. of Dayton (OH), J.D., 1982 • Roman Catholic •
M. Kelly Joyce, 3 ch **Cmte.** Appropriations • Ethics • Select
Committee on the Modernization of Congress
CoS. Anna Romeo   **LD.** Burke Smith
Sched. Kelsi Brogan (CD)   **PS.** Katherine Sears
Dist. Off. Mentor 440.352.3939 • Twinsburg 330.357.4139

R: 173 **T:** 5th 60%
Elected Year: 2012

⚘ Rep. Marcy C. Kaptur (KAP-tur)   D-OH-09   p 202.225.4146

Rm. RHOB 2186 **Web.** kaptur.house.gov   **f** 202.225.7711
Bio. 06/17/1946 • Toledo • Domestic Policy Staffer,
President Jimmy Carter; Urban Planner • Univ. of
Wisconsin, B.A., 1968; Univ. of Michigan, M.A., 1974 •
Catholic • S. **Cmte.** Appropriations • Select Economic
Disparity & Fairness in Growth • Veterans' Affairs
CoS. Steve Katich (CD)

                              PS. Christopher Dalton
Dist. Off. Cleveland 216.767.5933 • Lorain 440.288.1500 •
Toledo 419.259.7500

R: 5 **T:** 20th 63%
Elected Year: 1982

⌨ Rep. Bob E. Latta (LAT-uh)   R-OH-05   p 202.225.6405

Rm. RHOB 2467 **Web.** latta.house.gov   **f** 202.225.1985
Bio. 04/18/1956 • Bluffton • State Legislator; Attorney •
Bowling Green State Univ. (OH), B.A., 1978; Univ. of Toledo
College of Law (OH), J.D., 1981 • Roman Catholic • M.
Marcia Sloan Latta, 2 ch **Cmte.** Communications Standards
Commission • Energy & Commerce • Select Committee on
the Modernization of Congress
CoS. Drew Griffin   **LD.** Mike Davin
Sched. Jolie Brochin   **PS.** Rebecca Angelson
Dist. Off. Bowling Green 419.354.8700 • Defiance
419.782.1996 • Findlay 419.422.7791

R: 103 **T:** 8th 68%
Elected Year: 2006

⚘ Rep. Tim J. Ryan (RY-uhn)   D-OH-13   p 202.225.5261

Rm. LHOB 1126 **Web.** timryan.house.gov   **f** 202.225.3719
Bio. 07/16/1973 • Niles • State Senator • Bowling Green
State Univ. (OH), B.A., 1995; Franklin Pierce College Law
Center (NH), J.D., 2000 • Catholic • M. Andrea Zetts, 1 ch; 2
stepch **Cmte.** Appropriations
CoS. Ron Grimes   **LD.** Rachel Jenkins
Sched. Erin Isenberg   **PS.** Caty Payette
Dist. Off. Akron 330.630.7311 • Warren 330.373.0074 •
Youngstown 330.740.0193

R: 66 **T:** 10th 53%
Elected Year: 2012

OHIO

Rep. Mike R. Turner (TUR-nur)   R-OH-10   p 202.225.6465

Rm. RHOB 2082 **Web.** turner.house.gov   **f** 202.225.6754
Bio. 01/11/1960 • Dayton • Corporate Counsel; Mayor
(Dayton, OH) • Ohio Northern Univ., B.A., 1982; Case
Western Reserve Univ. School of Law, J.D., 1985; Univ.
of Dayton (OH), M.B.A., 1992 • Presbyterian • D. Majida
Mourad, 2 ch   **Cmte.** Armed Services • Permanent Select
on Intelligence
CoS. Adam Howard   **LD.** Michael Calcagni
Sched. Marty Heide (CD)   **PS.** MacKenzie Morales
Dist. Off. Dayton 937.225.2843

R: 69   **T:** 10th 58%
Elected Year: 2012

Rep. Brad R. Wenstrup (WEN-strup)   R-OH-02   p 202.225.3164

Rm. RHOB 2419 **Web.** wenstrup.house.gov   **f** 202.225.1992
Bio. 06/17/1958 • Cincinnati • Univ. of Cincinnati, B.A.,
1980; Rosalind Franklin Univ. (IL), B.S., 1985 • Roman
Catholic • M. Monica Klein, 2 ch   **Cmte.** Permanent Select
on Intelligence • Ways & Means
CoS. Greg Brooks   **LD.** Alexandra Igleheart
Sched. Anna Waterkotte   **PS.** Christopher Krepich
Dist. Off. Cincinnati 513.474.7777 • Peebles 513.605.1380

R: 196   **T:** 5th 61%
Elected Year: 2012

OKLAHOMA

Governor Kevin Stitt (stit)   p 405.521.2342

State Capitol Building   **C:** Oklahoma City
2300 N. Lincoln Blvd., Room 212   **P:** 3,943,079 (28)
Oklahoma City, OK 73105   **A:** 68,594.88 mi^2 (19th)
Website ok.gov
Fax 405.521.3353
Term Ends 2023
Lt. Governor
Matt Pinnell, R

U.S. Senators
James M. Inhofe, R
James P. Lankford, R
U.S. Representatives
01 / Kevin R. Hern, R
02 / Markwayne Mullin, R
03 / Frank D. Lucas, R
04 / Tom J. Cole, R
05 / Stephanie Bice, R

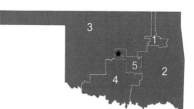

Sen. James M. Inhofe (IN-hahf)   R-OK-Sr.   p 202.224.4721

Rm. RSOB 205 **Web.** inhofe.senate.gov   **f** 202.228.0380
Bio. 11/17/1934 • Des Moines • U.S. Representative;
Insurance Executive • Army 1954-56 • Univ. of Tulsa (LK),
B.A., 1973 • Presbyterian • M. Kay Kirkpatrick Inhofe,
4 ch (1 deceased); 16 gr-ch   **Cmte.** Armed Services •
Environment & Public Works • Intelligence • Small Business
& Entrepreneurship
CoS. Luke Holland   **LD.** Daniel Hillenbrand
Sched. Wendi Price   **PS.** Leacy Burke
Dist. Off. Enid 580.234.5105 • Oklahoma City 405.208.8841
• Tulsa 918.748.5111

R: 7   **T:** 6th 63%
Elected Year: 1994
Next Election: 2026

♜ Sen. James P. Lankford (LANK-furd)　　　R-OK-Jr.　　p 202.224.5754

Rm. HSOB 316　**Web.** lankford.senate.gov　**f** 202.228.1015
Bio. 03/04/1968 • Dallas • Univ. of Texas, B.S., 1990;
Southwestern Theological Baptist Seminary (TX), M.Div.,
1994 • Baptist • M. Cindy Lankford, 2 ch　**Cmte.** Energy &
Natural Resources • Ethics • Finance • Homeland Security
& Government Affairs • Indian Affairs • Joint Congressional-
Executive Commission on China
CoS. Michelle Altman　　　**LD.** Sarah Seitz
Sched. Jaclyn O'Neil　　　**PS.** Aly Beley
Dist. Off. Oklahoma City 405.231.4941 • Tulsa
918.581.7651

R: 67　**T:** 2nd　68%
Elected Year: 2014
Next Election: 2022

♜ Rep. Stephanie Bice (bais)　　　R-OK-05　　p 202.225.2132

Rm. LHOB 1223　**Web.** bice.house.gov
Bio. 11/11/1973 • Oklahoma City • Oklahoma State Univ.,
B.S., 1995 • Catholic • M. Geoffrey Bice, 2 ch　**Cmte.** Armed
Services • Science, Space & Technology • Select Economic
Disparity & Fairness in Growth
CoS. Amy Albro (CD)　　　**LD.** Jett E. Thompson
Sched. Allison Smith　　　**PS.** Penny Seale (CD)
Dist. Off. Oklahoma City 405.300.6890

R: 373　**T:** 1st　52%
Elected Year: 2020

♜ Rep. Tom J. Cole (koal)　　　R-OK-04　　p 202.225.6165

Rm. RHOB 2207　**Web.** cole.house.gov　**f** 202.225.3512
Bio. 04/28/1949 • Shreveport • Chief of Staff, Republican
National Committee; Secretary of State • Grinnell College
(IA), B.A., 1971; Institute for Historical Research - London
(England), B.A., 1972; Yale Univ. (CT), M.A., 1974; Univ.
of Oklahoma (OK), Ph.D., 1984 • Methodist • M. Ellen
Elizabeth Decker Cole, 1 ch　**Cmte.** Appropriations • Rules
CoS. Josh Grogis　　　**LD.** Shane Hand
Sched. Sabrina Parker　　　**PS.** Sarah A. Corley
Dist. Off. Ada 580.436.5375 • Lawton 580.357.2131 •
Norman 405.329.6500

R: 61　**T:** 10th　68%
Elected Year: 2002

♜ Rep. Kevin R. Hern (hurn)　　　R-OK-01　　p 202.225.2211

Rm. LHOB 1019　**Web.** hern.house.gov　**f** 202.225.9187
Bio. 12/04/1961 • Belton • Univ. of Arkansas, B.S., 1986;
Univ. of Arkansas-Little Rock, M.B.A., 1999 • Evangelical • M.
Tammy Hern, 3 ch　**Cmte.** Ways & Means
CoS. Cameron Foster　　　**LD.** Dominique Yelinski
Sched. Anna Adamian　　　**PS.** Miranda Dabney
Dist. Off. Tulsa 918.935.3222

R: 292　**T:** 3rd　64%
Elected Year: 2017

♜ Rep. Frank D. Lucas (LOO-kuhss)　　　R-OK-03　　p 202.225.5565

Rm. RHOB 2405　**Web.** lucas.house.gov　**f** 202.225.8698
Bio. 01/06/1960 • Cheyenne • State Representative; Farmer/
Rancher • Oklahoma State Univ., B.S., 1982 • Baptist •
M. Lynda Bradshaw Lucas, 3 ch; 2 gr-ch　**Cmte.** Financial
Services • Science, Space & Technology
CoS. Stacey Glasscock (CD)　**LD.** Alison Slagell
Sched. Courtney Trigg　　　**PS.** Patrick Bond
Dist. Off. Yukon 405.373.1958

R: 27　**T:** 14th　79%
Elected Year: 2002

♜ Rep. Markwayne Mullin (MUHL-luhn)　　　R-OK-02　　p 202.225.2701

Rm. RHOB 2421　**Web.** mullin.house.gov　**f** 202.225.3038
Bio. 07/26/1977 • Tulsa • Oklahoma State Univ. Institute
of Technology, Assc. Deg., 2010 • Pentecostal • M. Christie
Mullin, 5 ch (twins)　**Cmte.** Energy & Commerce •
Permanent Select on Intelligence
CoS. Benjamin Cantrell　　　**LD.** Kaitlynn Skoog
Sched. Brooke Starr　　　**PS.** Meredith Blanford
Dist. Off. Claremore 918.283.6262 • McAlester
918.423.5951 • Muskogee 918.687.2533

R: 181　**T:** 5th　75%
Elected Year: 2012

OREGON

OREGON

🏛 **Governor Katherine Brown** ("brown")   p 503.378.4582

160 State Capitol
900 Court St. NE, Rm. 160
Salem, OR 97301-4047
Website oregon.gov
Fax 503.378.8970
Term Ends 2023

C: Salem
P: 4,190,713 (27)
A: 95,988.05 mi² (10th)

U.S. Senators
Ron Wyden, **D**
Jeff A. Merkley, **D**
U.S. Representatives
01 / Suzanne M. Bonamici, **D**
02 / Cliff S. Bentz, R
03 / Earl Blumenauer, **D**
04 / Peter A. DeFazio, **D**
05 / Kurt Schrader, **D**

🏛 **Sen. Jeff A. Merkley** (MURK-lee)   D-OR-Jr.   p 202.224.3753

Rm. HSOB 531 **Web.** merkley.senate.gov   **f** 202.228.3997
Bio. 10/24/1956 • Myrtle Creek • State Legislator • Stanford
Univ. (CA), B.A., 1979; Princeton Univ. Woodrow Wilson
School of Public and International Affairs (NJ), M.P.P., 1982 •
Lutheran • M. Mary Sorteberg, 2 ch **Cmte.** Appropriations
• Budget • Environment & Public Works • Foreign Relations
• Joint Congressional-Executive Commission on China •
Rules & Administration
CoS. Michael Zamore   **LD.** Elvia Montoya
Sched. Carly Vandegrift   **PS.** Martina McLennan
R: 35 **T:** 3rd 57%   **Dist. Off.** Baker City 541.278.1129 • Bend 541.318.1298 •
Elected Year: 2008   Eugene 541.465.6750 • Medford 541.608.9102 • Portland
Next Election: 2026   503.326.3386 • Salem 503.362.8102

🏛 **Sen. Ron Wyden** (WY-duhn)   D-OR-Sr.   p 202.224.5244

Rm. DSOB 221 **Web.** wyden.senate.gov   **f** 202.228.2717
Bio. 05/03/1949 • Wichita • Senior Citizen Advocacy Group
State Director; Professor, Gerontology • Stanford Univ. (CA),
B.A., 1971; Univ. of Oregon Law School, J.D., 1974 • Jewish
• M. Nancy Bass Wyden, 5 ch (2 from previous marriage)
Cmte. Budget • Energy & Natural Resources • Finance •
Intelligence • Joint Taxation
CoS. Jeffrey Michels   **LD.** Isaiah Akin
Sched. Aliyah Chance   **PS.** Keith Chu
R: 8 **T:** 5th 57%   **Dist. Off.** Bend 541.330.9142 • Eugene 541.431.0229 • La
Elected Year: 1996   Grande 541.962.7691 • Medford 541.858.5122 • Portland
Next Election: 2022   503.326.7525 • Salem 503.589.4555

🏛 **Rep. Cliff S. Bentz** (behnts)   R-OR-02   p 202.225.6730

Rm. LHOB 1239 **Web.** bentz.house.gov   **f** 202.225.5774
Bio. 01/12/1952 • Salem • Roman Catholic • M. Dr. Lindsay
Norman, 2 ch **Cmte.** Judiciary • Natural Resources
CoS. Nick Strader   **LD.** Katelyn Pay
Sched. Maggie Sayers   **PS.** Nick Clemens
Dist. Off. Medford 541.776.4646 • Ontario 541.709.2040

R: 372 **T:** 1st 60%
Elected Year: 2020

OREGON

⚓ Rep. Earl Blumenauer (BLOO-meh-nou-ur) D-OR-03 p 202.225.4811

Rm. LHOB 1111 **Web.** **f** 202.225.8941
blumenauer.house.gov
Bio. 08/16/1948 • Portland • Attorney • Northwestern
Law School, Lewis and Clark College (OR), B.A., 1970;
Northwestern Law School, Lewis and Clark College (OR),
J.D., 1976 • Unspecified/Other • M. Margaret Kirkpatrick
Blumenauer, 2 ch **Cmte.** Ways & Means
CoS. Willie Smith (CD) **LD.** Jon Bosworth
Sched. Zoe Walker **PS.** Janine Kritschgau
Dist. Off. Portland 503.231.2300

R: 32 **T:** 14th 73%
Elected Year: 1995

⚓ Rep. Suzanne M. Bonamici (baw-nuh-MEE-chee) D-OR-01 p 202.225.0855

Rm. RHOB 2231 **Web.** bonamici.house.gov **f** 202.225.9497
Bio. 10/14/1954 • Detroit • State Legislator; Attorney •
Lane Community College (OR), A.A., 1978; Univ. of Oregon,
B.A., 1980; Univ. of Oregon, B.A., 1980; Univ. of Oregon
Law School, J.D., 1983 • Episcopalian • M. Michael H.
Simon, 2 ch **Cmte.** Education & Labor • Science, Space &
Technology • Select Committee on the Climate Crisis
CoS. Rachael Bornstein **LD.** Joshua Izaak
Sched. Audrey Hazel **PS.** Natalie Crofts
Dist. Off. Beaverton 503.469.6010

R: 155 **T:** 6th 65%
Elected Year: 2011

⚓ Rep. Peter A. DeFazio (deh-FAH-zee-o) D-OR-04 p 202.225.6416

Rm. RHOB 2134 **Web.** defazio.house.gov **f** 202.226.3493
Bio. 05/27/1947 • Needham • Congressional Aide; Chair
Lane County Commission • Air Force 1967-71 • Tufts
Univ. (MA), B.A., 1969; Univ. of Oregon, M.S., 1977 •
Roman Catholic • M. Myrnie Daut **Cmte.** Transportation &
Infrastructure
CoS. Kristie M. Greco **LD.** Bobby Puckett
    Johnson
Sched. Kitra Moeny **PS.** King Green-Newton
Dist. Off. Coos Bay 541.269.2609 • Eugene 541.465.6732 •
    Roseburg 541.440.3523

R: 6 **T:** 18th 52%
Elected Year: 1986

⚓ Rep. Kurt Schrader (SHRAY-dur) D-OR-05 p 202.225.5711

Rm. RHOB 2431 **Web.** schrader.house.gov **f** 202.225.5699
Bio. 10/19/1951 • Bridgeport • State Legislator; Veterinarian
• Cornell Univ. (NY), B.A., 1973; Univ. of Illinois, B.A., 1975;
Univ. of Illinois College of Veterinary Medicine (IL), D.V.M.,
1977 • Episcopalian • D., 5 ch **Cmte.** Energy & Commerce
CoS. Chris Huckleberry **LD.** Kelly Nickel
Sched. Phoebe Miner **PS.** Molly Prescott
Dist. Off. Oregon City 503.557.1324 • Salem 503.588.9100

R: 115 **T:** 7th 52%
Elected Year: 2008

PENNSYLVANIA

⚓ Governor Thomas W. Wolf (wulf) p 717.787.2500

Main Capitol Building, Rm. 225 **C:** Harrisburg
Harrisburg, PA 17120 **P:** 12,807,060 (5)
Website pa.gov **A:** 44,742.66 mi² (32nd)
Fax 717.772.8284
Term Ends 2023
Lt. Governor
John Fetterman, D

U.S. Senators
Bob Casey, D
Pat J. Toomey, R
U.S. Representatives
01 / Brian Fitzpatrick, R
02 / Brendan F. Boyle, D
03 / Dwight Evans, D
04 / Madeleine Dean, D
05 / Mary Gay Scanlon, D
06 / Chrissy Jampoler Houlahan,
    D
07 / Susan Ellis Wild, D
08 / Matt Cartwright, D
09 / Dan P. Meuser, R

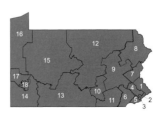

PENNSYLVANIA

PENNSYLVANIA

10 / Scott Perry, R	14 / Guy L. Reschenthaler, R
11 / Lloyd K. Smucker, R	15 / Glenn W. Thompson, R
12 / Fred B. Keller, R	16 / Mike Kelly, R
13 / John Joyce, R	17 / Conor Lamb, D
	18 / Mike F. Doyle, D

Sen. Bob Casey Jr. (KAY-see) — D-PA-Sr. — p 202.224.6324

Rm. RSOB 393 **Web.** casey.senate.gov **f** 202.228.0604
Bio. 04/13/1960 • Scranton • Teacher; Attorney • College of The Holy Cross (MA), B.A., 1982; Catholic Univ. of America (DC), J.D., 1988 • Roman Catholic • M. Terese Foppiano Casey, 4 ch; 1 gr-ch **Cmte.** Aging • Finance • Health, Education, Labor & Pensions • Intelligence
CoS. Kristen E. Gentile **LD.** Derek J. Miller
Sched. Landy Wade **PS.** Mairead Lynn
Dist. Off. Allentown 610.782.9470 • Bellefonte 814.357.0314 • Erie 814.874.5080 • Harrisburg 717.231.7540 • Philadelphia 215.405.9660 • Pittsburgh 412.803.7370 • Scranton 570.941.0930

R: 26 **T:** 3rd 56%
Elected Year: 2006
Next Election: 2024

Sen. Pat J. Toomey (TOO-mee) — R-PA-Jr. — p 202.224.4254

Rm. DSOB 455 **Web.** toomey.senate.gov **f** 202.228.0284
Bio. 11/17/1961 • Providence • Harvard Univ., B.A., 1984 • Roman Catholic • M. Kris Toomey, 3 ch **Cmte.** Banking, Housing & Urban Affairs • Budget • Finance • Joint Congressional Oversight Commission
CoS. Daniel Brandt **LD.** Theo Merkel
Sched. Danielle Quercia **PS.** Amy Hasenberg
Dist. Off. Allentown 610.434.1444 • Erie 814.453.3010 • Harrisburg 717.782.3951 • Johnstown 814.266.5970 • Philadelphia 215.241.1090 • Pittsburgh 412.803.3501 • Wilkes-Barre 570.820.4088

R: 44 **T:** 2nd 49%
Elected Year: 2010
Next Election: 2022

Rep. Brendan F. Boyle (BOY-uhl) — D-PA-02 — p 202.225.6111

Rm. LHOB 1133 **Web.** boyle.house.gov **f** 202.226.0611
Bio. 02/06/1977 • Philadelphia • Notre Dame Univ. St. Mary's College, B.A., 1999; Harvard Univ. John F. Kennedy School of Government (MA), M.P.P., 2005 • Roman Catholic • M. Jennifer Morgan, 1 ch **Cmte.** Budget • Ways & Means
CoS. Tim Barnes **LD.** Anthony Bellmon
Sched. Naomi Fecher-Davis **PS.** Sean Tobin
Dist. Off. Philadelphia 215.426.4616 • Philadelphia 215.982.1156

R: 210 **T:** 4th 73%
Elected Year: 2018

Rep. Matt Cartwright (KART-rite) — D-PA-08 — p 202.225.5546

Rm. RHOB 2102 **Web.** cartwright.house.gov **f** 202.226.0996
Bio. 05/01/1961 • Erie • Hamilton College (NY), A.B., 1983; Univ. of Pennsylvania, J.D., 1986 • Roman Catholic • M. Marion Munley, 2 ch **Cmte.** Appropriations
CoS. Hunter Ridgway **LD.** Rachel Cohen
Sched. Mia Robertson **PS.** Colleen Gerrity (CD)
Dist. Off. Hawley 570.576.8005 • Hazleton 570.751.0050 • Tannersville 570.355.1818

R: 166 **T:** 5th 52%
Elected Year: 2018

Rep. Madeleine Dean (deen) — D-PA-04 — p 202.225.4731

Rm. CHOB 120 **Web.** dean.house.gov **f** 202.225.0088
Bio. 06/06/1959 • Glenside • Montgomery County Community College, B.A.; La Salle Univ. (PA), B.A., 1981; Widener Univ. (PA), J.D., 1984 • Christian Church • M. Patrick J. Cunnane, 3 ch; 1 gr-ch **Cmte.** Financial Services • Judiciary
CoS. Colleen Carlos **LD.** Christopher McCann
Sched. Megan Ruane **PS.** Tim Mack
Dist. Off. Glenside 215.884.4300 • Norristown 610.382.1250

R: 308 **T:** 2nd 60%
Elected Year: 2018

PENNSYLVANIA

⚐ Rep. Mike F. Doyle Jr. (DOY-ull)   D-PA-18   p 202.225.2135

Rm. CHOB 270 **Web.** doyle.house.gov   **f** 202.225.3084
Bio. 08/05/1953 • Swissvale • Insurance Agency Co-owner; Congressional Aide • Pennsylvania State Univ., B.S., 1975 • Roman Catholic • M. Susan Erlandson Doyle, 4 ch **Cmte.** Energy & Commerce
CoS. David G. Lucas   **LD.** Kate Werley
Sched. Ellen Young   **PS.** Matt Dinkel
Dist. Off. Monroeville 412.856.3375

R: 29 **T:** 14th 69%
Elected Year: 2018

⚐ Rep. Dwight Evans (EH-vuhnz)   D-PA-03   p 202.225.4001

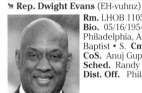

Rm. LHOB 1105 **Web.** evans.house.gov   **f** 202.225.5392
Bio. 05/16/1954 • Philadelphia • Community College of Philadelphia, A.A., 1973; La Salle College (PA), B.A., 1975 • Baptist • S. **Cmte.** Small Business • Ways & Means
CoS. Anuj Gupta (CD)   **LD.** Gillian Mueller
Sched. Randy Love   **PS.** Ben Turner
Dist. Off. Philadelphia 215.276.0340

R: 241 **T:** 4th 91%
Elected Year: 2018

▦ Rep. Brian Fitzpatrick (fits-PAT-rik)   R-PA-01   p 202.225.4276

Rm. CHOB 271 **Web.** brianfitzpatrick.house.gov   **f** 202.225.9511
Bio. 12/17/1973 • Levittown • LaSalle Univ., Bach. Deg., 1996; Pennsylvania State Univ., M.B.A., 2001; Pennsylvania State Univ. School of Law, J.D., 2001 • Roman Catholic • S. **Cmte.** Foreign Affairs • Joint Security & Cooperation in Europe • Permanent Select on Intelligence • Transportation & Infrastructure
CoS. Joseph Knowles
Sched. Emery Boylan   **PS.** Lauren Offenberg
Dist. Off. Langhorne 215.579.8102

R: 261 **T:** 3rd 57%
Elected Year: 2018

⚐ Rep. Chrissy Jampoler Houlahan (HOO-luh-han)D-PA-06   p 202.225.4315

Rm. LHOB 1218 **Web.** houlahan.house.gov
Bio. 06/05/1967 • Patuxent River • Stanford Univ. (CA), B.S., 1989; Massachusetts Institute of Technology, M.S., 1994 • Unspecified/Other • M. Bart Houlahan, 2 ch **Cmte.** Armed Services • Foreign Affairs • Small Business
CoS. Michelle Dorothy
Sched. Madeline Douglas
Dist. Off. Reading 610.295.0815 • West Chester 610.883.5050

R: 323 **T:** 2nd 56%
Elected Year: 2018

▦ Rep. John Joyce (joyss)   R-PA-13   p 202.225.2431

Rm. LHOB 1221 **Web.** johnjoyce.house.gov **f** 202.225.2486
Bio. 02/08/1957 • Altoona • Pennsylvania State Univ., Bach. Deg., 1979; Temple Univ. (PA), M.D., 1983 • Catholic • M. Alice Joyce, 3 ch **Cmte.** Energy & Commerce
CoS. Dante Cutrona   **LD.** Matt Tucker
Sched. Mallory Grove   **PS.** Ben Mullany
Dist. Off. Abbottstown 717.357.6320 • Altoona 814.656.6081 • Chambersburg 717.753.6344 • Somerset 814.485.6020

R: 325 **T:** 2nd 74%
Elected Year: 2018

▦ Rep. Fred B. Keller (KEH-lur)   R-PA-12   p 202.225.3731

Rm. LHOB 1717 **Web.** keller.house.gov   **f** 202.225.9594
Bio. 10/23/1965 • Page • Christian Church • M. Kay Keller, 2 ch; 1 gr-ch **Cmte.** Education & Labor • Oversight & Reform
CoS. Jon Anzur   **LD.** Kevin O'Keefe
Sched. Monica Zagame   **PS.** Nick Barley
Dist. Off. Selinsgrove 570.374.9469 • Tunkhannock 570.996.6550 • Williamsport 570.322.3961

R: 364 **T:** 2nd 71%
Elected Year: 2018

PENNSYLVANIA

◪ Rep. Mike Kelly Jr. (KEH-lee) R-PA-16 p 202.225.5406

Rm. LHOB 1707 **Web.** kelly.house.gov **f** 202.225.3103
Bio. 05/10/1948 • Pittsburgh • Univ. of Notre Dame (IN),
B.A., 1970 • Roman Catholic • M. Victoria Kelly, 4 ch; 10 gr-ch **Cmte.** Ways & Means
CoS. Tim Butler **LD.** Lori Prater
Sched. Jack Ciesinski **PS.** Matt Knoeller
Dist. Off. Erie 814.454.8190

R: 143 **T:** 6th 59%
Elected Year: 2018

⚑ Rep. Conor Lamb (lam) D-PA-17 p 202.225.2301

Rm. LHOB 1224 **Web.** lamb.house.gov **f** 202.225.1844
Bio. 06/27/1984 • Washington • Univ. of Pennsylvania, B.A.,
2006; Univ. of Pennsylvania Law School, J.D., 2009 • Catholic
• M. Hayley Haldeman **Cmte.** Science, Space & Technology
• Transportation & Infrastructure • Veterans' Affairs
CoS. Craig Kwiecinski **LD.** Christopher L. Bowman
Sched. Carly Krystyniak **PS.** Reenie Kuhlman (CD)
Dist. Off. Monaca 724.206.4860 • Pittsburgh 412.871.2060

R: 288 **T:** 3rd 51%
Elected Year: 2018

◪ Rep. Dan P. Meuser (MYOO-zur) R-PA-09 p 202.225.6511

Rm. CHOB 414 **Web.** meuser.house.gov
Bio. 02/10/1954 • Babylon • Cornell Univ. (NY), B.A., 1986;
Cornell Univ. (NY), B.A., 1986 • Catholic • M. Shelley Van
Acker, 3 ch **Cmte.** Foreign Affairs • Small Business
CoS. Tyler Menzler **LD.** Blake Deeley
  PS. Mary Owens
Dist. Off. Palmyra 717.473.5375 • Pottsville 570.871.6370 •
Reading 610.568.9959

R: 333 **T:** 2nd 66%
Elected Year: 2018

◪ Rep. Scott Perry (PAIR-ree) R-PA-10 p 202.225.5836

Rm. RHOB 2160 **Web.** perry.house.gov **f** 202.226.1000
Bio. 05/27/1962 • San Diego • U.S. Army War College (PA),
M.S.; Pennsylvania State Univ., B.S., 1991 • Church of the
United Brethren in Christ • M. Christy Perry, 2 ch **Cmte.**
Foreign Affairs • Transportation & Infrastructure
CoS. Lauren Muglia **LD.** Patrick Schilling
Sched. Carol Wiest (CD) **PS.** Jay Ostrich (CD)
Dist. Off. Harrisburg 717.603.4980 • York 717.893.7868

R: 182 **T:** 5th 53%
Elected Year: 2018

◪ Rep. Guy L. Reschenthaler (REH-shen-thaw-lur) R-PA-14 p 202.225.2065

Rm. CHOB 409 **Web.** **f** 202.225.5709
reschenthaler.house.gov
Bio. 04/17/1983 • Pittsburgh • Penn State Univ. Dickinson
School of Law (PA), B.A., 2004; Duquesne Univ., J.D., 2007
• Christian Church • S. **Cmte.** Appropriations • Rules •
Select Committee on the Modernization of Congress
CoS. Aaron R. Bonnaure **LD.** Emily Ackerman
Sched. Ashley Bailey
Dist. Off. Greensburg 724.219.4200 • Washington
724.206.4800

R: 343 **T:** 2nd 65%
Elected Year: 2018

⚑ Rep. Mary Gay Scanlon (scan-lin) D-PA-05 p 202.225.2011

Rm. LHOB 1227 **Web.** scanlon.house.gov **f** 202.226.0280
Bio. 08/30/1959 • Syracuse • Colgate Univ., B.A., 1980;
Univ. of Pennsylvania Law School, J.D., 1984 • Catholic
• M. Mark Scanlon, 3 ch **Cmte.** Administration •
Communications Standards Commission • Judiciary • Rules
CoS. Roddy Flynn **LD.** Armita Pedramrazi
Sched. Maddie Daly **PS.** Lauren Cox
Dist. Off. Chester 610.626.1913

R: 294 **T:** 3rd 65%
Elected Year: 2018

⚑ Rep. Lloyd K. Smucker (SMUH-kur)   R-PA-11   p 202.225.2411

Rm. CHOB 302 **Web.** smucker.house.gov   **f** 202.225.2013
Bio. 01/23/1964 • Lancaster • Lutheran • M. Cynthia
Smucker, 3 ch **Cmte.** Budget • Ways & Means
CoS. Kate Bonner   **LD.** Noelle Verhelst
Sched. Karen Cologne   **PS.** Eric Reath (CD)
Dist. Off. Hanover 717.969.6132 • Red Lion 717.969.6133

R: 281   **T:** 3rd   63%
Elected Year: 2016

⚑ Rep. Glenn W. Thompson Jr. (TOMP-suhn)   R-PA-15   p 202.225.5121

Rm. CHOB 400 **Web.** thompson.house.gov   **f** 202.225.5796
Bio. 07/27/1959 • Bellefonte • School Board Member;
Health Care Executive • Pennsylvania State Univ., B.S., 1981;
Temple Univ. (PA), M.Ed., 1998 • Protestant - Unspecified
Christian • M. Penny Thompson, 3 ch **Cmte.** Agriculture •
Education & Labor
CoS. Matthew Brennan   **LD.** Nick Rockwell
Sched. Lindsay Reusser   **PS.** Maddison Stone
Dist. Off. Ebensburg 814.419.8583

R: 116   **T:** 7th   74%
Elected Year: 2018

🐎 Rep. Susan Ellis Wild ("wild")   D-PA-07   p 202.225.6411

Rm. LHOB 1027 **Web.** wild.house.gov
Bio. 06/07/1957 • Wiesbaden • American Univ. (DC), B.A.,
1978; George Washington Univ. (DC), J.D., 1982 • Jewish •
D., 2 ch **Cmte.** Education & Labor • Ethics • Foreign Affairs
• Science, Space & Technology
CoS. Jed Ober   **LD.** Erin Meegan
Sched. Jessica Lindsay
Dist. Off. Allentown 484.781.6000 • Easton 610.333.1170 •
Stroudsburg 570.807.0333

R: 295   **T:** 3rd   52%
Elected Year: 2018

RHODE ISLAND

🐎 Governor Daniel McKee (mih-KEE)   p 401.222.2371

82 Smith St.   **C:** Providence
Providence, RI 02903   **P:** 1,057,315 (45)
Website ri.gov   **A:** 1,033.98 mi^2 (51st)
Fax 401.222.2012
Term Ends 2023
Lt. Governor
Sabina Matos, **D**

U.S. Senators
Jack F. Reed, **D**
Sheldon Whitehouse, **D**
U.S. Representatives
01 / David Cicilline, **D**
02 / Jim R. Langevin, **D**

🐎 Sen. Jack F. Reed (reed)   D-RI-Sr.   p 202.224.4642

Rm. HSOB 728 **Web.** reed.senate.gov   **f** 202.224.4680
Bio. 11/12/1949 • Cranston • Attorney; Professor at West
Point • Army 1967-79 • U.S. Military Academy (NY), B.S.,
1971; Harvard Univ. John F. Kennedy School of Government
(MA), M.P.P., 1973; Harvard Univ. School of Law (MA), J.D.,
1982 • Roman Catholic • M. Julia Hart Reed, 1 ch **Cmte.**
Appropriations • Armed Services • Banking, Housing &
Urban Affairs • Intelligence
CoS. Neil Campbell
Sched. Cara Gilbert   **PS.** Chip Unruh
Dist. Off. Cranston 401.943.3100 • Providence
401.528.5200

R: 10   **T:** 5th   67%
Elected Year: 1996
Next Election: 2026

RHODE ISLAND

🐦 Sen. Sheldon Whitehouse (WHITE-house)   D-RI-Jr.   p 202.224.2921

Rm. HSOB 530 **Web.** whitehouse.senate.gov **f** 202.228.6362
Bio. 10/20/1955 • New York City • Attorney • Yale Univ.
(CT), B.Arch., 1978; Univ. of Virginia Law School, J.D., 1982 •
Episcopalian • M. Sandra Thornton Whitehouse, 2 ch **Cmte.**
Budget • Environment & Public Works • Finance • Joint
Security & Cooperation in Europe • Judiciary
CoS. Monalisa Dugue   **LD.** Amalea Smirniotopoulos
Sched. Leah Seigle   **PS.** Richard Davidson
Dist. Off. Providence 401.453.5294

R: 28   **T:** 3rd   61%
Elected Year: 2006
Next Election: 2024

🐦 Rep. David Cicilline (sih-sih-LEE-nee)   D-RI-01   p 202.225.4911

Rm. RHOB 2233 **Web.** cicilline.house.gov   **f** 202.225.3290
Bio. 07/15/1961 • Providence • Brown Univ. (RI), B.A.,
1983; Georgetown Univ. Law Center (DC), J.D., 1986 •
Jewish • S. **Cmte.** Foreign Affairs • Judiciary
CoS. Peter Karafotas   **LD.** Megan Garcia
Sched. Leo Confalone   **PS.** Jennifer Bell
Dist. Off. Pawtucket 401.729.5600

R: 129   **T:** 6th   71%
Elected Year: 2010

🐦 Rep. Jim R. Langevin (LAN-jeh-vin)   D-RI-02   p 202.225.2735

Rm. RHOB 2077 **Web.** langevin.house.gov   **f** 202.225.5976
Bio. 04/22/1964 • Providence • RI Secretary of State; State
Representative • Rhode Island College, B.A., 1990; Harvard
Univ. John F. Kennedy School of Government (MA), M.P.A.,
1994 • Roman Catholic • S. **Cmte.** Armed Services •
Homeland Security
CoS. Nick JM Leiserson   **LD.** Caroline Goodson
Sched. Mark Galinsky   **PS.** Matt Fidel
Dist. Off. Warwick 401.732.9400

R: 53   **T:** 11th   58%
Elected Year: 2000

SOUTH CAROLINA

▥ Governor Henry McMaster (mik-MASS-tur)   p 803.734.2100

Office of the Governor
1205 Pendleton St.
Columbia, SC 29201
Website sc.gov
Fax 803.734.5167
Term Ends 2023
Lt. Governor
Pamela Evette, R

C: Columbia
P: 5,084,127 (23)
A: 30,060.74 mi^2 (40th)

U.S. Senators
Lindsey Graham, R
Tim E. Scott, R
U.S. Representatives
01 / Nancy Mace, R
02 / Joe Wilson, R
03 / Jeff D. Duncan, R
04 / William R. Timmons, R
05 / Ralph W. Norman, R
06 / James E. Clyburn, D
07 / Tom Rice, R

♙ Sen. Lindsey Graham (gram) R-SC-Sr. p 202.224.5972

Rm. RSOB 290 **Web.** lgraham.senate.gov **f** 202.224.3808
Bio. 07/09/1955 • Central • U.S. Representative • Air Force
Judge Advocate General Corps 1982-88; South Carolina Air
National Guard 1989-95, Air Force Reserve 1995-present •
Univ. of South Carolina, B.S., 1977; Univ. of South Carolina,
M.P.A., 1978; Univ. of South Carolina School of Law, J.D.,
1981 • Baptist • S. **Cmte.** Appropriations • Budget •
Environment & Public Works • Judiciary
CoS. Richard S. Perry **LD.** Craig R. Abele
Sched. Edward Mercer (CD) **PS.** Alice James
Dist. Off. Columbia 803.933.0112 • Florence 843.669.1505
• Greenville 864.250.1417 • Mount Pleasant 843.849.3887 •
Pendleton 864.646.4090 • Rock Hill 803.366.2828

R: 19 **T:** 4th 54%
Elected Year: 2002
Next Election: 2026

♙ Sen. Tim E. Scott (skaht) R-SC-Jr. p 202.224.6121

Rm. HSOB 104 **Web.** scott.senate.gov **f** 202.228.5143
Bio. 09/19/1965 • North Charleston • Charleston Southern
Univ. (SC), B.S., 1988 • Evangelical • S. **Cmte.** Aging •
Banking, Housing & Urban Affairs • Finance • Health,
Education, Labor & Pensions
CoS. Jennifer DeCasper **LD.** Chuck Cogar
Sched. Molly Venegas **PS.** Dominique G. McKay
Dist. Off. Columbia 803.771.6112 • Greenville
864.233.5366 • North Charleston 843.727.4525

R: 52 **T:** 3rd 61%
Elected Year: 2013
Next Election: 2022

♙ Rep. James E. Clyburn (KLY-burn) D-SC-06 p 202.225.3315

Rm. CHOB 274 **Web.** clyburn.house.gov **f** 202.225.2313
Bio. 07/21/1940 • Sumter • SC Human Affairs
Commissioner; Gubernatorial Assistant • South Carolina
State Univ., B.S., 1962; Univ. of South Carolina School of Law,
B.S., 1974 • African Methodist Episcopal • W. Emily England
Clyburn, 3 ch; 4 gr-ch
CoS. Yelberton R. Watkins **LD.** Ashleigh R. Wilson
Sched. Lindy Birch Kelly **PS.** Hope Derrick
Dist. Off. Columbia 803.799.1100 • Kingstree 843.355.1211
• Santee 803.854.4700

R: 18 **T:** 15th 68%
Elected Year: 1992

♙ Rep. Jeff D. Duncan (DUN-kuhn) R-SC-03 p 202.225.5301

Rm. RHOB 2229 **Web.** jeffduncan.house.gov **f** 202.225.3216
Bio. 01/07/1966 • Greenville • Clemson Univ. (SC), B.A.,
1988 • Baptist • M. Melody Duncan, 3 ch **Cmte.** Energy &
Commerce
CoS. Allen Klump **LD.** Joshua Gross
Sched. Thomas McAllister **PS.** Emily Wood
Dist. Off. Anderson 864.224.7401 • Clinton 864.681.1028

R: 132 **T:** 6th 71%
Elected Year: 2010

♙ Rep. Nancy Mace (mace) R-SC-01 p 202.225.3176

Rm. CHOB 212 **Web.** mace.house.gov
Bio. 12/04/1977 • Fayetteville • The Citadel Univ., B.A.,
1999; Univ. of Georgia, M.S., 2004 • Christian - Non-
Denominational • D. Curtis Jackson, 2 ch **Cmte.** Oversight
& Reform • Transportation & Infrastructure • Veterans'
Affairs
CoS. Mara Mellstrom **LD.** Dan Hanlon
Sched. Jazmin Anguiano
Dist. Off. Beaufort 843.521.2530 • Charleston 843.352.7572

R: 403 **T:** 1st 51%
Elected Year: 2020

🏛 Rep. Ralph W. Norman Jr. (NOR-muhn)　　　R-SC-05　　p 202.225.5501

Rm. CHOB 569　**Web.** norman.house.gov　**f** 202.225.0464
Bio. 06/20/1953 • York County • Presbyterian College (SC),
B.S., 1975 • Presbyterian • M. Elaine Rice, 4 ch; 16 gr-ch
Cmte. Homeland Security • Oversight & Reform
CoS. Mark Piland　　　　　**LD.** Jake Hilkin
Sched. Marie Price　　　　**PS.** Alex Crane
Dist. Off. Rock Hill 803.327.1114

R: 286　**T:** 3rd　60%
Elected Year: 2016

🏛 Rep. Tom Rice Jr. ("rice")　　　　　R-SC-07　　p 202.225.9895

Rm. CHOB 460　**Web.** rice.house.gov　**f** 202.225.9690
Bio. 08/04/1957 • Charleston • Univ. of South Carolina,
B.S., 1979; Univ. of South Carolina, Mast. Deg., 1982; Univ. of
South Carolina School of Law, J.D., 1982 • Episcopalian • M.
Wrenzie Rice, 3 ch　**Cmte.** Ways & Means
CoS. Jennifer Watson　　　**LD.** Philipp Clarke
Sched. Charlotte Bureau
Dist. Off. Florence 843.679.9781 • Myrtle Beach
843.445.6459

R: 185　**T:** 5th　62%
Elected Year: 2012

🏛 Rep. William R. Timmons IV (TIH-muhnz)　　R-SC-04　　p 202.225.6030

Rm. CHOB 267　**Web.** timmons.house.gov
Bio. 04/30/1984 • Greenville • George Washington Univ.
(DC), B.A., 2006; Univ. of South Carolina, Mast. Deg., 2009;
Univ. of South Carolina, J.D., 2010 • Church of Christ •
S.　Cmte. Financial Services • Select Committee on the
Modernization of Congress
CoS. Moutray McLaren　　　**LD.** Ann Thomas G.
　　　　　　　　　　　　　　　　　Johnston
Sched. Olivia Widenhouse　**PS.** Heather K. Smith
Dist. Off. Greer 864.241.0175

R: 356　**T:** 2nd　62%
Elected Year: 2018

🏛 Rep. Joe Wilson (WILL-suhn)　　　　　R-SC-02　　p 202.225.2452

Rm. LHOB 1436　**Web.** joewilson.house.gov　**f** 202.225.2455
Bio. 07/31/1947 • Charleston • State Senator; Attorney,
Founding Partner; Judge, Springdale • Army Reserve
1972-75; SC Army National Guard 1975-03 • Washington and
Lee Univ. (VA), B.A., 1969; Univ. of South Carolina, J.D., 1972
• Presbyterian • M. Roxanne Dusenbury McCrory Wilson, 4
ch; 7 gr-ch　**Cmte.** Armed Services • Education & Labor •
Foreign Affairs • Joint Security & Cooperation in Europe
CoS. Jonathan Day　　　　**LD.** Drew Kennedy
Sched. Stephanie Pendarvis　**PS.** David Snider
Dist. Off. Aiken 803.642.6416 • West Columbia
803.939.0041

R: 58　**T:** 11th　56%
Elected Year: 2000

🏛 Governor　Kristi Lynn Noem (noam)　　　　　p 605.773.3212

State Capitol
500 E. Capitol Ave.
Pierre, SD 57501-5070
Website sd.gov
Fax 605.773.4711
Term Ends 2023
Lt. Governor
Larry Rhoden, R

C: Pierre
P: 882,235 (47)
A: 75,811.13 mi^2 (16th)

SOUTH DAKOTA

U.S. Senators
John Thune, R
Mike Rounds, R
U.S. Representatives
01 / Dusty Johnson, R

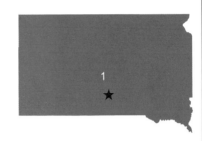

♦ Sen. Mike Rounds (rounz)   R-SD-Jr.   p 202.224.5842
Rm. HSOB 716 **Web.** rounds.senate.gov   **f** 202.224.7482
Bio. 10/24/1954 • Huron • Majority Leader, SD Senate;
Mbr., SD Senate • South Dakota State Univ., B.S., 1977 •
Roman Catholic • W. Jean Vedvei Rounds, 4 ch; 6 gr-ch
Cmte. Armed Services • Banking, Housing & Urban Affairs
• Foreign Relations • Indian Affairs • Veterans' Affairs
CoS. Kyle Chase   **LD.** Viraj Mirani
Sched. Erin Foth   **PS.** Dezmond Ward
Dist. Off. Aberdeen 605.225.0366 • Pierre 605.224.1450 •
Rapid City 605.343.5035 • Sioux Falls 605.336.0486

R: 70 **T:** 2nd 66%
Elected Year: 2014
Next Election: 2026

♦ Sen. John Thune (thoon)   R-SD-Sr.   p 202.224.2321
Rm. DSOB 511 **Web.** thune.senate.gov   **f** 202.228.5429
Bio. 01/07/1961 • Pierre • U.S. Representative;
Congressional Aide • Biola Univ., B.B.A., 1983; Univ. of
South Dakota, M.B.A., 1984 • Evangelical • M. Kimberley Joe
Weems Thune, 2 ch; 2 gr-ch **Cmte.** Agriculture, Nutrition &
Forestry • Commerce, Science & Transportation • Finance
CoS. Ryan Nelson   **LD.** Jessica McBride
Sched. Amy Barrera   **PS.** Ryan Wrasse
Dist. Off. Aberdeen 605.225.8823 • Rapid City
605.348.7551 • Sioux Falls 605.334.9596

R: 21 **T:** 3rd 72%
Elected Year: 2004
Next Election: 2022

♦ Rep. Dusty Johnson (JAHN-suhn)   R-SD-01   p 202.225.2801
Rm. LHOB 1714 **Web.**
dustyjohnson.house.gov
Bio. 09/30/1976 • Pierre • Univ. of South Dakota, B.A., 1999
• Christian Church • M. Jacquelyn Johnson, 3 ch **Cmte.**
Agriculture • Transportation & Infrastructure
CoS. Andrew Christianson   **LD.** John Weber
Sched. Alana Lomis   **PS.** Jazmine Kemp
Dist. Off. Aberdeen 605.622.1060 • Rapid City
605.646.6454 • Sioux Falls 605.275.2868

R: 324 **T:** 2nd 81%
Elected Year: 2018

TENNESSEE

TENNESSEE

♦ Governor Bill Lee (lee)   p 615.741.2001

Tennessee State Capitol, 1st Floor **C:** Nashville
Nashville, TN 37243   **P:** 6,770,010 (16)
Website tennessee.gov   **A:** 41,234.92 mi^2 (34th)
Fax 615.532.9711
Term Ends 2023
Lt. Governor
Rand McNally, R

U.S. Senators
Marsha Blackburn, R
Bill Hagerty, R
U.S. Representatives
01 / Diana Harshbarger, R
02 / Tim Burchett, R
03 / Chuck J. Fleischmann, R
04 / Scott E. DesJarlais, R
05 / Jim H.S. Cooper, D
06 / John W. Rose, R
07 / Mark E. Green, R

08 / David F. Kustoff, **R**
09 / Steve I. Cohen, **D**

▥ Sen. Marsha Blackburn (BLAK-burn)　　　R-TN-Sr.　　p 202.224.3344

Rm. DSOB 357　**Web.** blackburn.senate.gov　**f** 202.228.0566
Bio. 06/06/1952 • Laurel • Small Business Owner; State
Senator • Mississippi State Univ., B.S., 1973 • Presbyterian
• M. Chuck Blackburn, 2 ch; 2 gr-ch　**Cmte.** Armed Services
• Commerce, Science & Transportation • Judiciary •
Veterans' Affairs
CoS. Sean Farrell　　　　**LD.** Jon M. Adame
Sched. Grace Burch (CD)　**PS.** Spencer Hurwitz
Dist. Off. Chattanooga 423.541.2939 • Jackson
731.660.3971 • Jonesborough 423.753.4009 • Knoxville
865.540.3781 • Memphis 901.527.9199 • Nashville
629.800.6600

R: 83　**T:** 1st　55%
Elected Year: 2018
Next Election: 2024

▥ Sen. Bill Hagerty (HAG-gur-tee)　　　R-TN-Jr.　　p 202.224.4944

Rm. RSOB 248　**Web.** hagerty.senate.gov　**f** 202.228.3398
Bio. 08/14/1959 • Gallatin • Vanderbilt Univ. (TN),
B.A., 1981; Vanderbilt Univ. Law School (TN), J.D.,
1984 • Episcopalian • M. Chrissy Hagerty, 4 ch　**Cmte.**
Appropriations • Banking, Housing & Urban Affairs • Foreign
Relations • Rules & Administration
CoS. Adam Telle　　　　**LD.** Natalie McIntyre
Sched. Betsy Van Dam　　**PS.** Julia Hahn
Dist. Off. Blountville 423.325.6240 • Chattanooga
423.752.5337 • Cookeville 931.981.4874 • Jackson
731.234.9358 • Knoxville 865.545.4253 • Memphis
901.544.4224 • Nashville 615.736.5129

R: 92　**T:** 1st　62%
Elected Year: 2020
Next Election: 2026

▥ Rep. Tim Burchett (BUR-chuht)　　　R-TN-02　　p 202.225.5435

Rm. LHOB 1122　**Web.** burchett.house.gov　**f** 202.225.6440
Bio. 08/25/1964 • Knoxville • Univ. of Tennessee, B.S., 1988
• Presbyterian • M. Kelly Burchett, 1 ch　**Cmte.** Foreign
Affairs • Transportation & Infrastructure
CoS. Michael Grider　　　**LD.** Kelsey Wolfgram
Sched. Canon Woodward　　**PS.** William Bensur
Dist. Off. Knoxville 865.523.3772 • Maryville 865.984.5464

R: 301　**T:** 2nd　68%
Elected Year: 2018

▥ Rep. Steve I. Cohen (KO-uhn)　　　D-TN-09　　p 202.225.3265

Rm. RHOB 2104　**Web.** cohen.house.gov　**f** 202.225.5663
Bio. 05/24/1949 • Memphis • Attorney; State Representative
• Vanderbilt Univ. (TN), B.A., 1971; Memphis State Univ.
- Cecil C. Humphreys School of Law (TN), J.D., 1973
• Jewish • S.　**Cmte.** Joint Security & Cooperation in
Europe • Judiciary • Natural Resources • Transportation &
Infrastructure
CoS. Marilyn Dillihay　　　**LD.** Reisha Buster
Sched. Patti Marsh　　　　**PS.** Bart Sullivan
Dist. Off. Memphis 901.544.4131

R: 91　**T:** 8th　77%
Elected Year: 2006

▥ Rep. Jim H.S. Cooper (KOO-pur)　　　D-TN-05　　p 202.225.4311

Rm. LHOB 1536　**Web.** cooper.house.gov　**f** 202.226.1035
Bio. 06/19/1954 • Nashville • Investment banker; Attorney •
Univ. of North Carolina Chapel Hill (UNC), B.A., 1975; Oxford
Univ. (England), M.A., 1977; Harvard Univ. Law School (MA),
J.D., 1980 • Episcopalian • W. Martha Hays Cooper, 3 ch
Cmte. Armed Services • Budget • Oversight & Reform •
Permanent Select on Intelligence
CoS. Jason J. Lumia　　　**LD.** Christopher Jerrolds
Sched. Olivia Lee　　　　**PS.** Katie Feldhaus (CD)
Dist. Off. Nashville 615.736.5295

R: 15　**T:** 10th　100%
Elected Year: 2002

ᛗ Rep. Scott E. DesJarlais (deh-zhar-LAY)   R-TN-04   p 202.225.6831

Rm. RHOB 2304 **Web.** desjarlais.house.gov **f** 202.226.5172
Bio. 02/21/1964 • Des Moines • Univ. of South Dakota, B.S.,
1987; Univ. of South Dakota School of Medicine, M.D., 1991
• Episcopalian • M. Amy DesJarlais, 4 ch (1 from previous
marriage) **Cmte.** Agriculture • Armed Services
CoS. Richard Vaughn   **LD.** Hannah Russell
Sched. MeKenna Carman   **PS.** Alex Swisher
Dist. Off. Cleveland 423.472.7500 • Columbia 931.381.9920
• Murfreesboro 615.896.1986 • Winchester 931.962.3180

R: 131 **T:** 6th 67%
Elected Year: 2010

ᛗ Rep. Chuck J. Fleischmann (FLYSH-muhn)   R-TN-03   p 202.225.3271

Rm. CHOB 462 **Web.** fleischmann.house.gov **f** 202.225.3494
Bio. 10/11/1962 • New York • Univ. of Illinois, B.A., 1983;
Univ. of Tennessee College of Law, Knoxville, J.D., 1986 •
Roman Catholic • M. Brenda Fleischmann, 3 ch **Cmte.**
Appropriations
CoS. James Hill Hippe   **LD.** Daniel Tidwell
Sched. Nicolle Miranda   **PS.** Justin Doil
Dist. Off. Athens 423.745.4671 • Chattanooga 423.756.2342
• Oak Ridge 865.576.1976

R: 133 **T:** 6th 67%
Elected Year: 2010

ᛗ Rep. Mark E. Green (green)   R-TN-07   p 202.225.2811

Rm. RHOB 2446 **Web.** markgreen.house.gov **f** 202.225.3004
Bio. 11/08/1964 • Jacksonville • U.S. Military Academy -
West Point (NY), B.S., 1986; Univ. of Southern California,
Mast. Deg., 1987; Wright State Univ. (OH), M.D., 1999 •
Christian Church • M. Camilla Joy Guenther, 2 ch **Cmte.**
Armed Services • Foreign Affairs
CoS. Stephen Siao   **LD.** Jay Kronzer
Sched. Jerrica Proferes   **PS.** Rachel del Guidice
Dist. Off. Clarksville 931.266.4483 • Franklin 629.223.6050

R: 318 **T:** 2nd 70%
Elected Year: 2018

ᛗ Rep. Diana Harshbarger (HARSH-bar-gur)   R-TN-01   p 202.225.6356

Rm. CHOB 167 **Web.** harshbarger.house.gov
Bio. 01/01/1960 • Kingsport • East Tennessee State Univ.,
Bach. Deg.; Mercer Univ. (GA), Doct. Deg. • Baptist • M.
Robert Harshbarger, 1 ch **Cmte.** Education & Labor •
Homeland Security
CoS. Zachary Rutherford   **LD.** Susan Falconer
                                  PS. Mark Mansour
Dist. Off. Kingsport 423.398.5186 • Morristown
423.254.1400

R: 393 **T:** 1st 75%
Elected Year: 2020

ᛗ Rep. David F. Kustoff (KUS-tawf)   R-TN-08   p 202.225.4714

Rm. CHOB 560   **f** 202.225.1765
Bio. 10/08/1966 • Memphis • Univ. of Memphis, B.B.A.,
1989; Memphis State Univ. - Cecil C. Humphreys School of
Law (TN), J.D., 1992 • Jewish • M. Roberta Kustoff, 2 ch
Cmte. Financial Services
CoS. Justin E. Melvin   **LD.** Eliana Goodman
Sched. Anderson   **PS.** Kate Kelly
Okoniewski
Dist. Off. Dyersburg 731.412.1037 • Jackson 731.423.4848
• Martin 731.412.1043 • Memphis 901.682.4422

R: 272 **T:** 3rd 69%
Elected Year: 2016

ᛗ Rep. John W. Rose (roaz)   R-TN-06   p 202.225.4231

Rm. LHOB 1124 **Web.** johnrose.house.gov **f** 202.225.6887
Bio. 02/23/1965 • Cookeville • Tennessee Tech Univ., B.S.,
1988; Purdue Univ. (IN), M.S., 1990; Vanderbilt Univ. (TN),
J.D., 1993 • Christian Church • M. Chelsea Rose, 2 ch (1
deceased) **Cmte.** Financial Services
CoS. Van Hilleary   **LD.** Jason Kroitor
Sched. Leah Bane
Dist. Off. Cookeville 931.854.9430 • Gallatin 615.206.8204

R: 344 **T:** 2nd 74%
Elected Year: 2018

TEXAS

TEXAS

Governor Greg Abbott (A-buht) p 512.463.2000

PO Box 12428
Austin, TX 78711-2428
Website texas.gov
Fax 512.463.5571
Term Ends 2023
Lt. Governor
Dan Patrick, R

C: Austin
P: 28,701,845 (2)
A: 261,231.59 mi^2 (2nd)

U.S. Senators
John Cornyn, R
Ted Cruz, R
U.S. Representatives
01 / Louie B. Gohmert, R
02 / Daniel Crenshaw, R
03 / Van Taylor, R
04 / Pat Fallon, R
05 / Lance Gooden, R
06 / Jake Ellzey, R
07 / Lizzie Pannill Fletcher, **D**
08 / Kevin P. Brady, R
09 / Al Green, **D**
10 / Michael T. McCaul, R
11 / August L. Pfluger, R
12 / Kay N. Granger, R
13 / Ronny L. Jackson, R
14 / Randy Weber, R
15 / Vicente Gonzalez, **D**
16 / Veronica Escobar, **D**
17 / Pete A. Sessions, R
18 / Sheila Jackson Lee, **D**
19 / Jodey Cook Arrington, R
20 / Joaquin Castro, **D**
21 / Chip Roy, R
22 / Troy E. Nehls, R
23 / Tony Gonzales, R
24 / Beth A. Van Duyne, R
25 / Roger Williams, R
26 / Michael C. Burgess, R
27 / Michael J. Cloud, R

28 / Henry R. Cuellar, **D**
29 / Sylvia R. Garcia, **D**
30 / Eddie Bernice Bernice Johnson, **D**
31 / John R. Carter, R
32 / Colin Allred, **D**
33 / Marc A. Veasey, **D**
34 / Filemon B. Vela, **D**
35 / Lloyd A. Doggett, **D**
36 / Brian Babin, R

Sen. John Cornyn III (KOR-nuhn) R-TX-Sr. p 202.224.2934

Rm. HSOB 517 **Web.** cornyn.senate.gov **f** 202.228.2856
Bio. 02/02/1952 • Houston • State Attorney General; State
Supreme Court Judge • Trinity Univ. (TX), B.A., 1973; St.
Mary's School of Law (TX), J.D., 1977; Univ. of Virginia,
LL.M., 1995 • Church of Christ • M. Sandra Hansen Cornyn,
2 ch **Cmte.** Finance • Intelligence • Judiciary
CoS. Beth Jafari   **LD.** Stephen A. Tausend
Sched. Emily Ziegler   **PS.** Drew Brandewie
Dist. Off. Austin 512.469.6034 • Dallas 972.239.1310
• Harlingen 956.423.0162 • Houston 713.572.3337 •
Lubbock 806.472.7533 • San Antonio 210.224.7485 • Tyler
903.593.0902

R: 17 **T:** 4th 54%
Elected Year: 2002
Next Election: 2026

Sen. Ted Cruz (krooz) R-TX-Jr. p 202.224.5922

Rm. RSOB 127A **Web.** cruz.senate.gov **f** 202.228.0755
Bio. 12/22/1970 • Calgary • Princeton Univ. (NJ), A.B.,
1992; Harvard Law School (MA), J.D., 1995 • Southern
Baptist • M. Heidi Nelson, 2 ch **Cmte.** Commerce, Science
& Transportation • Foreign Relations • Joint Economic •
Judiciary • Rules & Administration
CoS. Steve Chartan   **LD.** Chris Jaarda
Sched. Sara L. Sylvester **PS.** Dave Vasquez
Dist. Off. Austin 512.916.5834 • Dallas 214.599.8749
• Houston 713.718.3057 • McAllen 956.686.7339 • San
Antonio 210.340.2885 • Tyler 903.593.5130

R: 59 **T:** 2nd 51%
Elected Year: 2012
Next Election: 2024

↘ Rep. Colin Allred (ALL-red) D-TX-32 p 202.225.2231

Rm. CHOB 114 **Web.** allred.house.gov
Bio. 04/15/1983 • Dallas • Baylor Univ. (TX), B.A.,
2005; Univ. of California, Berkeley, J.D., 2014 • M. Allred
Alexandra, 2 ch **Cmte.** Foreign Affairs • Transportation &
Infrastructure • Veterans' Affairs
CoS. Paige Hutchinson **LD.** Whitley O'Neal
Sched. Katie Payne **PS.** Joshua Stewart
Dist. Off. Richardson 972.972.7949

R: 297 **T:** 2nd 52%
Elected Year: 2018

⚑ Rep. Jodey Cook Arrington (AIR-ring-ten) R-TX-19 p 202.225.4005

Rm. LHOB 1107 **Web.** arrington.house.gov **f** 202.225.9615
Bio. 03/09/1972 • Kansas City • Texas Tech Univ., B.A.,
1994; Texas Tech Univ., M.P.A., 1997 • Presbyterian • M.
Anne Arrington, 3 ch **Cmte.** Joint Economic • Select
Economic Disparity & Fairness in Growth • Ways & Means
CoS. Elle Ciapciak **LD.** Mason Champion
Sched. McKenzie
Hammonds (CD)
Dist. Off. Abilene 325.675.9779 • Lubbock 806.763.1611

R: 244 **T:** 3rd 75%
Elected Year: 2016

⚑ Rep. Brian Babin (BA-bin) R-TX-36 p 202.225.1555

Rm. RHOB 2236 **Web.** babin.house.gov **f** 202.226.0396
Bio. Port Arthur • Lamar Univ., B.S., 1973; Univ. of Texas-
Houston, D.D.S., 1976 • Southern Baptist • M. Roxanne
Babin, 5 ch; 16 gr-ch **Cmte.** Science, Space & Technology
• Transportation & Infrastructure
CoS. Steve Janushkowsky **LD.** Lauren Ziegler
Sched. Nicole White **PS.** Sarah Reese
Dist. Off. Dayton 832.780.0966 • Deer Park 832.780.0966 •
Orange 409.883.8075 • Woodville 409.331.8066

R: 207 **T:** 4th 74%
Elected Year: 2014

⚑ Rep. Kevin P. Brady (BRAY-dee) R-TX-08 p 202.225.4901

Rm. LHOB 1011 **Web.** kevinbrady.house.gov **f** 202.225.5524
Bio. 04/11/1955 • Vermillion • State Representative;
Chamber of Commerce Executive • Univ. of South Dakota,
B.S., 1990 • Roman Catholic • M. Cathy Brady, 2 ch **Cmte.**
Joint Taxation • Ways & Means
CoS. David W. Davis **LD.** James O'Brien
Sched. Ashley Doyle **PS.** Janet M. Montesi
Dist. Off. Conroe 936.441.5700 • Huntsville 936.439.9532

R: 34 **T:** 13th 73%
Elected Year: 1996

⚑ Rep. Michael C. Burgess (BUR-juhs) R-TX-26 p 202.225.7772

Rm. RHOB 2161 **Web.** burgess.house.gov **f** 202.225.2919
Bio. 12/23/1950 • Rochester • Obstetrician • North Texas
State Univ., Dallas, B.S., 1972; North Texas State Univ., M.S.,
1976; Univ. of Texas-Houston, M.D., 1977; Univ. of Texas,
M.S., 2000 • Anglican • M. Laura Burgess, 3 ch; 2 gr-ch
Cmte. Budget • Energy & Commerce • Rules
CoS. James A. Decker **LD.** Rachel Huggins
Sched. Amanda Baldwin **PS.** Sarah-Anne Voyles
Dist. Off. Lake Dallas 940.497.5031

R: 59 **T:** 10th 61%
Elected Year: 2002

⚑ Rep. John R. Carter (KAR-tur) R-TX-31 p 202.225.3864

Rm. RHOB 2208 **Web.** carter.house.gov **f** 202.225.5886
Bio. 11/06/1941 • Houston • Williamson County District
Judge; Attorney • Texas Technical Univ., B.A., 1964; Univ. of
Texas School of Law, J.D., 1969 • Lutheran • M. Erika Carter,
4 ch; 6 gr-ch **Cmte.** Appropriations
CoS. Jonas Miller (CD) **LD.** Grady Bourn
Sched. Breely Peterson **PS.** Emily Dowdell (CD)
Dist. Off. Round Rock 512.246.1600 • Temple 254.933.1392

R: 60 **T:** 10th 53%
Elected Year: 2002

TEXAS

🐦 Rep. Joaquin Castro (KAS-tro)   D-TX-20   p 202.225.3236

Rm. RHOB 2241 **Web.** castro.house.gov   **f** 202.225.1915
Bio. 09/16/1974 • San Antonio • Stanford Univ. (CA), A.B.,
1996; Harvard Univ. Law School (MA), J.D., 2000 • Roman
Catholic • M. Anna Flores, 2 ch   **Cmte.** Education & Labor
• Foreign Affairs • Permanent Select on Intelligence
CoS. Ben Thomas   **LD.** Kaitlyn Montan
Sched. Maggie Pillis   **PS.** Geneva Kropper
Dist. Off. San Antonio 210.348.8216

R: 167   **T:** 5th   65%
Elected Year: 2012

🏛 Rep. Michael J. Cloud ("cloud")   R-TX-27   p 202.225.7742

Rm. CHOB 512 **Web.** cloud.house.gov   **f** 202.226.1134
Bio. 05/13/1975 • Baton Rouge • Oral Roberts Univ., Bach.
Deg. • M. Rosel Cloud, 3 ch   **Cmte.** Agriculture • Oversight
& Reform
CoS. Hugh Fike   **LD.** Abby McHan
Sched. Shelby Boswell   **PS.** Jeremy Crane
Dist. Off. Corpus Christi 361.884.2222 • Victoria
361.894.6446

R: 290   **T:** 3rd   63%
Elected Year: 2017

🏛 Rep. Daniel Crenshaw (KREN-shaw)   R-TX-02   p 202.225.6565

Rm. CHOB 413 **Web.** crenshaw.house.gov   **f** 202.225.5547
Bio. 03/14/1984 • Aberdeen • Tufts Univ. (MA), B.A., 2006 •
Methodist • M. Tara Crenshaw   **Cmte.** Energy & Commerce
• Select Committee on the Climate Crisis
CoS. Justin Discigil   **LD.** Matt Hodge
Dist. Off. Houston 281.640.7720 • Kingwood 713.860.1330

R: 305   **T:** 2nd   56%
Elected Year: 2018

🐦 Rep. Henry R. Cuellar (KWAY-ar)   D-TX-28   p 202.225.1640

Rm. RHOB 2372 **Web.** cuellar.house.gov   **f** 202.225.1641
Bio. 09/19/1955 • Laredo • State Representative; United
States Customs Broker • Laredo Community College (TX),
A.A., 1976; Georgetown Univ. (DC), B.S., 1978; Univ. of Texas
School of Law, J.D., 1981; Texas A and M International Univ.,
M.B.A., 1982; Univ. of Texas, Ph.D., 1998 • Roman Catholic •
M. Imelda Rios Cuellar, 2 ch   **Cmte.** Appropriations
CoS. Jacob Hochberg   **LD.** Travis Knight
Sched. Hannah Sztorc   **PS.** Dana Youngentob
Dist. Off. Laredo 956.725.0639 • Mission 956.424.3942 •
Rio Grande City 956.487.5603 • San Antonio 210.271.2851

R: 74   **T:** 9th   58%
Elected Year: 2004

🐦 Rep. Lloyd A. Doggett II (DAWG-eht)   D-TX-35   p 202.225.4865

Rm. RHOB 2307 **Web.** doggett.house.gov   **f** 202.225.3073
Bio. 10/06/1946 • Austin • State Supreme Court Justice;
Professor • Univ. of Texas, B.B.A., 1967; Univ. of Texas,
B.B.A., 1967 • Methodist • M. Libby Belk Doggett, 2 ch; 4 gr-
ch   **Cmte.** Budget • Joint Taxation • Ways & Means
CoS. Michael Mucchetti   **LD.** Afton Cissell
Sched. Johana Mata   **PS.** Kate Stotesbery
Dist. Off. Austin 512.916.5921 • San Antonio 210.704.1080

R: 28   **T:** 14th   65%
Elected Year: 2012

🏛 Rep. Jake Ellzey ()   R-TX-06   p 202.225.2002

Rm. LHOB 1725 **Web.** ellzey.house.gov
Bio. Potter County • U.S. Naval Academy (MD), Bach.
Deg. • M. Shelby Hoebeke, 2 ch   **Cmte.** Science, Space &
Technology • Veterans' Affairs
CoS. Robert Carretta   **LD.** Don Barber
Sched. Molly Harris-Stevens   **PS.** Scott Gilfillan (CD)
Dist. Off. Arlington 817.775.0370 • Corsicana 903.602.7860
• Waxahachie 469.550.7150

R: 431   **T:** 1st   53%
Elected Year: 2020

↘ Rep. Veronica Escobar (ess-ko-BAR) D-TX-16 p 202.225.4831

Rm. LHOB 1505 **Web.** escobar.house.gov
Bio. 09/15/1969 • El Paso • Univ. of Texas, El Paso, B.A., 1991; New York Univ., M.A., 1993 • Catholic • M. Michael Pleters, 2 ch **Cmte.** Armed Services • Ethics • Judiciary • Select Committee on the Climate Crisis
CoS. Eduardo Lerma **LD.** Zahraa Saheb
Sched. Jessica Andino **PS.** Elizabeth Lopez-Sandoval
Dist. Off. El Paso 915.541.1400

R: 310 **T:** 2nd 65%
Elected Year: 2018

▣ Rep. Pat Fallon (FAH-luhn) R-TX-04 p 202.225.6673

Rm. LHOB 1118 **Web.** fallon.house.gov
Bio. 12/19/1967 • Pittsfield • Univ. of Notre Dame (IN), B.A. • Roman Catholic • M. Susan Garner-Sherrill, 2 ch **Cmte.** Armed Services • Oversight & Reform
CoS. Shannan Sorrell **LD.** Shaun Taylor
Sched. Kaela Thompson **PS.** Austin Higginbotham
Dist. Off. Rockwall 972.771.0100 • Sherman 903.820.5170 • Texarkana 903.716.7500

R: 383 **T:** 1st 75%
Elected Year: 2020

↘ Rep. Lizzie Pannill Fletcher (FLEH-chur) D-TX-07 p 202.225.2571
  f 202.225.4381

Web. fletcher.house.gov
Bio. 02/13/1975 • Houston • Kenyon College (OH), B.A., 1997; William & Mary Law School (VA), J.D., 2006 • Methodist • M. Scott Fletcher PE, 2 stepch **Cmte.** Energy & Commerce • Science, Space & Technology
CoS. Sarah Kaplan **LD.** Ben Jackson (CD)
  Feinmann (CD)
Sched. Shannon McDermott **PS.** Clarissa Robles (CD) (CD)
Dist. Off. Houston 713.353.8680

R: 311 **T:** 2nd 51%
Elected Year: 2018

↘ Rep. Sylvia R. Garcia (gar-SEE-uh) D-TX-29 p 202.225.1688

Rm. LHOB 1620 **Web.** sylviagarcia.house.gov
Bio. 09/06/1950 • San Diego • Texas Woman's Univ., B.A., 1972; Texas Southern Univ., Thurgood Marshall School of Law, J.D., 1978 • Catholic • S. **Cmte.** Financial Services • Judiciary
CoS. John Chapa **LD.** Courtney Broderick
  Gorczynski
Sched. Tyler Hinkle
Dist. Off. Houston 832.325.3150

R: 314 **T:** 2nd 71%
Elected Year: 2018

▣ Rep. Louie B. Gohmert Jr. (GO-murt) R-TX-01 p 202.225.3035

Rm. RHOB 2269 **Web.** gohmert.house.gov f 202.226.1230
Bio. 08/18/1953 • Pittsburg • Chief Justice for the 12th Circuit Court of Appeals; Attorney • Texas Agricultural and Mechanical Univ., B.A., 1975; Baylor Univ. School of Law (TX), J.D., 1977 • Baptist • M. Kathy Gohmert, 3 ch **Cmte.** Judiciary • Natural Resources
CoS. Connie Hair **LD.** Suanne Edmiston
Sched. Chelsea Cohen
Dist. Off. Longview 903.236.8597 • Lufkin 936.632.3180 • Marshall 903.938.8386 • Nacogdoches 936.715.9514 • Tyler 903.561.6349

R: 77 **T:** 9th 73%
Elected Year: 2004

▣ Rep. Tony Gonzales II (gon-SAH-les) R-TX-23 p 202.225.4511

Rm. LHOB 1009 **Web.** gonzales.house.gov f 202.225.2237
Bio. Fort McClellan • Georgetown Univ. (DC), Bach. Deg.; American Public Univ. System, Mast. Deg.; Univ. of Southern Mississippi, Ph.D.; Chaminade Univ., A.A., 2005; Excelsior College, B.S., 2009 • Catholic • M. Angel Gonzales, 6 ch **Cmte.** Appropriations
CoS. Casey Contres **LD.** Chris Malen
Sched. Brandon T. Smith **PS.** Paige Lindgren
Dist. Off. Del Rio 830.308.6200 • Fort Stockton 432.299.6200 • San Antonio 210.806.9920 • Socorro 915.990.1500 • Uvalde 830.333.7410

R: 390 **T:** 1st 51%
Elected Year: 2020

Rep. Vicente Gonzalez (gon-SAH-les)   D-TX-15   p 202.225.2531

Rm. CHOB 113 **Web.** gonzalez.house.gov   **f** 202.225.5688
Bio. 09/04/1967 • Corpus Christi • Embry-Riddle
Aeronautical Univ., B.A., 1992; Texas A & M Univ. School of
Law (formerly Texas Wesleyan School of Law), J.D., 1996
• Catholic • M. Lorena Saenz   **Cmte.** Financial Services •
Foreign Affairs • Select Economic Disparity & Fairness in
Growth
CoS. Louise Colbath   **LD.** Chandler K. Smith
Bentsen
Sched. Paulina Carrillo   **PS.** James Rivera
Dist. Off. Benavides 888.217.0261 • Falfurrias 361.209.3027
• McAllen 956.682.5545 • San Diego 888.217.0261 • Seguin
888.217.0261

R: 264   T: 3rd   51%
Elected Year: 2016

Rep. Lance Gooden (GOOD-un)   R-TX-05   p 202.225.3484

Rm. LHOB 1722 **Web.** gooden.house.gov
Bio. 12/01/1982 • Terrell • Univ. of Texas, B.A., 2004 •
Church of Christ • M. Alexa Calligas, 2 ch   **Cmte.** Financial
Services
CoS. Mehgan Perez-Acosta   **LD.** Jordan Wood
Sched. Peyton Smith   **PS.** Dylan Chandler
Dist. Off. Canton 903.502.5300

R: 317   T: 2nd   62%
Elected Year: 2018

Rep. Kay N. Granger (GRAIN-jur)   R-TX-12   p 202.225.5071

Rm. LHOB 1026 **Web.** kaygranger.house.gov **f** 202.225.5683
Bio. 01/18/1943 • Greenville • Insurance Agent; Business
Owner; Mayor (Ft. Worth, TX) • Texas Wesleyan Univ., B.S.,
1965 • Methodist • D., 3 ch; 5 gr-ch   **Cmte.** Appropriations
CoS. Cole Rojewski   **LD.** Heather Campbell
Sched. Alex Dunn   **PS.** Valerie Nelson
Dist. Off. Fort Worth 817.338.0909

R: 37   T: 13th   64%
Elected Year: 1996

Rep. Al Green (green)   D-TX-09   p 202.225.7508

Rm. RHOB 2347 **Web.** algreen.house.gov   **f** 202.225.2947
Bio. 09/01/1947 • New Orleans • Attorney • Tuskegee Univ.
(AL), Bach. Deg.; Texas Southern Univ., Thurgood Marshall
School of Law, J.D., 1973 • Baptist • NS.   **Cmte.** Financial
Services • Homeland Security
CoS. Niha Razi
Sched. Christ-Shamma   **PS.** Lily Rodriguez (CD)
Matalbert
Dist. Off. Houston 713.383.9234

R: 78   T: 9th   76%
Elected Year: 2004

Rep. Ronny L. Jackson (JAK-suhn)   R-TX-13   p 202.225.3706

Rm. CHOB 118 **Web.** jackson.house.gov   **f** 202.225.3486
Bio. 05/04/1967 • Levelland • South Plains College (TX),
A.S., 1988; Texas A&M Univ. System, B.S., 1991; Univ. of
Texas Medical Branch, M.D., 1995 • Church of Christ • M.
Jane Ely, 3 ch   **Cmte.** Armed Services • Foreign Affairs
CoS. Jeff Billman   **LD.** Michael Martin
Sched. Kathy Zhu   **PS.** Casey Nelson
Dist. Off. Amarillo 806.641.5600 • Wichita Falls
940.285.8000

R: 396   T: 1st   79%
Elected Year: 2020

Rep. Sheila Jackson Lee (JAK-suhn-lee)   D-TX-18   p 202.225.3816

Rm. RHOB 2426 **Web.** jacksonlee.house.gov **f** 202.225.3317
Bio. 01/12/1950 • Jamaica • Judge; Attorney • Yale Univ.
(CT), B.A., 1972; Univ. of Virginia Law School, J.D., 1975
• Seventh-Day Adventist • M. Elwyn C. Lee, 2 ch; 2 gr-ch
(twins)   **Cmte.** Budget • Homeland Security • Judiciary
CoS. Lillie Coney   **LD.** Gregory Berry
Sched. LaDedra   **PS.** Jalelah Ahmed
Drummond
Dist. Off. Houston 713.227.7740 • Houston 713.655.0050 •
Houston 713.691.4882 • Houston 713.861.4070

R: 30   T: 14th   73%
Elected Year: 1994

↘ Rep. Eddie Bernice Bernice Johnson (JAHN-suhn) D-TX-30 p 202.225.8885

Rm. RHOB 2306 **Web.** ebjohnson.house.gov **f** 202.226.1477
Bio. 12/03/1935 • Waco • Nurse; State Legislator • Texas Christian Univ., B.S., 1967; Southern Methodist Univ., Dallas (TX), M.P.A., 1976 • Baptist • D., 1 ch; 3 gr-ch
Cmte. Science, Space & Technology • Transportation & Infrastructure
CoS. Murat Gokcigdem **LD.** Nawaid Ladak
  PS. Zachary Mitchiner
Dist. Off. Dallas 214.922.8885

R: 20 **T:** 15th 78%
Elected Year: 1992

↘ Rep. Michael T. McCaul (mih-KALL) R-TX-10 p 202.225.2401

Rm. RHOB 2001 **Web.** mccaul.house.gov **f** 202.225.5955
Bio. 01/14/1962 • Dallas • Attorney; Federal prosecutor • Trinity Univ. (TX), B.A., 1984; St. Mary's Univ. School of Law (TX), J.D., 1987 • Catholic • M. Linda McCaul, 5 ch (triplets)
Cmte. Foreign Affairs • Homeland Security
CoS. Chris Del Beccaro **LD.** Zachary Isakowitz
Sched. Carrie Coxen **PS.** Rachel Walker
Dist. Off. Austin 512.473.2357 • Brenham 979.830.8497 • Katy 281.505.6130

R: 80 **T:** 9th 53%
Elected Year: 2004

↘ Rep. Troy E. Nehls (nelz) R-TX-22 p 202.225.5951

Rm. LHOB 1104 **Web.** nehls.house.gov **f** 202.225.5241
Bio. 04/07/1968 • Beaver Dam • Liberty Univ. (VA), B.A.; Univ. of Houston (TX), M.A. • Christian - Non-Denominational • M. Jill Nehls, 3 ch **Cmte.** Transportation & Infrastructure • Veterans' Affairs
CoS. Robert Schroeder **LD.** Evan Bender
Sched. Christopher Giblin **PS.** Joel Gibbons
Dist. Off. Richmond 346.762.6600

R: 414 **T:** 1st 52%
Elected Year: 2020

↘ Rep. August L. Pfluger II (FLOO-gur) R-TX-11 p 202.225.3605

Rm. LHOB 1531 **Web.** pfluger.house.gov **f** 202.225.1783
Bio. 12/28/1977 • Harris County • United States Air Force Academy, Bach. Deg.; Georgetown Univ. (DC), M.S.; Embry-Riddle Aeronautical Univ., M.S.; United States Air Univ. (AL), Bach. Deg. • Christian - Non-Denominational • M. Camille Coley, 3 ch **Cmte.** Foreign Affairs • Homeland Security
CoS. John Byers **LD.** Preston Howey
Sched. Brooke Oliver **PS.** Lyssa Bell
Dist. Off. Brownwood 325.646.1950 • Granbury 682.936.2577 • Llano 325.247.2826 • Midland 432.687.2390 • Odessa 432.331.9667 • San Angelo 325.659.4010

R: 418 **T:** 1st 80%
Elected Year: 2020

↘ Rep. Chip Roy (roy) R-TX-21 p 202.225.4236

Web. roy.house.gov **f** 202.225.8628
Bio. 08/07/1972 • Bethesda • Univ. of Virginia, B.S., 1994; Univ. of Virginia, M.S., 1995; Univ. of Texas, J.D., 2003 • Baptist • M. Carrah Roy, 2 ch **Cmte.** Judiciary • Veterans' Affairs
CoS. Jason Rogers (CD) **LD.** Sabrina Hancock (CD)
Sched. Corinne Schillizzi **PS.** Nate Madden (CD)
  (CD)
Dist. Off. Austin 512.871.5959 • Kerrville 830.896.0154 • San Antonio 210.821.5024

R: 345 **T:** 2nd 52%
Elected Year: 2018

↘ Rep. Pete A. Sessions (SEH-shuhnz) R-TX-17 p 202.225.6105

Rm. RHOB 2204 **Web.** sessions.house.gov **f** 202.225.0350
Bio. 03/22/1955 • Waco • Telephone Company Executive • Southwestern Univ. (TX), B.S., 1978 • Methodist • M. Karen Sessions, 2 ch; 3 stepch **Cmte.** Financial Services • Oversight & Reform
CoS. Kirk Bell **LD.** Ryan Young
Sched. Lauren Read **PS.** Nicole Myers
Dist. Off. College Station 979.431.6340 • Waco 254.633.4500

R: 51 **T:** 1st 56%
Elected Year: 2020

TEXAS

🏛 Rep. Van Taylor (TAY-lur)   R-TX-03   p 202.225.4201

Rm. LHOB 1404 **Web.** vantaylor.house.gov   **f** 202.225.1485
Bio. 08/01/1972 • Dallas • Harvard College (MA), A.B.,
1995; Harvard Business School (MA), M.B.A., 2001 •
Episcopalian • M. Anne Taylor, 3 ch   **Cmte.** Financial
Services
CoS. Lonnie Dietz   **LD.** Laura Weldon
Sched. Sara Garcia   **PS.** Libby Schroeder
Dist. Off. Plano 972.202.4150

R: 355   **T:** 2nd 55%
Elected Year: 2018

🏛 Rep. Beth A. Van Duyne (van-DYN)   R-TX-24   p 202.225.6605

Rm. LHOB 1337 **Web.** vanduyne.house.gov   **f** 202.225.0074
Bio. 11/16/1970 • Ithaca • Cornell Univ. (NY), B.A.
• Episcopalian • D., 2 ch   **Cmte.** Select Committee
on the Modernization of Congress • Small Business •
Transportation & Infrastructure
CoS. Jake Olson   **LD.** Ryan Dilworth
Sched. Riley Bookout   **PS.** Sam Denham
Dist. Off. Dallas 972.966.5500

R: 426   **T:** 1st 49%
Elected Year: 2020

🏛 Rep. Marc A. Veasey (VEE-zee)   D-TX-33   p 202.225.9897

Rm. RHOB 2348 **Web.** veasey.house.gov   **f** 202.225.9702
Bio. 01/03/1971 • Tarrant County • Texas Wesleyan Univ.,
B.S., 1995 • Christian Church • M. Tonya Veasey, 1 ch   **Cmte.**
Armed Services • Energy & Commerce • Joint Security &
Cooperation in Europe
CoS. Nicole Varner   **LD.** Thaddeus S. Woody
Sched. Jane Phipps   **PS.** Emily Druckman
Dist. Off. Dallas 214.741.1387 • Fort Worth 817.920.9086

R: 191   **T:** 5th 67%
Elected Year: 2012

🏛 Rep. Filemon B. Vela Jr. (VEH-lah)   D-TX-34   p 202.225.9901

Rm. CHOB 307 **Web.** vela.house.gov   **f** 202.225.9770
Bio. 02/13/1963 • Harlingen • Georgetown Univ. (DC), B.A.,
1985; Univ. of Texas as Austin, J.D., 1987 • Roman Catholic •
M. Rose Vela. **Cmte.** Agriculture • Armed Services
CoS. Rebekah Solem   **LD.** Jennifer Haas
Sched. Hannah Followill   **PS.** Brenda Rangel (CD)
Dist. Off. Alice 361.230.9776 • Brownsville 956.544.8352 •
San Benito 956.276.4497 • Weslaco 956.520.8273

R: 192   **T:** 5th 55%
Elected Year: 2012

🏛 Rep. Randy Weber (WEH-bur)   R-TX-14   p 202.225.2831

Rm. CHOB 107 **Web.** weber.house.gov   **f** 202.225.0271
Bio. 07/02/1953 • Pearland • Alvin Community College
(TX), Assc. Deg., 1974; Univ. of Houston, Clear Lake (TX),
B.S., 1977 • Baptist • M. Brenda Weber, 3 ch; 8 gr-ch
Cmte. Science, Space & Technology • Transportation &
Infrastructure
CoS. Jeanette Whitener   **LD.** William Christian
Sched. Bradie Burnett (CD)   **PS.** Lisa Reynolds
Dist. Off. Beaumont 409.835.0108 • Lake Jackson
979.285.0231 • League City 281.316.0231

R: 195   **T:** 5th 62%
Elected Year: 2012

🏛 Rep. Roger Williams (WILL-yuhmz)   R-TX-25   p 202.225.9896

Rm. LHOB 1708 **Web.** williams.house.gov   **f** 202.225.9692
Bio. 09/13/1949 • Evanston • Texas Christian Univ., B.S.,
1972 • Disciples of Christ • M. Patty Williams, 2 ch   **Cmte.**
Financial Services • Small Business
CoS. John Etue   **LD.** Ben Johnson
Sched. Mary Kathryn   **PS.** Patrick Arlantico
Fedorchak
Dist. Off. Austin 512.473.8910 • Cleburne 817.774.2575

R: 197   **T:** 5th 56%
Elected Year: 2012

UTAH

⚑ **Governor Spencer J. Cox** (kahks)   p 801.538.1000

Utah State Capitol Complex
350 North State St., Suite 200
Salt Lake City, UT 84114-2220
Website utah.gov
Fax 801.538.1133
Term Ends 2025
Lt. Governor
Deidre Henderson, R

C: Salt Lake City
P: 3,161,105 (31)
A: 82,169.46 mi² (12th)

U.S. Senators
Mike Lee, R
Mitt Romney, R
U.S. Representatives
01 / Blake Moore, R
02 / Chris D. Stewart, R
03 / John R. Curtis, R
04 / Burgess Owens, R

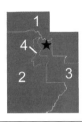

⚑ **Sen. Mike Lee** (lee)   R-UT-Sr.   p 202.224.5444

Rm. RSOB 361-A **Web.** lee.senate.gov   **f** 202.228.1168
Bio. 06/04/1971 • Mesa • Brigham Young Univ. (UT), B.A.,
1994; Brigham Young Univ. (UT), J.D., 1997 • Mormon •
M. Sharon Lee, 3 ch **Cmte.** Aging • Commerce, Science
& Transportation • Energy & Natural Resources • Joint
Economic • Judiciary
CoS. Allyson Bell   **LD.** Christy Woodruff
Sched. Mark Wait   **PS.** Lee Lonsberry
Dist. Off. Ogden 801.392.9633 • Salt Lake City
801.524.5933 • St. George 435.628.5514

R: 50   **T:** 2nd 68%
Elected Year: 2010
Next Election: 2022

⚑ **Sen. Mitt Romney** (RAHM-nee)   R-UT-Jr.   p 202.224.5251

Rm. RSOB 124 **Web.** romney.senate.gov   **f** 202.228.0836
Bio. 03/12/1947 • Detroit • Brigham Young Univ. (UT),
B.A., 1971; Harvard Univ. School of Business (MA), M.B.A.,
1975; Harvard Univ. Law School (MA), J.D., 1975 • Mormon
• M. Ann Davies, 5 ch **Cmte.** Budget • Foreign
Relations • Health, Education, Labor & Pensions •
Homeland Security & Government Affairs
CoS. Liz Johnson
Sched. Meagan Shepherd   **PS.** Brianna W. Manzelli
Dist. Off. Ogden 385.264.7885 • Salt Lake City
801.524.4380 • Spanish Fork 801.515.7230 • St. George
435.522.7100

R: 87   **T:** 1st 63%
Elected Year: 2018
Next Election: 2024

⚑ **Rep. John R. Curtis** (KUR-tiss)   R-UT-03   p 202.225.7751

Rm. RHOB 2400 **Web.** curtis.house.gov   **f** 202.225.5629
Bio. Salt Lake City • Brigham Young Univ. (UT), B.S., 1985
• Mormon • M. Sue Snarr, 6 ch; 5 gr-ch **Cmte.** Energy &
Commerce
CoS. Corey Norman   **LD.** Jake Bornstein
Sched. Sophie Draayer   **PS.** Adam Cloch
Dist. Off. Provo 801.922.5400

R: 287   **T:** 3rd 69%
Elected Year: 2016

⚑ **Rep. Blake Moore** (mor)   R-UT-01   p 202.225.0453

Rm. LHOB 1320 **Web.**   **f** 202.225.5857
blakemoore.house.gov
Bio. 06/22/1980 • Ogden • Utah State Univ., Bach. Deg.;
Northwestern Univ., M.P.P.; Univ. of Utah, Salt Lake City, B.A.
• Mormon • M. Jane Moore, 3 ch **Cmte.** Armed Services •
Natural Resources
CoS. Rachel Wagley   **LD.** Paul Johnson
Sched. Tara Kay Skeen   **PS.** Caroline Tucker
Dist. Off. Ogden 801.625.0107

R: 412   **T:** 1st 70%
Elected Year: 2020

UTAH

Rep. Burgess Owens (O-uhnz) R-UT-04 p 202.225.3011

Rm. LHOB 1039 **Web.** owens.house.gov
Bio. 08/02/1951 • Columbus • Univ. of Miami (FL)-
Teacher's Certificate, B.S. • Mormon • D., 6 ch **Cmte.**
Education & Labor • Judiciary
CoS. Keelie Broom **LD.** Miriam Harmer
  PS. Emma Hall
Dist. Off. West Jordan 801.999.9801

R: 417 **T:** 1st 48%
Elected Year: 2020

Rep. Chris D. Stewart (STOO-urt) R-UT-02 p 202.225.9730

Rm. CHOB 166 **Web.** stewart.house.gov **f** 202.225.5629
Bio. 07/15/1960 • Logan • Utah State Univ., B.S., 1984 •
Mormon • M. Evie Stewart, 6 ch **Cmte.** Appropriations •
Permanent Select on Intelligence
CoS. Clay White **LD.** Cam Madsen
Sched. Mark Coffield **PS.** Liam Anderson
Dist. Off. Bountiful 801.364.5550 • St. George 435.627.1500

R: 187 **T:** 5th 59%
Elected Year: 2012

VERMONT

VERMONT

Governor Phil Scott (skaht) p 802.828.3333

109 State Street Pavilion **C:** Montpelier
Montpelier, VT 05609-0101 **P:** 626,299 (51)
Website vermont.gov **A:** 9,216.64 mi^2 (43rd)
Fax 802.828.3339
Term Ends 2023
Lt. Governor
Molly Gray, **D**

U.S. Senators
Patrick Leahy, **D**
Bernie Sanders, **I**
U.S. Representatives
01 / Peter F. Welch, **D**

Sen. Patrick Leahy (LAY-hee) D-VT-Sr. p 202.224.4242

Rm. RSOB 437 **Web.** leahy.senate.gov **f** 202.224.3479
Bio. 03/31/1940 • Montpelier • Attorney; Prosecutor • St.
Michael's College (VT), B.A., 1961; Georgetown Univ. Law
Center (DC), J.D., 1964 • Roman Catholic • M. Marcelle
Pomerleau Leahy, 5 ch **Cmte.** Agriculture, Nutrition
& Forestry • Appropriations • Joint Library • Judiciary •
Rules & Administration
CoS. J.P. Dowd **LD.** Erica Chabot
Sched. Kevin McDonald **PS.** David Carle
Dist. Off. Burlington 802.863.2525 • Montpelier
802.229.0569

R: 1 **T:** 8th 60%
Elected Year: 1974
Next Election: 2022

Sen. Bernie Sanders (SAN-durz) I-VT-Jr. p 202.224.5141

Caucuses with Democratic Party **f** 202.228.0776
Rm. DSOB 332 **Web.** sanders.senate.gov
Bio. 09/08/1941 • Brooklyn • U.S. Representative • Univ. of
Chicago (IL), B.A., 1964 • Jewish • M. Jane O'Meara Driscoll,
1 ch; 3 stepch **Cmte.** Budget • Energy & Natural Resources
• Environment & Public Works • Health, Education, Labor &
Pensions • Veterans' Affairs
CoS. Misty Rebik **LD.** Billy Gendell
Sched. Jacob Gillison **PS.** Mike Casca
Dist. Off. Burlington 802.862.0697 • St. Johnsbury
802.332.6186

R: 24 **T:** 3rd 64%
Elected Year: 2006
Next Election: 2024

⌖ Rep. Peter F. Welch (welch)   D-VT-01   p 202.225.4115

Rm. RHOB 2187 **Web.** welch.house.gov   **f** 202.225.6790
Bio. 05/02/1947 • Springfield • Attorney • College of The
Holy Cross (MA), B.A., 1969; Univ. of California, Berkeley,
J.D., 1973 • Roman Catholic • M. Margaret Cheney, 5 ch; 3
stepch   **Cmte.** Energy & Commerce • Oversight & Reform
• Permanent Select on Intelligence
CoS. Patrick Satalin   **LD.** Meagan Foster
Sched. Elizabeth Haskell   **PS.** Arianna Jones
Dist. Off. Burlington 802.652.2450

R: 101   **T:** 8th   67%
Elected Year: 2006

▦ Governor Glenn Youngkin ()   p 804.786.2211

P.O. Box 1475   **C:** Richmond
Richmond, VA 23218   **P:** 8,517,685 (12)
Website virginia.gov   **A:** 39,490.13 mi^2 (36th)
Fax 804.371.6351
Term Ends 2026
Lt. Governor
Winsome Sears, R

U.S. Senators
Mark R. Warner, D
Tim M. Kaine, D
U.S. Representatives
01 / Rob J. Wittman, R
02 / Elaine G. Luria, D
03 / Bobby C. Scott, D
04 / A. Donald McEachin, D
05 / Bob Good, R
06 / Ben L. Cline, R
07 / Abigail D. Spanberger, D
08 / Don S. Beyer, D
09 / Morgan M. Griffith, R
10 / Jennifer T. Wexton, D   11 / Gerry E. Connolly, D

⌖ Sen. Tim M. Kaine (kain)   D-VA-Jr.   p 202.224.4024

Rm. RSOB 231 **Web.** kaine.senate.gov   **f** 202.228.6363
Bio. 02/26/1958 • St. Paul • Mayor, City of Richmond; Mbr.,
Richmond City Council; Lt. Governor & President of the
Senate, VA; Governor, Commonwealth of Virginia • Univ.
of Missouri, A.B., 1979; Harvard Law School (MA), J.D., 1983
• Roman Catholic • M. Anne Bright Holton, 3 ch   **Cmte.**
Armed Services • Budget • Foreign Relations • Health,
Education, Labor & Pensions
CoS. Mike Henry   **LD.** Nick Barbash
Sched. Kate McCarroll   **PS.** Katie Stuntz
Dist. Off. Abingdon 276.525.4790 • Fredericksburg

R: 58   **T:** 2nd   57%
Elected Year: 2012
Next Election: 2024

540.369.7667 • Manassas 703.361.3192 • Richmond
804.771.2221 • Roanoke 540.682.5693 • Virginia Beach
757.518.1674

⌖ Sen. Mark R. Warner (WAR-nur)   D-VA-Sr.   p 202.224.2023

Rm. HSOB 703 **Web.** warner.senate.gov   **f** 202.224.6920
Bio. 12/15/1954 • Indianapolis • Governor of Virginia
• George Washington Univ. (DC), B.A., 1977; Harvard
Univ. Law School (MA), J.D., 1980 • Presbyterian • M. Lisa
Collis, 3 ch   **Cmte.** Banking, Housing & Urban Affairs •
Budget • Finance • Intelligence • Joint Library • Rules &
Administration
CoS. Elizabeth Falcone   **LD.** Lauren Marshall
Sched. Malcolm Fouhy   **PS.** Rachel Cohen
Dist. Off. Abingdon 276.628.8158 • Norfolk 757.441.3079 •

R: 33   **T:** 3rd   56%
Elected Year: 2008
Next Election: 2026

Richmond 804.775.2314 • Roanoke 540.857.2676 • Vienna
703.442.0670

VIRGINIA

🏛 Rep. Don S. Beyer Jr. (BY-ur)　　　　　D-VA-08　　p 202.225.4376
　　Rm. LHOB 1119　**Web.** beyer.house.gov　　　**f** 202.225.0017
　　Bio. Trieste • Williams College, B.A., 1972 • Episcopalian
　　• M. Megan Carroll, 4 ch; 2 gr-ch　**Cmte.** Joint Economic •
　　Science, Space & Technology • Ways & Means
　　CoS. Zachary Cafritz　　　　**LD.** Kate Schisler
　　Sched. Barbara Hamlett　　　**PS.** Aaron Fritschner
　　Dist. Off. Arlington 703.658.5403

R: 208　**T:** 4th　76%
Elected Year: 2014

🏛 Rep. Ben L. Cline (kline)　　　　　　R-VA-06　　p 202.225.5431
　　Rm. RHOB 2443　**Web.** cline.house.gov　　　**f** 202.225.9681
　　Bio. 02/29/1972 • Stillwater • Bates College (ME), B.A.,
　　1994; Univ. of Richmond School of Law, J.D., 2007 •
　　Roman Catholic • M. Elizabeth Rocovich, 2 ch　**Cmte.**
　　Appropriations • Budget
　　CoS. Matt M. Miller　　　　**LD.** Nicole Manley
　　Sched. Meagan Jennings　　　**PS.** Matt Hanrahan
　　Dist. Off. Harrisonburg 540.432.2391 • Lynchburg
　　434.845.8306 • Roanoke 540.857.2672 • Staunton
　　540.885.3861

R: 303　**T:** 2nd　65%
Elected Year: 2018

🏛 Rep. Gerry E. Connolly (KAH-nuh-lee)　　D-VA-11　　p 202.225.1492
　　Rm. RHOB 2238　**Web.** connolly.house.gov　**f** 202.225.3071
　　Bio. 03/30/1950 • Boston • Transportation Commissioner;
　　US Senate Committee Staffer • Maryknoll College (IL), B.A.,
　　1971; Harvard Univ., M.P.A., 1979 • Roman Catholic • M.
　　Cathy Connolly, 1 ch　**Cmte.** Foreign Affairs • Oversight &
　　Reform
　　CoS. Jamie Smith　　　　**LD.** Collin Davenport
　　Sched. Lauren Covington
　　Dist. Off. Annandale 703.256.3071 • Woodbridge
　　571.408.4407

R: 108　**T:** 7th　71%
Elected Year: 2008

🏛 Rep. Bob Good (good)　　　　　　　R-VA-05　　p 202.225.4711
　　Rm. LHOB 1213　**Web.** good.house.gov　　　**f** 202.225.5681
　　Bio. 09/11/1965 • Wilkes Barre • Liberty Univ. (VA), Bach.
　　Deg., 1988; Liberty Univ. (VA), M.B.A., 2010 • Christian
　　Church • M. Tracey Good, 3 ch　**Cmte.** Budget • Education
　　& Labor
　　CoS. Mark Kelly　　　　**LD.** Joe Barry
　　Sched. Courtney Heath　　　**PS.** Mattie Nicholson
　　Dist. Off. Lynchburg 434.791.2596

R: 391　**T:** 1st　52%
Elected Year: 2020

🏛 Rep. Morgan M. Griffith (GRIH-fith)　　R-VA-09　　p 202.225.3861
　　Rm. RHOB 2202　**Web.**　　　　　　　**f** 202.225.0076
　　morgangriffith.house.gov
　　Bio. 03/15/1958 • Philadelphia • Emory and Henry College
　　(VA), B.A., 1980; Washington and Lee Univ. School of Law
　　(VA), J.D., 1983 • Episcopalian • M. Hilary Davis, 3 ch　**Cmte.**
　　Energy & Commerce
　　CoS. Kelly Lungren　　　**LD.** Emily Michael
　　　McCollum
　　Sched. Emma Ernst　　　**PS.** Kevin Baird
　　Dist. Off. Abingdon 276.525.1405 • Big Stone Gap
　　276.525.1405 • Christiansburg 540.381.5671

R: 136　**T:** 6th　94%
Elected Year: 2010

🏛 Rep. Elaine G. Luria (LUR-ree-uh)　　　D-VA-02　　p 202.225.4215
　　Rm. CHOB 412　**Web.** luria.house.gov
　　Bio. Birmingham • U.S. Naval Academy (MD), B.S., 1997;
　　Old Dominion Univ. (VA), M.E.M., 2004 • Jewish • M. Bob
　　Blondin, 1 ch; 2 stepch　**Cmte.** Armed Services • Homeland
　　Security • Select Investigate Jan 6 Attack on the U.S. Capitol
　　• Veterans' Affairs
　　CoS. Shira Siegel　　　　**LD.** John R. Brodtke
　　Sched. Tessa Cate　　　　**PS.** Jayce Genco
　　Dist. Off. Onley 757.364.7631 • Virginia Beach
　　757.364.7650 • Yorktown 757.364.7634

R: 330　**T:** 2nd　52%
Elected Year: 2018

⚑ Rep. A. Donald McEachin (muh-KEE-chuhn) D-VA-04 p 202.225.6365

Rm. CHOB 314 **Web.** mceachin.house.gov **f** 202.226.1170
Bio. 10/10/1961 • Nuremberg • American Univ. (DC),
B.S., 1982; Univ. of Virginia Law School, J.D., 1986; Virginia
Union Univ. Samuel DeWitt Proctor School of Theology,
M.Div., 2008 • Baptist • M. Colette Wallace McEachin, 3 ch
Cmte. Energy & Commerce • Natural Resources • Select
Committee on the Climate Crisis
CoS. Tara Rountree **LD.** Evan Chapman
Sched. Chris Nguyen **PS.** Shahid L. Ahmed
Dist. Off. Richmond 804.486.1840 • Suffolk 757.942.6050

R: 275 **T:** 3rd 62%
Elected Year: 2016

⚑ Rep. Bobby C. Scott (skaht) D-VA-03 p 202.225.8351

Rm. RHOB 2328 **Web.** bobbyscott.house.gov **f** 202.225.8354
Bio. 04/30/1947 • Washington • State Legislator • Army
Reserve 1970-74; Massachusetts National Guard 1974-76 •
Harvard Univ., B.A., 1969; Boston College Law School (MA),
J.D., 1973 • Episcopalian • D. **Cmte.** Budget • Education &
Labor
CoS. David Dailey **LD.** Paige Schwartz
Sched. Randi Petty **PS.** Austin Barbera
Dist. Off. Newport News 757.380.1000

R: 24 **T:** 15th 68%
Elected Year: 1992

⚑ Rep. Abigail D. Spanberger (SPAN-bur-gur) D-VA-07 p 202.225.2815

Rm. LHOB 1431 **Web.** spanberger.house.gov **f** 202.225.0011
Bio. 08/07/1979 • Red Bank • Univ. of Virginia, B.A., 2001
• Christian Church • M. Adam Spanberger, 3 ch **Cmte.**
Agriculture • Foreign Affairs
CoS. Bonnie Krenz **LD.** Samuel Wojcicki
Sched. Andrea Valverde **PS.** Connor Joseph
Dist. Off. Glen Allen 804.401.4110 • Spotsylvania
540.321.6130

R: 349 **T:** 2nd 51%
Elected Year: 2018

⚑ Rep. Jennifer T. Wexton (WEHK-stuhn) D-VA-10 p 202.225.5136

Rm. LHOB 1217 **Web.** wexton.house.gov **f** 202.225.0437
Bio. 05/27/1968 • Washington • Univ. of Maryland - College
Park, B.A., 1991; College of William and Mary - Marshall-
Wythe Law School (VA), J.D., 1995 • Unspecified/Other •
M. Andrew Wexton, 2 ch **Cmte.** Appropriations • Budget •
Joint Congressional-Executive Commission on China
CoS. Abby M. Carter **LD.** Mike Lucier
Sched. Meaghan Johnson **PS.** Justin McCartney
Dist. Off. Sterling 703.234.3800 • Winchester 703.236.1300

R: 363 **T:** 2nd 57%
Elected Year: 2018

⚑ Rep. Rob J. Wittman (WIT-muhn) R-VA-01 p 202.225.4261

Rm. RHOB 2055 **Web.** wittman.house.gov **f** 202.225.4382
Bio. 02/03/1959 • Washington • Mayor (Montrose Town,
VA); State Legislator • Virginia Polytechnic Institute, B.S.,
1981; Univ. of North Carolina in Chapel Hill, M.PH, 1990;
Virginia Commonwealth Univ., Ph.D., 2002 • Episcopalian
• M. Kathryn Jane Sisson Wittman, 2 ch; 4 gr-ch **Cmte.**
Armed Services • Natural Resources
CoS. Carolyn King **LD.** Christopher Hall
Sched. Jordan Wilson **PS.** Sarah Newsome
Dist. Off. Mechanicsville 804.730.6595 • Stafford
540.659.2734 • Tappahannock 804.443.0668

R: 104 **T:** 8th 58%
Elected Year: 2007

WASHINGTON

⚑ Governor Jay Inslee (INZ-lee) p 360.902.4111

PO Box 40002
Olympia, WA 98404-0002
Website wa.gov
Fax 360.753.4110
Term Ends 2025
Lt. Governor
Denny Heck, **D**

C: Olympia
P: 7,535,591 (13)
A: 66,455.49 mi^2 (20th)

WASHINGTON

U.S. Senators
Patty Murray, **D**
Maria Cantwell, **D**
U.S. Representatives
01 / Suzan K. DelBene, **D**
02 / Rick R. Larsen, **D**
03 / Jaime L. Herrera Beutler, **R**
04 / Dan M. Newhouse, **R**
05 / Cathy A. McMorris Rodgers, **R**
06 / Derek Kilmer, **D**
07 / Pramila Jayapal, **D**
08 / Kim Schrier, **D**
09 / Adam Smith, **D**
10 / Marilyn Strickland, **D**

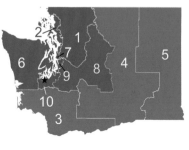

⚓ Sen. Maria Cantwell (KANT-wel)　　　　D-WA-Jr.　　p 202.224.3441

Rm. HSOB 511　**Web.** cantwell.senate.gov　**f** 202.228.0514
Bio. 10/13/1958 • Indianapolis • Representative • Miami
Univ. of Ohio, B.A., 1980 • Roman Catholic • S. **Cmte.**
Commerce, Science & Transportation • Energy & Natural
Resources • Finance • Indian Affairs • Joint Taxation •
Small Business & Entrepreneurship
CoS. Jami Burgess　　　　　**LD.** David Marten
Sched. Sheila M. Dwyer　　　**PS.** Ansley Lacitis
Dist. Off. Everett 425.303.0114 • Richland 509.946.8106
• Seattle 206.220.6400 • Spokane 509.353.2507 • Tacoma
253.572.2281 • Vancouver 360.696.7838

R: 16　**T:** 4th 58%
Elected Year: 2000
Next Election: 2024

⚓ Sen. Patty Murray (MUR-ree)　　　　　D-WA-Sr.　　p 202.224.2621

Rm. RSOB 154　**Web.** murray.senate.gov　**f** 202.224.0238
Bio. 10/11/1950 • Bothell • State Senator; Teacher •
Washington State Univ., B.A., 1972 • Roman Catholic • M.
Robert Randall Murray, 2 ch **Cmte.** Appropriations • Budget
• Health, Education, Labor & Pensions • Veterans' Affairs
CoS. Mindi Linquist　　　　**LD.** Benjamin Merkel
Sched. Meghan Mahoney　　**PS.** Helen Hare
Dist. Off. Everett 425.259.6515 • Seattle 206.553.5545 •
Spokane 509.624.9515 • Tacoma 253.572.3636 • Vancouver
360.696.7797 • Yakima 509.453.7462

R: 6　**T:** 5th 59%
Elected Year: 1992
Next Election: 2022

⚓ Rep. Suzan K. DelBene (del-BEH-nay)　　　D-WA-01　　p 202.225.6311

Rm. RHOB 2330　**Web.** delbene.house.gov　**f** 202.226.1606
Bio. 02/17/1962 • Selma • Reed College (OR), B.A., 1983;
Univ. of Washington, M.B.A., 1990 • Episcopalian • M. Kurt
Delbene, 2 ch **Cmte.** Ways & Means
CoS. Aaron Schmidt　　　　**LD.** Kyle Hill
Sched. Kelly Schulz　　　　**PS.** Nick Martin
Dist. Off. Kirkland 425.485.0085 • Mount Vernon
360.416.7879

R: 156　**T:** 6th 59%
Elected Year: 2011

⚓ Rep. Jaime L. Herrera Beutler (heh-RAIR-uh　R-WA-03　　p 202.225.3536
BUT-lur)

Rm. RHOB 2352　**Web.**　　　　　　　　　　**f** 202.225.3478
herrerabeutler.house.gov
Bio. 11/03/1978 • Glendale • Bellevue Community College
(WA), A.A., 2003; Univ. of Washington, B.A., 2004 • Christian
Church • M. Daniel Beutler, 3 ch **Cmte.** Appropriations •
Joint Economic
CoS. Casey Bowman (CD)　　**LD.** Jordan Evich
Sched. Angela Nguyen　　　　**PS.** Craig Wheeler
Dist. Off. Chehalis 360.695.6292 • Vancouver 360.695.6292

R: 139　**T:** 6th 56%
Elected Year: 2010

🦅 **Rep. Pramila Jayapal** (JIE-ah-pall) D-WA-07 p 202.225.3106

Rm. RHOB 2346 **f** 202.225.6197
Bio. Chennai • Georgetown Univ. (DC), A.B., 1986;
Northwestern Univ. Kellogg School Management (IL),
M.B.A., 1990 • Hinduism • M. Steve Williamson, 1 ch; 1
stepch **Cmte.** Budget • Education & Labor • Judiciary •
Select Economic Disparity & Fairness in Growth
CoS. Lilah Pomerance **LD.** Jennifer Chan
Sched. Naava Ellenberg **PS.** Chris Evans
Dist. Off. Seattle 206.674.0040

R: 268 **T:** 3rd 83%
Elected Year: 2016

🦅 **Rep. Derek Kilmer** (KILL-mur) D-WA-06 p 202.225.5916

Rm. RHOB 2059 **Web.** kilmer.house.gov **f** 202.226.3575
Bio. 01/01/1974 • Port Angeles • Princeton Univ. (NJ),
A.B., 1996; Univ. of Oxford (UK), Ph.D., 2003 • Methodist
• M. Jennifer Kilmer, 2 ch **Cmte.** Appropriations • Select
Committee on the Modernization of Congress
CoS. Rachel Kelly **LD.** Heather Painter
Sched. Tory Scordato **PS.** Andrew Wright
Dist. Off. Bremerton 360.373.9725 • Port Angeles
360.797.3623 • Tacoma 253.272.3515

R: 175 **T:** 5th 59%
Elected Year: 2012

🦅 **Rep. Rick R. Larsen** (LAR-suhn) D-WA-02 p 202.225.2605

Rm. RHOB 2163 **Web.** larsen.house.gov **f** 202.225.4420
Bio. 06/15/1965 • Arlington • Economic Development
official; Member, Snohomish County Council • Pacific
Lutheran Univ. (WA), B.A., 1987; Univ. of Minnesota, M.P.A.,
1990 • Methodist • M. Tiia Karlen Larsen, 2 ch **Cmte.**
Armed Services • Transportation & Infrastructure
CoS. Terra Sabag **LD.** Jonathan Z. Golden
Sched. Per Bergstrom **PS.** Joseph Tutino
Dist. Off. Bellingham 360.733.4500 • Everett 425.252.3188

R: 54 **T:** 11th 63%
Elected Year: 2000

🦅 **Rep. Cathy A. McMorris Rodgers** (mik-MOR-iss R-WA-05 p 202.225.2006
RAH-jurz)

Rm. LHOB 1035 **Web.** mcmorris.house.gov **f** 202.225.3392
Bio. 05/22/1969 • Salem • State Legislator • Pensacola
Christian College (FL), B.A., 1990; Univ. of Washington,
M.B.A., 2002 • Evangelical • M. Brian Rodgers, 3 ch **Cmte.**
Energy & Commerce
CoS. Jared Powell **LD.** Liz Payne
Sched. Karli Plucker **PS.** Kyle VonEnde
Dist. Off. Colville 509.684.3481 • Spokane 509.353.2374 •
Walla Walla 509.529.9358

R: 82 **T:** 9th 61%
Elected Year: 2004

🦅 **Rep. Dan M. Newhouse** (NOO-hous) R-WA-04 p 202.225.5816

Rm. CHOB 504 **Web.** newhouse.house.gov **f** 202.225.3251
Bio. 07/10/1955 • Sunnyside • Washington State Univ.,
B.S., 1977 • Presbyterian • M. Carol Newhouse, 2 ch **Cmte.**
Appropriations
CoS. Jessica Lynn Carter **LD.** Travis Martinez
Sched. Rick Nelson **PS.** Amanda Fitzmorris
Dist. Off. Grand Coulee 509.433.7760 • Richland
509.713.7374 • Yakima 509.452.3243

R: 228 **T:** 4th 66%
Elected Year: 2014

🦅 **Rep. Kim Schrier** (SHRY-uhr) D-WA-08 p 202.225.7761

Rm. LHOB 1123 **Web.** schrier.house.gov **f** 202.225.4282
Bio. 08/23/1968 • Los Angeles • Univ. of California,
Berkeley, B.A., 1991; Univ. of California, Davis, M.D., 1997
• Jewish • M. David Gowing, 1 ch **Cmte.** Agriculture •
Energy & Commerce
CoS. Erin O'Quinn **LD.** Jennifer E. Cash
Sched. Emilee Milborn **PS.** Elizabeth Carlson
Dist. Off. Issaquah 425.657.1001 • Wenatchee
509.850.5340

R: 346 **T:** 2nd 52%
Elected Year: 2018

WASHINGTON

🐦 Rep. Adam Smith (smith)   D-WA-09   p 202.225.8901

Rm. RHOB 2264 **Web.** adamsmith.house.gov
Bio. 06/15/1965 • Washington • Attorney • Fordham Univ. (NY), B.A., 1987; Univ. of Washington, J.D., 1990 • Christian Church • M. Sara Bickle-Eldridge Smith, 2 ch **Cmte.** Armed Services
CoS. Shana Chandler   **LD.** Connor Stubbs
                                  PS. Caleb Randall-Bodman
Dist. Off. Renton 425.793.5180

R: 42   **T:** 13th   74%
Elected Year: 1996

🐦 Rep. Marilyn Strickland (STRIK-luhnd)   D-WA-10   p 202.225.9740

Rm. LHOB 1004 **Web.** strickland.house.gov
Bio. 09/25/1962 • Seoul • Univ. of Washington, B.A.; Clark Atlanta Univ., M.B.A. • M. Pactrick Erwin, 2 stepch **Cmte.** Armed Services • Transportation & Infrastructure
CoS. Andrew Noh   **LD.** Hector Colon
Sched. Jesse Mayer
Dist. Off. Lacey 360.459.8514

R: 424   **T:** 1st   49%
Elected Year: 2020

WEST VIRGINIA

WEST VIRGINIA

🏛 Governor Jim Justice (JUHS-tiss)   p 304.558.2000

State Capitol
1900 Kanawha Blvd., East
Charleston, WV 25305
Website wv.gov
Fax 304.342.7025
Term Ends 2025
Lt. Governor
Craig Blair, R

C: Charleston
P: 1,805,832 (39)
A: 24,038.32 mi^2 (41st)

U.S. Senators
Joe Manchin, **D**
Shelley Moore Capito, **R**
U.S. Representatives
01 / David B. McKinley, **R**
02 / Alex X. Mooney, **R**
03 / Carol D. Miller, **R**

🏛 Sen. Shelley Moore Capito (KA-pih-toe)   R-WV-Jr.   p 202.224.6472

Rm. RSOB 172 **Web.** capito.senate.gov   **f** 202.224.7665
Bio. 11/26/1953 • Glen Dale • State Legislator • Duke Univ. (NC), B.S., 1975; Univ. of Virginia, M.Ed., 1976 • Presbyterian • M. Dr. Charles Lewis Capito, 3 ch; 4 gr-ch **Cmte.** Appropriations • Commerce, Science & Transportation • Environment & Public Works • Rules & Administration
CoS. Joel Brubaker   **LD.** Jeffrey T. Jezierski
Sched. Lauren Allen   **PS.** Kelley Moore
Dist. Off. Charleston 304.347.5372 • Martinsburg 304.262.9285 • Morgantown 304.292.2310

R: 64   **T:** 2nd   70%
Elected Year: 2014
Next Election: 2026

🔊 **Sen. Joe Manchin III** (MAN-shin) D-WV-Sr. p 202.224.3954

Rm. HSOB 306 **Web.** manchin.senate.gov **f** 202.228.0002
Bio. 08/24/1947 • Farmington • Candidate, Governor of West Virginia; President, Marion County Rescue Squad; Secretary of State, West Virginia; Mbr., WV House of Delegates; Mbr., WV Senate; Mbr., Marion County Airport Authority • West Virginia Univ., B.S., 1970 • Catholic • M. Gayle Conelly, 3 ch; 8 gr-ch **Cmte.** Appropriations • Armed Services • Energy & Natural Resources • Veterans' Affairs
CoS. Lance West   **LD.** Wes Kungel
Sched. Anne Raffaelli   **PS.** Sam Runyon (CD)
Dist. Off. Charleston 304.342.5855 • Fairmont 304.368.0567 • Martinsburg 304.264.4626

R: 38 **T:** 3rd 50%
Elected Year: 2010
Next Election: 2024

🏛 **Rep. David B. McKinley** (mih-KIN-lee) R-WV-01 p 202.225.4172

Rm. RHOB 2239 **Web.** mckinley.house.gov **f** 202.225.7564
Bio. 03/28/1947 • Wheeling • Purdue Univ. (IN), B.S., 1969 • Episcopalian • M. Mary McKinley, 4 ch; 6 gr-ch **Cmte.** Energy & Commerce
CoS. Mike Hamilton   **LD.** Jeannine M. Bender
                              PS. Kate Gianquinto
Dist. Off. Morgantown 304.284.8506 • Parkersburg 304.422.5972 • Wheeling 304.232.3801

R: 146 **T:** 6th 69%
Elected Year: 2010

🏛 **Rep. Carol D. Miller** (MIH-lur) R-WV-03 p 202.225.3452

Rm. CHOB 465 **Web.** miller.house.gov
Bio. 11/04/1950 • Columbus • Columbia College, B.S., 1972 • Baptist • M. Matt Miller, 2 ch **Cmte.** Select Committee on the Climate Crisis • Ways & Means
CoS. Lauren Billman   **LD.** Max Pedrotti
Sched. Shannon Joy Evans **PS.** Tatum Wallace
Dist. Off. Beckley 304.250.6177 • Bluefield 304.325.6800 • Huntington 304.522.2201

R: 334 **T:** 2nd 71%
Elected Year: 2018

🏛 **Rep. Alex X. Mooney** (MOON-ee) R-WV-02 p 202.225.2711

Rm. RHOB 2228 **Web.** mooney.house.gov **f** 202.225.7856
Bio. 06/07/1971 • Washington • Dartmouth College, A.B., 1993 • Roman Catholic • M. Grace Gonzalez, 3 ch **Cmte.** Financial Services
CoS. Michael J. Hough   **LD.** John Caddock
Sched. Meg Wagner   **PS.** Ryan Kelly
Dist. Off. Charleston 304.925.5964 • Martinsburg 304.264.8810

R: 226 **T:** 4th 63%
Elected Year: 2014

WISCONSIN

🔊 **Governor Tony Evers** (EV-urz) p 608.266.1212

115 E. Capitol
Madison, WI 53702
Website wisconsin.gov
Fax 608.267.8983
Term Ends 2023
Lt. Governor
Mandela Barnes, D

C: Madison
P: 5,813,568 (20)
A: 54,157.76 mi^2 (25th)

WISCONSIN

U.S. Senators
Ron H. Johnson, R
Tammy Baldwin, **D**
U.S. Representatives
01 / Bryan G. Steil, R
02 / Mark Pocan, **D**
03 / Ron J. Kind, **D**
04 / Gwen S. Moore, **D**
05 / Scott L. Fitzgerald, R
06 / Glenn S. Grothman, R
07 / Tom Tiffany, R
08 / Mike J. Gallagher, R

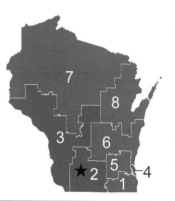

🐦 **Sen. Tammy Baldwin** (BALLD-win) D-WI-Jr. p 202.224.5653

Rm. HSOB 709 **Web.** baldwin.senate.gov **f** 202.224.9787
Bio. 02/11/1962 • Madison • City Council Member; Member,
State Assembly • Smith College (MA), A.B., 1984; Univ.
of Wisconsin Law School, J.D., 1989 • Unspecified/Other
• S. **Cmte.** Appropriations • Commerce, Science &
Transportation • Health, Education, Labor & Pensions
CoS. Ken B. Reidy **LD.** Dan M. McCarthy
Sched. Carolyn D. Walser **PS.** John W. Kraus
Dist. Off. Ashland 715.832.8424 • Eau Claire 715.832.8424
• Green Bay 920.498.2668 • La Crosse 608.796.0045 •
Madison 608.264.5338 • Milwaukee 414.297.4451

R: 53 **T:** 2nd 55%
Elected Year: 2012
Next Election: 2024

🐦 **Sen. Ron H. Johnson** (JAHN-suhn) R-WI-Sr. p 202.224.5323

Rm. HSOB 328 **Web.** ronjohnson.senate.gov **f** 202.228.6965
Bio. 05/08/1955 • Mankato • Univ. of Minnesota, B.S., 1977
• Lutheran • M. Jane Johnson, 3 ch; 2 gr-ch **Cmte.** Budget
• Commerce, Science & Transportation • Foreign Relations
• Homeland Security & Government Affairs
CoS. Sean Riley **LD.** Courtney Rutland
Sched. Chloe Pickle **PS.** Vanessa Ambrosini
Dist. Off. Madison 608.240.9629 • Milwaukee 414.276.7282
• Oshkosh 920.230.7250

R: 47 **T:** 2nd 50%
Elected Year: 2010
Next Election: 2022

🐦 **Rep. Scott L. Fitzgerald** (fits-JAIR-uld) R-WI-05 p 202.225.5101

Rm. LHOB 1507 **Web.** fitzgerald.house.gov
Bio. 11/16/1963 • Chicago • Univ. of Wisconsin - Oshkosh,
B.S., 1985 • Catholic • M. Lisa Fitzgerald, 3 ch **Cmte.**
Education & Labor • Judiciary • Small Business
CoS. Ryan McCormack **LD.** Robert N. Wagener
Sched. Jack Hogerty **PS.** Kelli Liegel
Dist. Off. Brookfield 262.784.1111

R: 386 **T:** 1st 60%
Elected Year: 2020

🐦 **Rep. Mike J. Gallagher** (GA-luh-gur) R-WI-08 p 202.225.5665

Rm. LHOB 1230 **Web.** gallagher.house.gov **f** 202.225.5729
Bio. 03/03/1984 • Green Bay • Princeton Univ. Woodrow
Wilson School of Public and International Affairs (NJ),
B.A., 2006; National Intelligence Univ. (DC), M.S., 2010;
Georgetown Univ. (DC), M.A., 2012; Georgetown Univ. (DC),
M.A., 2013; Georgetown Univ. (DC), Ph.D., 2015 • Catholic
• M. Holli A. Horak MD, 1 ch **Cmte.** Armed Services •
Transportation & Infrastructure
CoS. Taylor Andreae **LD.** Charles Morrison
Sched. Louise Brownell **PS.** Jordan Dunn
Dist. Off. De Pere 920.301.4500

R: 263 **T:** 3rd 64%
Elected Year: 2016

♜ Rep. Glenn S. Grothman ("GROWTH"-muhn)   R-WI-06   p 202.225.2476

Rm. LHOB 1427 **Web.** grothman.house.gov   **f** 202.225.2356
Bio. 07/03/1955 • Milwaukee • Univ. of Wisconsin -
Madison, B.B.A., 1977; Univ. of Wisconsin Law School,
J.D., 1983 • Lutheran • S. Growth Mulin **Cmte.** Budget •
Education & Labor • Oversight & Reform
CoS. Alan Ott (CD)   **LD.** Samantha Baker
Sched. Kayla Robson (CD)   **PS.** Timothy Svoboda
Dist. Off. Fond du Lac 920.907.0624

R: 218 **T:** 4th 59%
Elected Year: 2014

🐦 Rep. Ron J. Kind (kind)   D-WI-03   p 202.225.5506

Rm. LHOB 1502 **Web.** kind.house.gov   **f** 202.225.5739
Bio. 03/16/1963 • La Crosse • Attorney • Harvard Univ.,
Bach. Deg., 1985; London School of Economics (England),
M.A., 1987; Univ. of Minnesota, J.D., 1990 • Lutheran • M.
Tawni Zappa Kind, 2 ch **Cmte.** Ways & Means
CoS. Alex Eveland   **LD.** Ben Hutterer
Sched. Madeleine Mathias   **PS.** Carter MacLeod
Dist. Off. Eau Claire 715.831.9214 • La Crosse
608.782.2558

R: 38 **T:** 13th 51%
Elected Year: 1996

🐦 Rep. Gwen S. Moore (mor)   D-WI-04   p 202.225.4572

Rm. RHOB 2252 **Web.**   **f** 202.225.8135
gwenmoore.house.gov
Bio. 04/18/1951 • Racine • State Senator; Member, State
Assembly • Marquette Univ. (WI), B.A., 1978 • Baptist • S., 3
ch; 3 gr-ch **Cmte.** Joint Security & Cooperation in Europe •
Science, Space & Technology • Select Economic Disparity &
Fairness in Growth • Ways & Means
CoS. Sean Gard   **LD.** Christopher Goldson
Sched. Robert Montgomery   **PS.** Samara Sheff
Dist. Off. Milwaukee 414.297.1140

R: 83 **T:** 9th 75%
Elected Year: 2004

🐦 Rep. Mark Pocan (po-KAN)   D-WI-02   p 202.225.2906

Rm. LHOB 1727 **Web.** pocan.house.gov   **f** 202.225.6942
Bio. 08/14/1964 • Kenosha • Univ. of Wisconsin - Madison,
B.A., 1986 • Unspecified/Other • M. Philip Frank **Cmte.**
Appropriations • Education & Labor • Joint Economic
CoS. Glenn Wavrunek   **LD.** David Bagby
Sched. Maura Haydin   **PS.** Matthew Handverger
Dist. Off. Beloit 608.365.8001 • Madison 608.258.9800

R: 184 **T:** 5th 70%
Elected Year: 2012

♜ Rep. Bryan G. Steil ("style")   R-WI-01   p 202.225.3031

Rm. LHOB 1526 **Web.** steil.house.gov
Bio. 03/03/1981 • Janesville • Georgetown Univ. (DC), B.S.,
2003; Univ. of Wisconsin, J.D., 2007 • Catholic • S. **Cmte.**
Administration • Communications Standards Commission •
Financial Services • Select Economic Disparity & Fairness in
Growth
CoS. Ryan Carney   **LD.** David Goldfarb
Sched. Kristen Monterroso   **PS.** Grace White
Dist. Off. Janesville 608.752.4050

R: 352 **T:** 2nd 59%
Elected Year: 2018

♜ Rep. Tom Tiffany (TIF-uh-nee)   R-WI-07   p 202.225.3365

Rm. LHOB 1719 **Web.** tiffany.house.gov
Bio. 12/30/1957 • Wabasha • Univ. of Wisconsin, River
Falls, B.S., 1980 • M. Christine Sully, 3 ch **Cmte.** Judiciary •
Natural Resources
CoS. Jason Bauknecht   **LD.** Mac Zimmerman
Sched. Mary Galey   **PS.** Brigid Nealon
Dist. Off. Wausau 715.298.9344

R: 368 **T:** 2nd 61%
Elected Year: 2019

WYOMING

Governor Mark Gordon (GOR-duhn)   p 307.777.7434

State Capitol
200 W. 24th St.
Cheyenne, WY 82002-0010
Website wyoming.gov
Fax 307.632.3909
Term Ends 2023

C: Cheyenne
P: 577,737 (52)
A: 97,093.07 mi^2 (9th)

U.S. Senators
John A. Barrasso, R
Cynthia M. Lummis, R
U.S. Representatives
01 / Liz Cheney, R

Sen. John A. Barrasso (bah-RAH-so)   R-WY-Sr.   p 202.224.6441

Rm. DSOB 307 **Web.** barrasso.senate.gov   **f** 202.224.1724
Bio. 07/21/1952 • Reading • State Legislator; Orthopedic
Surgeon • Georgetown Univ. (DC), B.S., 1974; Georgetown
Univ. School of Medicine (DC), M.D., 1978 • Presbyterian •
M. Bobbi Brown, 3 ch (2 from previous marriage) **Cmte.**
Energy & Natural Resources • Finance • Foreign Relations
CoS. Dan Kunsman   **LD.** Amber Bland
Sched. Kathi Wise   **PS.** Laura Mengelkamp
Dist. Off. Casper 307.261.6413 • Cheyenne 307.772.2451
• Riverton 307.856.6642 • Rock Springs 307.362.5012 •
Sheridan 307.672.6456

R: 30 **T:** 4th 67%
Elected Year: 2007
Next Election: 2024

Sen. Cynthia M. Lummis (LUH-muhs)   R-WY-Jr.   p 202.224.3424

Web. lummis.senate.gov   **f** 202.228.0359
Bio. 09/10/1954 • Cheyenne • State Legislator; Attorney •
Univ. of Wyoming (WY), B.S., 1976; Univ. of Wyoming (WY),
B.S., 1978; Univ. of Wyoming College of Law, J.D., 1985 •
Lutheran • W., 1 ch; 1 gr-ch **Cmte.** Banking, Housing &
Urban Affairs • Commerce, Science & Transportation •
Environment & Public Works
CoS. Kristin Walker (CD)   **LD.** Darrin Munoz (CD)
Sched. Mikalah Skates (CD)   **PS.** Darin Miller (CD)
Dist. Off. Afton 307.248.1736 • Casper 307.261.6572 •
Cheyenne 307.772.2477 • Cody 307.527.9444 • Sheridan
307.439.7783 • Sundance 307.283.3461

R: 95 **T:** 1st 73%
Elected Year: 2020
Next Election: 2026

Rep. Liz Cheney (CHAY-nee)   R-WY-01   p 202.225.2311

Rm. CHOB 416 **Web.** cheney.house.gov   **f** 202.225.3057
Bio. 07/28/1966 • Madison • Colorado College, B.A.,
1988; Univ. of Chicago Law School, J.D., 1996 • Methodist
• M. Philip Perry, 5 ch **Cmte.** Armed Services • Select
Investigate Jan 6 Attack on the U.S. Capitol
CoS. Kara Ahern   **LD.** Andrew Meyer
Sched. Elizabeth Pearce   **PS.** Jeremy Adler
Dist. Off. Casper 307.261.6595 • Cheyenne 307.772.2595 •
Gillette 307.414.1677 • Riverton 307.463.0482

R: 254 **T:** 3rd 69%
Elected Year: 2016

AMERICAN SAMOA

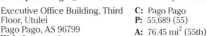

🔒 **Governor Lemanu Palepoi Mauga** ()   p 684.633.4116

Executive Office Building, Third
Floor, Utulei
Pago Pago, AS 96799
Website americansamoa.gov
Fax 684.633.2269
Term Ends 2025
Lt. Governor
Talauega Eleasalo Vaalele Ale, **D**

C: Pago Pago
P: 55,689 (55)
A: 76.45 mi² (55th)

Delegate

📷 **Del. Amata Coleman Radewagen** (RAD-eh-wag-R-AS-01   p 202.225.8577
uhn)

Rm. LHOB 1339 **Web.** radewagen.house.gov **f** 202.225.8757
Bio. Pago Pago • Univ. of Guam, B.S., 1975 • Roman
Catholic • M. Fred Radewagen, 3 ch; 1 gr-ch **Cmte.** Natural
Resources • Veterans' Affairs
CoS. Leafaina Yahn   **LD.** Richard Stanton
Sched. Nancy Dehlinger   **PS.** Joel Hannahs
Dist. Off. Fagatogo 684.633.3601

R: 4 **T:** 4th 83%
Elected Year: 2014

DISTRICT OF COLUMBIA

🔒 **Mayor Muriel Bowser** (BOU-zur)   p 202.727.2643

Executive Office of the Mayor
1350 Pennsylvania Avenue NW,
Suite 316
Washington, DC 20004
Website dc.gov
Fax 202.727.0505
Term Ends 2023

C: Washington
P: 702,455 (50)
A: 61.00 mi² (56th)

Delegate

🔒 **Del. Eleanor Holmes Norton** (NOR-tuhn)   D-DC-01   p 202.225.8050

Rm. RHOB 2136 **Web.** norton.house.gov   **f** 202.225.3002
Bio. 06/13/1937 • Washington • Professor; Employment
Commission Chair • Antioch College (OH), B.A., 1960; Yale
Univ. (CT), M.A., 1963; Yale Univ. Law School (CT), J.D.,
1964 • Episcopalian • D., 2 ch **Cmte.** Oversight & Reform •
Transportation & Infrastructure
CoS. Raven Reeder   **LD.** Bradley Truding
Sched. Try Onaghise-   **PS.** Sharon Eliza Nichols
Coburn
Dist. Off. Washington 202.408.9041 • Washington
202.678.8900

R: 1 **T:** 16th 86%
Elected Year: 1990

GUAM

🔒 **Governor Lou Leon Guerrero** (guh-RAIR-o)   p 671.472.8931

Richard J. Bordallo Governor's
Complex
Adelup, GU 96910
Website guam.gov
Fax 671.477.4826
Term Ends 2023
Lt. Governor
Josh Tenorio, **D**

C: Hagatna
P: 164,229 (53)
A: 209.65 mi² (52nd)

GUAM

Delegate

⚑ Del. Michael F.Q. San Nicolas (san nee-ko-LAH)   D-GU-01   p 202.225.1188

Rm. LHOB 1632 **Web.** sannicolas.house.gov
Bio. Talofofo • Univ. of Guam, B.A., 2004 • M. Kathryn
Santos Ko, 2 ch **Cmte.** Financial Services • Natural
Resources
CoS. Jennifer Winn (CD)
Sched. T'Nelta Mori
Dist. Off. Hagatna 671.475.6453

R: 6 **T:** 2nd 60%
Elected Year: 2018

MARIANA ISLANDS

⚑ Governor Ralph Torres (toe-ress)   p 670.664.2280

Juan Atalig Memorial Building
Isla Dr., Capitol Hill, Caller Box
10007
Saipan, MP 96950
Website gov.mp
Fax 670.664.2211
Term Ends 2023
Lt. Governor
Arnold Palacios, R

C: Saipan
P: 52,263 (56)
A: 182.24 mi^2 (53rd)

Delegate

⚑ Del. Gregorio Kilili Camacho Sablan (sah-   D-MP-01   p 202.225.2646
BLAHN)

Rm. RHOB 2267 **Web.** sablan.house.gov   **f** 202.226.4249
Bio. 01/19/1955 • Saipan • Public Administrator • Army
• Roman Catholic • M. Andrea C. Sablan, 6 ch **Cmte.**
Agriculture • Education & Labor • Natural Resources •
Veterans' Affairs
CoS. Robert Schwalbach   **LD.** Adam Tanga
Sched. John R.P. Del
Rosario
Dist. Off. Rota 670.532.2647 • Saipan 670.323.2647 •
Tinian 670.433.2647

R: 2 **T:** 6th 100%
Elected Year: 2008

PUERTO RICO

⚑ Governor Pedro R. Pierluisi (pee-air-loo-EE-see)   p 787.721.7000

PO Box 9023431
San Juan, PR 00902-0082
Website pr.gov
Fax 787.729.5072
Term Ends 2025

C: San Juan
P: 3,195,153 (30)
A: 3,423.95 mi^2 (49th)

Delegate

⚑ Del. Jenniffer A. Gonzalez-Colon (gon-SAH-les R-PR-01   p 202.225.2615
ko-LOAN)

Rm. RHOB 2338 **Web.** gonzalez-   **f** 202.225.2154
colon.house.gov
Bio. 08/05/1976 • San Juan • Univ. of Puerto Rico, Bach.
Deg.; Univ. of Puerto Rico, Bach. Deg.; Univ. of Puerto
Rico, Bach. Deg. • Unspecified/Other • S. **Cmte.** Natural
Resources • Transportation & Infrastructure
CoS. Gabriella Boffelli   **LD.** Ross Dietrich
Sched. Linoshka Luna   **PS.** Marieli Padro-Raldiris
(CD)
Dist. Off. San Juan 787.723.6333

R: 5 **T:** 2nd 41%
Elected Year: 2016

VIRGIN ISLANDS

⚑ Governor Albert Bryan (BRY-uhn)   p 340.774.0001

Government House
21-22 Kongens Gade, Charlotte
Amalie
St. Thomas, VI 00802
Website vi.gov
Fax 340.774.1361
Term Ends 2023
Lt. Governor
Tregenza Roach, **D**

C: Charlotte Amalie
P: 104,901 (54)
A: 134.36 mi^2 (54th)

Delegate

⚑ Del. Stacey E. Plaskett (PLAS-ket)   D-VI-01   p 202.225.1790

Rm. RHOB 2404 **Web.** plaskett.house.gov   **f** 202.225.5517
Bio. 05/13/1964 • New York • Georgetown Univ. Foreign
Service School (DC), B.S., 1984; American Univ., Washington
College of Law, J.D., 1994 • Lutheran • M. Jeremy Buckney
Small, 5 ch   **Cmte.** Agriculture • Budget • Ways & Means
CoS. Angeline Jabbar   **LD.** Jeffrey M. Nowill
Sched. Conrad R. Francois   **PS.** Michael J. McQuerry
Dist. Off. Frederiksted 340.778.5900 • St. Thomas
340.774.4408

R: 3   **T:** 4th 88%
Elected Year: 2014

VIRGIN ISLANDS

INDEX OF COMMITTEES AND SUBCOMMITTEES

Below is an alphabetical listing of all committees and subcommittees by name. Bold type indicates committee, non-bold type indicates subcommittee. Entries are grouped by Senate, Joint and House.

SENATE

SENATE COMMITTEES

Committee rosters are listed in order of ranking membership with the Chairman and Ranking Member indicated with "C" and "RM" respectively. The chairman and ranking member of each committee usually have membership status on all subcommittees of which they are not members. This is referred to as ex officio membership. These memberships are subject to the rules of the individual committees.

AGRICULTURE, NUTRITION & FORESTRY

Room: RSOB 328A
Website: www.agriculture.senate.gov
Phone: 202.224.2035
Ratio: 11 Democrats/11 Republicans
Subcommittees: 6

Majority:		Minority:	
C: Debbie Stabenow, MI	HSOB 731	RM: John Boozman, AR	HSOB 141
Patrick Leahy, VT	RSOB 437	Mitch McConnell, KY	RSOB 317
Sherrod Brown, OH	HSOB 503	John Hoeven, ND	RSOB 338
Amy Klobuchar, MN	DSOB 425	Joni Ernst, IA	HSOB 730
Michael Bennet, CO	RSOB 261	Cindy Hyde-Smith, MS	HSOB 702
Kirsten Gillibrand, NY	RSOB 478	Roger Marshall, KS	RSOB 479A
Tina Smith, MN	HSOB 720	Tommy Tuberville, AL	RSOB 142
Dick Durbin, IL	HSOB 711	Chuck Grassley, IA	HSOB 135
Cory Booker, NJ	HSOB 717	John Thune, SD	DSOB 511
Ben Ray Luján, NM	RSOB 498	Deb Fischer, NE	RSOB 454
Raphael Warnock, GA	RSOB 388	Mike Braun, IN	RSOB 374

Majority CoS: Joseph Shultz   **Minority CoS:** Fitzhugh Elder IV

——————————— Subcommittees ———————————

COMMODITIES, RISK MANAGEMENT & TRADE
Room:

Majority:		Minority:	
C: Raphael Warnock, GA	RSOB 388	RM: John Hoeven, ND	RSOB 338
Sherrod Brown, OH	HSOB 503	Mitch McConnell, KY	RSOB 317
Dick Durbin, IL	HSOB 711	Cindy Hyde-Smith, MS	HSOB 702
Tina Smith, MN	HSOB 720	Tommy Tuberville, AL	RSOB 142
Kirsten Gillibrand, NY	RSOB 478	Chuck Grassley, IA	HSOB 135
Ben Ray Luján, NM	RSOB 498	John Thune, SD	DSOB 511
Debbie Stabenow, MI	HSOB 731		

CONSERVATION, CLIMATE, FORESTRY & NATURAL RESOURCES
Room:

Majority:		Minority:	
C: Michael Bennet, CO	RSOB 261	RM: Roger Marshall, KS	RSOB 479A
Patrick Leahy, VT	RSOB 437	John Hoeven, ND	RSOB 338
Cory Booker, NJ	HSOB 717	Cindy Hyde-Smith, MS	HSOB 702
Ben Ray Luján, NM	RSOB 498	Tommy Tuberville, AL	RSOB 142
Sherrod Brown, OH	HSOB 503	John Thune, SD	DSOB 511
Amy Klobuchar, MN	DSOB 425	Mike Braun, IN	RSOB 374
Debbie Stabenow, MI	HSOB 731	John Boozman, AR	HSOB 141

FOOD & NUTRITION, SPECIALTY CROPS, ORGANICS & RESEARCH
Room:

Majority:		Minority:	
C: Cory Booker, NJ	HSOB 717	RM: Mike Braun, IN	RSOB 374
Patrick Leahy, VT	RSOB 437	Mitch McConnell, KY	RSOB 317
Amy Klobuchar, MN	DSOB 425	John Hoeven, ND	RSOB 338
Kirsten Gillibrand, NY	RSOB 478	Joni Ernst, IA	HSOB 730
Raphael Warnock, GA	RSOB 388	Roger Marshall, KS	RSOB 479A
Michael Bennet, CO	RSOB 261	Deb Fischer, NE	RSOB 454
Debbie Stabenow, MI	HSOB 731	John Boozman, AR	HSOB 141

LIVESTOCK, DAIRY, POULTRY, LOCAL FOOD SYS & FOOD SAFETY & SEC
Room:

Majority:		Minority:	
C: Kirsten Gillibrand, NY	RSOB 478	RM: Cindy Hyde-Smith, MS	HSOB 702
Patrick Leahy, VT	RSOB 437		
Tina Smith, MN	HSOB 720	Joni Ernst, IA	HSOB 730
Dick Durbin, IL	HSOB 711	Roger Marshall, KS	RSOB 479A
Cory Booker, NJ	HSOB 717	Chuck Grassley, IA	HSOB 135
Raphael Warnock, GA	RSOB 388	Deb Fischer, NE	RSOB 454
Debbie Stabenow, MI	HSOB 731	John Thune, SD	DSOB 511
		John Boozman, AR	HSOB 141

NUTRITION, AGRICULTURAL RESEARCH, AND SPECIALTY CROPS
Room:

Information for this committee, including membership, was not finalized as of the publication date and is therefore subject to change.

RURAL DEVELOPMENT & ENERGY
Room:

Majority:		Minority:	
C: Tina Smith, MN	HSOB 720	**RM: Joni Ernst, IA**	HSOB 730
Amy Klobuchar, MN	DSOB 425	Mitch McConnell, KY	RSOB 317
Ben Ray Luján, NM	RSOB 498	Tommy Tuberville, AL	RSOB 142
Sherrod Brown, OH	HSOB 503	Chuck Grassley, IA	HSOB 135
Michael Bennet, CO	RSOB 261	Deb Fischer, NE	RSOB 454
Dick Durbin, IL	HSOB 711	Mike Braun, IN	RSOB 374
Debbie Stabenow, MI	HSOB 731	John Boozman, AR	HSOB 141

APPROPRIATIONS

Room: The Capitol S-128
Website: www.appropriations.senate.gov
Phone: 202.224.7363
Ratio: 15 Democrats/15 Republicans
Subcommittees: 12

Majority:		Minority:	
C: Patrick Leahy, VT	RSOB 437	Richard Shelby, AL	RSOB 304
Patty Murray, WA	RSOB 154	Mitch McConnell, KY	RSOB 317
Dianne Feinstein, CA	HSOB 331	Susan Collins, ME	DSOB 413
Dick Durbin, IL	HSOB 711	Lisa Murkowski, AK	HSOB 522
Jack Reed, RI	HSOB 728	Lindsey Graham, SC	RSOB 290
Jon Tester, MT	HSOB 311	Roy Blunt, MO	RSOB 260
Jeanne Shaheen, NH	HSOB 506	Jerry Moran, KS	DSOB 521
Jeff Merkley, OR	HSOB 531	John Hoeven, ND	RSOB 338
Chris Coons, DE	RSOB 218	John Boozman, AR	HSOB 141
Brian Schatz, HI	HSOB 722	Shelley Capito, WV	RSOB 172
Tammy Baldwin, WI	HSOB 709	John Kennedy, LA	RSOB 416
Chris Murphy, CT	HSOB 136	Cindy Hyde-Smith, MS	HSOB 702
Joe Manchin, WV	HSOB 306	Mike Braun, IN	RSOB 374
Chris Van Hollen, MD	HSOB 110	Bill Hagerty, TN	RSOB 248
Martin Heinrich, NM	HSOB 303	Marco Rubio, FL	RSOB 284

Majority CoS: Charles E. Kieffer **Minority CoS:** William D. Duhnke III

———— Subcommittees ————

AGRICULTURE, RURAL DEVELOPMENT, FDA & RELATED AGENCIES
Room: DSOB 129
Phone: 202.224.8090

Majority:		Minority:	
C: Tammy Baldwin, WI	HSOB 709	**RM: John Hoeven, ND**	RSOB 338
Jeff Merkley, OR	HSOB 531	Mitch McConnell, KY	RSOB 317
Dianne Feinstein, CA	HSOB 331	Susan Collins, ME	DSOB 413
Jon Tester, MT	HSOB 311	Roy Blunt, MO	RSOB 260
Patrick Leahy, VT	RSOB 437	Jerry Moran, KS	DSOB 521
Brian Schatz, HI	HSOB 722	Cindy Hyde-Smith, MS	HSOB 702
Martin Heinrich, NM	HSOB 303	Mike Braun, IN	RSOB 374
		Richard Shelby, AL	RSOB 304

COMMERCE, JUSTICE, SCIENCE & RELATED AGENCIES
Room: DSOB 142
Phone: 202.224.5202

Majority:		Minority:	
C: Jeanne Shaheen, NH	HSOB 506	**RM: Jerry Moran, KS**	DSOB 521
Patrick Leahy, VT	RSOB 437	Lisa Murkowski, AK	HSOB 522
Dianne Feinstein, CA	HSOB 331	Susan Collins, ME	DSOB 413
Jack Reed, RI	HSOB 728	Lindsey Graham, SC	RSOB 290
Chris Coons, DE	RSOB 218	John Boozman, AR	HSOB 141
Brian Schatz, HI	HSOB 722	Shelley Capito, WV	RSOB 172
Joe Manchin, WV	HSOB 306	John Kennedy, LA	RSOB 416
Chris Van Hollen, MD	HSOB 110	Bill Hagerty, TN	RSOB 248
Jeff Merkley, OR	HSOB 531	Mike Braun, IN	RSOB 374
		Richard Shelby, AL	RSOB 304

DEPARTMENT OF DEFENSE
Room: DSOB 122
Phone: 202.224.6688

Majority:		Minority:	
C: Jon Tester, MT	HSOB 311	Richard Shelby, AL	RSOB 304
Dick Durbin, IL	HSOB 711	Mitch McConnell, KY	RSOB 317
Patrick Leahy, VT	RSOB 437	Susan Collins, ME	DSOB 413
Dianne Feinstein, CA	HSOB 331	Lisa Murkowski, AK	HSOB 522

Patty Murray, WA	RSOB 154	Lindsey Graham, SC	RSOB 290
Jack Reed, RI	HSOB 728	Roy Blunt, MO	RSOB 260
Brian Schatz, HI	HSOB 722	Jerry Moran, KS	DSOB 521
Tammy Baldwin, WI	HSOB 709	John Hoeven, ND	RSOB 338
Jeanne Shaheen, NH	HSOB 506	John Boozman, AR	HSOB 141

DEPARTMENT OF HOMELAND SECURITY
Room: DSOB 131
Phone: 202.224.8244

Majority:		Minority:	
C: Chris Murphy, CT	HSOB 136	**RM: Shelley Capito, WV**	RSOB 172
Jon Tester, MT	HSOB 311	Richard Shelby, AL	RSOB 304
Jeanne Shaheen, NH	HSOB 506	Lisa Murkowski, AK	HSOB 522
Patrick Leahy, VT	RSOB 437	John Hoeven, ND	RSOB 338
Patty Murray, WA	RSOB 154	John Kennedy, LA	RSOB 416
Tammy Baldwin, WI	HSOB 709	Cindy Hyde-Smith, MS	HSOB 702

DEPARTMENT OF THE INTERIOR, ENVIRONMENT & RELATED AGENCIES
Room: DSOB 142
Phone: 202.224.0774

Majority:		Minority:	
C: Jeff Merkley, OR	HSOB 531	**RM: Lisa Murkowski, AK**	HSOB 522
Dianne Feinstein, CA	HSOB 331	Roy Blunt, MO	RSOB 260
Patrick Leahy, VT	RSOB 437	Mitch McConnell, KY	RSOB 317
Jack Reed, RI	HSOB 728	Shelley Capito, WV	RSOB 172
Jon Tester, MT	HSOB 311	Cindy Hyde-Smith, MS	HSOB 702
Chris Van Hollen, MD	HSOB 110	Bill Hagerty, TN	RSOB 248
Martin Heinrich, NM	HSOB 303	Marco Rubio, FL	RSOB 284
		Richard Shelby, AL	RSOB 304

DOL, HHS & EDUCATION & RELATED AGENCIES
Room: DSOB 136
Phone: 202.224.9145

Majority:		Minority:	
C: Patty Murray, WA	RSOB 154	**RM: Roy Blunt, MO**	RSOB 260
Dick Durbin, IL	HSOB 711	Richard Shelby, AL	RSOB 304
Jack Reed, RI	HSOB 728	Lindsey Graham, SC	RSOB 290
Jeanne Shaheen, NH	HSOB 506	Jerry Moran, KS	DSOB 521
Jeff Merkley, OR	HSOB 531	Shelley Capito, WV	RSOB 172
Brian Schatz, HI	HSOB 722	John Kennedy, LA	RSOB 416
Tammy Baldwin, WI	HSOB 709	Cindy Hyde-Smith, MS	HSOB 702
Chris Murphy, CT	HSOB 136	Mike Braun, IN	RSOB 374
Joe Manchin, WV	HSOB 306	Marco Rubio, FL	RSOB 284
Patrick Leahy, VT	RSOB 437		

ENERGY & WATER DEVELOPMENT
Room: DSOB 131
Phone: 202.224.8119

Majority:		Minority:	
C: Dianne Feinstein, CA	HSOB 331	**RM: John Kennedy, LA**	RSOB 416
Patty Murray, WA	RSOB 154	Mitch McConnell, KY	RSOB 317
Jon Tester, MT	HSOB 311	Richard Shelby, AL	RSOB 304
Dick Durbin, IL	HSOB 711	Susan Collins, ME	DSOB 413
Jeanne Shaheen, NH	HSOB 506	Lisa Murkowski, AK	HSOB 522
Jeff Merkley, OR	HSOB 531	Lindsey Graham, SC	RSOB 290
Chris Coons, DE	RSOB 218	John Hoeven, ND	RSOB 338
Tammy Baldwin, WI	HSOB 709	Cindy Hyde-Smith, MS	HSOB 702
Martin Heinrich, NM	HSOB 303	Bill Hagerty, TN	RSOB 248
Patrick Leahy, VT	RSOB 437		

FINANCIAL SERVICES & GENERAL GOVERNMENT
Room: DSOB 133
Phone: 202.224.1133

Majority:		Minority:	
C: Chris Van Hollen, MD	HSOB 110	**RM: Cindy Hyde-Smith, MS**	HSOB 702
Chris Coons, DE	RSOB 218		
Dick Durbin, IL	HSOB 711	Jerry Moran, KS	DSOB 521
Joe Manchin, WV	HSOB 306	John Boozman, AR	HSOB 141
Patrick Leahy, VT	RSOB 437	John Kennedy, LA	RSOB 416
		Richard Shelby, AL	RSOB 304

LEGISLATIVE BRANCH
Room: The Capitol S-128
Phone: 202.224.7264

Majority:		Minority:	
C: Jack Reed, RI	HSOB 728	**RM: Mike Braun, IN**	RSOB 374
Chris Murphy, CT	HSOB 136	Richard Shelby, AL	RSOB 304
Martin Heinrich, NM	HSOB 303	Marco Rubio, FL	RSOB 284

Patrick Leahy, VT RSOB 437

MILITARY CONSTRUCTION & VETERAN AFFAIRS & RELATED AGENCIES
Room: DSOB 125
Phone: 202.224.8224

Majority:		Minority:	
C: Martin Heinrich, NM	HSOB 303	**RM: John Boozman, AR**	HSOB 141
Brian Schatz, HI	HSOB 722	Mitch McConnell, KY	RSOB 317
Jon Tester, MT	HSOB 311	Lisa Murkowski, AK	HSOB 522
Patty Murray, WA	RSOB 154	John Hoeven, ND	RSOB 338
Jack Reed, RI	HSOB 728	Susan Collins, ME	DSOB 413
Tammy Baldwin, WI	HSOB 709	Shelley Capito, WV	RSOB 172
Chris Coons, DE	RSOB 218	Marco Rubio, FL	RSOB 284
Joe Manchin, WV	HSOB 306	Bill Hagerty, TN	RSOB 248
Patrick Leahy, VT	RSOB 437	Richard Shelby, AL	RSOB 304

STATE, FOREIGN OPERATIONS & RELATED PROGRAMS
Room: DSOB 127
Phone: 202.224.7284

Majority:		Minority:	
C: Chris Coons, DE	RSOB 218	**RM: Lindsey Graham, SC**	RSOB 290
Patrick Leahy, VT	RSOB 437	Mitch McConnell, KY	RSOB 317
Dick Durbin, IL	HSOB 711	Roy Blunt, MO	RSOB 260
Jeanne Shaheen, NH	HSOB 506	John Boozman, AR	HSOB 141
Jeff Merkley, OR	HSOB 531	Jerry Moran, KS	DSOB 521
Chris Murphy, CT	HSOB 136	Marco Rubio, FL	RSOB 284
Chris Van Hollen, MD	HSOB 110	Bill Hagerty, TN	RSOB 248
		Richard Shelby, AL	RSOB 304

TRANSPORTATION, HUD & RELATED AGENCIES
Room: DSOB 184
Phone: 202.224.7281

Majority:		Minority:	
C: Brian Schatz, HI	HSOB 722	**RM: Susan Collins, ME**	DSOB 413
Jack Reed, RI	HSOB 728	Richard Shelby, AL	RSOB 304
Patty Murray, WA	RSOB 154	Roy Blunt, MO	RSOB 260
Dick Durbin, IL	HSOB 711	John Boozman, AR	HSOB 141
Dianne Feinstein, CA	HSOB 331	Shelley Capito, WV	RSOB 172
Chris Coons, DE	RSOB 218	Lindsey Graham, SC	RSOB 290
Chris Murphy, CT	HSOB 136	John Hoeven, ND	RSOB 338
Joe Manchin, WV	HSOB 306	John Kennedy, LA	RSOB 416
Chris Van Hollen, MD	HSOB 110	Mike Braun, IN	RSOB 374
Patrick Leahy, VT	RSOB 437		

ARMED SERVICES

Room: RSOB 228
Website: www.armed-services.senate.gov
Phone: 202.224.3871
Ratio: 13 Democrats/13 Republicans
Subcommittees: 7

Majority:		Minority:	
C: Jack Reed, RI	HSOB 728	**RM: James Inhofe, OK**	RSOB 205
Jeanne Shaheen, NH	HSOB 506	Roger Wicker, MS	DSOB 555
Kirsten Gillibrand, NY	RSOB 478	Deb Fischer, NE	RSOB 454
Richard Blumenthal, CT	HSOB 706	Tom Cotton, AR	RSOB 326
Mazie Hirono, HI	HSOB 109	Mike Rounds, SD	HSOB 716
Tim Kaine, VA	RSOB 231	Joni Ernst, IA	HSOB 730
Angus King, ME	HSOB 133	Thom Tillis, NC	DSOB 113
Elizabeth Warren, MA	HSOB 309	Dan Sullivan, AK	HSOB 302
Gary Peters, MI	HSOB 724	Kevin Cramer, ND	RSOB 400
Joe Manchin, WV	HSOB 306	Rick Scott, FL	HSOB 502
Tammy Duckworth, IL	HSOB 524	Marsha Blackburn, TN	DSOB 357
Jacky Rosen, NV	HSOB 713	Josh Hawley, MO	RSOB 212
Mark Kelly, AZ	HSOB 516	Tommy Tuberville, AL	RSOB 142

Majority CoS: Hon. Elizabeth L. King   **Minority CoS:** John Duane Wason
———————————— Subcommittees ————————————

AIRLAND
Room: RSOB 228
Phone: 202.224.3871

Majority:		Minority:	
C: Tammy Duckworth, IL	HSOB 524	**RM: Tom Cotton, AR**	RSOB 326
Angus King, ME	HSOB 133	Roger Wicker, MS	DSOB 555
Gary Peters, MI	HSOB 724	Thom Tillis, NC	DSOB 113
Joe Manchin, WV	HSOB 306	Dan Sullivan, AK	HSOB 302
Mark Kelly, AZ	HSOB 516	Rick Scott, FL	HSOB 502

Jacky Rosen, NV	HSOB 713	Josh Hawley, MO	RSOB 212
Jack Reed, RI	HSOB 728	James Inhofe, OK	RSOB 205

CYBERSECURITY
Room: RSOB 228
Phone: 202.224.3871

Majority:		Minority:	
C: Joe Manchin, WV	HSOB 306	**RM: Mike Rounds, SD**	HSOB 716
Kirsten Gillibrand, NY	RSOB 478	Roger Wicker, MS	DSOB 555
Richard Blumenthal, CT	HSOB 706	Joni Ernst, IA	HSOB 730
Jacky Rosen, NV	HSOB 713	Marsha Blackburn, TN	DSOB 357
Jack Reed, RI	HSOB 728	James Inhofe, OK	RSOB 205

EMERGING THREATS & CAPABILITIES
Room: RSOB 228
Phone: 202.224.3871

Majority:		Minority:	
C: Mark Kelly, AZ	HSOB 516	**RM: Joni Ernst, IA**	HSOB 730
Jeanne Shaheen, NH	HSOB 506	Deb Fischer, NE	RSOB 454
Tim Kaine, VA	RSOB 231	Kevin Cramer, ND	RSOB 400
Elizabeth Warren, MA	HSOB 309	Rick Scott, FL	HSOB 502
Gary Peters, MI	HSOB 724	Marsha Blackburn, TN	DSOB 357
Kirsten Gillibrand, NY	RSOB 478	Tommy Tuberville, AL	RSOB 142
Jack Reed, RI	HSOB 728	Josh Hawley, MO	RSOB 212

PERSONNEL
Room: RSOB 228
Phone: 202.224.3871

Majority:		Minority:	
C: Kirsten Gillibrand, NY	RSOB 478	**RM: Thom Tillis, NC**	DSOB 113
Mazie Hirono, HI	HSOB 109	Josh Hawley, MO	RSOB 212
Elizabeth Warren, MA	HSOB 309	Tommy Tuberville, AL	RSOB 142
Jack Reed, RI	HSOB 728	James Inhofe, OK	RSOB 205

READINESS & MANAGEMENT SUPPORT
Room: RSOB 228
Phone: 202.224.3871

Majority:		Minority:	
C: Tim Kaine, VA	RSOB 231	**RM: Dan Sullivan, AK**	HSOB 302
Jeanne Shaheen, NH	HSOB 506	Deb Fischer, NE	RSOB 454
Richard Blumenthal, CT	HSOB 706	Mike Rounds, SD	HSOB 716
Mazie Hirono, HI	HSOB 109	Joni Ernst, IA	HSOB 730
Tammy Duckworth, IL	HSOB 524	Marsha Blackburn, TN	DSOB 357
Jack Reed, RI	HSOB 728	James Inhofe, OK	RSOB 205

SEAPOWER
Room: RSOB 228
Phone: 202.224.3871

Majority:		Minority:	
C: Mazie Hirono, HI	HSOB 109	**RM: Kevin Cramer, ND**	RSOB 400
Jeanne Shaheen, NH	HSOB 506	Roger Wicker, MS	DSOB 555
Richard Blumenthal, CT	HSOB 706	Tom Cotton, AR	RSOB 326
Angus King, ME	HSOB 133	Thom Tillis, NC	DSOB 113
Tim Kaine, VA	RSOB 231	Rick Scott, FL	HSOB 502
Gary Peters, MI	HSOB 724	Josh Hawley, MO	RSOB 212
Jack Reed, RI	HSOB 728	James Inhofe, OK	RSOB 205

STRATEGIC FORCES
Room: RSOB 228
Phone: 202.224.3871

Majority:		Minority:	
C: Angus King, ME	HSOB 133	**RM: Deb Fischer, NE**	RSOB 454
Elizabeth Warren, MA	HSOB 309	Tom Cotton, AR	RSOB 326
Joe Manchin, WV	HSOB 306	Mike Rounds, SD	HSOB 716
Tammy Duckworth, IL	HSOB 524	Dan Sullivan, AK	HSOB 302
Jacky Rosen, NV	HSOB 713	Kevin Cramer, ND	RSOB 400
Mark Kelly, AZ	HSOB 516	Tommy Tuberville, AL	RSOB 142
Jack Reed, RI	HSOB 728	James Inhofe, OK	RSOB 205

BANKING, HOUSING & URBAN AFFAIRS

Room: DSOB 534
Website: www.banking.senate.gov
Phone: 202.224.7391
Ratio: 12 Democrats/12 Republicans
Subcommittees: 5

Majority:		Minority:	
C: Sherrod Brown, OH	HSOB 503	**RM: Pat Toomey, PA**	DSOB 455
Jack Reed, RI	HSOB 728	Richard Shelby, AL	RSOB 304

Bob Menendez, NJ	HSOB 528	Mike Crapo, ID	DSOB 239
Jon Tester, MT	HSOB 311	Tim Scott, SC	HSOB 104
Mark Warner, VA	HSOB 703	Mike Rounds, SD	HSOB 716
Elizabeth Warren, MA	HSOB 309	Thom Tillis, NC	DSOB 113
Chris Van Hollen, MD	HSOB 110	John Kennedy, LA	RSOB 416
Catherine Cortez Masto, NV	HSOB 313	Bill Hagerty, TN	RSOB 248
		Cynthia Lummis, WY	RSOB 124
Tina Smith, MN	HSOB 720	Jerry Moran, KS	DSOB 521
Kyrsten Sinema, AZ	HSOB 317	Kevin Cramer, ND	RSOB 400
Jon Ossoff, GA	RSOB 455	Steve Daines, MT	HSOB 320
Raphael Warnock, GA	RSOB 388		

Majority CoS: Laura Swanson   **Minority CoS:** Brad Grantz

————————— Subcommittees —————————

ECONOMIC POLICY
Room: RSOB 124
Phone: 202.224.2353

Majority:		Minority:	
C: Elizabeth Warren, MA	HSOB 309	**RM: John Kennedy, LA**	RSOB 416
Jack Reed, RI	HSOB 728	Tim Scott, SC	HSOB 104
Chris Van Hollen, MD	HSOB 110	Thom Tillis, NC	DSOB 113
Tina Smith, MN	HSOB 720	Kevin Cramer, ND	RSOB 400
Jon Ossoff, GA	RSOB 455	Steve Daines, MT	HSOB 320

FINANCIAL INSTITUTIONS & CONSUMER PROTECTION
Room:

Majority:		Minority:	
C: Raphael Warnock, GA	RSOB 388	**RM: Thom Tillis, NC**	DSOB 113
Bob Menendez, NJ	HSOB 528	Richard Shelby, AL	RSOB 304
Jon Tester, MT	HSOB 311	Tim Scott, SC	HSOB 104
Mark Warner, VA	HSOB 703	Mike Rounds, SD	HSOB 716
Elizabeth Warren, MA	HSOB 309	Bill Hagerty, TN	RSOB 248
Catherine Cortez Masto, NV	HSOB 313	Cynthia Lummis, WY	RSOB 124
		Jerry Moran, KS	DSOB 521
Chris Van Hollen, MD	HSOB 110	Kevin Cramer, ND	RSOB 400
Kyrsten Sinema, AZ	HSOB 317		

HOUSING, TRANSPORTATION & COMMUNITY DEVELOPMENT
Room: RSOB 455
Phone: 202.224.3521

Majority:		Minority:	
C: Tina Smith, MN	HSOB 720	**RM: Mike Rounds, SD**	HSOB 716
Jack Reed, RI	HSOB 728	Richard Shelby, AL	RSOB 304
Bob Menendez, NJ	HSOB 528	Mike Crapo, ID	DSOB 239
Jon Tester, MT	HSOB 311	Bill Hagerty, TN	RSOB 248
Catherine Cortez Masto, NV	HSOB 313	Cynthia Lummis, WY	RSOB 124
		Jerry Moran, KS	DSOB 521
Chris Van Hollen, MD	HSOB 110	Kevin Cramer, ND	RSOB 400
Jon Ossoff, GA	RSOB 455	Steve Daines, MT	HSOB 320
Raphael Warnock, GA	RSOB 388		

NATIONAL SECURITY & INTERNATIONAL TRADE & FINANCE
Room:

Majority:		Minority:	
C: Mark Warner, VA	HSOB 703	**RM: Bill Hagerty, TN**	RSOB 248
Jon Tester, MT	HSOB 311	Mike Crapo, ID	DSOB 239
Kyrsten Sinema, AZ	HSOB 317	John Kennedy, LA	RSOB 416
Jon Ossoff, GA	RSOB 455	Steve Daines, MT	HSOB 320

SECURITIES, INSURANCE & INVESTMENT
Room:

Majority:		Minority:	
C: Bob Menendez, NJ	HSOB 528	**RM: Tim Scott, SC**	HSOB 104
Jack Reed, RI	HSOB 728	Richard Shelby, AL	RSOB 304
Mark Warner, VA	HSOB 703	Mike Crapo, ID	DSOB 239
Elizabeth Warren, MA	HSOB 309	Mike Rounds, SD	HSOB 716
Catherine Cortez Masto, NV	HSOB 313	Thom Tillis, NC	DSOB 113
		John Kennedy, LA	RSOB 416
Tina Smith, MN	HSOB 720	Cynthia Lummis, WY	RSOB 124
Kyrsten Sinema, AZ	HSOB 317	Jerry Moran, KS	DSOB 521
Raphael Warnock, GA	RSOB 388		

BUDGET

Room: DSOB 624
Website: www.budget.senate.gov
Phone: 202.224.0642
Ratio: 11 Democrats/11 Republicans
Subcommittees: 0

Majority:		Minority:	
C: Bernie Sanders, VT	DSOB 332	**RM: Lindsey Graham, SC**	RSOB 290
Patty Murray, WA	RSOB 154	Chuck Grassley, IA	HSOB 135
Ron Wyden, OR	DSOB 221	Mike Crapo, ID	DSOB 239
Debbie Stabenow, MI	HSOB 731	Pat Toomey, PA	DSOB 455
Sheldon Whitehouse, RI	HSOB 530	Ron Johnson, WI	HSOB 328
Mark Warner, VA	HSOB 703	Mike Braun, IN	RSOB 374
Jeff Merkley, OR	HSOB 531	Rick Scott, FL	HSOB 502
Tim Kaine, VA	RSOB 231	Ben Sasse, NE	RSOB 107
Chris Van Hollen, MD	HSOB 110	Mitt Romney, UT	RSOB 124
Ben Ray Luján, NM	RSOB 498	John Kennedy, LA	RSOB 416
Alex Padilla, CA	HSOB 112	Kevin Cramer, ND	RSOB 400

Majority CoS: Warren Scott Gunnels   **Minority CoS:** Nick Myers

COMMERCE, SCIENCE & TRANSPORTATION

Room: RSOB 253
Website: www.commerce.senate.gov
Phone: 202.224.0411
Ratio: 14 Democrats/14 Republicans
Subcommittees: 7

Majority:		Minority:	
C: Maria Cantwell, WA	HSOB 511	**RM: Roger Wicker, MS**	DSOB 555
Amy Klobuchar, MN	DSOB 425	John Thune, SD	DSOB 511
Richard Blumenthal, CT	HSOB 706	Roy Blunt, MO	RSOB 260
Brian Schatz, HI	HSOB 722	Ted Cruz, TX	RSOB 127A
Ed Markey, MA	DSOB 255	Deb Fischer, NE	RSOB 454
Gary Peters, MI	HSOB 724	Jerry Moran, KS	DSOB 521
Tammy Baldwin, WI	HSOB 709	Dan Sullivan, AK	HSOB 302
Tammy Duckworth, IL	HSOB 524	Marsha Blackburn, TN	DSOB 357
Jon Tester, MT	HSOB 311	Todd Young, IN	DSOB 185
Kyrsten Sinema, AZ	HSOB 317	Mike Lee, UT	RSOB 361 A
Jacky Rosen, NV	HSOB 713	Ron Johnson, WI	HSOB 328
Ben Ray Luján, NM	RSOB 498	Shelley Capito, WV	RSOB 172
John Hickenlooper, CO	RSOB 374	Rick Scott, FL	HSOB 502
Raphael Warnock, GA	RSOB 388	Cynthia Lummis, WY	RSOB 124

Majority CoS: Melissa L. Porter   **Minority CoS:** John Keast

——————— Subcommittees ———————

AVIATION SAFETY, OPERATIONS & INNOVATIONS

Room: RSOB 253
Phone: 202.224.0411

Majority:		Minority:	
C: Kyrsten Sinema, AZ	HSOB 317	**RM: Ted Cruz, TX**	RSOB 127A
Tammy Duckworth, IL	HSOB 524	John Thune, SD	DSOB 511
Jon Tester, MT	HSOB 311	Roy Blunt, MO	RSOB 260
Jacky Rosen, NV	HSOB 713	Jerry Moran, KS	DSOB 521
John Hickenlooper, CO	RSOB 374	Mike Lee, UT	RSOB 361-A
Raphael Warnock, GA	RSOB 388	Shelley Capito, WV	RSOB 172
Maria Cantwell, WA	HSOB 511	Roger Wicker, MS	DSOB 555

COMMUNICATIONS, MEDIA & BROADBAND

Room: RSOB 253
Phone: 202.224.0411

Majority:		Minority:	
C: Ben Ray Luján, NM	RSOB 498	John Thune, SD	DSOB 511
Amy Klobuchar, MN	DSOB 425	Roy Blunt, MO	RSOB 260
Richard Blumenthal, CT	HSOB 706	Ted Cruz, TX	RSOB 127A
Brian Schatz, HI	HSOB 722	Deb Fischer, NE	RSOB 454
Ed Markey, MA	DSOB 255	Jerry Moran, KS	DSOB 521
Gary Peters, MI	HSOB 724	Dan Sullivan, AK	HSOB 302
Tammy Baldwin, WI	HSOB 709	Marsha Blackburn, TN	DSOB 357
Tammy Duckworth, IL	HSOB 524	Todd Young, IN	DSOB 185
Jon Tester, MT	HSOB 311	Mike Lee, UT	RSOB 361-A
Kyrsten Sinema, AZ	HSOB 317	Ron Johnson, WI	HSOB 328
Jacky Rosen, NV	HSOB 713	Shelley Capito, WV	RSOB 172
John Hickenlooper, CO	RSOB 374	Rick Scott, FL	HSOB 502
Raphael Warnock, GA	RSOB 388	Cynthia Lummis, WY	RSOB 124
Maria Cantwell, WA	HSOB 511	Roger Wicker, MS	DSOB 555

CONSUMER PROTECTION, PRODUCT SAFETY & DATA SECURITY

Room: RSOB 253
Phone: 202.224.0411

Majority:		Minority:	
C: Richard Blumenthal, CT	HSOB 706	**RM: Marsha Blackburn, TN**	DSOB 357
Amy Klobuchar, MN	DSOB 425	John Thune, SD	DSOB 511
Brian Schatz, HI	HSOB 722	Roy Blunt, MO	RSOB 260

Ed Markey, MA	DSOB 255	Jerry Moran, KS	DSOB 521
Tammy Baldwin, WI	HSOB 709	Todd Young, IN	DSOB 185
Ben Ray Luján, NM	RSOB 498	Mike Lee, UT	RSOB 361-A
Maria Cantwell, WA	HSOB 511	Roger Wicker, MS	DSOB 555

OCEANS, FISHERIES, CLIMATE CHANGE & MANUFACTURING
Room: RSOB 253
Phone: 202.224.0411

Majority:		Minority:	
C: Tammy Baldwin, WI	HSOB 709	RM: Dan Sullivan, AK	HSOB 302
Richard Blumenthal, CT	HSOB 706	Ted Cruz, TX	RSOB 127A
Brian Schatz, HI	HSOB 722	Deb Fischer, NE	RSOB 454
Ed Markey, MA	DSOB 255	Marsha Blackburn, TN	DSOB 357
Gary Peters, MI	HSOB 724	Todd Young, IN	DSOB 185
Ben Ray Luján, NM	RSOB 498	Ron Johnson, WI	HSOB 328
Maria Cantwell, WA	HSOB 511	Roger Wicker, MS	DSOB 555

SPACE & SCIENCE
Room: RSOB 253
Phone: 202.224.0411

Majority:		Minority:	
C: John Hickenlooper, CO	RSOB 374	RM: Cynthia Lummis, WY	RSOB 124
Richard Blumenthal, CT	HSOB 706	Ted Cruz, TX	RSOB 127A
Gary Peters, MI	HSOB 724	Deb Fischer, NE	RSOB 454
Kyrsten Sinema, AZ	HSOB 317	Todd Young, IN	DSOB 185
Ben Ray Luján, NM	RSOB 498	Mike Lee, UT	RSOB 361-A
Raphael Warnock, GA	RSOB 388	Rick Scott, FL	HSOB 502
Ed Markey, MA	DSOB 255	Jerry Moran, KS	DSOB 521
Maria Cantwell, WA	HSOB 511	Roger Wicker, MS	DSOB 555

SURFACE TRANSPORTATION, MARITIME FREIGHT & PORTS
Room: RSOB 253
Phone: 202.224.0411

Majority:		Minority:	
C: Gary Peters, MI	HSOB 724	RM: Deb Fischer, NE	RSOB 454
Amy Klobuchar, MN	DSOB 425	John Thune, SD	DSOB 511
Richard Blumenthal, CT	HSOB 706	Roy Blunt, MO	RSOB 260
Brian Schatz, HI	HSOB 722	Dan Sullivan, AK	HSOB 302
Ed Markey, MA	DSOB 255	Todd Young, IN	DSOB 185
Tammy Baldwin, WI	HSOB 709	Ron Johnson, WI	HSOB 328
Tammy Duckworth, IL	HSOB 524	Shelley Capito, WV	RSOB 172
Jon Tester, MT	HSOB 311	Rick Scott, FL	HSOB 502
Raphael Warnock, GA	RSOB 388	Cynthia Lummis, WY	RSOB 124
Maria Cantwell, WA	HSOB 511	Roger Wicker, MS	DSOB 555

TOURISM, TRADE & EXPORT PROMOTION
Room: RSOB 253
Phone: 202.224.0411

Majority:		Minority:	
C: Jacky Rosen, NV	HSOB 713	RM: Rick Scott, FL	HSOB 502
Amy Klobuchar, MN	DSOB 425	Dan Sullivan, AK	HSOB 302
Tammy Duckworth, IL	HSOB 524	Marsha Blackburn, TN	DSOB 357
Jon Tester, MT	HSOB 311	Ron Johnson, WI	HSOB 328
Kyrsten Sinema, AZ	HSOB 317	Shelley Capito, WV	RSOB 172
John Hickenlooper, CO	RSOB 374	Cynthia Lummis, WY	RSOB 124
Maria Cantwell, WA	HSOB 511	Roger Wicker, MS	DSOB 555

ENERGY & NATURAL RESOURCES
Room: DSOB 304
Website: www.energy.senate.gov
Phone: 202.224.4971
Ratio: 10 Democrats/10 Republicans
Subcommittees: 4

Majority:		Minority:	
C: Joe Manchin, WV	HSOB 306	RM: John Barrasso, WY	DSOB 307
Ron Wyden, OR	DSOB 221	James Risch, ID	RSOB 483
Maria Cantwell, WA	HSOB 511	Mike Lee, UT	RSOB 361 A
Bernie Sanders, VT	DSOB 332	Steve Daines, MT	HSOB 320
Martin Heinrich, NM	HSOB 303	Lisa Murkowski, AK	HSOB 522
Mazie Hirono, HI	HSOB 109	John Hoeven, ND	RSOB 338
Angus King, ME	HSOB 133	James Lankford, OK	HSOB 316
Catherine Cortez Masto, NV	HSOB 313	Bill Cassidy, LA	HSOB 520
		Cindy Hyde-Smith, MS	HSOB 702
Mark Kelly, AZ	HSOB 516	Roger Marshall, KS	RSOB 479A
John Hickenlooper, CO	RSOB 374		

Majority CoS: Renae Black   **Minority CoS:** Richard Russell

————————— Subcommittees —————————

ENERGY

Room:

Majority:		Minority:	
C: Mazie Hirono, HI	HSOB 109	RM: John Hoeven, ND	RSOB 338
Ron Wyden, OR	DSOB 221	James Risch, ID	RSOB 483
Bernie Sanders, VT	DSOB 332	Lisa Murkowski, AK	HSOB 522
Martin Heinrich, NM	HSOB 303	James Lankford, OK	HSOB 316
Angus King, ME	HSOB 133	Bill Cassidy, LA	HSOB 520
Catherine Cortez Masto, NV	HSOB 313	Cindy Hyde-Smith, MS	HSOB 702
		Roger Marshall, KS	RSOB 479A
John Hickenlooper, CO	RSOB 374	John Barrasso, WY	DSOB 307
Joe Manchin, WV	HSOB 306		

NATIONAL PARKS

Room:

Majority:		Minority:	
C: Angus King, ME	HSOB 133	RM: Steve Daines, MT	HSOB 320
Bernie Sanders, VT	DSOB 332	Mike Lee, UT	RSOB 361-A
Martin Heinrich, NM	HSOB 303	Lisa Murkowski, AK	HSOB 522
Mazie Hirono, HI	HSOB 109	John Hoeven, ND	RSOB 338
Mark Kelly, AZ	HSOB 516	James Lankford, OK	HSOB 316
Joe Manchin, WV	HSOB 306	John Barrasso, WY	DSOB 307

PUBLIC LANDS, FORESTS & MINING

Room:

Majority:		Minority:	
C: Catherine Cortez Masto, NV	HSOB 313	RM: Mike Lee, UT	RSOB 361-A
		James Risch, ID	RSOB 483
Ron Wyden, OR	DSOB 221	Steve Daines, MT	HSOB 320
Martin Heinrich, NM	HSOB 303	Lisa Murkowski, AK	HSOB 522
Mazie Hirono, HI	HSOB 109	James Lankford, OK	HSOB 316
Angus King, ME	HSOB 133	Bill Cassidy, LA	HSOB 520
Mark Kelly, AZ	HSOB 516	Cindy Hyde-Smith, MS	HSOB 702
John Hickenlooper, CO	RSOB 374	John Barrasso, WY	DSOB 307
Joe Manchin, WV	HSOB 306		

WATER & POWER

Room:

Majority:		Minority:	
C: Ron Wyden, OR	DSOB 221	RM: Cindy Hyde-Smith, MS	HSOB 702
Bernie Sanders, VT	DSOB 332		
Catherine Cortez Masto, NV	HSOB 313	James Risch, ID	RSOB 483
		Mike Lee, UT	RSOB 361-A
Mark Kelly, AZ	HSOB 516	John Hoeven, ND	RSOB 338
John Hickenlooper, CO	RSOB 374	Roger Marshall, KS	RSOB 479A
Joe Manchin, WV	HSOB 306	John Barrasso, WY	DSOB 307

ENVIRONMENT & PUBLIC WORKS

Room: DSOB 410
Website: www.epw.senate.gov
Phone: 202.224.8832
Ratio: 10 Democrats/10 Republicans
Subcommittees: 4

Majority:		Minority:	
C: Tom Carper, DE	HSOB 513	RM: Shelley Capito, WV	RSOB 172
Ben Cardin, MD	HSOB 509	James Inhofe, OK	RSOB 205
Bernie Sanders, VT	DSOB 332	Kevin Cramer, ND	RSOB 400
Sheldon Whitehouse, RI	HSOB 530	Cynthia Lummis, WY	RSOB 124
Jeff Merkley, OR	HSOB 531	Richard Shelby, AL	RSOB 304
Ed Markey, MA	DSOB 255	John Boozman, AR	HSOB 141
Tammy Duckworth, IL	HSOB 524	Roger Wicker, MS	DSOB 555
Debbie Stabenow, MI	HSOB 731	Dan Sullivan, AK	HSOB 302
Mark Kelly, AZ	HSOB 516	Joni Ernst, IA	HSOB 730
Alex Padilla, CA	HSOB 112	Lindsey Graham, SC	RSOB 290

Majority CoS: Mary Frances Repko   **Minority CoS:** Adam Tomlinson
———————————— Subcommittees ————————————

CHEM SAFETY, WASTE MNGMNT, ENVIRO JUSTICE & REG OVERSIGHT

Room: HSOB Suite 502
Phone: 202.224.5842

Majority:		Minority:	
C: Jeff Merkley, OR	HSOB 531	RM: Roger Wicker, MS	DSOB 555
Bernie Sanders, VT	DSOB 332	Richard Shelby, AL	RSOB 304
Ed Markey, MA	DSOB 255	Dan Sullivan, AK	HSOB 302
Mark Kelly, AZ	HSOB 516	Joni Ernst, IA	HSOB 730
Alex Padilla, CA	HSOB 112	Lindsey Graham, SC	RSOB 290

| Tom Carper, DE | HSOB 513 | Shelley Capito, WV | RSOB 172 |

CLEAN AIR, CLIMATE & NUCLEAR SAFETY
Room: RSOB B-85
Phone: 202.224.4814

Majority:		Minority:	
C: Ed Markey, MA	DSOB 255	RM: James Inhofe, OK	RSOB 205
Ben Cardin, MD	HSOB 509	Kevin Cramer, ND	RSOB 400
Bernie Sanders, VT	DSOB 332	Cynthia Lummis, WY	RSOB 124
Sheldon Whitehouse, RI	HSOB 530	Richard Shelby, AL	RSOB 304
Jeff Merkley, OR	HSOB 531	John Boozman, AR	HSOB 141
Tammy Duckworth, IL	HSOB 524	Roger Wicker, MS	DSOB 555
Debbie Stabenow, MI	HSOB 731	Joni Ernst, IA	HSOB 730
Alex Padilla, CA	HSOB 112	Lindsey Graham, SC	RSOB 290
Tom Carper, DE	HSOB 513	Shelley Capito, WV	RSOB 172

FISHERIES, WATER, AND WILDLIFE
Room: DSOB B40C
Phone: 202.224.2043

Majority:		Minority:	
C: Tammy Duckworth, IL	HSOB 524	RM: Cynthia Lummis, WY	RSOB 124
Ben Cardin, MD	HSOB 509	James Inhofe, OK	RSOB 205
Sheldon Whitehouse, RI	HSOB 530	Kevin Cramer, ND	RSOB 400
Ed Markey, MA	DSOB 255	John Boozman, AR	HSOB 141
Debbie Stabenow, MI	HSOB 731	Dan Sullivan, AK	HSOB 302
Mark Kelly, AZ	HSOB 516	Joni Ernst, IA	HSOB 730
Tom Carper, DE	HSOB 513	Shelley Capito, WV	RSOB 172

TRANSPORTATION & INFRASTRUCTURE
Room: RSOB 172
Phone: 202.224.6472

Majority:		Minority:	
C: Ben Cardin, MD	HSOB 509	RM: Kevin Cramer, ND	RSOB 400
Bernie Sanders, VT	DSOB 332	James Inhofe, OK	RSOB 205
Sheldon Whitehouse, RI	HSOB 530	Cynthia Lummis, WY	RSOB 124
Jeff Merkley, OR	HSOB 531	Richard Shelby, AL	RSOB 304
Tammy Duckworth, IL	HSOB 524	John Boozman, AR	HSOB 141
Debbie Stabenow, MI	HSOB 731	Roger Wicker, MS	DSOB 555
Mark Kelly, AZ	HSOB 516	Dan Sullivan, AK	HSOB 302
Alex Padilla, CA	HSOB 112	Lindsey Graham, SC	RSOB 290
Tom Carper, DE	HSOB 513	Shelley Capito, WV	RSOB 172

FINANCE
Room: DSOB 219
Website: www.finance.senate.gov
Phone: 202.224.4515
Ratio: 14 Democrats/14 Republicans
Subcommittees: 6

Majority:		Minority:	
C: Ron Wyden, OR	DSOB 221	RM: Mike Crapo, ID	DSOB 239
Debbie Stabenow, MI	HSOB 731	Chuck Grassley, IA	HSOB 135
Maria Cantwell, WA	HSOB 511	John Cornyn, TX	HSOB 517
Bob Menendez, NJ	HSOB 528	John Thune, SD	DSOB 511
Tom Carper, DE	HSOB 513	Richard Burr, NC	RSOB 217
Ben Cardin, MD	HSOB 509	Rob Portman, OH	RSOB 448
Sherrod Brown, OH	HSOB 503	Pat Toomey, PA	DSOB 455
Michael Bennet, CO	RSOB 261	Tim Scott, SC	HSOB 104
Bob Casey, PA	RSOB 393	Bill Cassidy, LA	HSOB 520
Mark Warner, VA	HSOB 703	James Lankford, OK	HSOB 316
Sheldon Whitehouse, RI	HSOB 530	Steve Daines, MT	HSOB 320
Maggie Hassan, NH	HSOB 324	Todd Young, IN	DSOB 185
Catherine Cortez Masto, NV	HSOB 313	Ben Sasse, NE	RSOB 107
Elizabeth Warren, MA	HSOB 309	John Barrasso, WY	DSOB 307

Majority CoS: Joshua L. Sheinkman   **Minority CoS:** Gregg Richard

—————— Subcommittees ——————

ENERGY, NATURAL RESOURCES & INFRASTRUCTURE
Room:

Majority:		Minority:	
C: Michael Bennet, CO	RSOB 261	RM: James Lankford, OK	HSOB 316
Tom Carper, DE	HSOB 513	John Cornyn, TX	HSOB 517
Mark Warner, VA	HSOB 703	Tim Scott, SC	HSOB 104
Sheldon Whitehouse, RI	HSOB 530	John Barrasso, WY	DSOB 307
Maggie Hassan, NH	HSOB 324	Steve Daines, MT	HSOB 320

FISCAL RESPONSIBILITY & ECONOMIC GROWTH
Room:

Majority:		Minority:	
C: Elizabeth Warren, MA	HSOB 309	**RM: Bill Cassidy, LA**	HSOB 520
Ron Wyden, OR	DSOB 221	Richard Burr, NC	RSOB 217

HEALTH CARE
Room:

Majority:		Minority:	
C: Debbie Stabenow, MI	HSOB 731	**RM: Steve Daines, MT**	HSOB 320
Bob Menendez, NJ	HSOB 528	Chuck Grassley, IA	HSOB 135
Tom Carper, DE	HSOB 513	John Thune, SD	DSOB 511
Ben Cardin, MD	HSOB 509	Richard Burr, NC	RSOB 217
Bob Casey, PA	RSOB 393	Pat Toomey, PA	DSOB 455
Mark Warner, VA	HSOB 703	Tim Scott, SC	HSOB 104
Sheldon Whitehouse, RI	HSOB 530	Bill Cassidy, LA	HSOB 520
Catherine Cortez Masto, NV	HSOB 313	James Lankford, OK	HSOB 316
		Todd Young, IN	DSOB 185
Maggie Hassan, NH	HSOB 324	John Barrasso, WY	DSOB 307
Elizabeth Warren, MA	HSOB 309		

INTERNATIONAL TRADE, CUSTOMS & GLOBAL COMPETITIVENESS
Room:

Majority:		Minority:	
C: Tom Carper, DE	HSOB 513	**RM: John Cornyn, TX**	HSOB 517
Ron Wyden, OR	DSOB 221	Chuck Grassley, IA	HSOB 135
Debbie Stabenow, MI	HSOB 731	John Thune, SD	DSOB 511
Bob Menendez, NJ	HSOB 528	Rob Portman, OH	RSOB 448
Ben Cardin, MD	HSOB 509	Pat Toomey, PA	DSOB 455
Sherrod Brown, OH	HSOB 503	Tim Scott, SC	HSOB 104
Michael Bennet, CO	RSOB 261	Steve Daines, MT	HSOB 320
Bob Casey, PA	RSOB 393	Todd Young, IN	DSOB 185
Mark Warner, VA	HSOB 703	Ben Sasse, NE	RSOB 107
Catherine Cortez Masto, NV	HSOB 313	John Barrasso, WY	DSOB 307

SOCIAL SECURITY, PENSIONS & FAMILY POLICY
Room:

Majority:		Minority:	
C: Sherrod Brown, OH	HSOB 503	**RM: Todd Young, IN**	DSOB 185
Ron Wyden, OR	DSOB 221	Rob Portman, OH	RSOB 448
Michael Bennet, CO	RSOB 261	Bill Cassidy, LA	HSOB 520
Bob Casey, PA	RSOB 393	James Lankford, OK	HSOB 316
Maggie Hassan, NH	HSOB 324	Ben Sasse, NE	RSOB 107

TAXATION & IRS OVERSIGHT
Room:

Majority:		Minority:	
C: Sheldon Whitehouse, RI	HSOB 530	**RM: John Thune, SD**	DSOB 511
		Chuck Grassley, IA	HSOB 135
Debbie Stabenow, MI	HSOB 731	John Cornyn, TX	HSOB 517
Bob Menendez, NJ	HSOB 528	Richard Burr, NC	RSOB 217
Ben Cardin, MD	HSOB 509	Rob Portman, OH	RSOB 448
Sherrod Brown, OH	HSOB 503	Pat Toomey, PA	DSOB 455
Catherine Cortez Masto, NV	HSOB 313	Ben Sasse, NE	RSOB 107
Elizabeth Warren, MA	HSOB 309		

FOREIGN RELATIONS

Room: DSOB 423
Website: www.foreign.senate.gov
Phone: 202.224.4651
Ratio: 11 Democrats/11 Republicans
Subcommittees: 7

Majority:		Minority:	
C: Bob Menendez, NJ	HSOB 528	**RM: James Risch, ID**	RSOB 483
Ben Cardin, MD	HSOB 509	Marco Rubio, FL	RSOB 284
Jeanne Shaheen, NH	HSOB 506	Ron Johnson, WI	HSOB 328
Chris Coons, DE	RSOB 218	Mitt Romney, UT	RSOB 124
Chris Murphy, CT	HSOB 136	Rob Portman, OH	RSOB 448
Tim Kaine, VA	RSOB 231	Rand Paul, KY	RSOB 167
Ed Markey, MA	DSOB 255	Todd Young, IN	DSOB 185
Jeff Merkley, OR	HSOB 531	John Barrasso, WY	DSOB 307
Cory Booker, NJ	HSOB 717	Ted Cruz, TX	RSOB 127A
Brian Schatz, HI	HSOB 722	Mike Rounds, SD	HSOB 716
Chris Van Hollen, MD	HSOB 110	Bill Hagerty, TN	RSOB 248

Majority CoS: Damian Murphy   **Minority CoS:** Chris Socha
———————————— Subcommittees ————————————

AFRICA & GLOBAL HEALTH POLICY

Room:

Majority:		Minority:	
C: Chris Van Hollen, MD	HSOB 110	**RM: Mike Rounds, SD**	HSOB 716
Cory Booker, NJ	HSOB 717	Marco Rubio, FL	RSOB 284
Tim Kaine, VA	RSOB 231	Todd Young, IN	DSOB 185
Jeff Merkley, OR	HSOB 531	John Barrasso, WY	DSOB 307
Chris Coons, DE	RSOB 218	Rand Paul, KY	RSOB 167

EAST ASIA, THE PACIFIC & INTERNATIONAL CYBERSECURITY POLICY

Room:

Majority:		Minority:	
C: Ed Markey, MA	DSOB 255	**RM: Mitt Romney, UT**	RSOB 124
Chris Coons, DE	RSOB 218	Ted Cruz, TX	RSOB 127A
Chris Murphy, CT	HSOB 136	Ron Johnson, WI	HSOB 328
Brian Schatz, HI	HSOB 722	Mike Rounds, SD	HSOB 716
Jeff Merkley, OR	HSOB 531	Bill Hagerty, TN	RSOB 248

EUROPE & REGIONAL SECURITY COOPERATION

Room:

Majority:		Minority:	
C: Jeanne Shaheen, NH	HSOB 506	**RM: Ron Johnson, WI**	HSOB 328
Ben Cardin, MD	HSOB 509	John Barrasso, WY	DSOB 307
Chris Murphy, CT	HSOB 136	Mitt Romney, UT	RSOB 124
Chris Van Hollen, MD	HSOB 110	Rob Portman, OH	RSOB 448
Chris Coons, DE	RSOB 218	Todd Young, IN	DSOB 185

INTERNAT'L DEV INSTIT & INTERNAT'L ECON, ENERGY & ENVIRON POLICY

Room:

Majority:		Minority:	
C: Chris Coons, DE	RSOB 218	**RM: Rob Portman, OH**	RSOB 448
Brian Schatz, HI	HSOB 722	Todd Young, IN	DSOB 185
Cory Booker, NJ	HSOB 717	Rand Paul, KY	RSOB 167
Ben Cardin, MD	HSOB 509	John Barrasso, WY	DSOB 307
Jeanne Shaheen, NH	HSOB 506	Mike Rounds, SD	HSOB 716

NEAR EAST, SOUTH ASIA, CENTRAL ASIA & COUNTERTERRORISM

Room:

Majority:		Minority:	
C: Chris Murphy, CT	HSOB 136	**RM: Todd Young, IN**	DSOB 185
Jeanne Shaheen, NH	HSOB 506	Rand Paul, KY	RSOB 167
Ed Markey, MA	DSOB 255	Ted Cruz, TX	RSOB 127A
Cory Booker, NJ	HSOB 717	Mitt Romney, UT	RSOB 124
Chris Van Hollen, MD	HSOB 110	Bill Hagerty, TN	RSOB 248

STATE DEPT & USAID MNGMNT, INTERNAT'L OPS & INTERNAT'L DEV

Room:

Majority:		Minority:	
C: Ben Cardin, MD	HSOB 509	**RM: Bill Hagerty, TN**	RSOB 248
Tim Kaine, VA	RSOB 231	Rand Paul, KY	RSOB 167
Brian Schatz, HI	HSOB 722	Ted Cruz, TX	RSOB 127A
Chris Murphy, CT	HSOB 136	Ron Johnson, WI	HSOB 328
Ed Markey, MA	DSOB 255	Marco Rubio, FL	RSOB 284

WEST HEM CRIME CIV SEC DEM RIGHTS & WOMEN'S ISSUES

Room:

Majority:		Minority:	
C: Tim Kaine, VA	RSOB 231	**RM: Marco Rubio, FL**	RSOB 284
Jeff Merkley, OR	HSOB 531	Rob Portman, OH	RSOB 448
Ben Cardin, MD	HSOB 509	John Barrasso, WY	DSOB 307
Jeanne Shaheen, NH	HSOB 506	Bill Hagerty, TN	RSOB 248
Ed Markey, MA	DSOB 255	Ted Cruz, TX	RSOB 127A

HEALTH, EDUCATION, LABOR & PENSIONS

Room: DSOB 428
Website: www.help.senate.gov
Phone: 202.224.0767
Ratio: 11 Democrats/11 Republicans
Subcommittees: 3

Majority:		Minority:	
C: Patty Murray, WA	RSOB 154	**RM: Richard Burr, NC**	RSOB 217
Bernie Sanders, VT	DSOB 332	Rand Paul, KY	RSOB 167
Bob Casey, PA	RSOB 393	Susan Collins, ME	DSOB 413
Tammy Baldwin, WI	HSOB 709	Bill Cassidy, LA	HSOB 520
Chris Murphy, CT	HSOB 136	Lisa Murkowski, AK	HSOB 522

Tim Kaine, VA	RSOB 231	Mike Braun, IN	RSOB 374
Maggie Hassan, NH	HSOB 324	Roger Marshall, KS	RSOB 479A
Tina Smith, MN	HSOB 720	Tim Scott, SC	HSOB 104
Jacky Rosen, NV	HSOB 713	Mitt Romney, UT	RSOB 124
Ben Ray Luján, NM	RSOB 498	Tommy Tuberville, AL	RSOB 142
John Hickenlooper, CO	RSOB 374	Jerry Moran, KS	DSOB 521

Majority CoS: Evan Schatz **Minority CoS:** David P. Cleary

———————— Subcommittees ————————

CHILDREN & FAMILIES
Room: DSOB 428
Phone: 202.224.5375

Majority:		**Minority:**	
C: Bob Casey, PA	RSOB 393	**RM: Bill Cassidy, LA**	HSOB 520
Bernie Sanders, VT	DSOB 332	Mitt Romney, UT	RSOB 124
Chris Murphy, CT	HSOB 136	Susan Collins, ME	DSOB 413
Tim Kaine, VA	RSOB 231	Lisa Murkowski, AK	HSOB 522
Maggie Hassan, NH	HSOB 324	Jerry Moran, KS	DSOB 521
Tina Smith, MN	HSOB 720	Roger Marshall, KS	RSOB 479A
John Hickenlooper, CO	RSOB 374	Tommy Tuberville, AL	RSOB 142
Patty Murray, WA	RSOB 154	Richard Burr, NC	RSOB 217

EMPLOYMENT & WORKPLACE SAFETY
Room: DSOB 428
Phone: 202.224.5375

Majority:		**Minority:**	
C: John Hickenlooper, CO	RSOB 374	**RM: Mike Braun, IN**	RSOB 374
Tammy Baldwin, WI	HSOB 709	Tommy Tuberville, AL	RSOB 142
Tina Smith, MN	HSOB 720	Rand Paul, KY	RSOB 167
Jacky Rosen, NV	HSOB 713	Tim Scott, SC	HSOB 104
Ben Ray Luján, NM	RSOB 498	Mitt Romney, UT	RSOB 124
Patty Murray, WA	RSOB 154	Richard Burr, NC	RSOB 217

PRIMARY HEALTH & RETIREMENT SECURITY
Room: DSOB 428
Phone: 202.224.5375

Majority:		**Minority:**	
C: Bernie Sanders, VT	DSOB 332	**RM: Susan Collins, ME**	DSOB 413
Bob Casey, PA	RSOB 393	Rand Paul, KY	RSOB 167
Tammy Baldwin, WI	HSOB 709	Lisa Murkowski, AK	HSOB 522
Chris Murphy, CT	HSOB 136	Roger Marshall, KS	RSOB 479A
Tim Kaine, VA	RSOB 231	Tim Scott, SC	HSOB 104
Maggie Hassan, NH	HSOB 324	Jerry Moran, KS	DSOB 521
Jacky Rosen, NV	HSOB 713	Bill Cassidy, LA	HSOB 520
Ben Ray Luján, NM	RSOB 498	Mike Braun, IN	RSOB 374
Patty Murray, WA	RSOB 154	Richard Burr, NC	RSOB 217

HOMELAND SECURITY & GOVERNMENT AFFAIRS
Room: DSOB 340
Website: www.hsgac.senate.gov
Phone: 202.224.2627
Ratio: 7 Democrats/7 Republicans
Subcommittees: 3

Majority:		**Minority:**	
C: Gary Peters, MI	HSOB 724	Rob Portman, OH	RSOB 448
Tom Carper, DE	HSOB 513	Ron Johnson, WI	HSOB 328
Maggie Hassan, NH	HSOB 324	Rand Paul, KY	RSOB 167
Kyrsten Sinema, AZ	HSOB 317	James Lankford, OK	HSOB 316
Jacky Rosen, NV	HSOB 713	Mitt Romney, UT	RSOB 124
Alex Padilla, CA	HSOB 112	Rick Scott, FL	HSOB 502
Jon Ossoff, GA	RSOB 455	Josh Hawley, MO	RSOB 212

Majority CoS: David Weinberg **Minority CoS:** Pam Thiessen
Majority Sched: April Beasley

———————— Subcommittees ————————

EMERGING THREATS & SPENDING OVERSIGHT
Room: DSOB 348
Phone: 202.224.7155

Majority:		**Minority:**	
C: Maggie Hassan, NH	HSOB 324	**RM: Rand Paul, KY**	RSOB 167
Kyrsten Sinema, AZ	HSOB 317	Mitt Romney, UT	RSOB 124
Jacky Rosen, NV	HSOB 713	Rick Scott, FL	HSOB 502
Jon Ossoff, GA	RSOB 455	Josh Hawley, MO	RSOB 212
Gary Peters, MI	HSOB 724	Rob Portman, OH	RSOB 448

GOVERNMENT OPERATIONS & BORDER MANAGEMENT
Room: HSOB 601
Phone: 202.224.4551

Majority:		Minority:	
C: Kyrsten Sinema, AZ	HSOB 317	RM: James Lankford, OK	HSOB 316
Tom Carper, DE	HSOB 513	Ron Johnson, WI	HSOB 328
Alex Padilla, CA	HSOB 112	Mitt Romney, UT	RSOB 124
Jon Ossoff, GA	RSOB 455	Josh Hawley, MO	RSOB 212
Gary Peters, MI	HSOB 724	Rob Portman, OH	RSOB 448

INVESTIGATIONS
Room: RSOB 199
Phone: 202.224.3721

Majority:		Minority:	
C: Jon Ossoff, GA	RSOB 455	RM: Ron Johnson, WI	HSOB 328
Tom Carper, DE	HSOB 513	Rand Paul, KY	RSOB 167
Maggie Hassan, NH	HSOB 324	James Lankford, OK	HSOB 316
Alex Padilla, CA	HSOB 112	Rick Scott, FL	HSOB 502
Gary Peters, MI	HSOB 724	Rob Portman, OH	RSOB 448

INDIAN AFFAIRS

Room: HSOB 838
Website: www.indian.senate.gov
Phone: 202.224.2251
Ratio: 6 Democrats/6 Republicans
Subcommittees: 0

Majority:		Minority:	
C: Brian Schatz, HI	HSOB 722	Lisa Murkowski, AK	HSOB 522
Maria Cantwell, WA	HSOB 511	John Hoeven, ND	RSOB 338
Jon Tester, MT	HSOB 311	James Lankford, OK	HSOB 316
Catherine Cortez Masto, NV	HSOB 313	Steve Daines, MT	HSOB 320
		Mike Rounds, SD	HSOB 716
Tina Smith, MN	HSOB 720	Jerry Moran, KS	DSOB 521
Ben Ray Luján, NM	RSOB 498		

Majority CoS: Jennifer Romero   **Minority CoS:** Kristi Nuna'q Williams

JUDICIARY

Room: DSOB 224
Website: www.judiciary.senate.gov
Phone: 202.224.7703
Ratio: 11 Democrats/11 Republicans
Subcommittees: 8

Majority:		Minority:	
C: Dick Durbin, IL	HSOB 711	RM: Chuck Grassley, IA	HSOB 135
Patrick Leahy, VT	RSOB 437	Lindsey Graham, SC	RSOB 290
Dianne Feinstein, CA	HSOB 331	John Cornyn, TX	HSOB 517
Sheldon Whitehouse, RI	HSOB 530	Mike Lee, UT	RSOB 361 A
Amy Klobuchar, MN	DSOB 425	Ted Cruz, TX	RSOB 127A
Chris Coons, DE	RSOB 218	Ben Sasse, NE	RSOB 107
Richard Blumenthal, CT	HSOB 706	Josh Hawley, MO	RSOB 212
Mazie Hirono, HI	HSOB 109	Tom Cotton, AR	RSOB 326
Cory Booker, NJ	HSOB 717	John Kennedy, LA	RSOB 416
Alex Padilla, CA	HSOB 112	Thom Tillis, NC	DSOB 113
Jon Ossoff, GA	RSOB 455	Marsha Blackburn, TN	DSOB 357

Majority CoS: Joseph R. Zogby   **Minority CoS:** Kolan L. Davis

——————— Subcommittees ———————

COMPETITION POLICY, ANTITRUST & CONSUMER RIGHTS
Room: DSOB 425
Phone: 202.224.3244

Majority:		Minority:	
C: Amy Klobuchar, MN	DSOB 425	RM: Mike Lee, UT	RSOB 361-A
Patrick Leahy, VT	RSOB 437	Josh Hawley, MO	RSOB 212
Richard Blumenthal, CT	HSOB 706	Tom Cotton, AR	RSOB 326
Cory Booker, NJ	HSOB 717	Thom Tillis, NC	DSOB 113
Jon Ossoff, GA	RSOB 455	Marsha Blackburn, TN	DSOB 357

CONSTITUTION
Room: HSOB 713
Phone: 202.224.6361

Majority:		Minority:	
C: Richard Blumenthal, CT	HSOB 706	RM: Ted Cruz, TX	RSOB 127A
		John Cornyn, TX	HSOB 517
Dianne Feinstein, CA	HSOB 331	Mike Lee, UT	RSOB 361-A
Sheldon Whitehouse, RI	HSOB 530	Ben Sasse, NE	RSOB 107
Jon Ossoff, GA	RSOB 455		

CRIMINAL JUSTICE & COUNTERTERRORISM
Room: DSOB 152
Phone: 202.224.2921

Majority:		Minority:	
C: Cory Booker, NJ	HSOB 717	**RM: Tom Cotton, AR**	RSOB 326
Patrick Leahy, VT	RSOB 437	Lindsey Graham, SC	RSOB 290
Dianne Feinstein, CA	HSOB 331	John Cornyn, TX	HSOB 517
Sheldon Whitehouse, RI	HSOB 530	Mike Lee, UT	RSOB 361-A
Amy Klobuchar, MN	DSOB 425	Ted Cruz, TX	RSOB 127A
Alex Padilla, CA	HSOB 112	Josh Hawley, MO	RSOB 212
Jon Ossoff, GA	RSOB 455	John Kennedy, LA	RSOB 416

FEDERAL COURTS, OVERSIGHT, AGENCY ACTION & FEDERAL RIGHTS

Room: HSOB 706
Phone: 202.224.2823

Majority:		Minority:	
C: Sheldon Whitehouse, RI	HSOB 530	**RM: John Kennedy, LA**	RSOB 416
		Lindsey Graham, SC	RSOB 290
Patrick Leahy, VT	RSOB 437	Mike Lee, UT	RSOB 361-A
Mazie Hirono, HI	HSOB 109	Ted Cruz, TX	RSOB 127A
Cory Booker, NJ	HSOB 717	Ben Sasse, NE	RSOB 107
Alex Padilla, CA	HSOB 112	Thom Tillis, NC	DSOB 113
Jon Ossoff, GA	RSOB 455		

HUMAN RIGHTS & THE LAW

Room: DSOB 224
Phone: 202.224.3841

Majority:		Minority:	
C: Dianne Feinstein, CA	HSOB 331	**RM: Josh Hawley, MO**	RSOB 212
Chris Coons, DE	RSOB 218	Ben Sasse, NE	RSOB 107
Richard Blumenthal, CT	HSOB 706	John Kennedy, LA	RSOB 416

IMMIGRATION, CITIZENSHIP & BORDER SECURITY

Room: DSOB 224
Phone: 202.224.6991

Majority:		Minority:	
C: Alex Padilla, CA	HSOB 112	**RM: John Cornyn, TX**	HSOB 517
Dianne Feinstein, CA	HSOB 331	Lindsey Graham, SC	RSOB 290
Amy Klobuchar, MN	DSOB 425	Ted Cruz, TX	RSOB 127A
Chris Coons, DE	RSOB 218	Tom Cotton, AR	RSOB 326
Richard Blumenthal, CT	HSOB 706	John Kennedy, LA	RSOB 416
Mazie Hirono, HI	HSOB 109	Thom Tillis, NC	DSOB 113
Cory Booker, NJ	HSOB 717	Marsha Blackburn, TN	DSOB 357

PRIVACY, TECHNOLOGY & THE LAW

Room: DSOB 224
Phone: 202.224.5042

Majority:		Minority:	
C: Chris Coons, DE	RSOB 218	**RM: Ben Sasse, NE**	RSOB 107
Sheldon Whitehouse, RI	HSOB 530	Lindsey Graham, SC	RSOB 290
Amy Klobuchar, MN	DSOB 425	Josh Hawley, MO	RSOB 212
Mazie Hirono, HI	HSOB 109	John Kennedy, LA	RSOB 416
Jon Ossoff, GA	RSOB 455	Marsha Blackburn, TN	DSOB 357

SUBCOMMITTEE ON INTELLECTUAL PROPERTY

Room: RSOB 127A
Phone: 202.224.5042

Majority:		Minority:	
C: Patrick Leahy, VT	RSOB 437	**RM: Thom Tillis, NC**	DSOB 113
Chris Coons, DE	RSOB 218	John Cornyn, TX	HSOB 517
Mazie Hirono, HI	HSOB 109	Tom Cotton, AR	RSOB 326
Alex Padilla, CA	HSOB 112	Marsha Blackburn, TN	DSOB 357

RULES & ADMINISTRATION

Room: RSOB 305
Website: www.rules.senate.gov
Phone: 202.224.6352
Ratio: 9 Democrats/9 Republicans
Subcommittees: 0

Majority:		Minority:	
C: Amy Klobuchar, MN	DSOB 425	**RM: Roy Blunt, MO**	RSOB 260
Dianne Feinstein, CA	HSOB 331	Mitch McConnell, KY	RSOB 317
Chuck Schumer, NY	HSOB 322	Richard Shelby, AL	RSOB 304
Mark Warner, VA	HSOB 703	Ted Cruz, TX	RSOB 127A
Patrick Leahy, VT	RSOB 437	Shelley Capito, WV	RSOB 172
Angus King, ME	HSOB 133	Roger Wicker, MS	DSOB 555
Jeff Merkley, OR	HSOB 531	Deb Fischer, NE	RSOB 454
Alex Padilla, CA	HSOB 112	Cindy Hyde-Smith, MS	HSOB 702
Jon Ossoff, GA	RSOB 455	Bill Hagerty, TN	RSOB 248

Majority CoS: Elizabeth Peluso   **Minority CoS:** Rachelle G. Schroeder

SMALL BUSINESS & ENTREPRENEURSHIP

Room: RSOB 428A
Website: www.sbc.senate.gov
Phone: 202.224.5175
Ratio: 10 Democrats/10 Republicans
Subcommittees: 0

Majority:		Minority:	
C: Ben Cardin, MD	HSOB 509	**RM: Rand Paul, KY**	RSOB 167
Maria Cantwell, WA	HSOB 511	Marco Rubio, FL	RSOB 284
Jeanne Shaheen, NH	HSOB 506	James Risch, ID	RSOB 483
Ed Markey, MA	DSOB 255	Rick Scott, FL	HSOB 502
Cory Booker, NJ	HSOB 717	Joni Ernst, IA	HSOB 730
Chris Coons, DE	RSOB 218	James Inhofe, OK	RSOB 205
Mazie Hirono, HI	HSOB 109	Todd Young, IN	DSOB 185
Tammy Duckworth, IL	HSOB 524	John Kennedy, LA	RSOB 416
Jacky Rosen, NV	HSOB 713	Josh Hawley, MO	RSOB 212
John Hickenlooper, CO	RSOB 374	Roger Marshall, KS	RSOB 479A

Majority CoS: Sean Moore   **Minority CoS:** Meredith D. West

VETERANS' AFFAIRS

Room: RSOB 412
Website: www.veterans.senate.gov
Phone: 202.224.9126
Ratio: 9 Democrats/9 Republicans
Subcommittees: 0

Majority:		Minority:	
C: Jon Tester, MT	HSOB 311	**RM: Jerry Moran, KS**	DSOB 521
Patty Murray, WA	RSOB 154	John Boozman, AR	HSOB 141
Bernie Sanders, VT	DSOB 332	Bill Cassidy, LA	HSOB 520
Sherrod Brown, OH	HSOB 503	Mike Rounds, SD	HSOB 716
Richard Blumenthal, CT	HSOB 706	Thom Tillis, NC	DSOB 113
Mazie Hirono, HI	HSOB 109	Dan Sullivan, AK	HSOB 302
Joe Manchin, WV	HSOB 306	Marsha Blackburn, TN	DSOB 357
Kyrsten Sinema, AZ	HSOB 317	Kevin Cramer, ND	RSOB 400
Maggie Hassan, NH	HSOB 324	Tommy Tuberville, AL	RSOB 142

Majority CoS: Tony McClain   **Minority CoS:** Jonathan A. Towers

SELECT AND SPECIAL COMMITTEES

AGING

Room: DSOB G-41
Website: www.aging.senate.gov
Phone: 202.224.0185
Ratio: 7 Democrats/7 Republicans
Subcommittees: 0

Majority:		Minority:	
C: Bob Casey, PA	RSOB 393	**RM: Tim Scott, SC**	HSOB 104
Kirsten Gillibrand, NY	RSOB 478	Susan Collins, ME	DSOB 413
Richard Blumenthal, CT	HSOB 706	Richard Burr, NC	RSOB 217
Elizabeth Warren, MA	HSOB 309	Marco Rubio, FL	RSOB 284
Jacky Rosen, NV	HSOB 713	Mike Braun, IN	RSOB 374
Mark Kelly, AZ	HSOB 516	Rick Scott, FL	HSOB 502
Raphael Warnock, GA	RSOB 388	Mike Lee, UT	RSOB 361 A

Majority CoS: Stacy Sanders   **Minority CoS:** Neri A. Martinez

ETHICS

Room:
Website: www.ethics.senate.gov
Ratio: 3 Democrats/3 Republicans
Subcommittees: 0

Majority:		Minority:	
C: Chris Coons, DE	RSOB 218	James Lankford, OK	HSOB 316
Brian Schatz, HI	HSOB 722	James Risch, ID	RSOB 483
Jeanne Shaheen, NH	HSOB 506	Deb Fischer, NE	RSOB 454

INTELLIGENCE

Room: HSOB 211
Website: www.intelligence.senate.gov
Phone: 202.224.1700
Ratio: 10 Democrats/10 Republicans
Subcommittees: 0

Majority:		Minority:	
C: Mark Warner, VA	HSOB 703	Marco Rubio, FL	RSOB 284
Dianne Feinstein, CA	HSOB 331	Richard Burr, NC	RSOB 217
Ron Wyden, OR	DSOB 221	James Risch, ID	RSOB 483
Martin Heinrich, NM	HSOB 303	Susan Collins, ME	DSOB 413
Angus King, ME	HSOB 133	Roy Blunt, MO	RSOB 260
Michael Bennet, CO	RSOB 261	Tom Cotton, AR	RSOB 326
Bob Casey, PA	RSOB 393	John Cornyn, TX	HSOB 517
Kirsten Gillibrand, NY	RSOB 478	Ben Sasse, NE	RSOB 107
Chuck Schumer, NY	HSOB 322	Mitch McConnell, KY	RSOB 317
Jack Reed, RI	HSOB 728	James Inhofe, OK	RSOB 205

Majority CoS: Chris A. Joyner   **Minority CoS:** Michael Colin Casey

JOINT COMMITTEES

JOINT CONGRESSIONAL COMMITTEE ON INAUGURAL CEREMONIES

Website: www.inaugural.senate.gov
Information for this committee, including membership, was not finalized as of the publication date and is therefore subject to change.

JOINT CONGRESSIONAL-EXECUTIVE COMMISSION ON CHINA

Website: www.cecc.gov

Majority U.S. Senate:		Minority U.S. Senate:	
C: Jeff Merkley, OR	HSOB 531	Marco Rubio, FL	RSOB 284
Dianne Feinstein, CA	HSOB 331	James Lankford, OK	HSOB 316
Angus King, ME	HSOB 133	Tom Cotton, AR	RSOB 326
Jon Ossoff, GA	RSOB 455	Steve Daines, MT	HSOB 320
Majority U.S. House:		**Minority U.S. House:**	
Co-C: Jim McGovern, MA-02		Chris Smith, NJ-04	RHOB 2373
	CHOB 370	Brian Mast, FL-18	RHOB 2182
Thomas Suozzi, NY-03	CHOB 407	Vicky Hartzler, MO-04	RHOB 2235
Tom Malinowski, NJ-07	LHOB 1318	Michelle Steel, CA-48	LHOB 1113
Rashida Tlaib, MI-13	LHOB 1628		
Jennifer Wexton, VA-10	LHOB 1217		

JOINT CONGRESSIONAL OVERSIGHT COMMISSION

Room: The Capitol ST-76
Website: www.coc.senate.gov
Phone: 202.224.5050

Majority U.S. Senate:		Minority U.S. Senate:	
Information not available as of press time.		Pat Toomey, PA	DSOB 455
Majority U.S. House:		**Minority U.S. House:**	
Information not available as of press time.		French Hill, AR-02	LHOB 1533

JOINT ECONOMIC

Website: www.jec.senate.gov

Majority U.S. Senate:		Minority U.S. Senate:	
VC: Martin Heinrich, NM	HSOB 303	RM: Mike Lee, UT	RSOB 361 A
Amy Klobuchar, MN	DSOB 425	Rob Portman, OH	RSOB 448
Maggie Hassan, NH	HSOB 324	Tom Cotton, AR	RSOB 326
Mark Kelly, AZ	HSOB 516	Bill Cassidy, LA	HSOB 520
Raphael Warnock, GA	RSOB 388	Ted Cruz, TX	RSOB 127A
Majority U.S. House:		**Minority U.S. House:**	
C: Don Beyer, VA-08	LHOB 1119	David Schweikert, AZ-06	CHOB 304
David Trone, MD-06	LHOB 1110	Jaime Herrera Beutler, WA-03	RHOB 2352
Joyce Beatty, OH-03	RHOB 2303		
Mark Pocan, WI-02	LHOB 1727	Ron Estes, KS-04	RHOB 2411
Scott Peters, CA-52	LHOB 1201	Jodey Arrington, TX-19	LHOB 1107
Sharice Davids, KS-03	LHOB 1541		

Majority CoS: Tamara Fucile **Minority CoS:** Vanessa Brown Calder

JOINT LIBRARY

Website: www.cha.house.gov

Majority U.S. Senate:		Minority U.S. Senate:	
VC: Amy Klobuchar, MN	DSOB 425	Roy Blunt, MO	RSOB 260
Patrick Leahy, VT	RSOB 437	Richard Shelby, AL	RSOB 304
Mark Warner, VA	HSOB 703		
Majority U.S. House:		**Minority U.S. House:**	
C: Zoe Lofgren, CA-19	LHOB 1401	Rodney Davis, IL-13	RHOB 2079
G.K. Butterfield, NC-01	RHOB 2080	Barry Loudermilk, GA-11	RHOB 2133
		Minority CoS: Tim Monahan	

JOINT PRINTING

Website: www.cha.house.gov

Majority U.S. Senate:		Minority U.S. Senate:	
C: Amy Klobuchar, MN	DSOB 425	Roy Blunt, MO	RSOB 260
Angus King, ME	HSOB 133	Roger Wicker, MS	DSOB 555
Alex Padilla, CA	HSOB 112		
Majority U.S. House:		**Minority U.S. House:**	
VC: Zoe Lofgren, CA-19	LHOB 1401	Rodney Davis, IL-13	RHOB 2079
Jamie Raskin, MD-08	RHOB 2242	Barry Loudermilk, GA-11	RHOB 2133
Teresa Leger Fernandez, NM-03	LHOB 1432		

JOINT SECURITY & COOPERATION IN EUROPE

Room: FHOB 234
Website: www.csce.gov
Phone: 202.225.1901

Majority U.S. Senate:		Minority U.S. Senate:	
C: Ben Cardin, MD	HSOB 509	Roger Wicker, MS	DSOB 555
Jeanne Shaheen, NH	HSOB 506	John Boozman, AR	HSOB 141
Sheldon Whitehouse, RI	HSOB 530	Marco Rubio, FL	RSOB 284

Richard Blumenthal, CT	HSOB 706	Thom Tillis, NC	DSOB 113
Tina Smith, MN	HSOB 720		
Majority U.S. House:		**Minority U.S. House:**	
Co-C: Steve Cohen,		**RM: Joe Wilson, SC-02**	LHOB 1436
TN-09	RHOB 2104	Robert Aderholt, AL-04	CHOB 266
Gwen Moore, WI-04	RHOB 2252	Brian Fitzpatrick, PA-01	CHOB 271
Emanuel Cleaver, MO-05	RHOB 2335	Richard Hudson, NC-08	RHOB 2112
Marc Veasey, TX-33	RHOB 2348		
Ruben Gallego, AZ-07	LHOB 1131		

JOINT TAXATION

Website: www.jct.gov

Majority U.S. Senate:		**Minority U.S. Senate:**	
C: Ron Wyden, OR	DSOB 221	Mike Crapo, ID	DSOB 239
Debbie Stabenow, MI	HSOB 731	Chuck Grassley, IA	HSOB 135
Maria Cantwell, WA	HSOB 511		
Majority U.S. House:		**Minority U.S. House:**	
VC: Richard Neal, MA-01	CHOB 372	Kevin Brady, TX-08	LHOB 1011
Lloyd Doggett, TX-35	RHOB 2307	Vern Buchanan, FL-16	RHOB 2110
Mike Thompson, CA-05	CHOB 268		

HOUSE COMMITTEES

Committee rosters are listed in order of ranking membership with the Chairman and Ranking Member indicated with "C" and "RM" respectively. The chairman and ranking member of each committee usually have membership status on all subcommittees of which they are not members. This is referred to as ex officio membership. These memberships are subject to the rules of the individual committees.

ADMINISTRATION

Room: LHOB 1309
Website: www.cha.house.gov
Phone: 202.225.2061
Ratio: 6 Democrats/3 Republicans
Subcommittees: 1

Majority:		Minority:	
C: Zoe Lofgren, CA-19	LHOB 1401	**RM: Rodney Davis, IL-13**	RHOB 2079
Jamie Raskin, MD-08	RHOB 2242	Barry Loudermilk, GA-11	RHOB 2133
G.K. Butterfield, NC-01	RHOB 2080	Bryan Steil, WI-01	LHOB 1526
Pete Aguilar, CA-31	CHOB 109		
Mary Scanlon, PA-05	LHOB 1227		
Teresa Leger Fernandez, NM-03	LHOB 1432		

Majority CoS: Jamie Fleet

Minority CoS: Tim Monahan
Minority Sched: Janet G. Schwalb

──────── Subcommittees ────────

ELECTIONS
Room: LHOB 1309
Phone: 202.225.2061

Majority:		Minority:	
C: G.K. Butterfield, NC-01	RHOB 2080	**RM: Bryan Steil, WI-01**	LHOB 1526
Pete Aguilar, CA-31	CHOB 109		
Teresa Leger Fernandez, NM-03	LHOB 1432		

AGRICULTURE

Room: LHOB 1301
Website: www.agriculture.house.gov
Phone: 202.225.2171
Ratio: 27 Democrats/24 Republicans
Subcommittees: 6

Majority:		Minority:	
C: David Scott, GA-13	CHOB 468	**RM: Glenn Thompson, PA-15**	CHOB 400
Alma Adams, NC-12	RHOB 2436	Austin Scott, GA-08	RHOB 2417
Jim Costa, CA-16	RHOB 2081	Rick Crawford, AR-01	RHOB 2422
Jim McGovern, MA-02	CHOB 370	Scott DesJarlais, TN-04	RHOB 2304
Filemon Vela, TX-34	CHOB 307	Vicky Hartzler, MO-04	RHOB 2235
Abigail Spanberger, VA-07	LHOB 1431	Doug LaMalfa, CA-01	CHOB 408
Jahana Hayes, CT-05	LHOB 1415	Rodney Davis, IL-13	RHOB 2079
Antonio Delgado, NY-19	LHOB 1007	Rick Allen, GA-12	CHOB 570
Shontel Brown, OH-11	RHOB 2344	David Rouzer, NC-07	RHOB 2333
Bobby Rush, IL-01	RHOB 2188	Trent Kelly, MS-01	RHOB 2243
Chellie Pingree, ME-01	RHOB 2162	Don Bacon, NE-02	LHOB 1024
Gregorio Sablan, MP-01	RHOB 2267	Dusty Johnson, SD-01	LHOB 1714
Ann Kuster, NH-02	CHOB 320	Jim Baird, IN-04	LHOB 1314
Cheri Bustos, IL-17	LHOB 1233	Jim Hagedorn, MN-01	LHOB 1433
Sean Maloney, NY-18	CHOB 464	Chris Jacobs, NY-27	CHOB 214
Stacey Plaskett, VI-01	RHOB 2404	Troy Balderson, OH-12	RHOB 2429
Tom O'Halleran, AZ-01	CHOB 318	Michael Cloud, TX-27	CHOB 512
Salud Carbajal, CA-24	RHOB 2331	Tracey Mann, KS-01	CHOB 522
Ro Khanna, CA-17	CHOB 306	Randy Feenstra, IA-04	LHOB 1440
Al Lawson, FL-05	RHOB 2437	Mary Miller, IL-15	LHOB 1529
Lou Correa, CA-46	RHOB 2301	Barry Moore, AL-02	LHOB 1504
Angie Craig, MN-02	RHOB 2442	Kat Cammack, FL-03	LHOB 1626
Josh Harder, CA-10	CHOB 209	Michelle Fischbach, MN-07	LHOB 1237
Cindy Axne, IA-03	LHOB 1034	Julia Letlow, LA-05	LHOB 1408
Kim Schrier, WA-08	LHOB 1123		
Jimmy Panetta, CA-20	CHOB 406		
Sanford Bishop, GA-02	RHOB 2407		

Majority CoS: Anne L. Simmons   **Minority CoS:** Parish M. Braden
──────── Subcommittees ────────

BIOTECHNOLOGY, HORTICULTURE & RESEARCH
Room:

Majority:		Minority:	
C: Stacey Plaskett, VI-01	RHOB 2404	RM: Jim Baird, IN-04	LHOB 1314
Antonio Delgado, NY-19	LHOB 1007	Austin Scott, GA-08	RHOB 2417
Shontel Brown, OH-11	RHOB 2344	Rick Crawford, AR-01	RHOB 2422
Kim Schrier, WA-08	LHOB 1123	Rodney Davis, IL-13	RHOB 2079
Jimmy Panetta, CA-20	CHOB 406	Don Bacon, NE-02	LHOB 1024
Chellie Pingree, ME-01	RHOB 2162	Jim Hagedorn, MN-01	LHOB 1433
Sean Maloney, NY-18	CHOB 464	Chris Jacobs, NY-27	CHOB 214
Salud Carbajal, CA-24	RHOB 2331	Troy Balderson, OH-12	RHOB 2429
Al Lawson, FL-05	RHOB 2437	Michelle Fischbach, MN-07	LHOB 1237
Josh Harder, CA-10	CHOB 209	Julia Letlow, LA-05	LHOB 1408
Lou Correa, CA-46	RHOB 2301	Glenn Thompson, PA-15	CHOB 400
David Scott, GA-13	CHOB 468		

COMMODITY EXCHANGES, ENERGY & CREDIT
Room:

Majority:		Minority:	
C: Antonio Delgado, NY-19	LHOB 1007	RM: Michelle Fischbach, MN-07	LHOB 1237
Sean Maloney, NY-18	CHOB 464	Austin Scott, GA-08	RHOB 2417
Stacey Plaskett, VI-01	RHOB 2404	Doug LaMalfa, CA-01	CHOB 408
Ro Khanna, CA-17	CHOB 306	Rodney Davis, IL-13	RHOB 2079
Cindy Axne, IA-03	LHOB 1034	Chris Jacobs, NY-27	CHOB 214
Bobby Rush, IL-01	RHOB 2188	Troy Balderson, OH-12	RHOB 2429
Angie Craig, MN-02	RHOB 2442	Michael Cloud, TX-27	CHOB 512
Ann Kuster, NH-02	CHOB 320	Randy Feenstra, IA-04	LHOB 1440
Cheri Bustos, IL-17	LHOB 1233	Kat Cammack, FL-03	LHOB 1626
David Scott, GA-13	CHOB 468	Glenn Thompson, PA-15	CHOB 400

CONSERVATION & FORESTRY
Room:

Majority:		Minority:	
C: Abigail Spanberger, VA-07	LHOB 1431	RM: Doug LaMalfa, CA-01	CHOB 408
		Scott DesJarlais, TN-04	RHOB 2304
Filemon Vela, TX-34	CHOB 307	Rick Allen, GA-12	CHOB 570
Chellie Pingree, ME-01	RHOB 2162	Trent Kelly, MS-01	RHOB 2243
Ann Kuster, NH-02	CHOB 320	Dusty Johnson, SD-01	LHOB 1714
Tom O'Halleran, AZ-01	CHOB 318	Mary Miller, IL-15	LHOB 1529
Jimmy Panetta, CA-20	CHOB 406	Barry Moore, AL-02	LHOB 1504
Lou Correa, CA-46	RHOB 2301	Glenn Thompson, PA-15	CHOB 400
Kim Schrier, WA-08	LHOB 1123		
David Scott, GA-13	CHOB 468		

GENERAL FARM COMMODITIES & RISK MANAGEMENT
Room:

Majority:		Minority:	
C: Cheri Bustos, IL-17	LHOB 1233	RM: Austin Scott, GA-08	RHOB 2417
Angie Craig, MN-02	RHOB 2442	Rick Crawford, AR-01	RHOB 2422
Filemon Vela, TX-34	CHOB 307	Rick Allen, GA-12	CHOB 570
Salud Carbajal, CA-24	RHOB 2331	David Rouzer, NC-07	RHOB 2333
Tom O'Halleran, AZ-01	CHOB 318	Tracey Mann, KS-01	CHOB 522
Al Lawson, FL-05	RHOB 2437	Mary Miller, IL-15	LHOB 1529
Sanford Bishop, GA-02	RHOB 2407	Glenn Thompson, PA-15	CHOB 400
David Scott, GA-13	CHOB 468		

LIVESTOCK & FOREIGN AGRICULTURE
Room:

Majority:		Minority:	
C: Jim Costa, CA-16	RHOB 2081	RM: Dusty Johnson, SD-01	LHOB 1714
Abigail Spanberger, VA-07	LHOB 1431		
Jahana Hayes, CT-05	LHOB 1415	Scott DesJarlais, TN-04	RHOB 2304
Lou Correa, CA-46	RHOB 2301	Vicky Hartzler, MO-04	RHOB 2235
Josh Harder, CA-10	CHOB 209	David Rouzer, NC-07	RHOB 2333
Ro Khanna, CA-17	CHOB 306	Trent Kelly, MS-01	RHOB 2243
Cindy Axne, IA-03	LHOB 1034	Don Bacon, NE-02	LHOB 1024
Bobby Rush, IL-01	RHOB 2188	Jim Baird, IN-04	LHOB 1314
Stacey Plaskett, VI-01	RHOB 2404	Jim Hagedorn, MN-01	LHOB 1433
Angie Craig, MN-02	RHOB 2442	Tracey Mann, KS-01	CHOB 522
Sanford Bishop, GA-02	RHOB 2407	Randy Feenstra, IA-04	LHOB 1440
David Scott, GA-13	CHOB 468	Barry Moore, AL-02	LHOB 1504
		Glenn Thompson, PA-15	CHOB 400

SUBCOMMITTEE NUTRITION, OVERSIGHT & DEPARTMENT OPERATIONS
Room: LHOB 1301
Phone: 202.225.2171

Majority:		Minority:	
C: Jahana Hayes, CT-05	LHOB 1415	RM: Don Bacon, NE-02	LHOB 1024

Alma Adams, NC-12	RHOB 2436	Rick Crawford, AR-01	RHOB 2422
Jim McGovern, MA-02	CHOB 370	Scott DesJarlais, TN-04	RHOB 2304
Shontel Brown, OH-11	RHOB 2344	Vicky Hartzler, MO-04	RHOB 2235
Bobby Rush, IL-01	RHOB 2188	Jim Baird, IN-04	LHOB 1314
Gregorio Sablan, MP-01	RHOB 2267	Chris Jacobs, NY-27	CHOB 214
Salud Carbajal, CA-24	RHOB 2331	Michael Cloud, TX-27	CHOB 512
Al Lawson, FL-05	RHOB 2437	Kat Cammack, FL-03	LHOB 1626
Ann Kuster, NH-02	CHOB 320	Glenn Thompson, PA-15	CHOB 400
Jimmy Panetta, CA-20	CHOB 406	Julia Letlow, LA-05	LHOB 1408
David Scott, GA-13	CHOB 468		

APPROPRIATIONS

Room: The Capitol H-307
Website: www.appropriations.house.gov
Phone: 202.225.2771
Ratio: 33 Democrats/25 Republicans
Subcommittees: 12

Majority:		Minority:	
C: Rosa DeLauro, CT-03	RHOB 2413	**RM: Kay Granger, TX-12**	LHOB 1026
Brenda Lawrence, MI-14	RHOB 2463	Tom Cole, OK-04	RHOB 2207
Marcy Kaptur, OH-09	RHOB 2186	Hal Rogers, KY-05	RHOB 2406
David Price, NC-04	RHOB 2108	Robert Aderholt, AL-04	CHOB 266
Lucille Roybal-Allard, CA-40	RHOB 2083	Mike Simpson, ID-02	RHOB 2084
		John Carter, TX-31	RHOB 2208
Sanford Bishop, GA-02	RHOB 2407	Ken Calvert, CA-42	RHOB 2205
Barbara Lee, CA-13	RHOB 2470	Mario Diaz-Balart, FL-25	CHOB 374
Betty McCollum, MN-04	RHOB 2256	Steve Womack, AR-03	RHOB 2412
Tim Ryan, OH-13	LHOB 1126	Chuck Fleischmann, TN-03	CHOB 462
Dutch Ruppersberger, MD-02	RHOB 2206	Jaime Herrera Beutler, WA-03	RHOB 2352
Debbie Wasserman Schultz, FL-23	LHOB 1114	Dave Joyce, OH-14	RHOB 2065
		Andy Harris, MD-01	RHOB 2334
Henry Cuellar, TX-28	RHOB 2372	Mark Amodei, NV-02	CHOB 101
Chellie Pingree, ME-01	RHOB 2162	Chris Stewart, UT-02	CHOB 166
Mike Quigley, IL-05	RHOB 2078	Steven Palazzo, MS-04	RHOB 2349
Derek Kilmer, WA-06	RHOB 2059	David Valadao, CA-21	LHOB 1728
Matt Cartwright, PA-08	RHOB 2102	Dan Newhouse, WA-04	CHOB 504
Grace Meng, NY-06	RHOB 2209	John Moolenaar, MI-04	CHOB 117
Mark Pocan, WI-02	LHOB 1727	John Rutherford, FL-04	LHOB 1711
Katherine Clark, MA-05	RHOB 2448	Ben Cline, VA-06	RHOB 2443
Pete Aguilar, CA-31	CHOB 109	Guy Reschenthaler, PA-14	CHOB 409
Lois Frankel, FL-21	RHOB 2305	Mike Garcia, CA-25	LHOB 1535
Cheri Bustos, IL-17	LHOB 1233	Ashley Hinson, IA-01	LHOB 1429
Bonnie Watson Coleman, NJ-12	CHOB 168	Tony Gonzales, TX-23	LHOB 1009
Norma Torres, CA-35	RHOB 2227		
Charlie Crist, FL-13	CHOB 215		
Ann Kirkpatrick, AZ-02	CHOB 309		
Ed Case, HI-01	RHOB 2210		
Adriano Espaillat, NY-13	RHOB 2332		
Josh Harder, CA-10	CHOB 209		
Jennifer Wexton, VA-10	LHOB 1217		
David Trone, MD-06	LHOB 1110		
Lauren Underwood, IL-14	LHOB 1130		
Susie Lee, NV-03	CHOB 365		

Majority CoS: Robin Juliano   **Minority CoS:** Anne Marie Chotvacs
——— Subcommittees ———

AGRICULTURE, RURAL DEVELOPMENT, FDA & RELATED AGENCIES
Room: RHOB 2362-A
Phone: 202.225.2638

Majority:		Minority:	
C: Sanford Bishop, GA-02	RHOB 2407	**RM: Andy Harris, MD-01**	RHOB 2334
Chellie Pingree, ME-01	RHOB 2162	Robert Aderholt, AL-04	CHOB 266
Mark Pocan, WI-02	LHOB 1727	David Valadao, CA-21	LHOB 1728
Lauren Underwood, IL-14	LHOB 1130	John Moolenaar, MI-04	CHOB 117
Barbara Lee, CA-13	RHOB 2470	Dan Newhouse, WA-04	CHOB 504
Betty McCollum, MN-04	RHOB 2256	Kay Granger, TX-12	LHOB 1026
Debbie Wasserman Schultz, FL-23	LHOB 1114		
Henry Cuellar, TX-28	RHOB 2372		
Grace Meng, NY-06	RHOB 2209		
Rosa DeLauro, CT-03	RHOB 2413		

COMMERCE, JUSTICE, SCIENCE & RELATED AGENCIES
Room: The Capitol H-310
Phone: 202.225.3351

Majority:		Minority:	
C: Matt Cartwright, PA-08	RHOB 2102	RM: Robert Aderholt, AL-04	CHOB 266
Charlie Crist, FL-13	CHOB 215	Steven Palazzo, MS-04	RHOB 2349
Grace Meng, NY-06	RHOB 2209	Ben Cline, VA-06	RHOB 2443
Ed Case, HI-01	RHOB 2210	Mike Garcia, CA-25	LHOB 1535
Dutch Ruppersberger, MD-02	RHOB 2206	Kay Granger, TX-12	LHOB 1026
Brenda Lawrence, MI-14	RHOB 2463		
David Trone, MD-06	LHOB 1110		
Rosa DeLauro, CT-03	RHOB 2413		

DEFENSE
Room: The Capitol H-405
Phone: 202.225.2847

Majority:		Minority:	
C: Betty McCollum, MN-04	RHOB 2256	RM: Ken Calvert, CA-42	RHOB 2205
Tim Ryan, OH-13	LHOB 1126	Hal Rogers, KY-05	RHOB 2406
Dutch Ruppersberger, MD-02	RHOB 2206	Tom Cole, OK-04	RHOB 2207
		Steve Womack, AR-03	RHOB 2412
Marcy Kaptur, OH-09	RHOB 2186	Robert Aderholt, AL-04	CHOB 266
Henry Cuellar, TX-28	RHOB 2372	John Carter, TX-31	RHOB 2208
Derek Kilmer, WA-06	RHOB 2059	Mario Diaz-Balart, FL-25	CHOB 374
Pete Aguilar, CA-31	CHOB 109	Kay Granger, TX-12	LHOB 1026
Cheri Bustos, IL-17	LHOB 1233		
Charlie Crist, FL-13	CHOB 215		
Ann Kirkpatrick, AZ-02	CHOB 309		
Rosa DeLauro, CT-03	RHOB 2413		

ENERGY & WATER DEVELOPMENT & RELATED AGENCIES
Room: RHOB 2362-B
Phone: 202.225.3421

Majority:		Minority:	
C: Marcy Kaptur, OH-09	RHOB 2186	RM: Mike Simpson, ID-02	RHOB 2084
Debbie Wasserman Schultz, FL-23	LHOB 1114	Ken Calvert, CA-42	RHOB 2205
		Chuck Fleischmann, TN-03	CHOB 462
Ann Kirkpatrick, AZ-02	CHOB 309	Dan Newhouse, WA-04	CHOB 504
Susie Lee, NV-03	CHOB 365	Jaime Herrera Beutler, WA-03	RHOB 2352
Tim Ryan, OH-13	LHOB 1126		
Derek Kilmer, WA-06	RHOB 2059	Guy Reschenthaler, PA-14	CHOB 409
Lois Frankel, FL-21	RHOB 2305	Kay Granger, TX-12	LHOB 1026
Cheri Bustos, IL-17	LHOB 1233		
Bonnie Watson Coleman, NJ-12	CHOB 168		
Rosa DeLauro, CT-03	RHOB 2413		

FINANCIAL SERVICES & GENERAL GOVERNMENT
Room: RHOB 2000
Phone: 202.225.7245

Majority:		Minority:	
C: Mike Quigley, IL-05	RHOB 2078	RM: Steve Womack, AR-03	RHOB 2412
Matt Cartwright, PA-08	RHOB 2102	Mark Amodei, NV-02	CHOB 104
Sanford Bishop, GA-02	RHOB 2407	Chris Stewart, UT-02	CHOB 166
Mark Pocan, WI-02	LHOB 1727	Dave Joyce, OH-14	RHOB 2065
Brenda Lawrence, MI-14	RHOB 2463	Kay Granger, TX-12	LHOB 1026
Norma Torres, CA-35	RHOB 2227		
Ann Kirkpatrick, AZ-02	CHOB 309		
Rosa DeLauro, CT-03	RHOB 2413		

HOMELAND SECURITY
Room: RHOB 2006
Phone: 202.225.5834

Majority:		Minority:	
C: Lucille Roybal-Allard, CA-40	RHOB 2083	RM: Chuck Fleischmann, TN-03	CHOB 462
Henry Cuellar, TX-28	RHOB 2372	Steven Palazzo, MS-04	RHOB 2349
Lauren Underwood, IL-14	LHOB 1130	John Rutherford, FL-04	LHOB 1711
David Price, NC-04	RHOB 2108	Ashley Hinson, IA-01	LHOB 1429
Dutch Ruppersberger, MD-02	RHOB 2206	Kay Granger, TX-12	LHOB 1026
Mike Quigley, IL-05	RHOB 2078		
Pete Aguilar, CA-31	CHOB 109		
Rosa DeLauro, CT-03	RHOB 2413		

INTERIOR, ENVIRONMENT & RELATED AGENCIES
Room: RHOB 2007
Phone: 202.225.3081

Majority:		Minority:	
C: Chellie Pingree, ME-01	RHOB 2162	RM: Dave Joyce, OH-14	RHOB 2065
Betty McCollum, MN-04	RHOB 2256	Mike Simpson, ID-02	RHOB 2084

Derek Kilmer, WA-06	RHOB 2059	Chris Stewart, UT-02	CHOB 166
Josh Harder, CA-10	CHOB 209	Mark Amodei, NV-02	CHOB 104
Susie Lee, NV-03	CHOB 365	Kay Granger, TX-12	LHOB 1026
Marcy Kaptur, OH-09	RHOB 2186		
Matt Cartwright, PA-08	RHOB 2102		
Rosa DeLauro, CT-03	RHOB 2413		

LABOR, HEALTH & HUMAN SERVICES, EDUCATION & RELATED AGENCIES
Room: RHOB 2358-B
Phone: 202.225.3508

Majority:		Minority:	
C: Rosa DeLauro, CT-03	RHOB 2413	**RM: Tom Cole, OK-04**	RHOB 2207
Lucille Roybal-Allard, CA-40	RHOB 2083	Andy Harris, MD-01	RHOB 2334
		Chuck Fleischmann, TN-03	CHOB 462
Barbara Lee, CA-13	RHOB 2470	Jaime Herrera Beutler, WA-03	RHOB 2352
Mark Pocan, WI-02	LHOB 1727		
Katherine Clark, MA-05	RHOB 2448	John Moolenaar, MI-04	CHOB 117
Lois Frankel, FL-21	RHOB 2305	Ben Cline, VA-06	RHOB 2443
Cheri Bustos, IL-17	LHOB 1233	Kay Granger, TX-12	LHOB 1026
Bonnie Watson Coleman, NJ-12	CHOB 168		
Brenda Lawrence, MI-14	RHOB 2463		
Josh Harder, CA-10	CHOB 209		

LEGISLATIVE BRANCH
Room: The Capitol H-306
Phone: 202.226.7252

Majority:		Minority:	
C: Tim Ryan, OH-13	LHOB 1126	**RM: Jaime Herrera Beutler, WA-03**	RHOB 2352
Katherine Clark, MA-05	RHOB 2448		
Ed Case, HI-01	RHOB 2210	Mark Amodei, NV-02	CHOB 104
Adriano Espaillat, NY-13	RHOB 2332	Dan Newhouse, WA-04	CHOB 504
Jennifer Wexton, VA-10	LHOB 1217	Kay Granger, TX-12	LHOB 1026
Rosa DeLauro, CT-03	RHOB 2413		

MILITARY CONSTRUCTION, VETERANS AFFAIRS & RELATED AGENCIES
Room: The Capitol HT-2
Phone: 202.225.3047

Majority:		Minority:	
C: Debbie Wasserman Schultz, FL-23	LHOB 1114	**RM: John Carter, TX-31**	RHOB 2208
		David Valadao, CA-21	LHOB 1728
Sanford Bishop, GA-02	RHOB 2407	John Rutherford, FL-04	LHOB 1711
Ed Case, HI-01	RHOB 2210	Tony Gonzales, TX-23	LHOB 1009
Chellie Pingree, ME-01	RHOB 2162	Kay Granger, TX-12	LHOB 1026
Charlie Crist, FL-13	CHOB 215		
David Trone, MD-06	LHOB 1110		
Susie Lee, NV-03	CHOB 365		
Rosa DeLauro, CT-03	RHOB 2413		

STATE, FOREIGN OPERATIONS & RELATED PROGRAMS
Room: The Capitol HT-Two
Phone: 202.225.2041

Majority:		Minority:	
C: Barbara Lee, CA-13	RHOB 2470	**RM: Hal Rogers, KY-05**	RHOB 2406
Grace Meng, NY-06	RHOB 2209	Mario Diaz-Balart, FL-25	CHOB 374
David Price, NC-04	RHOB 2108	Guy Reschenthaler, PA-14	CHOB 409
Lois Frankel, FL-21	RHOB 2305	Kay Granger, TX-12	LHOB 1026
Norma Torres, CA-35	RHOB 2227		
Adriano Espaillat, NY-13	RHOB 2332		
Jennifer Wexton, VA-10	LHOB 1217		
Rosa DeLauro, CT-03	RHOB 2413		

TRANSPORTATION, HUD & RELATED AGENCIES
Room: RHOB 2358-A
Phone: 202.225.2141

Majority:		Minority:	
C: David Price, NC-04	RHOB 2108	**RM: Mario Diaz-Balart, FL-25**	CHOB 374
Mike Quigley, IL-05	RHOB 2078		
Katherine Clark, MA-05	RHOB 2448	Steve Womack, AR-03	RHOB 2412
Bonnie Watson Coleman, NJ-12	CHOB 168	John Rutherford, FL-04	LHOB 1711
		Mike Garcia, CA-25	LHOB 1535
Norma Torres, CA-35	RHOB 2227	Ashley Hinson, IA-01	LHOB 1429
Pete Aguilar, CA-31	CHOB 109	Tony Gonzales, TX-23	LHOB 1009
Adriano Espaillat, NY-13	RHOB 2332	Kay Granger, TX-12	LHOB 1026
Jennifer Wexton, VA-10	LHOB 1217		
David Trone, MD-06	LHOB 1110		

Rosa DeLauro, CT-03   RHOB 2413

ARMED SERVICES

Room: RHOB 2216
Website: www.armedservices.house.gov
Phone: 202.225.4151
Ratio: 31 Democrats/28 Republicans
Subcommittees: 7

Majority:		Minority:	
C: Adam Smith, WA-09	RHOB 2264	RM: Mike Rogers, AL-03	RHOB 2469
Elaine Luria, VA-02	CHOB 412	Rob Wittman, VA-01	RHOB 2055
Jim Langevin, RI-02	RHOB 2077	Joe Wilson, SC-02	LHOB 1436
Rick Larsen, WA-02	RHOB 2163	Mike Turner, OH-10	RHOB 2082
Jim Cooper, TN-05	LHOB 1536	Doug Lamborn, CO-05	RHOB 2371
Joe Courtney, CT-02	RHOB 2449	Vicky Hartzler, MO-04	RHOB 2235
John Garamendi, CA-03	RHOB 2368	Austin Scott, GA-08	RHOB 2417
Jackie Speier, CA-14	RHOB 2465	Mo Brooks, AL-05	RHOB 2185
Donald Norcross, NJ-01	RHOB 2427	Sam Graves, MO-06	LHOB 1135
Ruben Gallego, AZ-07	LHOB 1131	Elise Stefanik, NY-21	RHOB 2211
Seth Moulton, MA-06	LHOB 1127	Scott DesJarlais, TN-04	RHOB 2304
Salud Carbajal, CA-24	RHOB 2331	Trent Kelly, MS-01	RHOB 2243
Anthony Brown, MD-04	LHOB 1323	Mike Gallagher, WI-08	LHOB 1230
Ro Khanna, CA-17	CHOB 306	Matt Gaetz, FL-01	LHOB 1721
Bill Keating, MA-09	RHOB 2351	Don Bacon, NE-02	LHOB 1024
Filemon Vela, TX-34	CHOB 307	Jim Banks, IN-03	LHOB 1713
Andy Kim, NJ-03	RHOB 2444	Liz Cheney, WY-01	CHOB 416
Chrissy Houlahan, PA-06	LHOB 1218	Jack Bergman, MI-01	CHOB 566
Jason Crow, CO-06	LHOB 1229	Mike Waltz, FL-06	CHOB 213
Elissa Slotkin, MI-08	LHOB 1210	Mike Johnson, LA-04	CHOB 568
Mikie Sherrill, NJ-11	LHOB 1414	Mark Green, TN-07	RHOB 2446
Veronica Escobar, TX-16	LHOB 1505	Stephanie Bice, OK-05	LHOB 1223
Jared Golden, ME-02	LHOB 1222	Scott Franklin, FL-15	LHOB 1517
Joseph Morelle, NY-25	LHOB 1317	Lisa McClain, MI-10	CHOB 218
Sara Jacobs, CA-53	LHOB 1232	Ronny Jackson, TX-13	CHOB 118
Kaiali'i Kahele, HI-02	LHOB 1205	Jerry Carl, AL-01	LHOB 1330
Marilyn Strickland, WA-10	LHOB 1004	Blake Moore, UT-01	LHOB 1320
Marc Veasey, TX-33	RHOB 2348	Pat Fallon, TX-04	LHOB 1118
Jimmy Panetta, CA-20	CHOB 406		
Stephanie Murphy, FL-07	LHOB 1710		
Steven Horsford, NV-04	CHOB 562		

Majority CoS: Paul Arcangeli   **Minority CoS:** Christopher Vieson

————————— Subcommittees —————————

CYBER, INNOVATIVE TECHNOLOGIES & INFORMATION SYSTEMS
Room: RHOB 2216
Phone: 202.225.4151

Majority:		Minority:	
C: Jim Langevin, RI-02	RHOB 2077	RM: Jim Banks, IN-03	LHOB 1713
Rick Larsen, WA-02	RHOB 2163	Elise Stefanik, NY-21	RHOB 2211
Seth Moulton, MA-06	LHOB 1127	Mo Brooks, AL-05	RHOB 2185
Ro Khanna, CA-17	CHOB 306	Matt Gaetz, FL-01	LHOB 1721
Bill Keating, MA-09	RHOB 2351	Mike Johnson, LA-04	CHOB 568
Andy Kim, NJ-03	RHOB 2444	Stephanie Bice, OK-05	LHOB 1223
Chrissy Houlahan, PA-06	LHOB 1218	Scott Franklin, FL-15	LHOB 1517
Jason Crow, CO-06	LHOB 1229	Blake Moore, UT-01	LHOB 1320
Elissa Slotkin, MI-08	LHOB 1210	Pat Fallon, TX-04	LHOB 1118
Veronica Escobar, TX-16	LHOB 1505		
Joseph Morelle, NY-25	LHOB 1317		

INTELLIGENCE & SPECIAL OPERATIONS
Room: RHOB 2340
Phone: 202.225.4151

Majority:		Minority:	
C: Ruben Gallego, AZ-07	LHOB 1131	RM: Trent Kelly, MS-01	RHOB 2243
Rick Larsen, WA-02	RHOB 2163	Doug Lamborn, CO-05	RHOB 2371
Jim Cooper, TN-05	LHOB 1536	Austin Scott, GA-08	RHOB 2417
Bill Keating, MA-09	RHOB 2351	Sam Graves, MO-06	LHOB 1135
Filemon Vela, TX-34	CHOB 307	Don Bacon, NE-02	LHOB 1024
Mikie Sherrill, NJ-11	LHOB 1414	Liz Cheney, WY-01	CHOB 416
Jimmy Panetta, CA-20	CHOB 406	Scott Franklin, FL-15	LHOB 1517
Stephanie Murphy, FL-07	LHOB 1710		

MILITARY PERSONNEL
Room:

Majority:		Minority:	
C: Jackie Speier, CA-14	RHOB 2465	RM: Mike Gallagher,	LHOB 1230
Andy Kim, NJ-03	RHOB 2444	WI-08	

Chrissy Houlahan, PA-06	LHOB 1218	Stephanie Bice, OK-05	LHOB 1223
Veronica Escobar, TX-16	LHOB 1505	Lisa McClain, MI-10	CHOB 218
Sara Jacobs, CA-53	LHOB 1232	Ronny Jackson, TX-13	CHOB 118
Marilyn Strickland, WA-10	LHOB 1004	Jerry Carl, AL-01	LHOB 1330
Marc Veasey, TX-33	RHOB 2348	Pat Fallon, TX-04	LHOB 1118

READINESS
Room:

Majority:		**Minority:**	
C: John Garamendi, CA-03	RHOB 2368	**RM: Mike Waltz, FL-06**	CHOB 213
		Joe Wilson, SC-02	LHOB 1436
Joe Courtney, CT-02	RHOB 2449	Austin Scott, GA-08	RHOB 2417
Jackie Speier, CA-14	RHOB 2465	Jack Bergman, MI-01	CHOB 566
Jason Crow, CO-06	LHOB 1229	Mike Johnson, LA-04	CHOB 568
Elissa Slotkin, MI-08	LHOB 1510	Mark Green, TN-07	RHOB 2446
Jared Golden, ME-02	LHOB 1222	Lisa McClain, MI-10	CHOB 218
Elaine Luria, VA-02	CHOB 412	Blake Moore, UT-01	LHOB 1320
Kaiali'i Kahele, HI-02	LHOB 1205		
Marilyn Strickland, WA-10	LHOB 1004		

SEAPOWER & PROJECTION FORCES
Room:

Majority:		**Minority:**	
C: Joe Courtney, CT-02	RHOB 2449	**RM: Rob Wittman, VA-01**	RHOB 2055
Jim Langevin, RI-02	RHOB 2077	Vicky Hartzler, MO-04	RHOB 2235
Jim Cooper, TN-05	LHOB 1536	Sam Graves, MO-06	LHOB 1135
Donald Norcross, NJ-01	RHOB 2427	Trent Kelly, MS-01	RHOB 2243
Anthony Brown, MD-04	LHOB 1323	Mike Gallagher, WI-08	LHOB 1230
Filemon Vela, TX-34	CHOB 307	Jim Banks, IN-03	LHOB 1713
Jared Golden, ME-02	LHOB 1222	Jack Bergman, MI-01	CHOB 566
Elaine Luria, VA-02	CHOB 412	Jerry Carl, AL-01	LHOB 1330
Sara Jacobs, CA-53	LHOB 1232		

STRATEGIC FORCES
Room:

Majority:		**Minority:**	
C: Jim Cooper, TN-05	LHOB 1536	**RM: Doug Lamborn, CO-05**	RHOB 2371
Jim Langevin, RI-02	RHOB 2077		
John Garamendi, CA-03	RHOB 2368	Joe Wilson, SC-02	LHOB 1436
Seth Moulton, MA-06	LHOB 1127	Mike Turner, OH-10	RHOB 2082
Salud Carbajal, CA-24	RHOB 2331	Mo Brooks, AL-05	RHOB 2185
Ro Khanna, CA-17	CHOB 306	Elise Stefanik, NY-21	RHOB 2211
Joseph Morelle, NY-25	LHOB 1317	Scott DesJarlais, TN-04	RHOB 2304
Jimmy Panetta, CA-20	CHOB 406	Liz Cheney, WY-01	CHOB 416
Steven Horsford, NV-04	CHOB 562	Mike Waltz, FL-06	CHOB 213

TACTICAL AIR & LAND FORCES
Room:

Majority:		**Minority:**	
C: Donald Norcross, NJ-01	RHOB 2427	**RM: Vicky Hartzler, MO-04**	RHOB 2235
Ruben Gallego, AZ-07	LHOB 1131	Mike Turner, OH-10	RHOB 2082
Salud Carbajal, CA-24	RHOB 2331	Rob Wittman, VA-01	RHOB 2055
Anthony Brown, MD-04	LHOB 1323	Scott DesJarlais, TN-04	RHOB 2304
Mikie Sherrill, NJ-11	LHOB 1414	Matt Gaetz, FL-01	LHOB 1721
Kaiali'i Kahele, HI-02	LHOB 1205	Don Bacon, NE-02	LHOB 1024
Marc Veasey, TX-33	RHOB 2348	Mark Green, TN-07	RHOB 2446
Stephanie Murphy, FL-07	LHOB 1710	Ronny Jackson, TX-13	CHOB 118
Steven Horsford, NV-04	CHOB 562		

BUDGET

Room: CHOB 204-E
Website: www.budget.house.gov
Phone: 202.226.7200
Ratio: 21 Democrats/16 Republicans
Subcommittees: 0

Majority:		**Minority:**	
C: John Yarmuth, KY-03	CHOB 402	**RM: Jason Smith, MO-08**	RHOB 2418
Hakeem Jeffries, NY-08	RHOB 2433	Trent Kelly, MS-01	RHOB 2243
Brian Higgins, NY-26	RHOB 2459	Tom McClintock, CA-04	RHOB 2312
Brendan Boyle, PA-02	LHOB 1133	Glenn Grothman, WI-06	LHOB 1427
Lloyd Doggett, TX-35	RHOB 2307	Lloyd Smucker, PA-11	CHOB 302
David Price, NC-04	RHOB 2108	Chris Jacobs, NY-27	CHOB 214
Jan Schakowsky, IL-09	RHOB 2367	Michael Burgess, TX-26	RHOB 2161
Dan Kildee, MI-05	CHOB 200	Buddy Carter, GA-01	RHOB 2432
Joseph Morelle, NY-25	LHOB 1317	Ben Cline, VA-06	RHOB 2443
Steven Horsford, NV-04	CHOB 562	Lauren Boebert, CO-03	LHOB 1609

Barbara Lee, CA-13	RHOB 2470	Byron Donalds, FL-19	CHOB 523
Judy Chu, CA-27	RHOB 2423	Randy Feenstra, IA-04	LHOB 1440
Stacey Plaskett, VI-01	RHOB 2404	Bob Good, VA-05	LHOB 1213
Jennifer Wexton, VA-10	LHOB 1217	Ashley Hinson, IA-01	LHOB 1429
Bobby Scott, VA-03	RHOB 2328	Jay Obernolte, CA-08	LHOB 1029
Sheila Jackson Lee, TX-18	RHOB 2426	Mike Carey, OH-15	RHOB 2234
Jim Cooper, TN-05	LHOB 1536		
Albio Sires, NJ-08	RHOB 2268		
Scott Peters, CA-52	LHOB 1201		
Seth Moulton, MA-06	LHOB 1127		
Pramila Jayapal, WA-07	RHOB 2346		

Majority CoS: Diana Meredith **Minority CoS:** Mark Roman
Majority Sched: Sheila A. McDowell

COMMUNICATIONS STANDARDS COMMISSION

Room: LHOB 1307
Website: www.cha.house.gov
Phone: 202.225.9337
Ratio: 3 Democrats/3 Republicans
Subcommittees: 0

Majority:		Minority:	
C: Mary Scanlon, PA-05	LHOB 1227	Kat Cammack, FL-03	LHOB 1626
Brad Sherman, CA-30	RHOB 2181	Bob Latta, OH-05	RHOB 2467
Mondaire Jones, NY-17	LHOB 1017	Bryan Steil, WI-01	LHOB 1526

Majority CoS: Matthew DeFreitas

EDUCATION & LABOR

Room: RHOB 2176
Website: www.edlabor.house.gov
Phone: 202.225.3725
Ratio: 29 Democrats/23 Republicans
Subcommittees: 5

Majority:		Minority:	
C: Bobby Scott, VA-03	RHOB 2328	RM: Virginia Foxx, NC-05	RHOB 2462
Jamaal Bowman, NY-16	LHOB 1605	Joe Wilson, SC-02	LHOB 1436
Raul Grijalva, AZ-03	LHOB 1511	Glenn Thompson, PA-15	CHOB 400
Joe Courtney, CT-02	RHOB 2449	Tim Walberg, MI-07	RHOB 2266
Gregorio Sablan, MP-01	RHOB 2267	Glenn Grothman, WI-06	LHOB 1427
Frederica Wilson, FL-24	RHOB 2445	Elise Stefanik, NY-21	RHOB 2211
Suzanne Bonamici, OR-01	RHOB 2231	Rick Allen, GA-12	CHOB 570
Mark Takano, CA-41	CHOB 420	Jim Banks, IN-03	LHOB 1713
Alma Adams, NC-12	RHOB 2436	James Comer, KY-01	RHOB 2410
Mark DeSaulnier, CA-11	CHOB 503	Russ Fulcher, ID-01	LHOB 1520
Donald Norcross, NJ-01	RHOB 2427	Fred Keller, PA-12	LHOB 1717
Pramila Jayapal, WA-07	RHOB 2346	Gregory Murphy, NC-03	CHOB 313
Joseph Morelle, NY-25	LHOB 1317	Mariannette Miller-Meeks,	LHOB 1716
Susan Wild, PA-07	LHOB 1027	IA-02	
Lucy McBath, GA-06	LHOB 1513	Burgess Owens, UT-04	LHOB 1039
Jahana Hayes, CT-05	LHOB 1415	Bob Good, VA-05	LHOB 1213
Andy Levin, MI-09	CHOB 312	Lisa McClain, MI-10	CHOB 218
Ilhan Omar, MN-05	LHOB 1730	Diana Harshbarger, TN-01	CHOB 167
Haley Stevens, MI-11	LHOB 1510	Mary Miller, IL-15	LHOB 1529
Teresa Leger Fernandez,	LHOB 1432	Victoria Spartz, IN-05	LHOB 1523
NM-03		Scott Fitzgerald, WI-05	LHOB 1507
Mondaire Jones, NY-17	LHOB 1017	Madison Cawthorn, NC-11	CHOB 102
Kathy Manning, NC-06	CHOB 415	Michelle Steel, CA-48	LHOB 1113
Frank Mrvan, IN-01	LHOB 1607	Julia Letlow, LA-05	LHOB 1408
Mark Pocan, WI-02	LHOB 1727		
Joaquin Castro, TX-20	RHOB 2241		
Mikie Sherrill, NJ-11	LHOB 1414		
Adriano Espaillat, NY-13	RHOB 2332		
Kweisi Mfume, MD-07	RHOB 2263		
Sheila Cherfilus-McCormick, FL-20	RHOB 2365		

Majority CoS: Veronique F. Pluviose **Minority CoS:** Cyrus Artz

———————————— Subcommittees ————————————

CIVIL RIGHTS & HUMAN SERVICES
Room: RHOB 2176
Phone: 202.225.3725

Majority:		Minority:	
C: Suzanne Bonamici, OR-01	RHOB 2231	RM: Russ Fulcher, ID-01	LHOB 1520
		Glenn Thompson, PA-15	CHOB 400
Alma Adams, NC-12	RHOB 2436	Lisa McClain, MI-10	CHOB 218
Jahana Hayes, CT-05	LHOB 1415	Victoria Spartz, IN-05	LHOB 1523
		Scott Fitzgerald, WI-05	LHOB 1507

Teresa Leger Fernandez, NM-03	LHOB 1432		
Frank Mrvan, IN-01	LHOB 1607		
Jamaal Bowman, NY-16	LHOB 1605		
Kweisi Mfume, MD-07	RHOB 2263		

EARLY CHILDHOOD, ELEMENTARY & SECONDARY EDUCATION

Room: RHOB 2101
Phone: 202.225.4527

Majority:		Minority:	
C: Gregorio Sablan, MP-01	RHOB 2267	**RM: Burgess Owens, UT-04**	LHOB 1039
Jahana Hayes, CT-05	LHOB 1415	Glenn Grothman, WI-06	LHOB 1427
Raul Grijalva, AZ-03	LHOB 1511	Rick Allen, GA-12	CHOB 570
Frederica Wilson, FL-24	RHOB 2445	Fred Keller, PA-12	LHOB 1717
Mark DeSaulnier, CA-11	CHOB 503	Mary Miller, IL-15	LHOB 1529
Joseph Morelle, NY-25	LHOB 1317	Madison Cawthorn, NC-11	CHOB 102
Lucy McBath, GA-06	LHOB 1513	Michelle Steel, CA-48	LHOB 1113
Andy Levin, MI-09	CHOB 312	Julia Letlow, LA-05	LHOB 1408
Kathy Manning, NC-06	CHOB 415		
Jamaal Bowman, NY-16	LHOB 1605		
Bobby Scott, VA-03	RHOB 2328		

HEALTH, EMPLOYMENT, LABOR & PENSIONS

Room: RHOB 2101
Phone: 202.225.4527

Majority:		Minority:	
C: Mark DeSaulnier, CA-11	CHOB 503	**RM: Rick Allen, GA-12**	CHOB 570
		Joe Wilson, SC-02	LHOB 1436
Joe Courtney, CT-02	RHOB 2449	Tim Walberg, MI-07	RHOB 2266
Donald Norcross, NJ-01	RHOB 2427	Jim Banks, IN-03	LHOB 1713
Joseph Morelle, NY-25	LHOB 1317	Diana Harshbarger, TN-01	CHOB 167
Susan Wild, PA-07	LHOB 1027	Mary Miller, IL-15	LHOB 1529
Lucy McBath, GA-06	LHOB 1513	Scott Fitzgerald, WI-05	LHOB 1507
Andy Levin, MI-09	CHOB 312		
Haley Stevens, MI-11	LHOB 1510		
Frank Mrvan, IN-01	LHOB 1607		

HIGHER EDUCATION & WORKFORCE INVESTMENT

Room: RHOB 2101
Phone: 202.225.4527

Majority:		Minority:	
C: Frederica Wilson, FL-24	RHOB 2445	Gregory Murphy, NC-03	CHOB 313
		Glenn Grothman, WI-06	LHOB 1427
Mark Takano, CA-41	CHOB 420	Elise Stefanik, NY-21	RHOB 2211
Pramila Jayapal, WA-07	RHOB 2346	Jim Banks, IN-03	LHOB 1713
Ilhan Omar, MN-05	LHOB 1730	James Comer, KY-01	RHOB 2410
Teresa Leger Fernandez, NM-03	LHOB 1432	Russ Fulcher, ID-01	LHOB 1520
Mondaire Jones, NY-17	LHOB 1017	Mariannette Miller-Meeks, IA-02	LHOB 1716
Kathy Manning, NC-06	CHOB 415	Bob Good, VA-05	LHOB 1213
Jamaal Bowman, NY-16	LHOB 1605	Lisa McClain, MI-10	CHOB 218
Mark Pocan, WI-02	LHOB 1727	Diana Harshbarger, TN-01	CHOB 167
Joaquin Castro, TX-20	RHOB 2241	Victoria Spartz, IN-05	LHOB 1523
Mikie Sherrill, NJ-11	LHOB 1414	Julia Letlow, LA-05	LHOB 1408
Adriano Espaillat, NY-13	RHOB 2332		
Raul Grijalva, AZ-03	LHOB 1511		
Joe Courtney, CT-02	RHOB 2449		
Suzanne Bonamici, OR-01	RHOB 2231		

WORKFORCE PROTECTIONS

Room: RHOB 2101
Phone: 202.225.3725

Majority:		Minority:	
C: Alma Adams, NC-12	RHOB 2436	**RM: Fred Keller, PA-12**	LHOB 1717
Mark Takano, CA-41	CHOB 420	Elise Stefanik, NY-21	RHOB 2211
Donald Norcross, NJ-01	RHOB 2427	Mariannette Miller-Meeks, IA-02	LHOB 1716
Pramila Jayapal, WA-07	RHOB 2346		
Ilhan Omar, MN-05	LHOB 1730	Burgess Owens, UT-04	LHOB 1039
Haley Stevens, MI-11	LHOB 1510	Bob Good, VA-05	LHOB 1213
Mondaire Jones, NY-17	LHOB 1017	Madison Cawthorn, NC-11	CHOB 102
Bobby Scott, VA-03	RHOB 2328	Michelle Steel, CA-48	LHOB 1113

ENERGY & COMMERCE

Room: RHOB 2125
Website: www.energycommerce.house.gov
Phone: 202.225.2927
Ratio: 32 Democrats/26 Republicans
Subcommittees: 6

Majority:		Minority:	
C: Frank Pallone, NJ-06	RHOB 2107	RM: Cathy McMorris Rodgers, WA-05	LHOB 1035
Robin Kelly, IL-02	RHOB 2416		
Bobby Rush, IL-01	RHOB 2188	Fred Upton, MI-06	RHOB 2183
Anna Eshoo, CA-18	CHOB 272	Michael Burgess, TX-26	RHOB 2161
Diana DeGette, CO-01	RHOB 2111	Steve Scalise, LA-01	RHOB 2049
Mike Doyle, PA-18	CHOB 270	Bob Latta, OH-05	RHOB 2467
Jan Schakowsky, IL-09	RHOB 2367	Brett Guthrie, KY-02	RHOB 2434
G.K. Butterfield, NC-01	RHOB 2080	David McKinley, WV-01	RHOB 2239
Doris Matsui, CA-06	RHOB 2311	Adam Kinzinger, IL-16	RHOB 2245
Kathy Castor, FL-14	RHOB 2052	Morgan Griffith, VA-09	RHOB 2202
John Sarbanes, MD-03	RHOB 2370	Gus Bilirakis, FL-12	RHOB 2354
Jerry McNerney, CA-09	RHOB 2265	Bill Johnson, OH-06	RHOB 2336
Peter Welch, VT-01	RHOB 2187	Billy Long, MO-07	RHOB 2454
Paul Tonko, NY-20	RHOB 2369	Larry Bucshon, IN-08	RHOB 2313
Yvette Clarke, NY-09	RHOB 2058	Markwayne Mullin, OK-02	RHOB 2421
Kurt Schrader, OR-05	RHOB 2431	Richard Hudson, NC-08	RHOB 2112
Tony Cardenas, CA-29	RHOB 2438	Tim Walberg, MI-07	RHOB 2266
Raul Ruiz, CA-36	RHOB 2342	Buddy Carter, GA-01	RHOB 2432
Scott Peters, CA-52	LHOB 1201	Jeff Duncan, SC-03	RHOB 2229
Debbie Dingell, MI-12	CHOB 116	Gary Palmer, AL-06	CHOB 170
Marc Veasey, TX-33	RHOB 2348	Neal Dunn, FL-02	CHOB 316
Ann Kuster, NH-02	CHOB 320	John Curtis, UT-03	RHOB 2400
Nanette Barragan, CA-44	RHOB 2246	Debbie Lesko, AZ-08	LHOB 1214
A. Donald McEachin, VA-04	CHOB 314	Greg Pence, IN-06	CHOB 211
Lisa Blunt Rochester, DE-01	LHOB 1724	Daniel Crenshaw, TX-02	CHOB 413
Darren Soto, FL-09	RHOB 2353	John Joyce, PA-13	LHOB 1221
Tom O'Halleran, AZ-01	CHOB 318	Kelly Armstrong, ND-01	LHOB 1740
Kathleen Rice, NY-04	RHOB 2435		
Angie Craig, MN-02	RHOB 2442		
Kim Schrier, WA-08	LHOB 1123		
Lori Trahan, MA-03	RHOB 2439		
Lizzie Fletcher, TX-07	CHOB 119		

Majority CoS: Tiffany Guarascio　　　**Minority CoS:** Nate Hodson
Majority Sched: Elizabeth B. Ertel

—————————————— Subcommittees ——————————————

COMMUNICATIONS & TECHNOLOGY

Room: RHOB 2125
Phone: 202.225.2927

Majority:		Minority:	
C: Mike Doyle, PA-18	CHOB 270	RM: Bob Latta, OH-05	RHOB 2467
Jerry McNerney, CA-09	RHOB 2265	Steve Scalise, LA-01	RHOB 2049
Yvette Clarke, NY-09	RHOB 2058	Brett Guthrie, KY-02	RHOB 2434
Marc Veasey, TX-33	RHOB 2348	Adam Kinzinger, IL-16	RHOB 2245
A. Donald McEachin, VA-04	CHOB 314	Gus Bilirakis, FL-12	RHOB 2354
Darren Soto, FL-09	RHOB 2353	Bill Johnson, OH-06	RHOB 2336
Tom O'Halleran, AZ-01	CHOB 318	Billy Long, MO-07	RHOB 2454
Kathleen Rice, NY-04	RHOB 2435	Richard Hudson, NC-08	RHOB 2112
Anna Eshoo, CA-18	CHOB 272	Markwayne Mullin, OK-02	RHOB 2421
G.K. Butterfield, NC-01	RHOB 2080	Tim Walberg, MI-07	RHOB 2266
Doris Matsui, CA-06	RHOB 2311	Buddy Carter, GA-01	RHOB 2432
Peter Welch, VT-01	RHOB 2187	Jeff Duncan, SC-03	RHOB 2229
Kurt Schrader, OR-05	RHOB 2431	John Curtis, UT-03	RHOB 2400
Tony Cardenas, CA-29	RHOB 2438	Cathy McMorris Rodgers, WA-05	LHOB 1035
Robin Kelly, IL-02	RHOB 2416		
Angie Craig, MN-02	RHOB 2442		
Lizzie Fletcher, TX-07	CHOB 119		
Frank Pallone, NJ-06	RHOB 2107		

CONSUMER PROTECTION & COMMERCE

Room: RHOB 2125
Phone: 202.225.2927

Majority:		Minority:	
C: Jan Schakowsky, IL-09	RHOB 2367	RM: Gus Bilirakis, FL-12	RHOB 2354
Bobby Rush, IL-01	RHOB 2188	Fred Upton, MI-06	RHOB 2183
Kathy Castor, FL-14	RHOB 2052	Bob Latta, OH-05	RHOB 2467
Lori Trahan, MA-03	RHOB 2439	Brett Guthrie, KY-02	RHOB 2434
Jerry McNerney, CA-09	RHOB 2265	Larry Bucshon, IN-08	RHOB 2313
Yvette Clarke, NY-09	RHOB 2058	Neal Dunn, FL-02	CHOB 316
Tony Cardenas, CA-29	RHOB 2438	Debbie Lesko, AZ-08	LHOB 1214

Debbie Dingell, MI-12	CHOB 116	Greg Pence, IN-06	CHOB 211
Robin Kelly, IL-02	RHOB 2416	Kelly Armstrong, ND-01	LHOB 1740
Darren Soto, FL-09	RHOB 2353	Cathy McMorris Rodgers,	LHOB 1035
Kathleen Rice, NY-04	RHOB 2435	WA-05	
Angie Craig, MN-02	RHOB 2442		
Lizzie Fletcher, TX-07	CHOB 119		
Frank Pallone, NJ-06	RHOB 2107		

ENERGY
Room: RHOB 2125
Phone: 202.225.2927

Majority:		Minority:	
C: Bobby Rush, IL-01	RHOB 2188	**RM: Fred Upton, MI-06**	RHOB 2183
Scott Peters, CA-52	LHOB 1201	Michael Burgess, TX-26	RHOB 2161
Mike Doyle, PA-18	CHOB 270	Bob Latta, OH-05	RHOB 2467
Jerry McNerney, CA-09	RHOB 2265	David McKinley, WV-01	RHOB 2239
Paul Tonko, NY-20	RHOB 2369	Adam Kinzinger, IL-16	RHOB 2245
Marc Veasey, TX-33	RHOB 2348	Morgan Griffith, VA-09	RHOB 2202
Kim Schrier, WA-08	LHOB 1123	Bill Johnson, OH-06	RHOB 2336
Diana DeGette, CO-01	RHOB 2111	Larry Bucshon, IN-08	RHOB 2313
G.K. Butterfield, NC-01	RHOB 2080	Tim Walberg, MI-07	RHOB 2266
Doris Matsui, CA-06	RHOB 2311	Jeff Duncan, SC-03	RHOB 2229
Kathy Castor, FL-14	RHOB 2052	Gary Palmer, AL-06	CHOB 170
Peter Welch, VT-01	RHOB 2187	Debbie Lesko, AZ-08	LHOB 1214
Kurt Schrader, OR-05	RHOB 2431	Greg Pence, IN-06	CHOB 211
Ann Kuster, NH-02	CHOB 320	Kelly Armstrong, ND-01	LHOB 1740
Nanette Barragan, CA-44	RHOB 2246	Cathy McMorris Rodgers,	LHOB 1035
A. Donald McEachin, VA-04	CHOB 314	WA-05	
Lisa Blunt Rochester, DE-01	LHOB 1724		
Tom O'Halleran, AZ-01	CHOB 318		
Frank Pallone, NJ-06	RHOB 2107		

ENVIRONMENT & CLIMATE CHANGE
Room: RHOB 2125
Phone: 202.225.2927

Majority:		Minority:	
C: Paul Tonko, NY-20	RHOB 2369	**RM: David McKinley,**	RHOB 2239
Diana DeGette, CO-01	RHOB 2111	**WV-01**	
Jan Schakowsky, IL-09	RHOB 2367	Bill Johnson, OH-06	RHOB 2336
John Sarbanes, MD-03	RHOB 2370	Markwayne Mullin, OK-02	RHOB 2421
Yvette Clarke, NY-09	RHOB 2058	Richard Hudson, NC-08	RHOB 2112
Raul Ruiz, CA-36	RHOB 2342	Buddy Carter, GA-01	RHOB 2432
Scott Peters, CA-52	LHOB 1201	Jeff Duncan, SC-03	RHOB 2229
Debbie Dingell, MI-12	CHOB 116	Gary Palmer, AL-06	CHOB 170
Nanette Barragan, CA-44	RHOB 2246	John Curtis, UT-03	RHOB 2400
A. Donald McEachin, VA-04	CHOB 314	Daniel Crenshaw, TX-02	CHOB 413
Lisa Blunt Rochester, DE-01	LHOB 1724	Cathy McMorris Rodgers,	LHOB 1035
Darren Soto, FL-09	RHOB 2353	WA-05	
Tom O'Halleran, AZ-01	CHOB 318		
Frank Pallone, NJ-06	RHOB 2107		

HEALTH
Room: RHOB 2125
Phone: 202.225.2927

Majority:		Minority:	
C: Anna Eshoo, CA-18	CHOB 272	**RM: Brett Guthrie, KY-02**	RHOB 2434
John Sarbanes, MD-03	RHOB 2370	Fred Upton, MI-06	RHOB 2183
G.K. Butterfield, NC-01	RHOB 2080	Michael Burgess, TX-26	RHOB 2161
Doris Matsui, CA-06	RHOB 2311	Morgan Griffith, VA-09	RHOB 2202
Kathy Castor, FL-14	RHOB 2052	Gus Bilirakis, FL-12	RHOB 2354
Peter Welch, VT-01	RHOB 2187	Billy Long, MO-07	RHOB 2454
Kurt Schrader, OR-05	RHOB 2431	Larry Bucshon, IN-08	RHOB 2313
Tony Cardenas, CA-29	RHOB 2438	Markwayne Mullin, OK-02	RHOB 2421
Raul Ruiz, CA-36	RHOB 2342	Richard Hudson, NC-08	RHOB 2112
Debbie Dingell, MI-12	CHOB 116	Buddy Carter, GA-01	RHOB 2432
Ann Kuster, NH-02	CHOB 320	Neal Dunn, FL-02	CHOB 316
Robin Kelly, IL-02	RHOB 2416	John Curtis, UT-03	RHOB 2400
Nanette Barragan, CA-44	RHOB 2246	Daniel Crenshaw, TX-02	CHOB 413
Lisa Blunt Rochester, DE-01	LHOB 1724	John Joyce, PA-13	LHOB 1221
Angie Craig, MN-02	RHOB 2442	Cathy McMorris Rodgers,	LHOB 1035
Kim Schrier, WA-08	LHOB 1123	WA-05	
Lori Trahan, MA-03	RHOB 2439		
Lizzie Fletcher, TX-07	CHOB 119		
Frank Pallone, NJ-06	RHOB 2107		

OVERSIGHT & INVESTIGATIONS
Room: RHOB 2125
Phone: 202.225.2927

Majority:		Minority:	
C: Diana DeGette, CO-01	RHOB 2111	**RM: Morgan Griffith,**	RHOB 2202
Ann Kuster, NH-02	CHOB 320	**VA-09**	
Kathleen Rice, NY-04	RHOB 2435	Michael Burgess, TX-26	RHOB 2161
Jan Schakowsky, IL-09	RHOB 2367	David McKinley, WV-01	RHOB 2239
Paul Tonko, NY-20	RHOB 2369	Billy Long, MO-07	RHOB 2454
Raul Ruiz, CA-36	RHOB 2342	Gary Palmer, AL-06	CHOB 170
Scott Peters, CA-52	LHOB 1201	Neal Dunn, FL-02	CHOB 316
Kim Schrier, WA-08	LHOB 1123	John Joyce, PA-13	LHOB 1221
Lori Trahan, MA-03	RHOB 2439	Cathy McMorris Rodgers,	LHOB 1035
Tom O'Halleran, AZ-01	CHOB 318	WA-05	
Frank Pallone, NJ-06	RHOB 2107		

ETHICS

Room: LHOB 1015
Website: www.ethics.house.gov
Phone: 202.225.7103
Ratio: 5 Democrats/5 Republicans
Subcommittees: 0

Majority:		Minority:	
C: Ted Deutch, FL-22	RHOB 2323	**RM: Jackie Walorski,**	CHOB 466
Susan Wild, PA-07	LHOB 1027	**IN-02**	
Dean Phillips, MN-03	RHOB 2452	Michael Guest, MS-03	CHOB 418
Veronica Escobar, TX-16	LHOB 1505	Dave Joyce, OH-14	RHOB 2065
Mondaire Jones, NY-17	LHOB 1017	John Rutherford, FL-04	LHOB 1711
		Kelly Armstrong, ND-01	LHOB 1740

FINANCIAL SERVICES

Room: RHOB 2129
Website: www.financialservices.house.gov
Phone: 202.225.4247
Ratio: 30 Democrats/24 Republicans
Subcommittees: 8

Majority:		Minority:	
C: Maxine Waters, CA-43	RHOB 2221	**RM: Patrick McHenry,**	RHOB 2004
Jake Auchincloss, MA-04	LHOB 1524	**NC-10**	
Carolyn Maloney, NY-12	RHOB 2308	Ann Wagner, MO-02	RHOB 2350
Nydia Velazquez, NY-07	RHOB 2302	Frank Lucas, OK-03	RHOB 2405
Brad Sherman, CA-30	RHOB 2181	Pete Sessions, TX-17	RHOB 2204
Gregory Meeks, NY-05	RHOB 2310	Bill Posey, FL-08	RHOB 2150
David Scott, GA-13	CHOB 468	Blaine Luetkemeyer,	RHOB 2230
Al Green, TX-09	RHOB 2347	MO-03	
Emanuel Cleaver, MO-05	RHOB 2335	Bill Huizenga, MI-02	RHOB 2232
Ed Perlmutter, CO-07	LHOB 1226	Andy Barr, KY-06	RHOB 2430
Jim Himes, CT-04	RHOB 2137	Roger Williams, TX-25	LHOB 1708
Bill Foster, IL-11	RHOB 2366	French Hill, AR-02	LHOB 1533
Joyce Beatty, OH-03	RHOB 2303	Tom Emmer, MN-06	CHOB 315
Juan Vargas, CA-51	RHOB 2244	Lee Zeldin, NY-01	RHOB 2441
Josh Gottheimer, NJ-05	CHOB 203	Barry Loudermilk, GA-11	RHOB 2133
Vicente Gonzalez, TX-15	CHOB 113	Alex Mooney, WV-02	RHOB 2228
Al Lawson, FL-05	RHOB 2437	Warren Davidson, OH-08	RHOB 2113
Michael San Nicolas, GU-01	LHOB 1632	Ted Budd, NC-13	CHOB 103
Cindy Axne, IA-03	LHOB 1034	David Kustoff, TN-08	CHOB 560
Sean Casten, IL-06	RHOB 2440	Trey Hollingsworth, IN-09	LHOB 1641
Ayanna Pressley, MA-07	LHOB 1108	Anthony Gonzalez, OH-16	RHOB 2458
Ritchie Torres, NY-15	CHOB 317	John Rose, TN-06	LHOB 1124
Stephen Lynch, MA-08	RHOB 2109	Bryan Steil, WI-01	LHOB 1526
Alma Adams, NC-12	RHOB 2436	Lance Gooden, TX-05	LHOB 1722
Rashida Tlaib, MI-13	LHOB 1628	William Timmons, SC-04	CHOB 267
Madeleine Dean, PA-04	CHOB 120	Van Taylor, TX-03	LHOB 1404
Alexandria Ocasio-Cortez, NY-14	CHOB 229		
Jesús Garcia, IL-04	LHOB 1519		
Sylvia Garcia, TX-29	LHOB 1620		
Nikema Williams, GA-05	LHOB 1406		

Majority CoS: Charla G. Ouertatani   **Minority CoS:** Matthew P. Hoffmann

———————————— Subcommittees ————————————

CONSUMER PROTECTION & FINANCIAL INSTITUTIONS
Room: RHOB 2129
Phone: 202.225.4247

Majority:		Minority:	
C: Ed Perlmutter, CO-07	LHOB 1226	**RM: Blaine Luetkemeyer,**	RHOB 2230
Ayanna Pressley, MA-07	LHOB 1108	**MO-03**	
Gregory Meeks, NY-05	RHOB 2310	David Kustoff, TN-08	CHOB 560
David Scott, GA-13	CHOB 468	Frank Lucas, OK-03	RHOB 2405

Nydia Velazquez, NY-07	RHOB 2302	Bill Posey, FL-08	RHOB 2150
Brad Sherman, CA-30	RHOB 2181	Andy Barr, KY-06	RHOB 2430
Al Green, TX-09	RHOB 2347	Roger Williams, TX-25	LHOB 1708
Bill Foster, IL-11	RHOB 2366	Barry Loudermilk, GA-11	RHOB 2133
Juan Vargas, CA-51	RHOB 2244	Ted Budd, NC-13	CHOB 103
Al Lawson, FL-05	RHOB 2437	John Rose, TN-06	LHOB 1124
Michael San Nicolas, GU-01	LHOB 1632	William Timmons, SC-04	CHOB 267
Sean Casten, IL-06	RHOB 2440		
Ritchie Torres, NY-15	CHOB 317		

DIVERSITY & INCLUSION
Room: RHOB 2129
Phone: 202.225.4247

Majority:		Minority:	
C: Joyce Beatty, OH-03	RHOB 2303	**RM: Ann Wagner, MO-02**	RHOB 2350
Sylvia Garcia, TX-29	LHOB 1620	Anthony Gonzalez, OH-16	RHOB 2458
Ayanna Pressley, MA-07	LHOB 1108	Frank Lucas, OK-03	RHOB 2405
Stephen Lynch, MA-08	RHOB 2109	Ted Budd, NC-13	CHOB 103
Rashida Tlaib, MI-13	LHOB 1628	John Rose, TN-06	LHOB 1124
Madeleine Dean, PA-04	CHOB 120	Lance Gooden, TX-05	LHOB 1722
Nikema Williams, GA-05	LHOB 1406	William Timmons, SC-04	CHOB 267
Jake Auchincloss, MA-04	LHOB 1524		

HOUSING, COMMUNITY DEVELOPMENT & INSURANCE
Room: RHOB 2129
Phone: 202.225.4247

Majority:		Minority:	
C: Emanuel Cleaver, MO-05	RHOB 2335	**RM: French Hill, AR-02**	LHOB 1533
		Bryan Steil, WI-01	LHOB 1526
Cindy Axne, IA-03	LHOB 1034	Bill Posey, FL-08	RHOB 2150
Nydia Velazquez, NY-07	RHOB 2302	Bill Huizenga, MI-02	RHOB 2232
Brad Sherman, CA-30	RHOB 2181	Lee Zeldin, NY-01	RHOB 2441
Joyce Beatty, OH-03	RHOB 2303	Trey Hollingsworth, IN-09	LHOB 1641
Al Green, TX-09	RHOB 2347	John Rose, TN-06	LHOB 1124
Vicente Gonzalez, TX-15	CHOB 113	Lance Gooden, TX-05	LHOB 1722
Carolyn Maloney, NY-12	RHOB 2308	Van Taylor, TX-03	LHOB 1404
Juan Vargas, CA-51	RHOB 2244		
Al Lawson, FL-05	RHOB 2437		
Ritchie Torres, NY-15	CHOB 317		

INVESTOR PROTECTION, ENTREPRENEURSHIP & CAPITAL MARKETS
Room: RHOB 2129
Phone: 202.225.4247

Majority:		Minority:	
C: Brad Sherman, CA-30	RHOB 2181	**RM: Bill Huizenga, MI-02**	RHOB 2232
Sean Casten, IL-06	RHOB 2440	Trey Hollingsworth, IN-09	LHOB 1641
Carolyn Maloney, NY-12	RHOB 2308	Ann Wagner, MO-02	RHOB 2350
David Scott, GA-13	CHOB 468	French Hill, AR-02	LHOB 1533
Jim Himes, CT-04	RHOB 2137	Tom Emmer, MN-06	CHOB 315
Bill Foster, IL-11	RHOB 2366	Alex Mooney, WV-02	RHOB 2228
Gregory Meeks, NY-05	RHOB 2310	Warren Davidson, OH-08	RHOB 2113
Juan Vargas, CA-51	RHOB 2244	Anthony Gonzalez, OH-16	RHOB 2458
Josh Gottheimer, NJ-05	CHOB 203	Bryan Steil, WI-01	LHOB 1526
Vicente Gonzalez, TX-15	CHOB 113	Van Taylor, TX-03	LHOB 1404
Michael San Nicolas, GU-01	LHOB 1632		
Cindy Axne, IA-03	LHOB 1034		
Emanuel Cleaver, MO-05	RHOB 2335		

NAT'L SECURITY, INTERNATIONAL DEVELOPMENT & MONETARY POLICY
Room: RHOB 2129
Phone: 202.225.4247

Majority:		Minority:	
C: Jim Himes, CT-04	RHOB 2137	**RM: Andy Barr, KY-06**	RHOB 2430
Josh Gottheimer, NJ-05	CHOB 203	Pete Sessions, TX-17	RHOB 2204
Michael San Nicolas, GU-01	LHOB 1632	Roger Williams, TX-25	LHOB 1708
Ritchie Torres, NY-15	CHOB 317	French Hill, AR-02	LHOB 1533
Stephen Lynch, MA-08	RHOB 2109	Lee Zeldin, NY-01	RHOB 2441
Madeleine Dean, PA-04	CHOB 120	Warren Davidson, OH-08	RHOB 2113
Alexandria Ocasio-Cortez, NY-14	CHOB 229	Anthony Gonzalez, OH-16	RHOB 2458
Jesús Garcia, IL-04	LHOB 1519		
Jake Auchincloss, MA-04	LHOB 1524		

OVERSIGHT & INVESTIGATIONS
Room: RHOB 2129
Phone: 202.225.4247

HOUSE COMMITTEES

Majority:		Minority:	
C: Al Green, TX-09	RHOB 2347	**RM: Tom Emmer, MN-06**	CHOB 315
Nikema Williams, GA-05	LHOB 1406	William Timmons, SC-04	CHOB 267
Emanuel Cleaver, MO-05	RHOB 2335	Barry Loudermilk, GA-11	RHOB 2133
Alma Adams, NC-12	RHOB 2436	Alex Mooney, WV-02	RHOB 2228
Rashida Tlaib, MI-13	LHOB 1628	David Kustoff, TN-08	CHOB 560
Jesús Garcia, IL-04	LHOB 1519		
Sylvia Garcia, TX-29	LHOB 1620		

TASK FORCE ON ARTIFICIAL INTELLIGENCE
Room: RHOB 2129
Phone: 202.225.4247

Majority:		Minority:	
C: Bill Foster, IL-11	RHOB 2366	**RM: Anthony Gonzalez,**	RHOB 2458
Brad Sherman, CA-30	RHOB 2181	**OH-16**	
Sean Casten, IL-06	RHOB 2440	Barry Loudermilk, GA-11	RHOB 2133
Ayanna Pressley, MA-07	LHOB 1108	Ted Budd, NC-13	CHOB 103
Alma Adams, NC-12	RHOB 2436	Trey Hollingsworth, IN-09	LHOB 1641
Sylvia Garcia, TX-29	LHOB 1620	Van Taylor, TX-03	LHOB 1404
Jake Auchincloss, MA-04	LHOB 1524		

TASK FORCE ON FINANCIAL TECHNOLOGY
Room: RHOB 2129
Phone: 202.225.4247

Majority:		Minority:	
C: Stephen Lynch, MA-08	RHOB 2109	**RM: Warren Davidson,**	RHOB 2113
Jim Himes, CT-04	RHOB 2137	**OH-08**	
Josh Gottheimer, NJ-05	CHOB 203	Pete Sessions, TX-17	RHOB 2204
Al Lawson, FL-05	RHOB 2437	Blaine Luetkemeyer,	RHOB 2230
Michael San Nicolas, GU-01	LHOB 1632	MO-03	
Ritchie Torres, NY-15	CHOB 317	Tom Emmer, MN-06	CHOB 315
Nikema Williams, GA-05	LHOB 1406	Bryan Steil, WI-01	LHOB 1526

FOREIGN AFFAIRS

Room: RHOB 2170
Website: www.foreignaffairs.house.gov
Phone: 202.225.5021
Ratio: 27 Democrats/24 Republicans
Subcommittees: 6

Majority:		Minority:	
C: Gregory Meeks, NY-05	RHOB 2310	**RM: Michael McCaul,**	RHOB 2001
Tom Malinowski, NJ-07	LHOB 1318	**TX-10**	
Brad Sherman, CA-30	RHOB 2181	Ann Wagner, MO-02	RHOB 2350
Albio Sires, NJ-08	RHOB 2268	Chris Smith, NJ-04	RHOB 2373
Gerry Connolly, VA-11	RHOB 2238	Steve Chabot, OH-01	RHOB 2408
Ted Deutch, FL-22	RHOB 2323	Joe Wilson, SC-02	LHOB 1436
Karen Bass, CA-37	RHOB 2021	Scott Perry, PA-10	RHOB 2160
Bill Keating, MA-09	RHOB 2351	Darrell Issa, CA-50	LHOB 2300
David Cicilline, RI-01	RHOB 2233	Adam Kinzinger, IL-16	RHOB 2245
Ami Bera, CA-07	CHOB 172	Lee Zeldin, NY-01	RHOB 2441
Joaquin Castro, TX-20	RHOB 2241	Brian Mast, FL-18	RHOB 2182
Dina Titus, NV-01	RHOB 2464	Brian Fitzpatrick, PA-01	CHOB 271
Ted Lieu, CA-33	CHOB 403	Ken Buck, CO-04	RHOB 2455
Susan Wild, PA-07	LHOB 1027	Tim Burchett, TN-02	LHOB 1122
Dean Phillips, MN-03	RHOB 2452	Mark Green, TN-07	RHOB 2446
Ilhan Omar, MN-05	LHOB 1730	Andy Barr, KY-06	RHOB 2430
Colin Allred, TX-32	CHOB 114	Greg Steube, FL-17	RHOB 2457
Andy Levin, MI-09	CHOB 312	Dan Meuser, PA-09	CHOB 414
Abigail Spanberger, VA-07	LHOB 1431	Claudia Tenney, NY-22	LHOB 1410
Chrissy Houlahan, PA-06	LHOB 1218	August Pfluger, TX-11	LHOB 1531
Andy Kim, NJ-03	RHOB 2444	Peter Meijer, MI-03	LHOB 1508
Sara Jacobs, CA-53	LHOB 1232	Nicole Malliotakis, NY-11	CHOB 417
Kathy Manning, NC-06	CHOB 415	Ronny Jackson, TX-13	CHOB 118
Jim Costa, CA-16	RHOB 2081	Young Kim, CA-39	LHOB 1306
Juan Vargas, CA-51	RHOB 2244	Maria Salazar, FL-27	LHOB 1616
Vicente Gonzalez, TX-15	CHOB 113		
Brad Schneider, IL-10	CHOB 300		

Majority CoS: Sophia Lafargue   **Minority CoS:** Brendan P. Shields
———————————— Subcommittees ————————————

AFRICA, GLOBAL HEALTH & GLOBAL HUMAN RIGHTS
Room: RHOB 2170
Phone: 202.225.5021

Majority:		Minority:	
C: Karen Bass, CA-37	RHOB 2021	**RM: Chris Smith, NJ-04**	RHOB 2373
Ilhan Omar, MN-05	LHOB 1730	Darrell Issa, CA-50	LHOB 2300
Dean Phillips, MN-03	RHOB 2452	Greg Steube, FL-17	RHOB 2457

Ami Bera, CA-07	CHOB 172	Dan Meuser, PA-09	CHOB 414
Susan Wild, PA-07	LHOB 1027	Young Kim, CA-39	LHOB 1306
Tom Malinowski, NJ-07	LHOB 1318	Ronny Jackson, TX-13	CHOB 118
Sara Jacobs, CA-53	LHOB 1232		
David Cicilline, RI-01	RHOB 2233		

ASIA, THE PACIFIC, CENTRAL ASIA, NONPROLIFERATION
Room: RHOB 2170
Phone: 202.225.5021

Majority:		**Minority:**	
C: Ami Bera, CA-07	CHOB 172	**RM: Steve Chabot, OH-01**	RHOB 2408
Brad Sherman, CA-30	RHOB 2181	Scott Perry, PA-10	RHOB 2160
Dina Titus, NV-01	RHOB 2464	Ann Wagner, MO-02	RHOB 2350
Andy Levin, MI-09	CHOB 312	Ken Buck, CO-04	RHOB 2455
Chrissy Houlahan, PA-06	LHOB 1218	Tim Burchett, TN-02	LHOB 1122
Andy Kim, NJ-03	RHOB 2444	Mark Green, TN-07	RHOB 2446
Gerry Connolly, VA-11	RHOB 2238	Andy Barr, KY-06	RHOB 2430
Ted Lieu, CA-33	CHOB 403	Young Kim, CA-39	LHOB 1306
Abigail Spanberger, VA-07	LHOB 1431		
Kathy Manning, NC-06	CHOB 415		

EUROPE, ENERGY, THE ENVIRONMENT & CYBER
Room: RHOB 2170
Phone: 202.225.5021

Majority:		**Minority:**	
C: Bill Keating, MA-09	RHOB 2351	**RM: Brian Fitzpatrick,**	CHOB 271
Susan Wild, PA-07	LHOB 1027	**PA-01**	
Abigail Spanberger, VA-07	LHOB 1431	Ann Wagner, MO-02	RHOB 2350
Albio Sires, NJ-08	RHOB 2268	Adam Kinzinger, IL-16	RHOB 2245
Ted Deutch, FL-22	RHOB 2323	Brian Mast, FL-18	RHOB 2182
David Cicilline, RI-01	RHOB 2233	Dan Meuser, PA-09	CHOB 414
Dina Titus, NV-01	RHOB 2464	Claudia Tenney, NY-22	LHOB 1410
Dean Phillips, MN-03	RHOB 2452	August Pfluger, TX-11	LHOB 1531
Jim Costa, CA-16	RHOB 2081	Nicole Malliotakis, NY 11	CHOB 417
Vicente Gonzalez, TX-15	CHOB 113	Peter Meijer, MI-03	LHOB 1508
Brad Schneider, IL-10	CHOB 300		

INTERN'L DEV'T, INTERN'L ORGS & GLOBAL CORPORATE SOCIAL IMPACT
Room: RHOB 2170
Phone: 202.225.5021

Majority:		**Minority:**	
C: Joaquin Castro, TX-20	RHOB 2241	**RM: Nicole Malliotakis,**	CHOB 417
Chrissy Houlahan, PA-06	LHOB 1218	**NY-11**	
Sara Jacobs, CA-53	LHOB 1232	Darrell Issa, CA-50	LHOB 2300
Brad Sherman, CA-30	RHOB 2181	Lee Zeldin, NY-01	RHOB 2441
Ilhan Omar, MN-05	LHOB 1730	Claudia Tenney, NY-22	LHOB 1410
Andy Kim, NJ-03	RHOB 2444		

MIDDLE EAST, NORTH AFRICA & GLOBAL COUNTERTERRORISM
Room: RHOB 2170
Phone: 202.225.5021

Majority:		**Minority:**	
C: Ted Deutch, FL-22	RHOB 2323	**RM: Joe Wilson, SC-02**	LHOB 1436
Tom Malinowski, NJ-07	LHOB 1318	Scott Perry, PA-10	RHOB 2160
Gerry Connolly, VA-11	RHOB 2238	Adam Kinzinger, IL-16	RHOB 2245
David Cicilline, RI-01	RHOB 2233	Lee Zeldin, NY-01	RHOB 2441
Ted Lieu, CA-33	CHOB 403	Brian Mast, FL-18	RHOB 2182
Colin Allred, TX-32	CHOB 114	Tim Burchett, TN-02	LHOB 1122
Kathy Manning, NC-06	CHOB 415	Greg Steube, FL-17	RHOB 2457
Bill Keating, MA-09	RHOB 2351	Ronny Jackson, TX-13	CHOB 118
Brad Sherman, CA-30	RHOB 2181	Maria Salazar, FL-27	LHOB 1616
Juan Vargas, CA-51	RHOB 2244		
Brad Schneider, IL-10	CHOB 300		

WEST HEM, CIV SEC, MIGRATION, & INTERN'L ECON POLICY
Room: RHOB 2170
Phone: 202.225.5021

Majority:		**Minority:**	
Joaquin Castro, TX-20	RHOB 2241	**RM: Mark Green, TN-07**	RHOB 2446
Andy Levin, MI-09	CHOB 312	August Pfluger, TX-11	LHOB 1531
Vicente Gonzalez, TX-15	CHOB 113	Maria Salazar, FL-27	LHOB 1616
Juan Vargas, CA-51	RHOB 2244		

HOMELAND SECURITY

Room: FHOB H2-176
Website: www.homeland.house.gov
Phone: 202.226.2616
Ratio: 19 Democrats/16 Republicans
Subcommittees: 6

Majority:		Minority:	
C: Bennie Thompson, MS-02	RHOB 2466	**RM: John Katko, NY-24**	RHOB 2457
		Michael Guest, MS-03	CHOB 418
Ritchie Torres, NY-15	CHOB 317	Michael McCaul, TX-10	RHOB 2001
Sheila Jackson Lee, TX-18	RHOB 2426	Clay Higgins, LA-03	CHOB 572
Jim Langevin, RI-02	RHOB 2077	Dan Bishop, NC-09	LHOB 1207
Donald Payne, NJ-10	CHOB 106	Jefferson Van Drew, NJ-02	RHOB 2447
Elissa Slotkin, MI-08	LHOB 1210	Ralph Norman, SC-05	CHOB 569
Emanuel Cleaver, MO-05	RHOB 2335	Mariannette Miller-Meeks, IA-02	LHOB 1716
Al Green, TX-09	RHOB 2347	Diana Harshbarger, TN-01	CHOB 167
Yvette Clarke, NY-09	RHOB 2058	Andrew Clyde, GA-09	CHOB 521
Eric Swalwell, CA-15	CHOB 174	Carlos Gimenez, FL-26	CHOB 419
Dina Titus, NV-01	RHOB 2464	Jake LaTurner, KS-02	LHOB 1630
Bonnie Watson Coleman, NJ-12	CHOB 168	Peter Meijer, MI-03	LHOB 1508
		Kat Cammack, FL-03	LHOB 1626
Kathleen Rice, NY-04	RHOB 2435	August Pfluger, TX-11	LHOB 1531
Val Demings, FL-10	CHOB 217	Andrew Garbarino, NY-02	LHOB 1516
Nanette Barragan, CA-44	RHOB 2246		
Josh Gottheimer, NJ-05	CHOB 203		
Elaine Luria, VA-02	CHOB 412		
Tom Malinowski, NJ-07	LHOB 1318		

Majority CoS: Hope E. Goins   **Minority CoS:** Kyle D. Klein

——————————————— Subcommittees ———————————————

BORDER SECURITY, FACILITATION & OPERATIONS
Room: FHOB H2-176
Phone: 202.226.2616

Majority:		Minority:	
C: Nanette Barragan, CA-44	RHOB 2246	**RM: Clay Higgins, LA-03**	CHOB 572
		Michael Guest, MS-03	CHOB 418
Lou Correa, CA-46	RHOB 2301	Dan Bishop, NC-09	LHOB 1207
Emanuel Cleaver, MO-05	RHOB 2335	Andrew Clyde, GA-09	CHOB 521
Al Green, TX-09	RHOB 2347	John Katko, NY-24	RHOB 2457
Yvette Clarke, NY-09	RHOB 2058		
Bennie Thompson, MS-02	RHOB 2466		

CYBERSECURITY, INFRASTRUCTURE PROTECTION & INNOVATION
Room: FHOB H2-176
Phone: 202.226.2616

Majority:		Minority:	
C: Yvette Clarke, NY-09	RHOB 2058	**RM: Andrew Garbarino, NY-02**	LHOB 1516
Sheila Jackson Lee, TX-18	RHOB 2426		
Jim Langevin, RI-02	RHOB 2077	Ralph Norman, SC-05	CHOB 569
Elissa Slotkin, MI-08	LHOB 1210	Diana Harshbarger, TN-01	CHOB 167
Kathleen Rice, NY-04	RHOB 2435	Andrew Clyde, GA-09	CHOB 521
Ritchie Torres, NY-15	CHOB 317	Jake LaTurner, KS-02	LHOB 1630
Bennie Thompson, MS-02	RHOB 2466	John Katko, NY-24	RHOB 2457

EMERGENCY PREPAREDNESS, RESPONSE & RECOVERY
Room: FHOB H2-176
Phone: 202.226.2616

Majority:		Minority:	
C: Val Demings, FL-10	CHOB 217	**RM: Kat Cammack, FL-03**	LHOB 1626
Sheila Jackson Lee, TX-18	RHOB 2426	Clay Higgins, LA-03	CHOB 572
Donald Payne, NJ-10	CHOB 106	Mariannette Miller-Meeks, IA-02	LHOB 1716
Al Green, TX-09	RHOB 2347	Andrew Garbarino, NY-02	LHOB 1516
Bonnie Watson Coleman, NJ-12	CHOB 168	John Katko, NY-24	RHOB 2457
Bennie Thompson, MS-02	RHOB 2466		

INTELLIGENCE & COUNTERTERRORISM
Room: FHOB H2-176
Phone: 202.226.2616

Majority:		Minority:	
C: Elissa Slotkin, MI-08	LHOB 1210	**RM: August Pfluger, TX-11**	LHOB 1531
Sheila Jackson Lee, TX-18	RHOB 2426	Michael Guest, MS-03	CHOB 418
Jim Langevin, RI-02	RHOB 2077	Jefferson Van Drew, NJ-02	RHOB 2447
Eric Swalwell, CA-15	CHOB 174	Jake LaTurner, KS-02	LHOB 1630
Josh Gottheimer, NJ-05	CHOB 203	Peter Meijer, MI-03	LHOB 1508
Tom Malinowski, NJ-07	LHOB 1318	John Katko, NY-24	RHOB 2457

Bennie Thompson, MS-02   RHOB 2466

OVERSIGHT, MANAGEMENT & ACCOUNTABILITY

Room: FHOB H2-176
Phone: 202.226.2616

Majority:		Minority:	
C: Lou Correa, CA-46	RHOB 2301	**RM: Peter Meijer, MI-03**	LHOB 1508
Donald Payne, NJ-10	CHOB 106	Dan Bishop, NC-09	LHOB 1207
Dina Titus, NV-01	RHOB 2464	Diana Harshbarger, TN-01	CHOB 167
Ritchie Torres, NY-15	CHOB 317	John Katko, NY-24	RHOB 2457
Bennie Thompson, MS-02	RHOB 2466		

TRANSPORTATION & MARITIME SECURITY

Room: FHOB H2-176
Phone: 202.226.2616

Majority:		Minority:	
C: Bonnie Watson	CHOB 168	**RM: Carlos Gimenez,**	CHOB 419
Coleman, NJ-12		**FL-26**	
Donald Payne, NJ-10	CHOB 106	Jefferson Van Drew, NJ-02	RHOB 2447
Dina Titus, NV-01	RHOB 2464	Ralph Norman, SC-05	CHOB 569
Josh Gottheimer, NJ-05	CHOB 203	Mariannette Miller-Meeks,	LHOB 1716
Elaine Luria, VA-02	CHOB 412	IA-02	
Bennie Thompson, MS-02	RHOB 2466	John Katko, NY-24	RHOB 2457

JUDICIARY

Room: RHOB 2138
Website: www.judiciary.house.gov
Phone: 202.225.3951
Ratio: 25 Democrats/19 Republicans
Subcommittees: 5

Majority:		Minority:	
C: Jerry Nadler, NY-10	RHOB 2132	**RM: Jim Jordan, OH-04**	RHOB 2056
Madeleine Dean, PA-04	CHOB 120	Steve Chabot, OH-01	RHOB 2408
Zoe Lofgren, CA-19	LHOB 1401	Louie Gohmert, TX-01	RHOB 2269
Sheila Jackson Lee, TX-18	RHOB 2426	Darrell Issa, CA-50	LHOB 2300
Steve Cohen, TN-09	RHOB 2104	Ken Buck, CO-04	RHOB 2455
Hank Johnson, GA-04	RHOB 2240	Matt Gaetz, FL-01	LHOB 1721
Ted Deutch, FL-22	RHOB 2323	Mike Johnson, LA-04	CHOB 568
Karen Bass, CA-37	RHOB 2021	Andy Biggs, AZ-05	CHOB 171
Hakeem Jeffries, NY-08	RHOB 2433	Tom McClintock, CA-04	RHOB 2312
David Cicilline, RI-01	RHOB 2233	Greg Steube, FL-17	RHOB 2457
Eric Swalwell, CA-15	CHOB 174	Tom Tiffany, WI-07	LHOB 1719
Ted Lieu, CA-33	CHOB 403	Thomas Massie, KY-04	RHOB 2453
Jamie Raskin, MD-08	RHOB 2242	Chip Roy, TX-21	LHOB 1005
Pramila Jayapal, WA-07	RHOB 2346	Dan Bishop, NC-09	LHOB 1207
Val Demings, FL-10	CHOB 217	Michelle Fischbach, MN-07	LHOB 1237
Lou Correa, CA-46	RHOB 2301	Victoria Spartz, IN-05	LHOB 1523
Mary Scanlon, PA-05	LHOB 1227	Scott Fitzgerald, WI-05	LHOB 1507
Sylvia Garcia, TX-29	LHOB 1620	Cliff Bentz, OR-02	LHOB 1239
Joe Neguse, CO-02	LHOB 1419	Burgess Owens, UT-04	LHOB 1039
Lucy McBath, GA-06	LHOB 1513		
Greg Stanton, AZ-09	CHOB 207		
Veronica Escobar, TX-16	LHOB 1505		
Mondaire Jones, NY-17	LHOB 1017		
Deborah Ross, NC-02	LHOB 1208		
Cori Bush, MO-01	CHOB 563		

Majority CoS: Aaron Hiller   **Minority CoS:** Christopher Hixon

――――――――― Subcommittees ―――――――――

ANTITRUST, COMMERCIAL & ADMINISTRATIVE LAW

Room: Thomas P. O'Neill Federal Bldg. 6240
Phone: 202.226.7680

Majority:		Minority:	
C: David Cicilline, RI-01	RHOB 2233	**RM: Ken Buck, CO-04**	RHOB 2455
Pramila Jayapal, WA-07	RHOB 2346	Darrell Issa, CA-50	LHOB 2300
Joe Neguse, CO-02	LHOB 1419	Matt Gaetz, FL-01	LHOB 1721
Eric Swalwell, CA-15	CHOB 174	Mike Johnson, LA-04	CHOB 568
Mondaire Jones, NY-17	LHOB 1017	Greg Steube, FL-17	RHOB 2457
Ted Deutch, FL-22	RHOB 2323	Dan Bishop, NC-09	LHOB 1207
Hakeem Jeffries, NY-08	RHOB 2433	Michelle Fischbach, MN-07	LHOB 1237
Jamie Raskin, MD-08	RHOB 2242	Victoria Spartz, IN-05	LHOB 1523
Val Demings, FL-10	CHOB 217	Scott Fitzgerald, WI-05	LHOB 1507
Mary Scanlon, PA-05	LHOB 1227	Cliff Bentz, OR-02	LHOB 1239
Lucy McBath, GA-06	LHOB 1513	Burgess Owens, UT-04	LHOB 1039
Madeleine Dean, PA-04	CHOB 120		
Hank Johnson, GA-04	RHOB 2240		

HOUSE COMMITTEES

CONSTITUTION, CIVIL RIGHTS & CIVIL LIBERTIES
Room:

Majority:		Minority:	
C: Steve Cohen, TN-09	RHOB 2104	**RM: Mike Johnson, LA-04**	CHOB 568
Deborah Ross, NC-02	LHOB 1208	Tom McClintock, CA-04	RHOB 2312
Jamie Raskin, MD-08	RHOB 2242	Chip Roy, TX-21	LHOB 1005
Hank Johnson, GA-04	RHOB 2240	Michelle Fischbach, MN-07	LHOB 1237
Sylvia Garcia, TX-29	LHOB 1620	Burgess Owens, UT-04	LHOB 1039
Cori Bush, MO-01	CHOB 563		
Sheila Jackson Lee, TX-18	RHOB 2426		

COURTS, INTELLECTUAL PROPERTY & INTERNET
Room: Thomas P. O'Neill Federal Bldg. 6310
Phone: 202.225.5741

Majority:		Minority:	
C: Hank Johnson, GA-04	RHOB 2240	**RM: Darrell Issa, CA-50**	LHOB 2300
Mondaire Jones, NY-17	LHOB 1017	Steve Chabot, OH-01	RHOB 2408
Ted Deutch, FL-22	RHOB 2323	Louie Gohmert, TX-01	RHOB 2269
Hakeem Jeffries, NY-08	RHOB 2433	Matt Gaetz, FL-01	LHOB 1721
Ted Lieu, CA-33	CHOB 403	Mike Johnson, LA-04	CHOB 568
Greg Stanton, AZ-09	CHOB 207	Tom Tiffany, WI-07	LHOB 1719
Zoe Lofgren, CA-19	LHOB 1401	Thomas Massie, KY-04	RHOB 2453
Steve Cohen, TN-09	RHOB 2104	Dan Bishop, NC-09	LHOB 1207
Karen Bass, CA-37	RHOB 2021	Michelle Fischbach, MN-07	LHOB 1237
Eric Swalwell, CA-15	CHOB 174	Scott Fitzgerald, WI-05	LHOB 1507
Deborah Ross, NC-02	LHOB 1208	Cliff Bentz, OR-02	LHOB 1239
Joe Neguse, CO-02	LHOB 1419		

CRIME, TERRORISM & HOMELAND SECURITY
Room:

Majority:		Minority:	
C: Sheila Jackson Lee, TX-18	RHOB 2426	**RM: Andy Biggs, AZ-05**	CHOB 171
		Steve Chabot, OH-01	RHOB 2408
Cori Bush, MO-01	CHOB 563	Louie Gohmert, TX-01	RHOB 2269
Karen Bass, CA-37	RHOB 2021	Greg Steube, FL-17	RHOB 2457
Val Demings, FL-10	CHOB 217	Tom Tiffany, WI-07	LHOB 1719
Lucy McBath, GA-06	LHOB 1513	Thomas Massie, KY-04	RHOB 2453
Madeleine Dean, PA-04	CHOB 120	Victoria Spartz, IN-05	LHOB 1523
Mary Scanlon, PA-05	LHOB 1227	Scott Fitzgerald, WI-05	LHOB 1507
David Cicilline, RI-01	RHOB 2233	Burgess Owens, UT-04	LHOB 1039
Ted Lieu, CA-33	CHOB 403		
Lou Correa, CA-46	RHOB 2301		
Veronica Escobar, TX-16	LHOB 1505		
Steve Cohen, TN-09	RHOB 2104		

IMMIGRATION & CITIZENSHIP
Room:

Majority:		Minority:	
C: Zoe Lofgren, CA-19	LHOB 1401	**RM: Tom McClintock, CA-04**	RHOB 2312
Joe Neguse, CO-02	LHOB 1419		
Pramila Jayapal, WA-07	RHOB 2346	Ken Buck, CO-04	RHOB 2455
Lou Correa, CA-46	RHOB 2301	Andy Biggs, AZ-05	CHOB 171
Sylvia Garcia, TX-29	LHOB 1620	Tom Tiffany, WI-07	LHOB 1719
Veronica Escobar, TX-16	LHOB 1505	Chip Roy, TX-21	LHOB 1005
Sheila Jackson Lee, TX-18	RHOB 2426	Victoria Spartz, IN-05	LHOB 1523
Mary Scanlon, PA-05	LHOB 1227		

NATURAL RESOURCES

Room: LHOB 1324
Website: www.naturalresources.house.gov
Phone: 202.225.6065
Ratio: 26 Democrats/21 Republicans
Subcommittees: 5

Majority:		Minority:	
C: Raul Grijalva, AZ-03	LHOB 1511	**RM: Bruce Westerman, AR-04**	CHOB 202
Jesús Garcia, IL-04	LHOB 1519		
Grace Napolitano, CA-32	LHOB 1610	Louie Gohmert, TX-01	RHOB 2269
Jim Costa, CA-16	RHOB 2081	Don Young, AK-01	RHOB 2314
Gregorio Sablan, MP-01	RHOB 2267	Doug Lamborn, CO-05	RHOB 2371
Jared Huffman, CA-02	LHOB 1527	Rob Wittman, VA-01	RHOB 2055
Alan Lowenthal, CA-47	CHOB 108	Tom McClintock, CA-04	RHOB 2312
Ruben Gallego, AZ-07	LHOB 1131	Garret Graves, LA-06	RHOB 2402
Joe Neguse, CO-02	LHOB 1419	Jody Hice, GA-10	CHOB 404
Mike Levin, CA-49	LHOB 1030	Amata Radewagen, AS-01	LHOB 1339
Katie Porter, CA-45	LHOB 1117	Daniel Webster, FL-11	RHOB 2184
Teresa Leger Fernandez, NM-03	LHOB 1432	Jenniffer Gonzalez-Colon, PR-01	RHOB 2338

Melanie Stansbury, NM-01	LHOB 1421	Russ Fulcher, ID-01	LHOB 1520
Nydia Velazquez, NY-07	RHOB 2302	Pete Stauber, MN-08	CHOB 461
Diana DeGette, CO-01	RHOB 2111	Tom Tiffany, WI-07	LHOB 1719
Julia Brownley, CA-26	RHOB 2262	Jerry Carl, AL-01	LHOB 1330
Debbie Dingell, MI-12	CHOB 116	Matt Rosendale, MT-01	LHOB 1037
A. Donald McEachin, VA-04	CHOB 314	Blake Moore, UT-01	LHOB 1320
Darren Soto, FL-09	RHOB 2353	Yvette Herrell, NM-02	LHOB 1305
Michael San Nicolas, GU-01	LHOB 1632	Lauren Boebert, CO-03	LHOB 1609
Ed Case, HI-01	RHOB 2210	Jay Obernolte, CA-08	LHOB 1029
Betty McCollum, MN-04	RHOB 2256	Cliff Bentz, OR-02	LHOB 1239
Steve Cohen, TN-09	RHOB 2104		
Paul Tonko, NY-20	RHOB 2369		
Rashida Tlaib, MI-13	LHOB 1628		
Lori Trahan, MA-03	RHOB 2439		

Majority CoS: David Watkins **Minority CoS:** Vivian Moeglein
———————————— Subcommittees ————————————

ENERGY & MINERAL RESOURCES
Room:

Majority:		Minority:	
C: Alan Lowenthal, CA-47	CHOB 108	**RM: Pete Stauber, MN-08**	CHOB 461
A. Donald McEachin, VA-04	CHOB 314	Yvette Herrell, NM-02	LHOB 1305
Mike Levin, CA-49	LHOB 1030	Garret Graves, LA-06	RHOB 2402
Katie Porter, CA-45	LHOB 1117	Doug Lamborn, CO-05	RHOB 2371
Diana DeGette, CO-01	RHOB 2111	Tom Tiffany, WI-07	LHOB 1719
Betty McCollum, MN-04	RHOB 2256	Bruce Westerman, AR-04	CHOB 202
Jared Huffman, CA-02	LHOB 1527		
Debbie Dingell, MI-12	CHOB 116		
Raul Grijalva, AZ-03	LHOB 1511		

INDIGENOUS PEOPLES OF THE UNITED STATES
Room: LHOB 1324
Phone: 202.225.6065

Majority:		Minority:	
C: Teresa Leger Fernandez, NM-03	LHOB 1432	**RM: Don Young, AK-01**	RHOB 2314
		Jay Obernolte, CA-08	LHOB 1029
Ruben Gallego, AZ-07	LHOB 1131	Amata Radewagen, AS-01	LHOB 1339
Darren Soto, FL-09	RHOB 2353	Jerry Carl, AL-01	LHOB 1330
Betty McCollum, MN-04	RHOB 2256	Matt Rosendale, MT-01	LHOB 1037
Michael San Nicolas, GU-01	LHOB 1632	Lauren Boebert, CO-03	LHOB 1609
Ed Case, HI-01	RHOB 2210	Cliff Bentz, OR-02	LHOB 1239
Alan Lowenthal, CA-47	CHOB 108	Bruce Westerman, AR-04	CHOB 202
Jesús Garcia, IL-04	LHOB 1519		
Melanie Stansbury, NM-01	LHOB 1421		
Raul Grijalva, AZ-03	LHOB 1511		

NATIONAL PARKS, FORESTS & PUBLIC LANDS
Room: LHOB 1324
Phone: 202.225.6065

Majority:		Minority:	
C: Joe Neguse, CO-02	LHOB 1419	**RM: Russ Fulcher, ID-01**	LHOB 1520
Gregorio Sablan, MP-01	RHOB 2267	Tom Tiffany, WI-07	LHOB 1719
Diana DeGette, CO-01	RHOB 2111	Louie Gohmert, TX-01	RHOB 2269
Paul Tonko, NY-20	RHOB 2369	Doug Lamborn, CO-05	RHOB 2371
Rashida Tlaib, MI-13	LHOB 1628	Tom McClintock, CA-04	RHOB 2312
Lori Trahan, MA-03	RHOB 2439	Jody Hice, GA-10	CHOB 404
Ruben Gallego, AZ-07	LHOB 1131	Matt Rosendale, MT-01	LHOB 1037
Teresa Leger Fernandez, NM-03	LHOB 1432	Blake Moore, UT-01	LHOB 1320
		Yvette Herrell, NM-02	LHOB 1305
Debbie Dingell, MI-12	CHOB 116	Jay Obernolte, CA-08	LHOB 1029
Ed Case, HI-01	RHOB 2210	Bruce Westerman, AR-04	CHOB 202
Michael San Nicolas, GU-01	LHOB 1632		
Katie Porter, CA-45	LHOB 1117		
Raul Grijalva, AZ-03	LHOB 1511		

OVERSIGHT & INVESTIGATIONS
Room:

Majority:		Minority:	
C: Katie Porter, CA-45	LHOB 1117	Blake Moore, UT-01	LHOB 1320
Nydia Velazquez, NY-07	RHOB 2302	Louie Gohmert, TX-01	RHOB 2269
Jesús Garcia, IL-04	LHOB 1519	Jody Hice, GA-10	CHOB 404
Steve Cohen, TN-09	RHOB 2104	Bruce Westerman, AR-04	CHOB 202
Jared Huffman, CA-02	LHOB 1527		
Raul Grijalva, AZ-03	LHOB 1511		

WATER, OCEANS & WILDLIFE
Room: LHOB 1324
Phone: 202.225.6065

Majority:		Minority:	
C: Jared Huffman, CA-02	LHOB 1527	RM: Cliff Bentz, OR-02	LHOB 1239
Grace Napolitano, CA-32	LHOB 1610	Jerry Carl, AL-01	LHOB 1330
Jim Costa, CA-16	RHOB 2081	Don Young, AK-01	RHOB 2314
Mike Levin, CA-49	LHOB 1030	Rob Wittman, VA-01	RHOB 2055
Julia Brownley, CA-26	RHOB 2262	Tom McClintock, CA-04	RHOB 2312
Debbie Dingell, MI-12	CHOB 116	Garret Graves, LA-06	RHOB 2402
Ed Case, HI-01	RHOB 2210	Amata Radewagen, AS-01	LHOB 1339
Alan Lowenthal, CA-47	CHOB 108	Daniel Webster, FL-11	RHOB 2184
Steve Cohen, TN-09	RHOB 2104	Jenniffer Gonzalez-Colon, PR-01	RHOB 2338
Darren Soto, FL-09	RHOB 2353		
Raul Grijalva, AZ-03	LHOB 1511	Russ Fulcher, ID-01	LHOB 1520
Nydia Velazquez, NY-07	RHOB 2302	Lauren Boebert, CO-03	LHOB 1609
Melanie Stansbury, NM-01	LHOB 1421	Bruce Westerman, AR-04	CHOB 202

OVERSIGHT & REFORM

Room: RHOB 2157
Website: www.oversight.house.gov
Phone: 202.225.5051
Ratio: 25 Democrats/19 Republicans
Subcommittees: 6

Majority:		Minority:	
C: Carolyn Maloney, NY-12	RHOB 2308	RM: James Comer, KY-01	RHOB 2410
		Jim Jordan, OH-04	RHOB 2056
Jimmy Gomez, CA-34	LHOB 1530	Virginia Foxx, NC-05	RHOB 2462
Eleanor Norton, DC-01	RHOB 2136	Jody Hice, GA-10	CHOB 404
Stephen Lynch, MA-08	RHOB 2109	Glenn Grothman, WI-06	LHOB 1427
Jim Cooper, TN-05	LHOB 1536	Michael Cloud, TX-27	CHOB 512
Gerry Connolly, VA-11	RHOB 2238	Bob Gibbs, OH-07	RHOB 2217
Raja Krishnamoorthi, IL-08	CHOB 115	Clay Higgins, LA-03	CHOB 572
Jamie Raskin, MD-08	RHOB 2242	Ralph Norman, SC-05	CHOB 569
Ro Khanna, CA-17	CHOB 306	Pete Sessions, TX-17	RHOB 2204
Kweisi Mfume, MD-07	RHOB 2263	Fred Keller, PA-12	LHOB 1717
Alexandria Ocasio-Cortez, NY-14	CHOB 229	Andy Biggs, AZ-05	CHOB 171
		Andrew Clyde, GA-09	CHOB 521
Rashida Tlaib, MI-13	LHOB 1628	Nancy Mace, SC-01	CHOB 212
Katie Porter, CA-45	LHOB 1117	Scott Franklin, FL-15	LHOB 1517
Cori Bush, MO-01	CHOB 563	Jake LaTurner, KS-02	LHOB 1630
Shontel Brown, OH-11	RHOB 2344	Pat Fallon, TX-04	LHOB 1118
Danny Davis, IL-07	RHOB 2159	Yvette Herrell, NM-02	LHOB 1305
Debbie Wasserman Schultz, FL-23	LHOB 1114	Byron Donalds, FL-19	CHOB 523
Peter Welch, VT-01	RHOB 2187		
Hank Johnson, GA-04	RHOB 2240		
John Sarbanes, MD-03	RHOB 2370		
Jackie Speier, CA-14	RHOB 2465		
Robin Kelly, IL-02	RHOB 2416		
Brenda Lawrence, MI-14	RHOB 2463		
Mark DeSaulnier, CA-11	CHOB 503		
Ayanna Pressley, MA-07	LHOB 1108		

Majority CoS: Ben Harney   **Minority CoS:** Mark D. Marin

———————— Subcommittees ————————

GOVERNMENT OPERATIONS
Room: RHOB 2157
Phone: 202.225.5051

Majority:		Minority:	
C: Gerry Connolly, VA-11	RHOB 2238	RM: Jody Hice, GA-10	CHOB 404
Katie Porter, CA-45	LHOB 1117	Fred Keller, PA-12	LHOB 1717
Eleanor Norton, DC-01	RHOB 2136	Andrew Clyde, GA-09	CHOB 521
Danny Davis, IL-07	RHOB 2159	Andy Biggs, AZ-05	CHOB 171
John Sarbanes, MD-03	RHOB 2370	Nancy Mace, SC-01	CHOB 212
Brenda Lawrence, MI-14	RHOB 2463	Jake LaTurner, KS-02	LHOB 1630
Stephen Lynch, MA-08	RHOB 2109	Yvette Herrell, NM-02	LHOB 1305
Jamie Raskin, MD-08	RHOB 2242		
Ro Khanna, CA-17	CHOB 306		
Shontel Brown, OH-11	RHOB 2344		

NATIONAL SECURITY
Room:

Majority:		Minority:	
C: Stephen Lynch, MA-08	RHOB 2109	RM: Glenn Grothman, WI-06	LHOB 1427
Kweisi Mfume, MD-07	RHOB 2263		
Peter Welch, VT-01	RHOB 2187	Virginia Foxx, NC-05	RHOB 2462
Hank Johnson, GA-04	RHOB 2240	Bob Gibbs, OH-07	RHOB 2217
Mark DeSaulnier, CA-11	CHOB 503	Clay Higgins, LA-03	CHOB 572

| Debbie Wasserman Schultz, FL-23 | LHOB 1114 |
| Jackie Speier, CA-14 | RHOB 2465 |

SELECT INVESTIGATIVE ON THE CORONAVIRUS CRISIS
Room: RHOB 2157
Phone: 202.225.4400

Majority:		Minority:	
C: James Clyburn, SC-06	CHOB 274	RM: Steve Scalise, LA-01	RHOB 2049
Maxine Waters, CA-43	RHOB 2221	Jim Jordan, OH-04	RHOB 2056
Carolyn Maloney, NY-12	RHOB 2308	Mark Green, TN-07	RHOB 2446
Nydia Velazquez, NY-07	RHOB 2302	Nicole Malliotakis, NY-11	CHOB 417
Bill Foster, IL-11	RHOB 2366	Mariannette Miller-Meeks, IA-02	LHOB 1716
Jamie Raskin, MD-08	RHOB 2242		
Raja Krishnamoorthi, IL-08	CHOB 115		

SUBCOMMITTEE ON CIVIL RIGHTS & CIVIL LIBERTIES
Room: RHOB 2157
Phone: 202.225.5051

Majority:		Minority:	
C: Jamie Raskin, MD-08	RHOB 2242	RM: Nancy Mace, SC-01	CHOB 212
Alexandria Ocasio-Cortez, NY-14	CHOB 229	Jim Jordan, OH-04	RHOB 2056
		Clay Higgins, LA-03	CHOB 572
Kweisi Mfume, MD-07	RHOB 2263	Pete Sessions, TX-17	RHOB 2204
Debbie Wasserman Schultz, FL-23	LHOB 1114	Andy Biggs, AZ-05	CHOB 171
		Scott Franklin, FL-15	LHOB 1517
Robin Kelly, IL-02	RHOB 2416	Byron Donalds, FL-19	CHOB 523
Ayanna Pressley, MA-07	LHOB 1108		
Eleanor Norton, DC-01	RHOB 2136		
Rashida Tlaib, MI-13	LHOB 1628		
Danny Davis, IL-07	RHOB 2159		

SUBCOMMITTEE ON ECONOMIC & CONSUMER POLICY
Room: RHOB 2157
Phone: 202.225.5051

Majority:		Minority:	
C: Raja Krishnamoorthi, IL-08	CHOB 115	RM: Michael Cloud, TX-27	CHOB 512
		Fred Keller, PA-12	LHOB 1717
Ayanna Pressley, MA-07	LHOB 1108	Scott Franklin, FL-15	LHOB 1517
Katie Porter, CA-45	LHOB 1117	Andrew Clyde, GA-09	CHOB 521
Cori Bush, MO-01	CHOB 563	Byron Donalds, FL-19	CHOB 523
Jackie Speier, CA-14	RHOB 2465		
Hank Johnson, GA-04	RHOB 2240		
Mark DeSaulnier, CA-11	CHOB 503		
Shontel Brown, OH-11	RHOB 2344		

SUBCOMMITTEE ON ENVIRONMENT
Room: RHOB 2157
Phone: 202.225.5051

Majority:		Minority:	
C: Ro Khanna, CA-17	CHOB 306	RM: Ralph Norman, SC-05	CHOB 569
Rashida Tlaib, MI-13	LHOB 1628	Bob Gibbs, OH-07	RHOB 2217
Jim Cooper, TN-05	LHOB 1536	Pat Fallon, TX-04	LHOB 1118
Alexandria Ocasio-Cortez, NY-14	CHOB 229	Yvette Herrell, NM-02	LHOB 1305
Jimmy Gomez, CA-34	LHOB 1530		
Raja Krishnamoorthi, IL-08	CHOB 115		
Cori Bush, MO-01	CHOB 563		

RULES

Room: The Capitol H-312
Website: www.rules.house.gov
Phone: 202.225.9091
Ratio: 9 Democrats/4 Republicans
Subcommittees: 3

Majority:		Minority:	
C: Jim McGovern, MA-02	CHOB 370	RM: Tom Cole, OK-04	RHOB 2207
Norma Torres, CA-35	RHOB 2227	Michael Burgess, TX-26	RHOB 2161
Ed Perlmutter, CO-07	LHOB 1226	Guy Reschenthaler, PA-14	CHOB 409
Jamie Raskin, MD-08	RHOB 2242	Michelle Fischbach, MN-07	LHOB 1237
Mary Scanlon, PA-05	LHOB 1227		
Joseph Morelle, NY-25	LHOB 1317		
Mark DeSaulnier, CA-11	CHOB 503		
Deborah Ross, NC-02	LHOB 1208		
Joe Neguse, CO-02	LHOB 1419		

Majority CoS: Donald C. Sisson

Minority CoS: Kelly A. Dixon Chambers

─────────────── Subcommittees ───────────────

EXPEDITED PROCEDURES
Room: The Capitol H-312
Phone: 202.225.9091

Majority:		Minority:	
C: Jamie Raskin, MD-08	RHOB 2242	**RM: Michelle Fischbach,**	LHOB 1237
Deborah Ross, NC-02	LHOB 1208	**MN-07**	
Norma Torres, CA-35	RHOB 2227	Tom Cole, OK-04	RHOB 2207
Mark DeSaulnier, CA-11	CHOB 503		
Jim McGovern, MA-02	CHOB 370		

LEGISLATIVE & BUDGET PROCESS
Room:

Majority:		Minority:	
C: Joseph Morelle, NY-25	LHOB 1317	**RM: Michael Burgess,**	RHOB 2161
Mary Scanlon, PA-05	LHOB 1227	**TX-26**	
Deborah Ross, NC-02	LHOB 1208	Tom Cole, OK-04	RHOB 2207
Joe Neguse, CO-02	LHOB 1419		
Jim McGovern, MA-02	CHOB 370		

RULES & ORGANIZATION OF THE HOUSE
Room:

Majority:		Minority:	
C: Norma Torres, CA-35	RHOB 2227	**RM: Guy Reschenthaler,**	CHOB 409
Ed Perlmutter, CO-07	LHOB 1226	**PA-14**	
Mary Scanlon, PA-05	LHOB 1227	Tom Cole, OK-04	RHOB 2207
Joe Neguse, CO-02	LHOB 1419		
Jim McGovern, MA-02	CHOB 370		

SCIENCE, SPACE & TECHNOLOGY

Room: RHOB 2321
Website: www.science.house.gov
Phone: 202.225.6375
Ratio: 23 Democrats/18 Republicans
Subcommittees: 5

Majority:		Minority:	
C: Eddie Bernice	RHOB 2306	**RM: Frank Lucas, OK-03**	RHOB 2405
Johnson, TX-30		Mo Brooks, AL-05	RHOB 2185
Zoe Lofgren, CA-19	LHOB 1401	Bill Posey, FL-08	RHOB 2150
Suzanne Bonamici, OR-01	RHOB 2231	Randy Weber, TX-14	CHOB 107
Ami Bera, CA-07	CHOB 172	Brian Babin, TX-36	RHOB 2236
Haley Stevens, MI-11	LHOB 1510	Anthony Gonzalez, OH-16	RHOB 2458
Mikie Sherrill, NJ-11	LHOB 1414	Mike Waltz, FL-06	CHOB 213
Jamaal Bowman, NY-16	LHOB 1605	Jim Baird, IN-04	LHOB 1314
Melanie Stansbury, NM-01	LHOB 1421	Daniel Webster, FL-11	RHOB 2184
Brad Sherman, CA-30	RHOB 2181	Mike Garcia, CA-25	LHOB 1535
Ed Perlmutter, CO-07	LHOB 1226	Stephanie Bice, OK-05	LHOB 1223
Jerry McNerney, CA-09	RHOB 2265	Young Kim, CA-39	LHOB 1306
Paul Tonko, NY-20	RHOB 2369	Randy Feenstra, IA-04	LHOB 1440
Bill Foster, IL-11	RHOB 2366	Jake LaTurner, KS-02	LHOB 1630
Donald Norcross, NJ-01	RHOB 2427	Carlos Gimenez, FL-26	CHOB 419
Don Beyer, VA-08	LHOB 1119	Jay Obernolte, CA-08	LHOB 1029
Charlie Crist, FL-13	CHOB 215	Peter Meijer, MI-03	LHOB 1508
Sean Casten, IL-06	RHOB 2440	Jake Ellzey, TX-06	LHOB 1725
Conor Lamb, PA-17	LHOB 1224		
Deborah Ross, NC-02	LHOB 1208		
Gwen Moore, WI-04	RHOB 2252		
Dan Kildee, MI-05	CHOB 200		
Susan Wild, PA-07	LHOB 1027		
Lizzie Fletcher, TX-07	CHOB 119		

Majority CoS: Richard Obermann   **Minority CoS:** Josh Mathis
─────────────── Subcommittees ───────────────

ENERGY
Room:

Majority:		Minority:	
C: Jamaal Bowman, NY-16	LHOB 1605	**RM: Randy Weber, TX-14**	CHOB 107
Suzanne Bonamici, OR-01	RHOB 2231	Jim Baird, IN-04	LHOB 1314
Haley Stevens, MI-11	LHOB 1510	Mike Garcia, CA-25	LHOB 1535
Melanie Stansbury, NM-01	LHOB 1421	Randy Feenstra, IA-04	LHOB 1440
Jerry McNerney, CA-09	RHOB 2265	Carlos Gimenez, FL-26	CHOB 419
Donald Norcross, NJ-01	RHOB 2427	Peter Meijer, MI-03	LHOB 1508
Sean Casten, IL-06	RHOB 2440	Jay Obernolte, CA-08	LHOB 1029
Conor Lamb, PA-17	LHOB 1224		
Deborah Ross, NC-02	LHOB 1208		

ENVIRONMENT
Room:

Majority:		Minority:	
C: Mikie Sherrill, NJ-11	LHOB 1414	**RM: Stephanie Bice, OK-05**	LHOB 1223
Suzanne Bonamici, OR-01	RHOB 2231		
Dan Kildee, MI-05	CHOB 200	Anthony Gonzalez, OH-16	RHOB 2458
Lizzie Fletcher, TX-07	CHOB 119	Randy Feenstra, IA-04	LHOB 1440
Charlie Crist, FL-13	CHOB 215	Carlos Gimenez, FL-26	CHOB 419
Sean Casten, IL-06	RHOB 2440		

INVESTIGATIONS & OVERSIGHT
Room:

Majority:		Minority:	
C: Bill Foster, IL-11	RHOB 2366	**RM: Jay Obernolte, CA-08**	LHOB 1029
Ed Perlmutter, CO-07	LHOB 1226	Stephanie Bice, OK-05	LHOB 1223
Ami Bera, CA-07	CHOB 172		
Gwen Moore, WI-04	RHOB 2252		
Sean Casten, IL-06	RHOB 2440		

RESEARCH & TECHNOLOGY
Room:

Majority:		Minority:	
C: Haley Stevens, MI-11	LHOB 1510	**RM: Mike Waltz, FL-06**	CHOB 213
Melanie Stansbury, NM-01	LHOB 1421	Anthony Gonzalez, OH-16	RHOB 2458
Paul Tonko, NY-20	RHOB 2369	Jim Baird, IN-04	LHOB 1314
Gwen Moore, WI-04	RHOB 2252	Jake LaTurner, KS-02	LHOB 1630
Susan Wild, PA-07	LHOB 1027	Peter Meijer, MI-03	LHOB 1508
Bill Foster, IL-11	RHOB 2366	Jake Ellzey, TX-06	LHOB 1725
Conor Lamb, PA-17	LHOB 1224		
Deborah Ross, NC-02	LHOB 1208		

SPACE & AERONAUTICS
Room:

Majority:		Minority:	
C: Don Beyer, VA-08	LHOB 1119	**RM: Brian Babin, TX-36**	RHOB 2236
Zoe Lofgren, CA-19	LHOB 1401	Mo Brooks, AL-05	RHOB 2185
Ami Bera, CA-07	CHOB 172	Bill Posey, FL-08	RHOB 2150
Brad Sherman, CA-30	RHOB 2181	Daniel Webster, FL-11	RHOB 2184
Ed Perlmutter, CO-07	LHOB 1226	Young Kim, CA-39	LHOB 1306
Charlie Crist, FL-13	CHOB 215		
Donald Norcross, NJ-01	RHOB 2427		

SMALL BUSINESS

Room: RHOB 2361
Website: www.smallbusiness.house.gov
Phone: 202.225.4038
Ratio: 15 Democrats/12 Republicans
Subcommittees: 5

Majority:		Minority:	
C: Nydia Velazquez, NY-07	RHOB 2302	**RM: Blaine Luetkemeyer, MO-03**	RHOB 2230
Kweisi Mfume, MD-07	RHOB 2263		
Jared Golden, ME-02	LHOB 1222	Roger Williams, TX-25	LHOB 1708
Jason Crow, CO-06	LHOB 1229	Jim Hagedorn, MN-01	LHOB 1433
Sharice Davids, KS-03	LHOB 1541	Pete Stauber, MN-08	CHOB 461
Dean Phillips, MN-03	RHOB 2452	Dan Meuser, PA-09	CHOB 414
Marie Newman, IL-03	LHOB 1022	Claudia Tenney, NY-22	LHOB 1410
Carolyn Bourdeaux, GA-07	LHOB 1319	Andrew Garbarino, NY-02	LHOB 1516
Troy Carter, LA-02	CHOB 506	Young Kim, CA-39	LHOB 1306
Judy Chu, CA-27	RHOB 2423	Beth Van Duyne, TX-24	LHOB 1337
Dwight Evans, PA-03	LHOB 1105	Byron Donalds, FL-19	CHOB 523
Antonio Delgado, NY-19	LHOB 1007	Maria Salazar, FL-27	LHOB 1616
Chrissy Houlahan, PA-06	LHOB 1218	Scott Fitzgerald, WI-05	LHOB 1507
Andy Kim, NJ-03	RHOB 2444		
Angie Craig, MN-02	RHOB 2442		

Majority CoS: Melissa Jung **Minority CoS:** David M. Planning
Majority Sched: Mory Garcia

——————— Subcommittees ———————

CONTRACTING & INFRASTRUCTURE
Room: RHOB 2361
Phone: 202.225.4038

Majority:		Minority:	
C: Kweisi Mfume, MD-07	RHOB 2263	**RM: Maria Salazar, FL-27**	LHOB 1616
Jared Golden, ME-02	LHOB 1222	Jim Hagedorn, MN-01	LHOB 1433
Andy Kim, NJ-03	RHOB 2444	Pete Stauber, MN-08	CHOB 461
Marie Newman, IL-03	LHOB 1022	Dan Meuser, PA-09	CHOB 414
		Scott Fitzgerald, WI-05	LHOB 1507

ECONOMIC GROWTH, TAX & CAPITAL ACCESS
Room: RHOB 2361
Phone: 202.225.4038

Majority:		Minority:	
C: Sharice Davids, KS-03	LHOB 1541	**RM: Dan Meuser, PA-09**	CHOB 414
Marie Newman, IL-03	LHOB 1022	Andrew Garbarino, NY-02	LHOB 1516
Judy Chu, CA-27	RHOB 2423	Young Kim, CA-39	LHOB 1306
Dwight Evans, PA-03	LHOB 1105	Beth Van Duyne, TX-24	LHOB 1337
Andy Kim, NJ-03	RHOB 2444	Byron Donalds, FL-19	CHOB 523
Carolyn Bourdeaux, GA-07	LHOB 1319		

INNOVATION, ENTREPRENEURSHIP & WORKFORCE DEVELOPMENT
Room: RHOB 2361
Phone: 202.225.4038

Majority:		Minority:	
C: Jason Crow, CO-06	LHOB 1229	**RM: Young Kim, CA-39**	LHOB 1306
Carolyn Bourdeaux, GA-07	LHOB 1319	Roger Williams, TX-25	LHOB 1708
Chrissy Houlahan, PA-06	LHOB 1218	Claudia Tenney, NY-22	LHOB 1410
Sharice Davids, KS-03	LHOB 1541	Andrew Garbarino, NY-02	LHOB 1516
Dean Phillips, MN-03	RHOB 2452	Maria Salazar, FL-27	LHOB 1616
Marie Newman, IL-03	LHOB 1022		

OVERSIGHT, INVESTIGATIONS & REGULATIONS
Room: RHOB 2361
Phone: 202.225.4038

Majority:		Minority:	
C: Dean Phillips, MN-03	RHOB 2452	**RM: Beth Van Duyne, TX-24**	LHOB 1337
Angie Craig, MN-02	RHOB 2442		
Kweisi Mfume, MD-07	RHOB 2263	Jim Hagedorn, MN-01	LHOB 1433
Judy Chu, CA-27	RHOB 2423	Dan Meuser, PA-09	CHOB 414
Dwight Evans, PA-03	LHOB 1105	Byron Donalds, FL-19	CHOB 523
Sharice Davids, KS-03	LHOB 1541	Scott Fitzgerald, WI-05	LHOB 1507

UNDERSERVED, AGRICULTURAL & RURAL BUSINESS DEVELOPMENT
Room: RHOB 2361
Phone: 202.225.4038

Majority:		Minority:	
C: Jared Golden, ME-02	LHOB 1222	**RM: Jim Hagedorn, MN-01**	LHOB 1433
Antonio Delgado, NY-19	LHOB 1007		
Troy Carter, LA-02	CHOB 506	Roger Williams, TX-25	LHOB 1708
		Pete Stauber, MN-08	CHOB 461
		Claudia Tenney, NY-22	LHOB 1410
		Maria Salazar, FL-27	LHOB 1616

TRANSPORTATION & INFRASTRUCTURE
Room: RHOB 2165
Website: www.transportation.house.gov
Phone: 202.225.4472
Ratio: 37 Democrats/32 Republicans
Subcommittees: 6

Majority:		Minority:	
C: Peter DeFazio, OR-04	RHOB 2134	**RM: Sam Graves, MO-06**	LHOB 1135
Sharice Davids, KS-03	LHOB 1541	Don Young, AK-01	RHOB 2314
Eleanor Norton, DC-01	RHOB 2136	Rick Crawford, AR-01	RHOB 2422
Eddie Bernice Johnson, TX-30	RHOB 2306	Bob Gibbs, OH-07	RHOB 2217
		Daniel Webster, FL-11	RHOB 2184
Rick Larsen, WA-02	RHOB 2163	Thomas Massie, KY-04	RHOB 2453
Grace Napolitano, CA-32	LHOB 1610	Scott Perry, PA-10	RHOB 2160
Steve Cohen, TN-09	RHOB 2104	Rodney Davis, IL-13	RHOB 2079
Albio Sires, NJ-08	RHOB 2268	John Katko, NY-24	RHOB 2457
John Garamendi, CA-03	RHOB 2368	Brian Babin, TX-36	RHOB 2236
Hank Johnson, GA-04	RHOB 2240	Garret Graves, LA-06	RHOB 2402
Andre Carson, IN-07	RHOB 2135	David Rouzer, NC-07	RHOB 2333
Dina Titus, NV-01	RHOB 2464	Mike Bost, IL-12	LHOB 1211
Sean Maloney, NY-18	CHOB 464	Randy Weber, TX-14	CHOB 107
Jared Huffman, CA-02	LHOB 1527	Doug LaMalfa, CA-01	CHOB 408
Julia Brownley, CA-26	RHOB 2262	Bruce Westerman, AR-04	CHOB 202
Frederica Wilson, FL-24	RHOB 2445	Brian Mast, FL-18	RHOB 2182
Donald Payne, NJ-10	CHOB 106	Mike Gallagher, WI-08	LHOB 1230
Alan Lowenthal, CA-47	CHOB 108	Brian Fitzpatrick, PA-01	CHOB 271
Mark DeSaulnier, CA-11	CHOB 503	Jenniffer Gonzalez-Colon, PR-01	RHOB 2338
Stephen Lynch, MA-08	RHOB 2109		
Salud Carbajal, CA-24	RHOB 2331	Troy Balderson, OH-12	RHOB 2429
Anthony Brown, MD-04	LHOB 1323	Pete Stauber, MN-08	CHOB 461
Tom Malinowski, NJ-07	LHOB 1318	Tim Burchett, TN-02	LHOB 1122

Greg Stanton, AZ-09	CHOB 207	Dusty Johnson, SD-01	LHOB 1714
Colin Allred, TX-32	CHOB 114	Jefferson Van Drew, NJ-02	RHOB 2447
Jesús Garcia, IL-04	LHOB 1519	Michael Guest, MS-03	CHOB 418
Antonio Delgado, NY-19	LHOB 1007	Troy Nehls, TX-22	LHOB 1104
Chris Pappas, NH-01	CHOB 319	Nancy Mace, SC-01	CHOB 212
Conor Lamb, PA-17	LHOB 1224	Nicole Malliotakis, NY-11	CHOB 417
Seth Moulton, MA-06	LHOB 1127	Beth Van Duyne, TX-24	LHOB 1337
Jake Auchincloss, MA-04	LHOB 1524	Carlos Gimenez, FL-26	CHOB 419
Carolyn Bourdeaux, GA-07	LHOB 1319	Michelle Steel, CA-48	LHOB 1113
Kaiali'i Kahele, HI-02	LHOB 1205		
Marilyn Strickland, WA-10	LHOB 1004		
Nikema Williams, GA-05	LHOB 1406		
Marie Newman, IL-03	LHOB 1022		
Troy Carter, LA-02	CHOB 506		

Majority CoS: Kathy Dedrick **Minority CoS:** Paul J. Sass
———————— Subcommittees ————————

AVIATION
Room: RHOB 2165
Phone: 202.225.4472

Majority:		Minority:	
C: Rick Larsen, WA-02	RHOB 2163	**RM: Garret Graves, LA-06**	RHOB 2402
Sharice Davids, KS-03	LHOB 1541	Don Young, AK-01	RHOB 2314
Steve Cohen, TN-09	RHOB 2104	Thomas Massie, KY-04	RHOB 2453
Andre Carson, IN-07	RHOB 2135	Scott Perry, PA-10	RHOB 2160
Kaiali'i Kahele, HI-02	LHOB 1205	John Katko, NY-24	RHOB 2457
Nikema Williams, GA-05	LHOB 1406	Brian Mast, FL-18	RHOB 2182
Hank Johnson, GA-04	RHOB 2240	Mike Gallagher, WI-08	LHOB 1230
Dina Titus, NV-01	RHOB 2464	Brian Fitzpatrick, PA-01	CHOB 271
Sean Maloney, NY-18	CHOB 464	Troy Balderson, OH-12	RHOB 2429
Julia Brownley, CA-26	RHOB 2262	Pete Stauber, MN-08	CHOB 461
Donald Payne, NJ-10	CHOB 106	Tim Burchett, TN-02	LHOB 1122
Mark DeSaulnier, CA-11	CHOB 503	Jefferson Van Drew, NJ-02	RHOB 2447
Stephen Lynch, MA-08	RHOB 2109	Troy Nehls, TX-22	LHOB 1104
Anthony Brown, MD-04	LHOB 1323	Nancy Mace, SC-01	CHOB 212
Greg Stanton, AZ-09	CHOB 207	Beth Van Duyne, TX-24	LHOB 1337
Colin Allred, TX-32	CHOB 114	Carlos Gimenez, FL-26	CHOB 419
Conor Lamb, PA-17	LHOB 1224	Michelle Steel, CA-48	LHOB 1113
Eleanor Norton, DC-01	RHOB 2136	Sam Graves, MO-06	LHOB 1135
Eddie Bernice Johnson, TX-30	RHOB 2306		
John Garamendi, CA-03	RHOB 2368		
Peter DeFazio, OR-04	RHOB 2134		

COAST GUARD & MARITIME TRANSPORTATION
Room: RHOB 2165
Phone: 202.225.4472

Majority:		Minority:	
C: Salud Carbajal, CA-24	RHOB 2331	**RM: Bob Gibbs, OH-07**	RHOB 2217
Rick Larsen, WA-02	RHOB 2163	Don Young, AK-01	RHOB 2314
Jake Auchincloss, MA-04	LHOB 1524	Randy Weber, TX-14	CHOB 107
Sean Maloney, NY-18	CHOB 464	Mike Gallagher, WI-08	LHOB 1230
Alan Lowenthal, CA-47	CHOB 108	Jefferson Van Drew, NJ-02	RHOB 2447
Anthony Brown, MD-04	LHOB 1323	Nicole Malliotakis, NY-11	CHOB 417
Chris Pappas, NH-01	CHOB 319	Sam Graves, MO-06	LHOB 1135
Peter DeFazio, OR-04	RHOB 2134		

ECONOMIC DEV'T, PUBLIC BUILDINGS & EMERGENCY MANAGEMENT
Room: RHOB 2165
Phone: 202.225.4472

Majority:		Minority:	
C: Dina Titus, NV-01	RHOB 2464	**RM: Daniel Webster, FL-11**	RHOB 2184
Eleanor Norton, DC-01	RHOB 2136		
Sharice Davids, KS-03	LHOB 1541	Thomas Massie, KY-04	RHOB 2453
Chris Pappas, NH-01	CHOB 319	Jenniffer Gonzalez-Colon, PR-01	RHOB 2338
Grace Napolitano, CA-32	LHOB 1610		
John Garamendi, CA-03	RHOB 2368	Michael Guest, MS-03	CHOB 418
Peter DeFazio, OR-04	RHOB 2134	Beth Van Duyne, TX-24	LHOB 1337
		Carlos Gimenez, FL-26	CHOB 419
		Sam Graves, MO-06	LHOB 1135

HIGHWAYS & TRANSIT
Room: RHOB 2165
Phone: 202.225.4472

Majority:		Minority:	
Eleanor Norton, DC-01	RHOB 2136	**RM: Rodney Davis, IL-13**	RHOB 2079
		Don Young, AK-01	RHOB 2314

Eddie Bernice Johnson, TX-30	RHOB 2306	Rick Crawford, AR-01	RHOB 2422
		Bob Gibbs, OH-07	RHOB 2217
Albio Sires, NJ-08	RHOB 2268	Thomas Massie, KY-04	RHOB 2453
John Garamendi, CA-03	RHOB 2368	Scott Perry, PA-10	RHOB 2160
Hank Johnson, GA-04	RHOB 2240	John Katko, NY-24	RHOB 2457
Sean Maloney, NY-18	CHOB 464	Brian Babin, TX-36	RHOB 2236
Julia Brownley, CA-26	RHOB 2262	David Rouzer, NC-07	RHOB 2333
Frederica Wilson, FL-24	RHOB 2445	Mike Bost, IL-12	LHOB 1211
Alan Lowenthal, CA-47	CHOB 108	Doug LaMalfa, CA-01	CHOB 408
Mark DeSaulnier, CA-11	CHOB 503	Bruce Westerman, AR-04	CHOB 202
Stephen Lynch, MA-08	RHOB 2109	Mike Gallagher, WI-08	LHOB 1230
Anthony Brown, MD-04	LHOB 1323	Brian Fitzpatrick, PA-01	CHOB 271
Greg Stanton, AZ-09	CHOB 207	Jenniffer Gonzalez-Colon, PR-01	RHOB 2338
Colin Allred, TX-32	CHOB 114		
Jesús Garcia, IL-04	LHOB 1519	Troy Balderson, OH-12	RHOB 2429
Antonio Delgado, NY-19	LHOB 1007	Pete Stauber, MN-08	CHOB 461
Chris Pappas, NH-01	CHOB 319	Tim Burchett, TN-02	LHOB 1122
Conor Lamb, PA-17	LHOB 1224	Dusty Johnson, SD-01	LHOB 1714
Jake Auchincloss, MA-04	LHOB 1524	Michael Guest, MS-03	CHOB 418
Carolyn Bourdeaux, GA-07	LHOB 1319	Troy Nehls, TX-22	LHOB 1104
Marilyn Strickland, WA-10	LHOB 1004	Nancy Mace, SC-01	CHOB 212
Grace Napolitano, CA-32	LHOB 1610	Nicole Malliotakis, NY-11	CHOB 417
Jared Huffman, CA-02	LHOB 1527	Beth Van Duyne, TX-24	LHOB 1337
Salud Carbajal, CA-24	RHOB 2331	Carlos Gimenez, FL-26	CHOB 419
Sharice Davids, KS-03	LHOB 1541	Michelle Steel, CA-48	LHOB 1113
Seth Moulton, MA-06	LHOB 1127	Sam Graves, MO-06	LHOB 1135
Kaiali'i Kahele, HI-02	LHOB 1205		
Nikema Williams, GA-05	LHOB 1406		
Marie Newman, IL-03	LHOB 1022		
Steve Cohen, TN-09	RHOB 2104		
Peter DeFazio, OR-04	RHOB 2134		

RAILROADS, PIPELINES & HAZARDOUS MATERIALS

Room: RHOB 2165
Phone: 202.225.4472

Majority:		Minority:	
C: Donald Payne, NJ-10	CHOB 106	**RM: Rick Crawford, AR-01**	RHOB 2422
Marilyn Strickland, WA-10	LHOB 1004	Scott Perry, PA-10	RHOB 2160
Tom Malinowski, NJ-07	LHOB 1318	Rodney Davis, IL-13	RHOB 2079
Seth Moulton, MA-06	LHOB 1127	Mike Bost, IL-12	LHOB 1211
Marie Newman, IL-03	LHOB 1022	Randy Weber, TX-14	CHOB 107
Steve Cohen, TN-09	RHOB 2104	Doug LaMalfa, CA-01	CHOB 408
Albio Sires, NJ-08	RHOB 2268	Bruce Westerman, AR-04	CHOB 202
Andre Carson, IN-07	RHOB 2135	Brian Fitzpatrick, PA-01	CHOB 271
Frederica Wilson, FL-24	RHOB 2445	Troy Balderson, OH-12	RHOB 2429
Jesús Garcia, IL-04	LHOB 1519	Pete Stauber, MN-08	CHOB 461
Grace Napolitano, CA-32	LHOB 1610	Tim Burchett, TN-02	LHOB 1122
Hank Johnson, GA-04	RHOB 2240	Dusty Johnson, SD-01	LHOB 1714
Dina Titus, NV-01	RHOB 2464	Troy Nehls, TX-22	LHOB 1104
Jared Huffman, CA-02	LHOB 1527	Michelle Steel, CA-48	LHOB 1113
Stephen Lynch, MA-08	RHOB 2109	Sam Graves, MO-06	LHOB 1135
Jake Auchincloss, MA-04	LHOB 1524		
Troy Carter, LA-02	CHOB 506		
Peter DeFazio, OR-04	RHOB 2134		

WATER RESOURCES & ENVIRONMENT

Room: RHOB 2165
Phone: 202.225.4472

Majority:		Minority:	
C: Grace Napolitano, CA-32	LHOB 1610	**RM: David Rouzer, NC-07**	RHOB 2333
		Daniel Webster, FL-11	RHOB 2184
Jared Huffman, CA-02	LHOB 1527	John Katko, NY-24	RHOB 2457
Eddie Bernice Johnson, TX-30	RHOB 2306	Brian Babin, TX-36	RHOB 2236
		Garret Graves, LA-06	RHOB 2402
John Garamendi, CA-03	RHOB 2368	Mike Bost, IL-12	LHOB 1211
Alan Lowenthal, CA-47	CHOB 108	Randy Weber, TX-14	CHOB 107
Tom Malinowski, NJ-07	LHOB 1318	Doug LaMalfa, CA-01	CHOB 408
Antonio Delgado, NY-19	LHOB 1007	Bruce Westerman, AR-04	CHOB 202
Chris Pappas, NH-01	CHOB 319	Brian Mast, FL-18	RHOB 2182
Carolyn Bourdeaux, GA-07	LHOB 1319	Jenniffer Gonzalez-Colon, PR-01	RHOB 2338
Frederica Wilson, FL-24	RHOB 2445		
Salud Carbajal, CA-24	RHOB 2331	Nancy Mace, SC-01	CHOB 212
Greg Stanton, AZ-09	CHOB 207	Sam Graves, MO-06	LHOB 1135
Eleanor Norton, DC-01	RHOB 2136		
Steve Cohen, TN-09	RHOB 2104		
Peter DeFazio, OR-04	RHOB 2134		

VETERANS' AFFAIRS

Room: CHOB 364
Website: www.veterans.house.gov
Phone: 202.225.9756
Ratio: 17 Democrats/13 Republicans
Subcommittees: 5

Majority:		Minority:	
C: Mark Takano, CA-41	CHOB 420	RM: Mike Bost, IL-12	LHOB 1211
Mike Levin, CA-49	LHOB 1030	Amata Radewagen, AS-01	LHOB 1339
Julia Brownley, CA-26	RHOB 2262	Jack Bergman, MI-01	CHOB 566
Conor Lamb, PA-17	LHOB 1224	Jim Banks, IN-03	LHOB 1713
Chris Pappas, NH-01	CHOB 319	Chip Roy, TX-21	LHOB 1005
Elaine Luria, VA-02	CHOB 412	Tracey Mann, KS-01	CHOB 522
Frank Mrvan, IN-01	LHOB 1607	Barry Moore, AL-02	LHOB 1504
Sheila Cherfilus-McCormick, FL-20	RHOB 2365	Nancy Mace, SC-01	CHOB 212
		Madison Cawthorn, NC-11	CHOB 102
Gregorio Sablan, MP-01	RHOB 2267	Troy Nehls, TX-22	LHOB 1104
Lauren Underwood, IL-14	LHOB 1130	Matt Rosendale, MT-01	LHOB 1037
Colin Allred, TX-32	CHOB 114	Mariannette Miller-Meeks, IA-02	LHOB 1716
Lois Frankel, FL-21	RHOB 2305		
Elissa Slotkin, MI-08	LHOB 1210	Jake Ellzey, TX-06	LHOB 1725
David Trone, MD-06	LHOB 1110		
Marcy Kaptur, OH-09	RHOB 2186		
Raul Ruiz, CA-36	RHOB 2342		
Ruben Gallego, AZ-07	LHOB 1131		

Majority CoS: Matthew N. Reel   **Minority CoS:** Maria C. Tripplaar
Majority Sched: Carol Murray

———————————— Subcommittees ————————————

DISABILITY ASSISTANCE & MEMORIAL AFFAIRS
Room:

Majority:		Minority:	
C: Elaine Luria, VA-02	CHOB 412	RM: Troy Nehls, TX-22	LHOB 1104
Elissa Slotkin, MI-08	LHOB 1210	Barry Moore, AL-02	LHOB 1504
Marcy Kaptur, OH-09	RHOB 2186	Mariannette Miller-Meeks, IA-02	LHOB 1716
Raul Ruiz, CA-36	RHOB 2342		
David Trone, MD-06	LHOB 1110	Jake Ellzey, TX-06	LHOB 1725

ECONOMIC OPPORTUNITY
Room:

Majority:		Minority:	
C: Mike Levin, CA-49	LHOB 1030	RM: Barry Moore, AL-02	LHOB 1504
Chris Pappas, NH-01	CHOB 319	Tracey Mann, KS-01	CHOB 522
David Trone, MD-06	LHOB 1110	Nancy Mace, SC-01	CHOB 212
Ruben Gallego, AZ-07	LHOB 1131	Madison Cawthorn, NC-11	CHOB 102

HEALTH
Room:

Majority:		Minority:	
C: Julia Brownley, CA-26	RHOB 2262	RM: Jack Bergman, MI-01	CHOB 566
Frank Mrvan, IN-01	LHOB 1607	Amata Radewagen, AS-01	LHOB 1339
Conor Lamb, PA-17	LHOB 1224	Chip Roy, TX-21	LHOB 1005
Mike Levin, CA-49	LHOB 1030	Matt Rosendale, MT-01	LHOB 1037
Gregorio Sablan, MP-01	RHOB 2267	Mariannette Miller-Meeks, IA-02	LHOB 1716
Lauren Underwood, IL-14	LHOB 1130		
Colin Allred, TX-32	CHOB 114		
Lois Frankel, FL-21	RHOB 2305		

OVERSIGHT & INVESTIGATIONS
Room: CHOB 364
Phone: 202.225.9756

Majority:		Minority:	
C: Chris Pappas, NH-01	CHOB 319	RM: Tracey Mann, KS-01	CHOB 522
Conor Lamb, PA-17	LHOB 1224	Amata Radewagen, AS-01	LHOB 1339
Elaine Luria, VA-02	CHOB 412	Jack Bergman, MI-01	CHOB 566
Lauren Underwood, IL-14	LHOB 1130		

TECHNOLOGY MODERNIZATION
Room:

Majority:		Minority:	
C: Frank Mrvan, IN-01	LHOB 1607	RM: Matt Rosendale, MT-01	LHOB 1037
Mark Takano, CA-41	CHOB 420	Jim Banks, IN-03	LHOB 1713

HOUSE COMMITTEES

WAYS & MEANS

Room: LHOB 1102
Website: www.waysandmeans.house.gov
Phone: 202.225.3625
Ratio: 25 Democrats/18 Republicans
Subcommittees: 6

Majority:		Minority:	
C: Richard Neal, MA-01	CHOB 372	RM: Kevin Brady, TX-08	LHOB 1011
Suzan DelBene, WA-01	RHOB 2330	Vern Buchanan, FL-16	RHOB 2110
Lloyd Doggett, TX-35	RHOB 2307	Adrian Smith, NE-03	CHOB 502
Mike Thompson, CA-05	CHOB 268	Tom Reed, NY-23	LHOB 1203
John Larson, CT-01	LHOB 1501	Mike Kelly, PA-16	LHOB 1707
Earl Blumenauer, OR-03	LHOB 1111	Jason Smith, MO-08	RHOB 2418
Bill Pascrell, NJ-09	RHOB 2409	Tom Rice, SC-07	CHOB 460
Danny Davis, IL-07	RHOB 2159	David Schweikert, AZ-06	CHOB 304
Linda Sanchez, CA-38	RHOB 2329	Jackie Walorski, IN-02	CHOB 466
Brian Higgins, NY-26	RHOB 2459	Darin LaHood, IL-18	LHOB 1424
Terri Sewell, AL-07	RHOB 2201	Brad Wenstrup, OH-02	RHOB 2419
Judy Chu, CA-27	RHOB 2423	Jodey Arrington, TX-19	LHOB 1107
Gwen Moore, WI-04	RHOB 2252	Drew Ferguson, GA-03	LHOB 1032
Dan Kildee, MI-05	CHOB 200	Ron Estes, KS-04	RHOB 2411
Brendan Boyle, PA-02	LHOB 1133	Lloyd Smucker, PA-11	CHOB 302
Don Beyer, VA-08	LHOB 1119	Kevin Hern, OK-01	LHOB 1019
Dwight Evans, PA-03	LHOB 1105	Carol Miller, WV-03	CHOB 465
Brad Schneider, IL-10	CHOB 300	Gregory Murphy, NC-03	CHOB 313
Thomas Suozzi, NY-03	CHOB 407		
Jimmy Panetta, CA-20	CHOB 406		
Stephanie Murphy, FL-07	LHOB 1710		
Jimmy Gomez, CA-34	LHOB 1530		
Steven Horsford, NV-04	CHOB 562		
Stacey Plaskett, VI-01	RHOB 2404		

Majority CoS: Brandon Casey   **Minority CoS:** Gary J. Andres
———————————— Subcommittees ————————————

HEALTH
Room:

Majority:		Minority:	
C: Lloyd Doggett, TX-35	RHOB 2307	RM: Vern Buchanan,	RHOB 2110
Mike Thompson, CA-05	CHOB 268	FL-16	
Ron Kind, WI-03	LHOB 1502	Adrian Smith, NE-03	CHOB 502
Earl Blumenauer, OR-03	LHOB 1111	Tom Reed, NY-23	LHOB 1203
Brian Higgins, NY-26	RHOB 2459	Mike Kelly, PA-16	LHOB 1707
Terri Sewell, AL-07	RHOB 2201	Jason Smith, MO-08	RHOB 2418
Judy Chu, CA-27	RHOB 2423	David Schweikert, AZ-06	CHOB 304
Dwight Evans, PA-03	LHOB 1105	Brad Wenstrup, OH-02	RHOB 2419
Brad Schneider, IL-10	CHOB 300	Gregory Murphy, NC-03	CHOB 313
Jimmy Gomez, CA-34	LHOB 1530		
Steven Horsford, NV-04	CHOB 562		

OVERSIGHT
Room:

Majority:		Minority:	
C: Bill Pascrell, NJ-09	RHOB 2409	RM: Tom Rice, SC-07	CHOB 460
Thomas Suozzi, NY-03	CHOB 407	Jackie Walorski, IN-02	CHOB 466
Judy Chu, CA-27	RHOB 2423	Gregory Murphy, NC-03	CHOB 313
Brad Schneider, IL-10	CHOB 300	Drew Ferguson, GA-03	LHOB 1032
Stacey Plaskett, VI-01	RHOB 2404	Carol Miller, WV-03	CHOB 465
Lloyd Doggett, TX-35	RHOB 2307		
Dwight Evans, PA-03	LHOB 1105		
Steven Horsford, NV-04	CHOB 562		

SELECT REVENUE MEASURES
Room: LHOB 1102
Phone: 202.225.3625

Majority:		Minority:	
C: Mike Thompson, CA-05	CHOB 268	RM: Mike Kelly, PA-16	LHOB 1707
Lloyd Doggett, TX-35	RHOB 2307	Tom Rice, SC-07	CHOB 460
John Larson, CT-01	LHOB 1501	David Schweikert, AZ-06	CHOB 304
Linda Sanchez, CA-38	RHOB 2329	Darin LaHood, IL-18	LHOB 1424
Suzan DelBene, WA-01	RHOB 2330	Jodey Arrington, TX-19	LHOB 1107
Gwen Moore, WI-04	RHOB 2252	Drew Ferguson, GA-03	LHOB 1032
Brendan Boyle, PA-02	LHOB 1133	Kevin Hern, OK-01	LHOB 1019
Don Beyer, VA-08	LHOB 1119	Ron Estes, KS-04	RHOB 2411
Thomas Suozzi, NY-03	CHOB 407		
Stacey Plaskett, VI-01	RHOB 2404		
Terri Sewell, AL-07	RHOB 2201		

SOCIAL SECURITY
Room:

Majority:		Minority:	
C: John Larson, CT-01	LHOB 1501	**RM: Tom Reed, NY-23**	LHOB 1203
Bill Pascrell, NJ-09	RHOB 2409	Kevin Hern, OK-01	LHOB 1019
Linda Sanchez, CA-38	RHOB 2329	Tom Rice, SC-07	CHOB 460
Brian Higgins, NY-26	RHOB 2459	Jodey Arrington, TX-19	LHOB 1107
Steven Horsford, NV-04	CHOB 562	Ron Estes, KS-04	RHOB 2411
Earl Blumenauer, OR-03	LHOB 1111		
Terri Sewell, AL-07	RHOB 2201		
Gwen Moore, WI-04	RHOB 2252		

TRADE
Room:

Majority:		Minority:	
C: Earl Blumenauer, OR-03	LHOB 1111	**RM: Adrian Smith, NE-03**	CHOB 502
		Vern Buchanan, FL-16	RHOB 2110
Ron Kind, WI-03	LHOB 1502	Darin LaHood, IL-18	LHOB 1424
Danny Davis, IL-07	RHOB 2159	Jodey Arrington, TX-19	LHOB 1107
Brian Higgins, NY-26	RHOB 2459	Drew Ferguson, GA-03	LHOB 1032
Dan Kildee, MI-05	CHOB 200	Ron Estes, KS-04	RHOB 2411
Jimmy Panetta, CA-20	CHOB 406	Carol Miller, WV-03	CHOB 465
Stephanie Murphy, FL-07	LHOB 1710	Lloyd Smucker, PA-11	CHOB 302
Suzan DelBene, WA-01	RHOB 2330		
Don Beyer, VA-08	LHOB 1119		
Linda Sanchez, CA-38	RHOB 2329		
Brendan Boyle, PA-02	LHOB 1133		

WORKER & FAMILY SUPPORT
Room:

Majority:		Minority:	
C: Danny Davis, IL-07	RHOB 2159	**RM: Jackie Walorski, IN-02**	CHOB 466
Judy Chu, CA-27	RHOB 2423		
Gwen Moore, WI-04	RHOB 2252	Brad Wenstrup, OH-02	RHOB 2419
Dwight Evans, PA-03	LHOB 1105	Carol Miller, WV-03	CHOB 465
Stephanie Murphy, FL-07	LHOB 1710	Lloyd Smucker, PA-11	CHOB 302
Jimmy Gomez, CA-34	LHOB 1530	Kevin Hern, OK-01	LHOB 1019
Dan Kildee, MI-05	CHOB 200		
Jimmy Panetta, CA-20	CHOB 406		

SELECT AND SPECIAL COMMITTEES

PERMANENT SELECT ON INTELLIGENCE

Room: The Capitol Visitors Center HVC-304
Website: www.intelligence.house.gov
Phone: 202.225.7690
Ratio: 13 Democrats/9 Republicans
Subcommittees: 4

Majority:		Minority:	
C: Adam Schiff, CA-28	RHOB 2309	**RM: Mike Turner, OH-10**	RHOB 2082
Jim Himes, CT-04	RHOB 2137	Brad Wenstrup, OH-02	RHOB 2419
Andre Carson, IN-07	RHOB 2135	Chris Stewart, UT-02	CHOB 166
Jackie Speier, CA-14	RHOB 2465	Rick Crawford, AR-01	RHOB 2422
Mike Quigley, IL-05	RHOB 2078	Elise Stefanik, NY-21	RHOB 2211
Eric Swalwell, CA-15	CHOB 174	Markwayne Mullin, OK-02	RHOB 2421
Joaquin Castro, TX-20	RHOB 2241	Trent Kelly, MS-01	RHOB 2243
Peter Welch, VT-01	RHOB 2187	Darin LaHood, IL-18	LHOB 1424
Sean Maloney, NY-18	CHOB 464	Brian Fitzpatrick, PA-01	CHOB 271
Val Demings, FL-10	CHOB 217		
Raja Krishnamoorthi, IL-08	CHOB 115		
Jim Cooper, TN-05	LHOB 1536		
Jason Crow, CO-06	LHOB 1229		

Majority CoS: Jeff Lowenstein   **Minority CoS:** George J. Pappas

—————————————— Subcommittees ——————————————

COUNTERTERRORISM, COUNTERINTELLIGENCE & COUNTERPROLIFERATION

Room: Capitol Visitor Center HVC-304
Phone: 202.225.7690

Majority:		Minority:	
C: Andre Carson, IN-07	RHOB 2135	**RM: Rick Crawford, AR-01**	RHOB 2422
Mike Quigley, IL-05	RHOB 2078	Brad Wenstrup, OH-02	RHOB 2419
Joaquin Castro, TX-20	RHOB 2241	Chris Stewart, UT-02	CHOB 166
Peter Welch, VT-01	RHOB 2187	Elise Stefanik, NY-21	RHOB 2211
Sean Maloney, NY-18	CHOB 464	Darin LaHood, IL-18	LHOB 1424
Val Demings, FL-10	CHOB 217		

DEFENSE INTELLIGENCE & WARFIGHTER SUPPORT

Room: Capitol Visitor Center HVC-304
Phone: 202.225.7690

Majority:		Minority:	
C: Peter Welch, VT-01	RHOB 2187	**RM: Brad Wenstrup, OH-02**	RHOB 2419
Jim Himes, CT-04	RHOB 2137		
Jackie Speier, CA-14	RHOB 2465	Rick Crawford, AR-01	RHOB 2422
Mike Quigley, IL-05	RHOB 2078	Markwayne Mullin, OK-02	RHOB 2421
Sean Maloney, NY-18	CHOB 464	Trent Kelly, MS-01	RHOB 2243
Jason Crow, CO-06	LHOB 1229	Brian Fitzpatrick, PA-01	CHOB 271

INTELLIGENCE MODERNIZATION & READINESS

Room: Capitol Visitor Center HVC-304
Phone: 202.225.7690

Majority:		Minority:	
C: Eric Swalwell, CA-15	CHOB 174	**RM: Markwayne Mullin, OK-02**	RHOB 2421
Val Demings, FL-10	CHOB 217		
Raja Krishnamoorthi, IL-08	CHOB 115	Trent Kelly, MS-01	RHOB 2243
Jim Cooper, TN-05	LHOB 1536	Darin LaHood, IL-18	LHOB 1424
Jason Crow, CO-06	LHOB 1229	Brian Fitzpatrick, PA-01	CHOB 271

STRATEGIC TECHNOLOGIES & ADVANCED RESEARCH

Room: Capitol Visitor Center HVC-304
Phone: 202.225.7690

Majority:		Minority:	
C: Jackie Speier, CA-14	RHOB 2465	**RM: Chris Stewart, UT-02**	CHOB 166
Jim Himes, CT-04	RHOB 2137	Mike Turner, OH-10	RHOB 2082
Andre Carson, IN-07	RHOB 2135	Elise Stefanik, NY-21	RHOB 2211
Joaquin Castro, TX-20	RHOB 2241	Markwayne Mullin, OK-02	RHOB 2421
Raja Krishnamoorthi, IL-08	CHOB 115		
Jim Cooper, TN-05	LHOB 1536		

SELECT COMMITTEE ON THE CLIMATE CRISIS

Room: FHOB H2-359
Website: www.climatecrisis.house.gov
Phone: 202.225.1106
Ratio: 9 Democrats/7 Republicans
Subcommittees: 0

Majority:		Minority:	
C: Kathy Castor, FL-14	RHOB 2052	**RM: Garret Graves, LA-06**	RHOB 2402
Suzanne Bonamici, OR-01	RHOB 2231	Gary Palmer, AL-06	CHOB 170
Julia Brownley, CA-26	RHOB 2262	Buddy Carter, GA-01	RHOB 2432
Jared Huffman, CA-02	LHOB 1527	Carol Miller, WV-03	CHOB 465

A. Donald McEachin, VA-04	CHOB 314	Kelly Armstrong, ND-01	LHOB 1740
Mike Levin, CA-49	LHOB 1030	Daniel Crenshaw, TX-02	CHOB 413
Sean Casten, IL-06	RHOB 2440	Anthony Gonzalez, OH-16	RHOB 2458
Joe Neguse, CO-02	LHOB 1419		
Veronica Escobar, TX-16	LHOB 1505		

Majority CoS: Dr. Ana Unruh Cohen **Minority CoS:** Sarah Jorgenson

SELECT COMMITTEE ON THE MODERNIZATION OF CONGRESS

Room: CHOB 164
Website: www.modernizecongress.house.gov
Phone: 202.225.1530
Ratio: 6 Democrats/6 Republicans
Subcommittees: 0

Majority:		Minority:	
C: Derek Kilmer, WA-06	RHOB 2059	William Timmons, SC-04	CHOB 267
Emanuel Cleaver, MO-05	RHOB 2335	Rodney Davis, IL-13	RHOB 2079
Zoe Lofgren, CA-19	LHOB 1401	Bob Latta, OH-05	RHOB 2467
Ed Perlmutter, CO-07	LHOB 1226	Guy Reschenthaler, PA-14	CHOB 409
Dean Phillips, MN-03	RHOB 2452	Beth Van Duyne, TX-24	LHOB 1337
Nikema Williams, GA-05	LHOB 1406	Dave Joyce, OH-14	RHOB 2065

SELECT ECONOMIC DISPARITY & FAIRNESS IN GROWTH

Room: Thomas P. O'Neill Federal Bldg. 3470
Website: www.speaker.gov
Phone: 202.225.5990
Ratio: 8 Democrats/6 Republicans
Subcommittees: 0

Majority:		Minority:	
C: Jim Himes, CT-04	RHOB 2137	**RM: Bryan Steil, WI-01**	LHOB 1526
Marcy Kaptur, OH-09	RHOB 2186	Warren Davidson, OH-08	RHOB 2113
Gwen Moore, WI-04	RHOB 2252	Jodey Arrington, TX-19	LHOB 1107
Vicente Gonzalez, TX-15	CHOB 113	Stephanie Bice, OK-05	LHOB 1223
Pramila Jayapal, WA-07	RHOB 2346	Kat Cammack, FL-03	LHOB 1626
Angie Craig, MN-02	RHOB 2442	Byron Donalds, FL-19	CHOB 523
Alexandria Ocasio-Cortez, NY-14	CHOB 229		
Sara Jacobs, CA-53	LHOB 1232		

SELECT INVESTIGATE JAN 6 ATTACK ON THE U.S. CAPITOL

Room: RHOB 2466
Website:
Phone: 202.225.7800
Ratio: 7 Democrats/2 Republicans
Subcommittees: 0

Majority:		Minority:	
C: Bennie Thompson, MS-02	RHOB 2466	Liz Cheney, WY-01	CHOB 416
Zoe Lofgren, CA-19	LHOB 1401	Adam Kinzinger, IL-16	RHOB 2245
Adam Schiff, CA-28	RHOB 2309		
Pete Aguilar, CA-31	CHOB 109		
Stephanie Murphy, FL-07	LHOB 1710		
Jamie Raskin, MD-08	RHOB 2242		
Elaine Luria, VA-02	CHOB 412		

EXECUTIVE BRANCH

The Executive Branch of the U.S. government was formed through Article II of the U.S. Constitution. The Executive Branch is primarily composed of the President (who is also the Commander-in-Chief of the armed services), the White House staff, the Executive Office of the President, the Vice President, as well as the 14 Federal departments, the heads of which form the President's Cabinet.

Also included under the purview of the Executive Branch are the various subordinate divisions of the Federal departments, independent Federal agencies, the independent Federal reserve system, and several permanent and ad hoc agencies, boards, commissions and committees. The Executive Branch is responsible for carrying out and enforcing the federal laws and protecting the people of the United States.

President of the United States **Joseph R. Biden Jr. (D)** p **202.456.1111**

1600 Pennsylvania Ave. NW
Washington, DC 20500
Bio. 11/20/1942 • Scranton, PA • University of Delaware, B.A., 1965; University of Delaware, B.A., 1965; Syracuse University - College of Law (NY), J.D., 1968 • Catholic • M. Jill Biden, 4 ch (2 deceased); 5 gr-ch
Salary $400,000

Vice President **Kamala D. Harris (D)** p **202.456.1111**

1600 Pennsylvania Ave. NW
Washington, DC 20500
Bio. 10/20/1964 • Oakland, CA • Howard University, B.A.; University of California, Hastings, J.D. • Baptist • M. Douglas Emhoff, 2 stepch
Salary $235,100

THE OFFICE OF THE PRESIDENT

www.whitehouse.gov

President
Joseph R. Biden Jr. 202.456.0373

Chief of Staff
Ron Klain

Counselor to the President
Jeff Zients

Counselor to the President
Steve Ricchetti 202.456.0373

Deputy Chief of Staff
Bruce Reed

Director of Communications
Kate Bedingfield 202.456.0373

National Security Advisor
Jake Sullivan 202.456.2744

Press Secretary
Jen Psaki 202.456.4673

Senior Advisor
Gene Sperling

Senior Advisor
Michael C. Donilon

Senior Advisor
Mitch Landrieu

Senior Advisor
Neera Tanden

Senior Advisor
Rep. Cedric Richmond

THE OFFICE OF THE VICE PRESIDENT

www.whitehouse.gov/vicepresident

Vice President
Kamala D. Harris

Chief of Staff
Hartina Flournoy

Second Gentleman
Douglas Emhoff

THE OFFICE OF THE FIRST LADY

www.whitehouse.gov/firstlady

First Lady
Jill Biden

202.456.7458

Chief of Staff
Julissa Reynoso Pantaleón

EXECUTIVE OFFICE OF THE PRESIDENT

www.whitehouse.gov

Through the U.S. Code's Reorganization Act of 1939, authority over a variety of Federal agencies was transferred to the Executive Branch, which has since formed the Executive Office of the President. The composition of the Executive Office customarily changes with each administration to reflect the policy goals of the President.

The President, through the Office of Management and Budget (OMB), manages the Executive Office of the President. It is through the OMB that the Executive Branch's departments, agency programs, policies and expenditures are shaped. In addition to OMB, the following agencies comprise the Executive Office of the President.

Council on Environmental Quality
1600 Pennsylvania Ave. NW
Washington, DC 20500

202.456.1111

Council on Environmental Quality (CEQ)
Eisenhower Executive Office Bldg. (EEOB)
1600 Pennsylvania Ave. NW
Washington, WV 20500
Chairman: Brenda Mallory

202.456.1111

Domestic Policy Council (DPC)
1600 Pennsylvania Ave. NW
Washington, WA 20500
Director: Susan Rice

202.456.1111

National Economic Council (NEC)
Eisenhower Executive Office Bldg. (EEOB)
1600 Pennsylvania Ave. NW
Washington, WA 20500
Director: Brian Deese

202.456.1111

National Security Council (NSC)
1600 Pennsylvania Ave. NW
Washington, WA 20500
Jake Sullivan

202.456.1111

Office of Administration
1600 Pennsylvania Ave. NW
Washington, DC 20500

202.456.1111

Office of Faith-Based and Neighborhood Partnerships
1600 Pennsylvania Ave. NW
Washington, DC 20500

202.456.1111

Office of Intergovernmental Affairs
1600 Pennsylvania Ave. NW
Washington, DC 20500
Director: Julie Chavez Rodriguez

202.456.1111

Office of Management and Budget (OMB)
725 17th St. NW
Washington, DC 20503

202.395.3080

Office of National AIDS Policy
The White House
1600 Pennsylvania Ave. NW
Washington, DC 20500

202.456.4533

Office of National Drug Control Policy
1600 Pennsylvania Ave. NW
Washington, WA 20500
Acting Director: Regina LaBelle

202.456.1111

Office of Public Engagement
1600 Pennsylvania Ave. NW
Washington, DC 20500
Director: Rep. Cedric Richmond

202.456.1111

Office of Science and Technology Policy
Eisenhower Executive Office Building
1600 Pennsylvania Ave. NW
Washington, DC 20504

202.456.4444

Office of Social Innovation and Civic Participation
1600 Pennsylvania Ave. NW
Washington, DC 20500

202.456.1111

Office of the U.S. Trade Representative
600 17th St. NW
Washington, DC 20508

202.395.2870

President's Intelligence Advisory Board
1600 Pennsylvania Ave. NW
Washington, DC 20500

202.456.1111

White House Military Office
1600 Pennsylvania Ave. NW
Washington, DC 20500

202.456.1111

THE CABINET

The Executive Branch's 14 department Secretaries form the President's Cabinet. The President appoints each Secretary, who must be confirmed by the Senate. The Cabinet advises the President on various aspects of the Executive Branch and then proceed as the president directs. The annual salary for Department Secretaries is $203,700.

The President also has the authority to appoint members of the Executive Office of the President and other officials to Cabinet-level rank, The Vice President and the President's chief of staff are considered members of the Cabinet. Under the Biden administration, the following administrators also are considered members of the Cabinet.

Director, Office of Management and Budget
Shalanda Young
Chief of Staff
Ron Klain
Trade Representative
Katherine C. Tai
Director, National Intelligence
Avril Haines
Chairman, Council of Economic Advisors
Cecilia Elena Rouse
Ambassador to the United Nations
Linda Thomas Greenfield
Administrator, Environmental Protection Agency
Michael S. Regan
Administrator, Small Business Adminstration
Isabel Guzman
Director, Office of Science and Technology Policy
Eric Lander

Department of Agriculture (USDA)

Secretary Thomas J. Vilsack (VIL-sak)　　　　　　p 202.720.2791

1400 Independence Ave., S.W.
Washington, DC 20250
Website usda.gov
Bio. 12/12/1950 • Pittsburgh, PA • Governor (Iowa); State Senator; Mayor • Hamilton College (NY), B.A., 1972; Albany Law School, J.D., 1975 • Catholic • M. Christie Bell, 2 ch; 2 gr-ch

Department of Commerce (DOC)

Gov. Gina Raimondo (ruh-MON-doh)　　　　　　p 202.482.2000

1401 Constitution Ave NW
Washington, DC 20230
Website commerce.gov
Bio. 05/17/1971 • Smithfield, RI • General Treasurer (RI); Chair of Democratic Governors Association; Governor (RI) • Harvard University, B.A., 1993; Yale University (CT), J.D., 1998; University of Oxford (UK), M.A., 2002; University of Oxford (UK), Ph.D., 2002 • Catholic • M. Andrew Moffit, 2 ch

Department of Defense (DOD)

Lloyd Austin (AW-stuhn)　　　　　　p 703.571.3343

1400 Defense Pentagon
Washington, DC 20301
Website defense.gov
Bio. 08/08/1953 • Mobile, AL • Vice Chief of Staff of the U.S. Army; Commander of the U.S. Central Command • U.S. Military Academy - West Point (NY), B.S., 1975; Auburn University, M.A., 1986; Webster University (MO), M.B.A., 1989 • Catholic • M. Charlene Banner, 2 stepch

Department of Education (ED)
Dr. Miguel Cardona (KAR-dohn-ah) **p 202.401.2000**

400 Maryland Avenue, SW
Washington, DC 20202
Website ed.gov
Bio. 07/11/1975 • Meriden, CT • Education Commissioner
(CT) • Central Connecticut State University (CT), B.S.,
1997; University of Connecticut, M.S., 2001; University of
Connecticut, Ed.D., 2011 • M. Marissa Peréz, 2 ch

Department of Energy (DOE)
Jennifer M. Granholm (GRAHN-"home") **p 202.586.5000**

1000 Independence Ave., SW
Washington, DC 20585
Website energy.gov
Bio. 02/05/1959 • VancouverCorporation Counsel, Wayne
County ; Michigan Attorney General; Mbr., Natl. Governors
Assn. • University of California, Berkeley, B.A., 1984; Harvard
University, J.D., 1987 • Catholic • M. Daniel Mulhern, 3 ch

Department of Health and Human Services (HHS)
Xavier Becerra (beh-SEH-rah) **p 202.690.7000**

200 Independence Avenue, S.W.
Washington, DC 20201
Website hhs.gov
Bio. 01/26/1958 • Sacramento, CA • State Deputy Attorney;
Attorney; State Legislator • Stanford University (CA), B.A.,
1980; Stanford University Law School (CA), J.D., 1984 •
Roman Catholic • M. Dr. Carolina Reyes, 3 ch

Department of Homeland Security (DHS)
Alejandro Mayorkas (mai-YOR-kus) **p 202.282.8000**

245 Murray Lane, SW
Washington, DC 20528
Website dhs.gov
Bio. 11/24/1959 • HavanaU.S. Attorney (Central District of
CA); Director, U.S. Citizenship and Immigration Services;
Deputy Secretary of Homeland Security • University of
California, Berkeley, B.A., 1981; Loyola Marymount University,
J.D., 1985 • M. , 2 ch

Department of Housing and Urban Development (HUD)
Rep. Marcia L. Fudge (fuhj) **p 202.708.1112**

451 7th St., SW
Washington, DC 20410
Website hud.gov
Bio. 10/29/1952 • Cleveland, OH • Mayor (Warrensville
Heights); Congressional Staffer; Attorney • Ohio State
University, B.S., 1975; Cleveland State University Marshall
College of Law (OH), J.D., 1983 • Baptist • S.

Department of Justice (DOJ)
Merrick Garland (GAR-lend) **p 202.514.2000**

950 Pennsylvania Ave. NW
Washington, DC 20530
Website justice.gov
Bio. 11/13/1952 • Chicago, IL • Judge, U.S. Court of Appeals;
Chief Judge, U.S. Court of Appeals • Harvard University,
B.A., 1974; Harvard University, J.D., 1977 • Jewish • M. Lynn
Rosenman, 2 ch

Department of Labor (DOL)

Marty Walsh (walsh) p **866.487.2365**

200 Constitution Ave NW
Washington, DC 20210
Bio. 04/10/1967 • Boston, MA • Member, House of
Representatives (MA); Mayor of Boston • Boston College
(MA), B.A., 2009 • Roman Catholic • S.

Department of State (DOS)

Anthony Blinken p **202.647.4000**

2201 C St., NW
Washington, DC 20520
Bio. 04/16/1962 • Yonkers, NY • National Security Advisor to
the Vice President; U.S. Deputy National Security Advisor; U.S.
Deputy Secretary of State • Harvard University, B.A., 1984;
Columbia University (NY), J.D., 1988 • Jewish • M. Evan Ryan,
2 ch

Department of the Interior (DOI)

Rep. Deb A. Haaland (HAH-lund) p **202.208.3100**

1849 C St., NW
Washington, DC 20240
Website doi.gov
Bio. 12/02/1960 • Winslow, AZ • Chair, New Mexico
Democratic Party; Member, U.S. House of Representatives
(NM) • University of New Mexico, B.A., 1994; University of
New Mexico Law School, J.D., 2006 • Catholic • S. , 1 ch

Department of Transportation (DOT)

Pete Buttigieg (BOO-tuh-jej) p **202.366.4000**

1200 New Jersey Ave, SE
Washington, DC 20590
Website transportation.gov
Bio. 01/19/1982 • South Bend, IN • U.S. Navy Lieutenant;
Mayor of South Bend (IN) • Harvard University, B.A., 2004;
Pembroke College at Oxford University, England, B.A., 2007 •
M. Chasten Glezman

Department of Treasury

Janet L. Yellen (YEHL-len) p **202.622.2000**

1500 Pennsylvania Avenue, NW
Washington, DC 20220
Website home.treasury.gov
Bio. 08/13/1946 • Brooklyn, NY • Chair, Council of Economic
Advisors; President, Federal Reserve Bank of San Francisco;
Member, Federal Reserve Board of Governors; Vice Chair,
Federal Reserve; Chair, Federal Reserve • Brown University
(RI), B.A., 1967; Yale University (CT), Ph.D., 1971 • Jewish • M.
George Akerlof, 1 ch

Department of Veterans Affairs (VA)

Denis R. McDonough (mik-DUH-nuh)   p **202.724.5454**

441 4th Street, NW
Washington, DE 20001
Website va.gov
Bio. 12/02/1969 • Stillwater, MN • U.S. Deputy National
Security Advisor; White House Chief of Staff • St. John's
University (MN), B.A., 1992; Georgetown University (DC), M.S.,
1996 • Catholic • M. Karin Hillstrom, 3 ch

SELECTED FEDERAL AGENCIES

American Battle Monuments Commission   abmc.gov
2300 Clarendon Blvd.   **703.584.1501**
Courthouse Plaza II., Suite 500
Arlington, VA 22201

AMTRAK - Natl Railroad Passenger Corporation   amtrak.com
60 Massachusetts Ave. NE   **202.906.3000**
Washington, DC 20002

Bureau of Alcohol, Tobacco, Firearms and   atf.gov
Explosives (ATF)   **202.648.8500**
Department of Justice (DOJ)
99 New York Ave. NE
Washington, DC 20226

Bureau of Indian Affairs (BIA)   bia.gov
Department of the Interior (DOI)   **202.208.5116**
1849 C St. NW
MS-4606
Washington, DC 20240

Bureau of Land Management (BLM)   blm.gov
Department of the Interior (DOI)   **202.208.3801**
1849 C St. NW
Room 5665
Washington, DC 20240

Bureau of Ocean Energy Management   boem.gov
Department of the Interior (DOI)   **202.208.6474**
1849 C St. NW
Office of Public Affairs
Washington, DC 20240

Central Intelligence Agency (CIA)   cia.gov
Office of Public Affairs   **703.482.0623**
Washington, DC 20505

Commodity Futures Trading Commission (CFTC)   cftc.gov
1155 21st St. NW   **202.418.5000**
Three Lafayette Centre
Washington, DC 20581

Congressional Budget Office (CBO)   cbo.gov
Second & D Streets, SW   **202.226.2602**
Fourth Floor
Washington, DC 20515-6925

Corporation for National & Community Service   nationalservice.gov
250 E St. SW   **202.606.9390**
Suite 4100
Washington, DC 20525

Director of National Intelligence (ODNI)   dni.gov
Office of the Director of National Intelligence   **703.733.8600**
Washington, DC 20511

Election Assistance Commission (EAC)   eac.gov
633 Third St. NW   **301.563.3919**
Suite 200
Washington, DC 20001

Export-Import Bank of the United States   exim.gov
811 Vermont Ave. NW   **202.565.3946**
Washington, DC 20571

Farm Credit Administration   fca.gov
1501 Farm Credit Dr.   **703.883.4056**
McLean, VA 22102-5090

Federal Accounting Standards Advisory Board   fasab.gov
(FASAB)   **202.512.7350**
441 G St. NW
Suite 1155
Washington, DC 20548

Federal Aviation Administration (FAA)
800 Independence Ave. SW
Washington, DC 20591
faa.gov
866.835.5322

Federal Bureau of Investigation (FBI)
Department of Justice (DOJ)
935 Pennsylvania Ave. NW
Washington, DC 20535-0001
fbi.gov
202.324.3000

Federal Communications Commission
45 L St. NE
Washington, DC 20554
fcc.gov
202.418.1122

Federal Deposit Insurance Corporation
550 17th St. NW
Washington, DC 20429-9990
fdic.gov
877.275.3342

Federal Election Commission (FEC)
1050 First St. NE
Washington, DC 20463
fec.gov
202.694.1000

Federal Emergency Management Agency (FEMA)
Department of Homeland Security (DHS)
500 C St. SW
Washington, DC 20472
fema.gov
202.646.2500

Federal Energy Regulatory Commission
888 First St. NE
Washington, DC 20426
ferc.gov
202.502.6088

Federal Highway Administration (FHA)
1200 New Jersey Ave. SE
Washington, DC 20590
fhwa.dot.gov
202.366.4000

Federal Housing Finance Agency
400 Seventh St. SW
Constitution Center
Washington, DC 20219
fhfa.gov
202.649.3800

Federal Labor Relations Authority (FLRA)
1400 K St. NW
Washington, DC 20424
flra.gov
202.218.7770

Federal Maritime Commission
800 N. Capitol St. NW
Washington, DC 20573
fmc.gov
202.523.5725

Federal Mediation & Conciliation Service
2100 K St. NW
Washington, DC 20427
fmcs.gov
202.606.8100

Federal Railroad Administration
1200 New Jersey Ave. SE
Washington, DC 20590
fra.dot.gov
202.493.6014

Federal Reserve System
20th St. & Constitution Ave. NW
Washington, DC 20551
federalreserve.gov
202.452.3000

Federal Trade Commission (FTC)
600 Pennsylvania Ave. NW
Washington, DC 20580
ftc.gov
202.326.2222

Federal Transit Administration
1200 New Jersey Ave. SE
Washington, DC 20590
fta.dot.gov
202.366.4043

Forest Service
1400 Independence Ave. SW
Washington, DC 20250
fs.fed.us
800.832.1355

Government Accountability Office
441 G St. NW
Washington, DC 20548
gao.gov
202.512.3000

Government National Mortgage Association
451 Seventh St. SW
Room B-133
Washington, DC 20410
ginniemae.gov
202.475.4930

Government Printing Office (GPO)
732 N. Capitol St. NW
Washington, DC 20401
gpo.gov
202.512.1800

Institute of Museum and Library Services (IMLS)
955 L'Enfant Plaza North SW
Suite 4000
Washington, DC 20024-2135
imls.gov
202.653.4657

Inter-American Foundation
1331 Pennsylvania Ave. NW
Suite 1200 North
Washington, DC 20004
iaf.gov
202.360.4530

Internal Revenue Service (IRS)
1750 Forest Dr.
Suite 110
Annapolis, MD 21401
irs.gov
410.224.5000

Legal Services Corporation
3333 K St. NW
Washington, DC 20007
lsc.gov
202.295.1500

Library of Congress (LOC)
101 Independence Ave. SE
Washington, DC 20540
loc.gov
202.707.5000

Medicare Payment Advisory Commission (MedPAC)
425 I St. NW
Suite 701
Washington, DC 20001
medpac.gov
202.220.3700

Merit Systems Protection Board
1615 M St. NW
Washington, DC 20419
mspb.gov
202.653.7200

National Aeronautics and Space Administration
300 E St. SW
Suite 5R30
Washington, DC 20546
nasa.gov
202.358.0001

National Archives and Records Administration
8601 Adelphi Rd.
College Park, MD 20740-6001
archives.gov
866.272.6272

National Council on Disability
1331 F St. NW
Suite 850
Washington, DC 20004
ncd.gov
202.272.2004

National Credit Union Administration
1775 Duke St.
Alexandria, VA 22314-3428
ncua.gov
703.518.6300

National Endowment For the Arts
400 Seventh St. SW
Washington, DC 20506-0001
arts.gov
202.682.5400

National Highway Traffic Safety Administration (NHTSA)
1200 New Jersey Ave. SE
Washington, DC 20590
nhtsa.gov
888.327.4236

National Indian Gaming Commission
Department of the Interior (DOI)
90 K St. NE
Suite 200
Washington, DC 20002
nigc.gov
202.632.7003

National Labor Relations Board
1015 Half St. SE
Washington, DC 20570-0001
nlrb.gov
202.273.1000

National Mediation Board
1301 K St. NW
Suite 250 East
Washington, DC 20005-7011
nmb.gov
202.692.5000

National Park Service (NPS)
Department of the Interior (DOI)
1849 C St. NW
Washington, DC 20240
nps.gov
202.208.6843

National Science Foundation
2415 Eisenhower Ave.
Alexandria, VA 22314
nsf.gov
703.292.5111

National Transportation Safety Board
490 L'Enfant Plaza SW
Washington, DC 20594
ntsb.gov
202.314.6000

Occupational Safety and Health Administration
200 Constitution Ave. NW
Room Number N3626
Washington, DC 20210
osha.gov
800.321.6742

Office of Government Ethics (OGE)
1201 New York Ave. NW
Suite 500
Washington, DC 20005
oge.gov
202.482.9300

Office of Housing
Department of Housing and Urban Development (HUD)
451 7th St SW
Washington, DC 20410
202.708.1112

Office of Housing and Urban Development
451 Seventh St. SW
Washington, DC 20410
hud.gov
202.708.1112

Office of Special Counsel
1730 M St. NW
Suite 218
Washington, DC 20036-4505
osc.gov
202.254.3600

Office of the Comptroller of the Currency
400 Seventh St. SW
Washington, DC 20219
occ.gov
202.649.6800

Overseas Private Investment Corp (OPIC)
1100 New York Ave. NW
Washington, DC 20527
opic.gov
202.336.8400

Peace Corps
1275 First St. NE
Washington, DC 20526
peacecorps.gov
855.855.1961

Pension Benefit Guaranty Corporation
P.O. Box 151750
Alexandria, VA 22315-1750
pbgc.gov
202.326.4000

Postal Regulatory Commission
901 New York Ave. NW
Suite 200
Washington, DC 20268-0001
prc.gov
202.789.6800

Selective Service System
P.O. Box 94638
Palatine, IL 60094-4638
sss.gov
847.688.6888

Smithsonian Institution
P.O. Box 37012
Room 153, MRC 010
Washington, DC 20013-7012
si.edu
202.633.1000

Social Security Administration
6401 Security Blvd.
1100 West High Rise
Baltimore, MD 21235
ssa.gov
800.772.1213

Trade & Development Agency (TDA)
1101 Wilson Blvd.
Suite 1100
Arlington, VA 22209
ustda.gov
703.875.4357

U.S. Agency for International Development
1300 Pennsylvania Ave. NW
Washington, DC 20523
usaid.gov
202.712.1150

U.S. Census Bureau
Department of Commerce (DOC)
4600 Silver Hill Road
Washington, DC 20233
301.763.4636

U.S. Chemical Safety & Hazard Investigation Board
1750 Pennsylvania Ave. NW
Suite 910
Washington, DC 20006
csb.gov
202.261.7600

U.S. Citizenship and Immigration Services
Department of Homeland Security (DHS)
5900 Capital Gateway Dr.
Suite 1S100, First Floor
Suitland, MD 20746
uscis.gov
800.375.5283

U.S. Commission of Fine Arts
401 F St. NW
Suite 312
Washington, DC 20001-2728
cfa.gov
202.504.2200

U.S. Commission on Civil Rights
1331 Pennsylvania Ave. NW
Suite 1150
Washington, DC 20425
usccr.gov
202.376.7700

U.S. Consumer Product Safety Commission
4330 East West Hwy.
Bethesda, MD 20814
cpsc.gov
800.638.2772

U.S. Copyright Office
101 Independence Ave. SE
Washington, DC 20559-6000
copyright.gov
202.707.3000

U.S. Customs & Border Protection
Department of Homeland Security (DHS)
1300 Pennsylvania Ave. NW
Washington, DC 20229
cbp.gov
202.325.8000

U.S. Drug Enforcement Administration
Department of Justice (DOJ)
800 K St. NW
Suite 500
Washington, DC 20001
dea.gov
202.305.8500

U.S. Environmental Protection Agency
1200 Pennsylvania Ave. NW
Washington, DC 20460
epa.gov
202.564.4700

U.S. Equal Employment Opportunity Commission
131 M St. NE
Washington, DC 20507
eeoc.gov
202.663.4900

U.S. Fish and Wildlife Service
Department of the Interior (DOI)
1849 C St. NW
Washington, DC 20240
fws.gov
202.208.6541

U.S. General Services Administration
1800 F St. NW
Washington, DC 20405
gsa.gov
202.208.4949

U.S. Institute of Peace
2301 Constitution Ave. NW
Washington, DC 20037
usip.org
202.457.1700

U.S. International Trade Commission
500 E St. SW
Washington, DC 20436
usitc.gov
202.205.2000

U.S. Marshals Service
Department of Justice (DOJ)
Third & Constitution Ave. NW
Room 1103
Washington, DC 20001
usmarshals.gov
202.353.0600

U.S. Mint
801 Ninth St. NW
Washington, DC 20220-0012
usmint.gov
800.872.6468

U.S. Nuclear Regulatory Commission
11555 Rockville Pike
One White Flint North
Rockville, MD 20852-2738
nrc.gov
301.415.7000

U.S. Office of Personnel Management
1900 E St. NW
Washington, DC 20415-1000
opm.gov
202.606.1800

U.S. Postal Service
475 L'Enfant Plaza SW
Room 1P830
Washington, DC 20260-1101
usps.gov
202.268.2608

U.S. Secret Service
Department of Homeland Security (DHS)
245 Murray Ln. SW
Bldg. T-Five
Washington, DC 20223
secretservice.gov
202.406.5708

U.S. Securities and Exchange Commission
100 F St. NE
Washington, DC 20549
sec.gov
202.942.8088

U.S. Small Business Administration
409 Third St. SW
Washington, DC 20416
sba.gov
800.827.5722

Veterans Employment & Training Service
200 Constitution Ave. NW
Room S-1325
Washington, DC 20210
dol.gov
866.487.2365

Violence Against Women Program
Department of Justice (DOJ)
145 N St. NE
Suite 10W.121
Washington, DC 20530
ovw.usdoj.gov
202.307.6026

THE SUPREME COURT OF THE UNITED STATES

One First St. NE
Washington, DC 20543
202.479.3000
www.supremecourt.gov

Court Officers

Clerk	Scott Harris
Counselor to the Chief Justice	Jeffrey P. Minear
Court Counsel	Ethan Torrey
Curator	Catherine Fitts
Director of Information Technology	Robert J. Hawkins
Librarian	Linda Maslow
Marshal	Gail Curley
Public Information Officer	Patricia McCabe
Reporter of Decisions	Rebecca A. Womeldorf

U.S. Supreme Court and Federal Court Resources

Federal Judicial Center	**fjc.gov**
Federal Judiciary	**uscourts.gov**
Supreme Court Historical Society	**supremecourthistory.org**
U.S. Court of Appeals for the Federal Circuit	**cafc.uscourts.gov**
U.S. Supreme Court Opinion Announcements	**202.479.3360**
U.S. Supreme Court Public Information Office	**202.479.3211**
U.S. Supreme Court Visitor Information Line	**202.479.3030**

2022 UNITED STATES SUPREME COURT

Chief Justice John G. Roberts (RAH bertz)

Nominated by George W. Bush, 2005
Bio. 01/27/1955 • Buffalo, NY • United States Court of Appeals for the District of Columbia Circuit; Private Practicing Attorney; U.S. Department of Justice; Office of the White House Counsel • Harvard College (MA), A.B, 1976; Harvard University Law School (MA), J.D., 1979 • Catholic • M. Jane Marie Sullivan Roberts, 2 ch
Law Clerks Samuel Adkission • Christina Gay • Maxwell Gottschall • Dennis Howe
Salary $263,300
Jurisdiction United States Court of Appeals for the District of Columbia, Fourth and Federal Circuits

Associate Justice Clarence Thomas (TOM as)

Nominated by George H.W. Bush, 1991
Bio. 06/23/1948 • Pin Point, GA • Judge, U.S. Court of Appeals for the DC Circuit; Chair, U.S. Equal Opportunity Employment Commission; Assistant Secretary, U.S. Department of Education; Assistant Attorney General of Missouri • College of The Holy Cross (MA), A.B; Yale University Law School (CT), J.D., 1974 • Catholic • M. Virginia 'Ginni' Lamp Thomas, 1 ch
Law Clerks Christopher Goodnow • Steven Lindsay • Michael Proctor • Jose Valle
Salary $251,800
Jurisdiction U.S. Court of Appeals for the Eleventh Circuit

Associate Justice Stephen G. Breyer (BRY er)

Nominated by William J. Clinton, 1994
Bio. 08/15/1938 • San Francisco, CA • Chief Judge and Judge, U.S. Court of Appeals for the First District; Law Professor, Harvard University • Stanford University (CA), A.B; Oxford University (England), B.A.; Harvard University, LL.B. • Jewish • M. Joanna Hare Breyer, 3 ch; 5 gr-ch
Law Clerks Elizabeth Deutsch • Erika Hoglund • Diana Kim • Joel Wacks
Salary $251,800
Jurisdiction U.S. Court of Appeals for the First Circuit

Associate Justice Samuel A. Alito (Ah LEE tow)

Nominated by George W. Bush, 2006
Bio. 04/01/1950 • Trenton, NJ • Judge, U.S. Court of Appeals for the Third District; Law Professor; U.S. Attorney; Deputy Assistant Attorney General; Assistant to the Solicitor General; Assistant U.S. Attorney; Law Clerk • Princeton University (NJ), A.B; Yale University Law School (CT), J.D. • Catholic • M. Martha-Ann Bomgardner Alito, 2 ch
Law Clerks Shelby Baird • Thomas Gaiser • Eric Palmer • Edward West Jr.
Salary $251,800
Jurisdiction U.S. Court of Appeals for the Third and Fifth Circuits

Associate Justice Sonia M. Sotomayor (so-"toe"-my-YOR)

Nominated by Barack H. Obama, 2009
Bio. 06/25/1954 • The Bronx, NY • Judge, U.S. District Court of Appeals for the Second District; Judge, U.S. District Court for the Southern District of New York • Princeton University (NJ), A.B, 1976; Yale University Law School (CT), J.D., 1979 • Catholic • D.
Law Clerks Whitney Brown • Amit Jain • Katherine Munyan • Kelley Schiffman
Salary $251,800
Jurisdiction U.S. Court of Appeals for the Second Circuit

Associate Justice Elena Kagan (KAY-guhn)

Nominated by Barack H. Obama, 2010
Bio. 04/28/1960 • New York, NY • Law Professor and Dean, Harvard Law School; US Solicitor General • Princeton Universtiy, A.B, 1981; Oxford University (England), M.Phil, 1983; Harvard University Law School (MA), J.D., 1986 • Jewish • S.
Law Clerks Jennifer Fischell • Alexandra Lim • Christine Smith • Andrew Waks
Salary $251,800
Jurisdiction U.S. Court of Appeals for the Ninth Circuit

Associate Justice Neil M. Gorsuch (GOR-such)

Nominated by Donald J. Trump, 2017
Bio. 08/29/1967 • Denver, CO • United States Court of Appeals for the Tenth Circuit; Judicial Clerk (1991-1994); Attorney • Oxford University (England), DPhil; Columbia University (NY), B.A., 1988; Harvard University Law School (MA), J.D., 1991 • Episcopalian • M. Louise Gorsuch, 2 ch
Law Clerks Stephanie Barclay • Louis Capozzi • Mark Storslee • John Thompson
Salary $251,800
Jurisdiction U.S. Court of Appeals for the Tenth Circuit

Associate Justice Brett M. Kavanaugh (cah vuh NAW)

Nominated by Donald J. Trump, 2018
Bio. 02/12/1965 • Washington, DC • Yale University (CT), B.A.; Yale University (CT), J.D • Catholic • M. Ashley Estes Kavanaugh, 2 ch
Law Clerks Alexa Baltes • Athanasia Livas • Jennifer Pavelec • Sarah Welch
Salary $251,800
Jurisdiction U.S. Court of Appeals for the Sixth and Eighth Circuit

Associate Justice Amy Coney Barrett (kow-nee beh-ruht)

Nominated by Donald J. Trump, 2020
Bio. 01/28/1972 • New Orleans, LA • Judge, U.S. Court of Appeals; Law Professor • Rhodes College, B.A.; University of Notre Dame (IN), J.D • Catholic • M. , 7 ch
Law Clerks Libby Baird • Mike Heckmann • Max Schulman • Zachary Tyree
Salary $251,800
Jurisdiction U.S. Court of Appeals for the Seventh Circuits

The Electoral College was established in Article II of the U.S. Constitution. The Electoral College requires that the President and Vice President be elected through a group of electors based on state population rather than by popular vote. This ensures that less populated states, such as Vermont and North Dakota, will have a bearing on the results of the national election, rather than the election being determined primarily by the more populated states such as California and New York.

For example, the Electoral College ensures that candidates must visit all of the states, as an election cannot be won based on winning only the most populated states. A candidate must therefore make an effort to visit and win a majority of states in order to win an election.

Each state has an amount of electors equal to the number of their Members in Congress. Therefore, each state has at least three electors (the District of Columbia also receives three electors for a national total of 538 electors). Though laws vary from state to state, the state parties typically choose electors. Electors in some states cast their ballot based on the popular vote of the state and others cast their vote based on the party candidate. However, rarely will an elector vote opposite of the vote of the people.

Electors in each state meet in their respective state capitals in December to cast their votes for President and Vice President. Once these ballots have been cast, they are sent to Congress, where they are counted by the President of the Senate on January 6 (or the following day if January 6 falls on a Sunday). The candidate with an absolute majority prevails. If no candidate receives an absolute majority of electoral votes, the House of Representatives selects the next President and the Senate selects the next Vice President.

For more information on the Electoral College, contact the National Archives and Records Administration at **www.archives.gov**.

The Electoral College
Total: 538
Majority Needed to Elect: 270

NOTES

NOTES